DEATH
IN
YELLOWSTONE

DEATH
IN
YELLOWSTONE

ACCIDENTS AND FOOLHARDINESS
IN THE FIRST NATIONAL PARK

SECOND EDITION

Lee H. Whittlesey

A ROBERTS RINEHART BOOK
Lanham • Boulder • New York • Toronto • Plymouth, UK

Published by Roberts Rinehart Publishers
An imprint of Rowman & Littlefield
4501 Forbes Boulevard, Suite 200, Lanham, Maryland 20706
www.rowman.com

10 Thornbury Road, Plymouth PL6 7PP, United Kingdom

Distributed by NATIONAL BOOK NETWORK

British Library Cataloguing in Publication Information Available

Library of Congress Cataloging-in-Publication Data

Whittlesey, Lee H., 1950–
  Death in Yellowstone : accidents and foolhardiness in the first national park / Lee H. Whittlesey. — Second edition.
    pages cm
  Summary: "Covering the sometimes gruesome but always tragic ways people have died in Yellowstone National Park, this updated edition of a classic includes calamities in Yellowstone from the past sixteen years"— Provided by publisher.
  Includes bibliographical references and index.
  ISBN 978-1-57098-450-1 (pbk.) — ISBN 978-1-57098-451-8 (electronic) 1. Violent deaths—Yellowstone National Park—Anecdotes. 2. Accidents—Yellowstone National Park—Anecdotes. 3. Yellowstone National Park—History—Anecdotes. 4. Accidents—Yellowstone National Park—Prevention. I. Title.
  F722.W588 2014
  978.7'52—dc23
                                                                                    2013030035

♾️™ The paper used in this publication meets the minimum requirements of American National Standard for Information Sciences—Permanence of Paper for Printed Library Materials, ANSI/NISO Z39.48-1992.

Printed in the United States of America

To Tamela Whittlesey, a remarkable partner in a wonderful journey with our daughter Tess.

To Julie Gayde Benden, who suggested the whole project.

"[In the wilderness] You're never very far away from the edge, and if you take it for granted, it will come up and bite you!"

—Elliot Brown, 1993 rescued cross-country
ski party, Aspen, Colorado

"What fools these mortals be!"

—Shakespeare, *A Midsummer Night's Dream*

Contents

Part Two: Death by Man

ACKNOWLEDGMENTS

A BOOK LIKE THIS IS DIFFICULT TO WRITE, not only because of the emotional impacts on author and interviewees and the delicacy of subject matter, but also because in researching and publishing it, I risk reopening old wounds or renewing grieving processes. Certainly it has not been my intention to do either of these things. But as an historian, I am keenly aware that pieces of history can become lost when people do not want to talk about something. And for talking, writing, and helping me find obscure materials, I have numerous folks to thank.

All Yellowstone historians owe debts to Aubrey L. Haines for so skillfully showing us the way during his forty-plus years of researching the history of this region. I will always think of myself as his student and of him as the great master. One of his remarks to us is a classic for pointing out the ephemeral nature of people and events: "History is something we have agreed to believe in."

A number of "Yellowstone Nation" residents provided me with information for the original manuscript based on their personal experiences. Former and present Yellowstone rangers Gerry Mernin, Bonnie Gafney, Andrew Mitchell, Jeff Henry, Mike Pflaum, Bruce Blair, John Lounsbury, Stephen Dobert, Jerry Ryder, Paul Miller, Mike Robinson, Melanie Weeks, Kerry Murphy, Bob Carnes, Bobbie Seaquist, Mark Marschall, Rick Fey, Brian O'Dea, and Dan Reinhart all advised me on their roles in various incidents. Former and present T. W. Services (later Amfac Parks and Resorts and, still later, Xanterra) personnel have been equally important: Andrea Paul, Leon Brunton, Leslie Quinn, Ruth Lira Quinn, Paul Shea, John Richardson, Steve Blakeley, Diane Ihle Renkin, George Bornemann, Jill Fitterer, Chris Marshall, Tom Woods, Mike Keller, Liz Kearney, Diane Papineau, Tim Baymiller, and Sue Plummer. My fellow employees in the park's Division of Interpretation were kind enough to read and comment upon the original manuscript: Greg Kroll, Steve

Eide, Tom Tankersley, Linda Tankersley, and Sandy Snell-Dobert. Members of the park research staff have also been gracious: John Varley, Don Despain, Bob Crabtree, and Rick Hutchinson. Park chief ranger Dan Sholly was kind enough to read and comment upon the original manuscript. Other park employees who were helpful were Jennifer Whipple Hutchinson, Curtis Whittlesey, and Paul Rubinstein, whose photo graced the cover of the first edition of this book. Dr. Mary Meagher of the National Park Service read the original manuscript and offered me the benefit of her many years of wisdom, and I regret omitting her name in oversight from acknowledgments in the first edition.

Descendants such as Dale Dose, Davenport, Iowa; John Fogerty, Lake City, California; Isabel Squire, Seattle, Washington; and Bruce Graham, Livingston, Montana, provided family information.

As usual, library personnel were indispensable: Barb Zafft and Bev Whitman at Yellowstone, Nathan Bender at Montana State University, David Walters at the Montana Historical Society, Tamsen Emerson Hert at the University of Wyoming, and Bonnie Travis, Eleanor Schweigert, and June Phillips at Livingston Public Library.

Walt Stebbins of Gardiner, Montana; Doris Whithorn of Livingston, Montana; Beth Bittner of Sun Valley, Idaho; Joni and Don Hofmann of Gardiner, Montana; John Tyers, Bozeman, Montana; Todd Wilkinson, Livingston, Montana; Gerard Pesman, Bozeman, Montana; Florence Crossen, Gardiner, Montana; Warren Hutchings, Livingston, Montana; Lee Silliman, Deer Lodge, Montana; Bob Murphy, Livingston, Montana; and M. A. Bellingham, Billings, Montana, provided details that only they could know. Dr. Susan Neel of Montana State University and Rocco Paperiello of Billings, Montana, both provided important perspective.

For this second edition, Lyn Stallings, director at the Park County (Wyoming) Archives, helped me, as did Jessica Gerdes and Jackie Jerla at the Yellowstone Research Library. Archivists and museum staff at Yellowstone have been very efficient, too: Colleen Curry, Anne Foster, Bridgette Guild, Shawn Bawden, Lee Steiner, Mariah Robertson, John Wachstetter, Charissa Reid, and Jared Infanger. Marsha Karle and Jon Dahlheim in Yellowstone's Public Affairs Office were always kind and helpful, as were their "descendants" who helped me years later: Al Nash and Amy Bartlett. My history interns and VIPs (volunteers in parks) have been good at turning up obscure items that I filed away for later: M. A. Bellingham, Theresa and Steve Fisher, Michael Fox, Rachelle Schrader, Brad Snow, Julie Robinson, and Alyssa Krekemeier.

Special Yellowstone experts must be acknowledged. My friend Paul Schullery of Bozeman, Montana, read the original manuscript and as usual offered invaluable comments and suggestions. He and my longtime lawyer-

and-historian friend, Steve Mishkin of Olympia, Washington, both read this new edition, and their careful examinations improved the manuscript. Historian Jeremy Johnston from the Buffalo Bill Historical Center in Cody, Wyoming; Xanterra interpretive specialist Leslie Quinn of Gardiner, Montana; Kerry Gunther, Yellowstone bear biologist; and thirty-year Yellowstone veteran Randy Ingersoll also read parts of the manuscript. Thanks to all of them.

For this new edition of *Death in Yellowstone*, the following people made much appreciated efforts to contact me with additional details on the fatalities presented in the original book or with completely new fatalities, and those extra details about events and people (mentioned here in parentheses) appear in this edition: Aubrey L. Haines, Tucson, Arizona (Ed Wilson, Charles White, Vern Keiser); Paul Schullery, Bozeman, Montana (Matthew Carey); Mike Robinson, Bozeman, Montana (Brigitta Fredenhagen and James Lee Hamer); Bruce Graham, Livingston, Montana (Charles Walter Pring); John Dracon, White Sulphur Springs, Montana (Explorer Scouts drowning); H. Kim Jones, Lovettsville, Virginia (Explorer Scouts drowning); Mary Eleanor Foutz, Gallup, New Mexico (Burris Wollsieffer); Steve B. Elliott (descendant of Ninian T. Elliott); Tamra Phelps, Somerset, Kentucky (descendant of Oliver Adkins); Diana Sears, Somerset, Kentucky (descendant of Oliver Adkins); Sally Kloppenburg, Corvallis, Oregon (Madison Stedman); Kent Morby, Salt Lake City, Utah (M. D. Scott); Jim Barton, Three Rivers, California (a baby at Lewis Lake); Bob Flather, Galeta, California (the army station on Wickiup Creek); Sandy Bennett, San Jose, California (Don Cressey); Shannon Wilson, Tracy, California (Don Cressey); Barbara Oxford Bettevy, Pollock, Louisiana (Don Cressey); Kimberly Mohney, Centralia, Washington (Edgar Gibson); Susan McFeatters, New York, New York (Eliza and Louise Zabriskie); Jean Lewis Ryland (Danny Lewis); Alan Dunefsky, New Paltz, New York (Brian Parsons); Mark Rockmore, Bethesda, Maryland (Brian Parsons); Scott Wonder, Bellevue, Washington (Rick Reid); Pam Haner, Redmond, Washington (Rick Reid); John Morawetz, Cincinnati, Ohio (gasses); Earl Johnson, Roundup, Montana (Bill Nelson, Dick Meyers, Joe Tribble); Judson M. Rhoads, Fort Collins, Colorado (his grandfather, Judson M. Rhoads); Kyle Hannon, Elkhart, Indiana (Shane Rich); Bob Haraden, Bozeman, Montana (Mark Swift, Hugh Galusha); James V. Court, Billings, Montana (lightning); John Criger, Denver, Colorado (unknown Gardner River drowning; unknown carbon monoxide death at Lamar); Rick Fey, Lake, Wyoming (drowning impressions); M. Evelyn Rose, San Francisco, California (Mary J. Foster); Shirley Rush, Heyburn, Idaho (Mary J. Foster); Janice Weekley, Tulsa, Oklahoma (Sarry E. Bolding); Donalene O'Neill, Neihart, Montana (1950 Gardiner fire and bear story); Gary S. Bradak, Logan, Utah (Bessie Rowbottom); Earl Felix, Veradale, Washington (Bessie Rowbottom); Lee Silliman, Deer Lodge, Montana (Vincent Zappala); Jim Hepburn,

Emigrant, Montana (C. J. Carpenter); Cheryl Williams Cummings, Wetumpka, Alabama (John Mark Williams); Mary Link, New Berlin, Wisconsin (Frank Welch); Larry C. Stokes, Wichita Falls, Texas (Joseph "Frenchy" Duret); Jim Hepburn, Emigrant, Montana (C. J. Carpenter); Dr. Yolanda Youngs, Pocatello, Idaho (W. L. Escher); Elizabeth "Betsy" Watry, Bozeman, Montana (George Trischman), Kerry Gunther, Gardiner, Montana (William Tesinsky, John Wallace), and Jeff Koechling, Boston, Massachusetts (Diane Dustman).

Finally, by way of disclaimer I must mention that although I have been a permanent employee of the National Park Service since 1989, in this book I do not represent the NPS either formally or informally. I originally wrote this book on my own time before I came to my present job, and for this revised edition I have done the same thing. In researching it, I have used no information that is not available to any other writer; my sources are given in the endnotes. Interested researchers should know that the informational resources of Yellowstone are as vast as its natural and cultural resources (in fact, they are arguably a cultural resource on their own). I especially recommend the great wealth of material in the library, museum, and archives collections at the Yellowstone Heritage and Research Center in Gardiner, Montana. Other outstanding Yellowstone collections that I have used through the years may be found at Montana State University in Bozeman; the University of Wyoming in Laramie; the Montana Historical Society in Helena; Brigham Young University Library in Provo, Utah; the University of Oklahoma in Norman; and of course the Library of Congress and the National Archives in Washington, DC.

Introduction to the Second Edition

Ⅰ**T HAS BEEN ALMOST EIGHTEEN YEARS** since Roberts Rinehart published the first edition of this book, and during that time I have found that the book has held up fairly well in its information. In my original introduction, I asked readers to write if they knew of additional fatalities that I had missed. Sure enough, a few people provided me with actual "new" cases of old deaths. Bruce Graham, a researcher in Livingston, Montana, turned up an additional (and early! 1898!) thermal-burn fatality that I now include here. Paul Schullery of Bozeman found the early drowning of Matthew Carey, as well as an 1881 death by freezing. Bob Haraden of Bozeman reminded me of deaths I had omitted involving Mark Swift and Hugh Galusha. Janice Weekley of Tulsa put me on the trail of solving the long-elusive death of Sarry Bolding. And many other correspondents provided me with additional details for already known incidents. Their names appear in the acknowledgments, and those new details are now presented in this edition.

As I expected in 1995, I missed a few Yellowstone fatalities that were buried deeply in history. I turned up many of these myself during the past seventeen years from the emerging Internet (especially in newspapers—more on that in a moment). It is good for the record that these stories can now be presented here. Alongside these new stories, my original reasons for writing the book remain in place. I wrote it (1) because all the stories represent fascinating history, (2) because the stories have legal ramifications for park managers, and (3) because the book teaches important safety lessons.

I would like to believe that the original version of this book has influenced the park's safety record, if only in small ways. Regardless, the onward march of such incidents in Yellowstone has continued, and so this new edition chronicles more than sixty additional human deaths. Many are from the recent period 1996 through 2012, but a fair number are older ones formerly buried in history. I reiterate here that the book does not address human deaths from auto, motorcycle, or snowmobile wrecks, nor does it address high-elevation heart attacks or deaths from illness. Far too many of those exist for me to pursue them all.[1]

Those kinds of fatalities continue to keep our law enforcement rangers busy in Yellowstone during all seasons, but we can now prevent some of them from becoming fatalities. By way of example, several park rangers at Fishing Bridge RV Park, aided by a neighbor with a defibrillator, were able to save the life of a 67-year-old heart-attack victim on July 19, 2012. The man was not breathing and his heart had not been beating (perhaps for as long as twenty minutes) when life-support personnel recovered a pulse.[2]

Since my original *Death in Yellowstone* was published in 1995, other authors have joined me in writing about deaths and injuries in other national parks, and in at least one of those cases I spoke on the telephone to an author. My friend Butch Farabee joined Michael Ghiglieri to produce *Off the Wall: Death in Yosemite* (2007), and Ghiglieri also produced *Over the Edge: Death in Grand Canyon* (2001). We swapped some information, and I thank those authors for that.

Almost as interesting to me as the many death incidents themselves are references I found to the way that early Yellowstone residents and writers responded generally to the subject of deaths in the first national park. A New Jersey subscriber to the *Livingston* (MT) *Post* wrote to that newspaper in 1892 asking "if any tourists were ever murdered in the Yellowstone National Park." James C. McCartney—one of the founders of the village of Mammoth Hot Springs in 1871 and the credited founder of the town of Gardiner, Montana, in 1880—responded to the inquiry by stating that he knew of no such murders except for the ones that occurred during the Nez Perce war of 1877. McCartney mentioned Charles Kenck and Richard Dietrich without mentioning the violent deaths of at least two members of the Nez Perce tribe—an old woman and a teenaged boy—whose names we do not know but who are now chronicled in this book.[3] Just as interesting is the full-page newspaper article that appeared in the *Washington* (DC) *Times* in late 1905, provoked by the thermal death of Fannie Weeks a month earlier. The article was "Dangers of the Yellowstone Park Where a Washington Woman Has Just Lost Her Life." "In exchange for the great pleasure [nature] gives in this marvelous workshop," wrote the author, who was probably John E. Sheridan, "she exacts her price . . . and the price is high. It is death." Written in a style calculated to scare, this long article must have terrified its readers! "Under every hands-breadth of the beauty," warned the writer about Yellowstone, "lies a pitfall." But then the writer ventured into unproven science when he claimed that vapors from the geysers were generally poisonous and produced a "narcotic effect" that must have "stupefied" Miss Weeks into a "semiconscious state," causing her to fall into boiling water. That was stretching it, and so was the writer's statement that the brink of Lower Falls was a spot where "many venturesome sightseers have lost their lives." The writer correctly warned of the beautiful colors of hot springs and geysers and the panoramic vistas that attracted visitors into venturing too closely onto thin crusts and near to dangerous drop-offs. He ended with a note of horrific warning for his readers: "Somebody from time to time must be drawn down into the fires to pay Mother Nature's price of a life for the delight of the thousands." Regardless of his tendency to deeply dramatize, this writer knew that caution was required in Yellowstone—as it still is today.[4]

As that article illustrates and as I stated in the first edition of this book, the nation's newspapers have been and continue to be fertile sources of park history. More and more of these tales are coming to light as a vibrant Internet makes them available to us, and because of it, I am able to present many "new" (actually old) stories in this revised volume. Through the lens of this emerging mass of historic material, I am constantly reminded that Yellowstone visitors from all fifty states and from many other countries returned home to write interesting accounts of their trips for their local newspapers. Thousands of those accounts have been turning up for the past seven to ten years, and I hope I live long enough to see many of the others that will so emerge through time. Meanwhile, I am presenting and citing many of the "new" old ones here for you in addition to chronicling the more recent fatal incidents that occurred in Yellowstone from 1995 through 2012.

ORIGINAL INTRODUCTION
AND RECENT ADDITIONS

"The Park Can Kill"

A child has died in a particularly horrible fashion in Yellowstone Park. He wandered off the boardwalk at a geyser basin and fell into a boiling hot spring.

Our hearts suffer with the parents.

But we know that there may be other deaths in the park this year from less rare incidents such as bear maulings.

Death is a frequent visitor in raw nature. And Yellowstone Park, despite the cabins and roads, is raw nature. The Park is the untamed and unfenced wildlife and the amoral energy of thermal wonders.

It cannot be treated lightly; when it is it erupts in death.

We have seen other visitors in the park who left the paths and boardwalks. We have seen visitors in the park who sat their children on bears in order to take a picture. They were lucky.

The park is not Disneyland, Rocky Mountain version. Nor is it a zoo with moats and fences separating the wild and the domesticated.

For all the trappings of men, it is wilderness. And the man who fails to accept it as such dies.

More money for more rangers to enforce the Park's rules would help.

But until that time we urge all visitors, and urge all Montana and Wyoming residents to warn visitors again and again to obey signs in the park, to remember that Yellowstone Park is wild.

The Park is raw nature.

And it can kill.

—editorial, *Billings Gazette,* July 1, 1970

THAT SOBERING EDITORIAL SUMMED UP some of the dangers in Yellowstone National Park and noted that wilderness itself can bring death. Certainly no one who comes to Yellowstone expects death or injury to visit. Indeed, death seems antithetical to the reason for the park's being. Yellowstone was created in 1872 "as a public park or pleasuring ground for the benefit and enjoyment of the people," and the park seems to proclaim life. But there are very real dangers in true wilderness, and that is part of our fascination with it. A longtime researcher of wilderness areas has noted in defining them that places where one cannot be killed by a wild animal *are not* wilderness areas. In fact, the word *wilderness* comes from *wilder*, a wild animal. Yellowstone National Park, of course, is managed as a wilderness area.

Many visitors to Yellowstone and other national parks enter the gates with a false sense of security. These persons wrongly believe that the animals are tame and that the place surely is a lot like a city park, with swings, horseshoe pits, golf courses, swimming pools, and total safety—a place where lawns are watered and mowed regularly and fallen tree branches are picked up and carted away, all nicely managed, nicely sanitized. But national parks are not like that; they are places where nature and history are preserved intact. And intact nature includes dangers.

Why would anyone write a book like this? The obvious answers are these: there are illuminating safety lessons to be learned, there is fascinating history in the stories, and there are legal ramifications for park managers. Certainly the stories are heart-wrenching. But they teach us.

I first became interested in this subject during my quest for information while I was a bus tour guide and later a park ranger at Yellowstone. My interest continued at law school, where I studied many wrongful deaths and personal injury cases involving Yellowstone National Park. Death is a subject that often comes up on any Yellowstone tour or in any naturalist question-and-answer session, because this oldest of national parks does have some dangerous facets. While not pleasant, the subject is always relevant, timely, and interesting. It serves to illustrate why the park has rules and regulations and why we must exercise reasonable care in our play.

As I delved into the subject of fatalities and injuries in Yellowstone, it became at once apparent that there were those caused by nature and those caused by man. In the latter category are car and snowmobile wrecks. These number in the hundreds and are not terribly interesting, so I have omitted them. But some in the man-caused category, such as murders, airplane crashes, and stagecoach accidents, are novel, interesting, and instructive, and so I have included them here. Of course, all of the nature-caused fatalities are novel and instructive. After all, how often in contemporary America does someone get killed by a grizzly bear or by falling into a boiling pool?

In other national parks, deaths and injuries occur in some of the same ways: drownings, falls, falling trees, falling rocks, lightning, and so on. But Yellowstone adds the novel ones: hot springs, grizzly bears, bison, and poisonous gas. Most parks simply do not have the great variety of dangers of Yellowstone. Zion National Park (Utah) reports falls from rock climbing and a few drownings, but not much else. In Tennessee's Great Smoky Mountains National Park, deaths from falls, falling trees, lightning, and a few freezings are the rule. In Yosemite, Grand Teton, Mount McKinley, and Rocky Mountain National Parks mountain-climbing incidents occur commonly. And in California's Sequoia National Park, drownings are the leading cause of violent death, but there are some instances of each of a few others. At the time of this book's original writing, a visitor who was struck by lightning in Sequoia was suing that park for failing to provide notice of such danger, failing to warn of the storm, and failing to provide lightning protection. The judge ruled that such notice, warning, and protection fell within the discretionary function exception to the Federal Tort Claims Act and dismissed the case.[1]

In 2011, Yosemite National Park occupied the spotlight for deaths in national parks. By late August of that year, sixteen people had died there from falls, drownings, and other causes. Following the philosophies presented in the earlier edition of this book, a national writer decried attempts to make nature "tame and lawyer-vetted." "There will always be steep cliffs, deep water, and ornery and unpredictable animals," wrote Timothy Egan, "in that messy part of the national habitat not crossed by climate-controlled malls and processed-food emporiums. If people expect a grizzly bear to be benign, or think a glacier is just another variant of a theme-park slide, it's not the fault of the government when something goes fatally wrong."[2] Upon reading that column, a coworker of mine wondered whether there should be "stupid meters" erected at each park entrance gate. That is, of course, a gentle poke at visitors who are naive or not paying attention or hiking barefoot on a wet and steep slope, but some visitors need to be reminded that nature can be dangerous. Meanwhile, the fatal goring of hiker Robert Boardman in 2010 by a rogue mountain goat in Olympic National Park resulted in a lawsuit against that park. A U.S. district judge dismissed this case in late 2012 based upon governmental immunity under the discretionary exception to the Federal Tort Claims Act, but plaintiffs still had the right to appeal to the Ninth Circuit.[3]

Dangers and wilderness go hand in hand. That is part of the attraction of wilderness, and danger is part of the allure. The fundamental way in which we in America view wilderness, with its raw man-against-nature aspects and the potential for adventure, is rooted in the idea that wilderness has dangers. Many would argue, "God save us from sanitized wilderness experiences!" Indeed, where would the inspiration, the adventure, the interest—in short, the fun—be without some risks? In the final analysis, it is impossible to "safety proof" a national park, and those parks are often more akin to Jurassic Park than to Disneyland.

Although the title of this book uses the word *accidents* for the sake of communication, I want to make it clear that most of these incidents were caused by foolhardiness or negligence, or (in the cases of suicide and murder) were purposeful. Stupidity and negligence have been big elements in these stories; very few were true "accidents," especially in the "Death by Nature" section. Yet no one still living wants to be blamed for or feel guilty about one of these incidents. So in recounting their stories about death incidents, most of those still living will go to great lengths to avoid blame or guilt by rationalizing their actions, by claiming the incident was a total "accident" rather than due to anyone's negligence, or even by fabricating parts of a story. I am not condemning anyone for this. I am simply stating that it happens. Many lawyers believe that true accidents ("acts of God") occur very rarely, and that someone's individual negligence is more often a factor in a death incident. Perhaps that is one reason the public does not like lawyers, because we do not wish to believe that. But in researching this book, I have come to the conclusion that, at least in most of these Yellowstone cases, the lawyers are correct. Many people do not understand the sometimes subtle difference between negligence and a true accident ("act of God"). In negligence, a person who had a legal duty to another person breaches that duty and as a result causes harm. In an "act of God," a true coincidence happens, and no one can be blamed.[4]

My friend Butch Farabee and his coauthor Michael Ghiglieri, who wrote *Off the Wall: Death in Yosemite*, have counted at least forty-eight deaths in that park since 1914 from people falling over waterfalls, including three in one incident in 2011. Like me, these authors attribute many of those deaths to the victims' personal negligence. People attempt brutal hikes in extreme heat or ski in extreme cold. They hike or ski alone. They drink too little water or too much alcohol. They go rafting without life jackets. They climb over guardrails and disregard signs. They go rock climbing alone in sandals. They hike barefoot on steep and even wet slopes. They enter rivers to cool off even when they cannot swim. And Ghiglieri, a near-forty-year veteran of wilderness guiding, also blames carelessness when people are taking photographs and when they are making jokes about falling (with the joke itself sometimes *causing* an actual fall!). Family members of a victim sometimes want to blame someone besides the victim, but the victim is often the one at fault.

Considerable research was necessary to turn up much of this material, as Yellowstone National Park itself does not have complete records. I utilized all of the annual reports of the superintendent, and all of the monthly reports of the superintendent, which unfortunately exist only for the period 1917–1967. I also used all known park press releases, and those case incident reports that were reachable under the Freedom of Information Act. Finally, I utilized area newspapers in great measure and personal interviews, as well as the large bibliography I amassed in writing other books and articles. Newspapers, as every historian knows, must be used with care, most often as a supplement to more reliable sources. Unfortunately, with all of their potential inaccuracies, caused by deadlines, distance, and other factors, newspapers are sometimes our only sources for fleeting bits of history, pieces that get too easily lost in the forward march of time, and pieces of strictly local history that get published nowhere else. So it is with some of my stories; they are fragmentary and nearly lost, rescued here only by means of scattered sources. For the more recent incidents, I have tried to save the details by interviewing participants where I knew of them.

Well over three hundred deaths are chronicled here and I, of course, instinctually realize something very important about this: every one of these deaths is or was an intensely emotional story for someone. I have learned a great deal about that from this research. I have learned about the delicate, almost tender, approach that is necessary when a writer is required to deal with the emotions of some very good people in order to find out the facts. I have learned that perceptions and memories can vary even among the very persons who were present at a given incident. I have learned that the incidents and their attendant circumstances can be exceedingly complex and open to vastly different interpretations, even among fellow participants. I have learned that memories fade over time and that reminiscences can be fallible, but that we must consult them both in order to be fair to the parties involved and to try to do justice to the story's correctness. And I have learned to beware of the "armchair quarterback" comments of those persons who were not present at a given incident.

It is logical to assume that the record, as presented here, even after extensive efforts, is incomplete. There may well be a number of instances of someone being injured in Yellowstone Park and then dying later in some faraway location. In those cases, the park may never have been notified of the death, and I have no way to find it. If you know of such a fatality involving Yellowstone, please write to me at PO Box 228, Yellowstone National Park, Wyoming, 82190.

Finally, the central messages of this book, aside from fascinating history, must be these: *play safely*, and think before you act.

I

DEATH BY NATURE

1

HOLD FAST TO YOUR CHILDREN
DEATH IN HOT WATER

He maketh the deep to boil like a pot.

—Job 41:31

IT IS A MYSTERY WHY ANYONE would dive headfirst into a Yellowstone hot spring merely to save a dog, but that is precisely what happened on July 20, 1981. David Allen Kirwan, 24, of La Canada, California, and his friend Ronald Ratliff, 25, of Thousand Oaks, parked their truck at Yellowstone's Fountain Paint Pot parking lot at around one o'clock that afternoon. While the men looked at the hot springs, Ratliff's dog Moosie, a large mastiff or Great Dane, escaped from the vehicle and jumped into nearby Celestine Pool, a hot spring later measured at 202 degrees Fahrenheit. The dog began yelping, and someone nearby quipped, "Oh, look, the poor thing!" Kirwan and Ratliff rushed to the spring and stood on the edge of it. Ratliff and another bystander both saw that Kirwan was preparing to go into the spring, and the bystander yelled, "Don't go in there!" Kirwan yelled back, "Like hell I won't!" Several more people yelled not to go in, but Kirwan took two steps into the pool then dove headfirst into the boiling water. One witness described it as a flying, swimming-pool-type dive.

Visitor Earl Welch of Annistow, Alabama, saw Kirwan actually swim to the dog and attempt to take it to shore, go completely underwater again, then release the dog, and begin trying to climb out. Ronald Ratliff pulled Kirwan from the spring, sustaining second-degree burns to his feet. Welch saw Kirwan appear to stagger backward, so the visitor hastened to him and said, "Give me your hand." Kirwan offered his hand, and Welch directed, "Come to the sidewalk."

As they moved slowly toward the walk, Kirwan managed to say, "That was stupid. How bad am I?" Welch tried to reassure him, and before they reached the walkway Kirwan again spoke softly. "That was a stupid thing I did."

Welch was suddenly overwhelmed with the feeling that he was walking with a corpse. He could see that Kirwan's entire body was badly burned, as the skin was already peeling off. It seemed to Welch that Kirwan was blind, for his eyes appeared totally white. Another man ran up and began to remove one of Kirwan's shoes, and the men watched horrified as the skin came off with it. "Don't do that!" said Welch, and Kirwan responded very tiredly, "It doesn't matter." Near the spring, rangers found two large pieces of skin shaped like human hands.

Kirwan experienced third-degree burns over 100 percent of his body including his entire head. He was taken to the clinic at Old Faithful, where a burn specialist who was coincidentally on duty could do little for him other than to pump in intravenous fluids at a high rate. Bob Carnes, a ranger who saw him at the clinic, remembers thinking that Kirwan did not have a chance for survival. "He was blind and most of his skin was coming off." Tony Sisto, Old Faithful's acting subdistrict ranger, was also there, and he agreed. "He had no vision," said Sisto, "but was fully conscious. He talked amiably with his caretakers, in no pain, asking the nurses to save his belt while they cut off what remained of his clothes." Ronald Ratliff's dog died in the pool and was not rescued. Oils from its body later made the hot spring have small eruptions. Kirwan died the following morning in a Salt Lake City hospital. In the men's truck, rangers found the park's warning literature and pamphlets. Kirwan and Ratliff had not read any of them.[1]

The idea of being boiled to death in a hot spring is a truly terrifying one to any rational person. Notwithstanding the *Billings Gazette* editorial at the beginning of this book, hot-spring deaths have occurred much more commonly in Yellowstone National Park than have grizzly bear deaths. The park has around ten thousand hot springs, geysers, mudpots, and steam vents scattered over its mountain plateau. Though collectively called thermal features today, all are technically hot springs. Most are hotter than 150 degrees Fahrenheit (sixty-six degrees Celsius), and many reach temperatures of 185–205 degrees Fahrenheit (eighty-five to ninety-six degrees Celsius). (Water boils at around 198 degrees Fahrenheit at this elevation.) These hot springs are dramatic and exquisitely beautiful features that are also very dangerous. The 1905 writer mentioned in the introduction spent great amounts of space warning of thermal dangers and then stated that the beautiful color of hot springs was an attractant: "Death lurks in the path of those who venture near, fascinated by the dazzling array of hues." Out of twenty known human deaths from hot springs in Yellowstone, eight have been children (not including three teenagers). Generally, these children were not being closely supervised by their parents in dangerous thermal areas at the times of their deaths. Because children are often oblivious to dangers around them, it is imperative that parents watch them closely in the park. Adults, too, can be oblivious, so we must hold fast to our children, regardless of their ages.

Injuries from hot springs in Yellowstone began early. Although no known records exist of fur trappers (1822–1840) or prospectors (1863–1869) being injured or killed by Yellowstone's hot springs, perhaps it happened. Nor do we know of Native American injuries or deaths from hot springs. But beginning in 1870, with the party that received credit for discovering Yellowstone, people began to be injured in the area's hot springs, and the injuries were nearly always as a result of their own carelessness. Truman Everts, of the 1870 Washburn Expedition, was separated from the main party. Lost for thirty-seven days, he wandered to Heart Lake to seek warmth from the hot springs there and inadvertently burned his hip in one of them.[2]

In 1871, the first known thermal injury occurred when Macon Josey and photographer H. B. Calfee entered the area. In attempting to help a deer out of a similar predicament, Josey fell almost completely into a "horrible seething pool" in Upper Geyser Basin near Old Faithful. His partner Calfee noted: "I assisted my companion as quickly as possible but in one half minute he was badly scalded from his waist down. He was so badly scalded that when I pulled his boots and socks off the flesh rolled off with them."

Calfee pulled Josey out and constructed a travois to carry him on, dabbing their remaining flour onto "his raw and bleeding burns." The travois proved unsatisfactory for "this pathless country," so Calfee rigged an arrangement in which Josey could sit with his legs crossed over the horse's neck to prevent pain to his burns. They traveled west in that manner to an old settler's place on the Madison River and then north to the Gallatin Valley and Bozeman, Montana. I have tried unsuccessfully to find Macon Josey's grave (probably somewhere in Montana) or anything else about him that would reveal whether or not he died from his injuries, for they were severe. If he died shortly after leaving Yellowstone, he would represent the first human death from a hot spring in park history. But for now, Josey's fate remains a mystery.[3]

As the numbers of tourists in Yellowstone Park increased, so did the chances of visitor injury. One possible thermal-injury incident, if it is true, is known for 1882. According to a lengthy 1882 newspaper article, traveler Walter Watson fell into a long and deep geyser tube "about 2½ miles from Fire Hole River" that summer, while accompanied by three other men, who gave him up for dead and left. According to Watson, the water into which he fell, some fifty feet below, was only warm, not hot—a most unusual situation in Yellowstone thermal areas. He stated that the geyser began to rise a few hours later, carrying him to the top of the well just before it got very hot and erupted. If the whole thing was a tall tale, it was a long and detailed one.[4]

At least two thermal injuries are known of for 1883.[5] One of the injured was former U.S. senator Roscoe Conkling of New York, who visited Mammoth Hot Springs that summer. A lover of hot baths, Conkling asked park resident G. L. Henderson for the use of his bathhouse near Capitol Hill. Unfortunately, Conkling did not know that cold water had to be added, and believing all to be in readiness, stepped into the tub. He immediately sprang out, crying, "Great God, I am scalded!" Henderson rushed to his assistance, dumping a bucket of snow into the bath, and ordered Conkling back into it. After some time, Conkling was much better.[6]

Hot-spring injuries began occurring in greater numbers in the 1880s as visitors to Yellowstone increased. A Mr. Crossman was scalded in the Fountain Paintpot in 1884, a young boy that same summer who convalesced at Marshall's Hotel,[7] and another man in the Artists' Paintpots in 1888.[8] A lady visitor was burned in 1888[9] and another, a Mrs. Dwyer, in 1890.[10] Henry Muedeking, a concessioner employee at West Thumb in August of 1893, started a long parade of thermal injuries and deaths at that location when he "strolled out one moonlit evening to the Thumb geyser, in company with two hotel girls." While "monkeying around" on the formation, he broke through the crust into boiling water, badly burning his legs. Taken to Fort Yellowstone, he spent two months in the hospital there before riding the train home to Saint Paul. Muedeking would not be the last employee to be injured at West Thumb. Ross P. White of Ames, Iowa, a tour guide and reportedly also Wylie Camp manager there, was guiding a group at Thumb on or about September 18, 1913, and fell into a hot spring while simultaneously walking backward and talking to his group. Ross White was badly injured. A newspaper article stated that the spring burned "almost every particle of skin" from the body of the college senior.[11] Army soldiers were not exempt from injuries in the hot springs which they were supposed to be guarding. One was burned in 1896,[12] another in 1899,[13] and a third in 1900.[14] A mother and daughter were badly scalded at Thumb Paintpots in 1901 and a Chinese visitor in the same place the same year.[15]

The two women injured in 1901 made newspapers around the country, for they were from a well-known New York family. Traveler/writer G. S. Turrill chronicled their "deaths" in Thumb Paintpots, but the victims did not die. Instead, the death story Turrill heard from his brother-in-law was simply an embellishment of their injury. The incident occurred at Thumb Paintpots on July 6, 1901. Eliza Garvin (Mrs. John L.) Zabriskie, age about 64, and her daughter Louise G. Zabriskie of Brooklyn, New York, were walking near the paintpots when Mrs. Zabriskie fell into one mud spring up to her armpits. Her daughter rushed up, grabbed the mother's skirts, and attempted to pull her out. The fabric gave way, however, and the daughter fell backward into the paintpot behind her, landing in a sitting position. The two ladies, badly burned, were hastily washed off with warm water, dabbed with witch hazel by persons at the nearby lunch station, wrapped in blankets, and taken on the steamboat *Zillah* to Lake Hotel. Mrs. Zabriskie was in the worse shape of the two, burned across her breast and shoulder along with her legs and hands, while her daughter was burned mainly on her legs. The women were conveyed to Mammoth Hot Springs, where surgeon J. B. Ferguson of Fort Yellowstone cared for them. According to later newspaper reports, both survived but spent months convalescing. The two women were from a prominent Brooklyn family, such that the woman's son (Dr. John B. Zabriskie), upon receiving a telegram from Dr. Ferguson, immediately boarded a train and headed for Yellowstone. The women's names were misspelled (often as "LaBriskie") in many newspapers until their hometown paper picked up the story.[16]

One of the worst alleged death incidents from hot springs in Yellowstone involved four Chinese laundrymen in 1889, but the best guess is that it never happened. For one thing, it supposedly occurred in the winter, a time when almost no one was historically present in the interior of Yellowstone (let alone four Chinese men running a laundry) and for another, the injury supposedly occurred "in Canyon City, near the Yellowstone Park . . . a new mining town." This geography was obviously confused, for there is no "Canyon City" in or

Photo of hot mud at West Thumb, where the Zabriskie women were injured in 1901, and a boat at dock that took them to Lake Hotel (NPS scrapbook photo 32-JN, YNP Archives)

near Yellowstone and there are no accessible thermal springs at the location known as Canyon in the park. At least two newspapers picked up the story in early February, slugging it "Cheyenne, Wyoming Territory" and proclaiming that "Yet Sing had established a wash house in a tent directly over a boiling spring." The story claimed that the spring suddenly erupted as a geyser one night, scalding the four men to death and throwing their bodies some distance away. A week later, *Illustrated Police News*—the nineteenth century's *National Enquirer*—picked up the story in garish style and trumpeted it as "Boiled Chinamen in the Yellowstone Park Region," even including a large woodcut drawing of bodies, pigtails, and washtubs being spouted into the air and stating that it was "a most singular fatality by which four Chinamen lost their lives." This ridiculousness can be no other than a retelling and expanding of the Chinese-laundry fable that was already making the rounds in Yellowstone by 1889. In that tall tale, a Chinese man running a laundry at Old Faithful supposedly was "blown to Shanghai" when the spring, over which he had pitched his laundry tent, erupted.[17]

But reality is much more serious. As of 2013, at least twenty persons are known to have died from hot-spring injuries in or near Yellowstone National Park, including the David Allen Kirwan fatality. The first three were children.

The details of the first human death from a hot spring in Yellowstone seem to be lost. But relatives of little James Joseph Stumbo are convinced that it happened. James was born November 21, 1882, at Rock Creek, Wyoming, and moved with his family to Livingston, Montana, in 1886. He died February 22, 1890, at the age of 7. According to descendants of his family, who still live in Livingston, James died after falling into a hot spring in Yellowstone National Park. That information appears in the *History of Park County, Montana 1984* and in a local tour book. A search of 1889–1890 issues of the *Livingston Enterprise* and the *Livingston Post* newspapers fails to turn up the details of the story. However, descendants told me it has been known in their family for more than a hundred years that little James's death happened that way. Unfortunately we currently know nothing else about it. But apparently it began the long, heart-wrenching history of human deaths from hot springs in Yellowstone.[18]

The second such known fatality was also that of a child, and it occurred on October 5, 1898. On that day, 9-year-old Charles Walter Pring of Stacy (in Custer County near Miles City), Montana, traveled with his parents by wagon to Yellowstone. The *Livingston Enterprise* reported:

> The family [was] in the vicinity of Norris Geyser Basin Wednesday of last week when the youth preferring to walk for a change, had preceded the vehicle and on reaching the geyser basin was walking by use of a

cane over the formation. He reached a point where the crust near a boiling spring gave way, precipitating him into the water. He was alone and relying on his own efforts succeeded in climbing out onto the solid formation where he was found by his parents. Both legs and his left arm and side were horribly scalded. The surgeon from Fort Yellowstone was summoned, the wounds dressed and the boy removed to the Cottage hotel at Mammoth Hot Springs where he lingered in agony until relieved by death last Saturday [October 8]. The body was brought to this city Monday evening and interred in Mountain view cemetery.[19]

The *Livingston Post* newspaper added that the family had driven its wagon up from Custer County but that "since the unfortunate occurrence resulting in the death of their son, they have decided not to return to their former home, but will locate in another part of the state."[20] Those devastated parents would not be the last to change their home location to a different one because of a death incident in Yellowstone National Park (see David Childers, chapter 11).

Little Lester LaDuke, 4, was scalded to death at LaDuke Hot Springs (eight miles north of the park) on July 23, 1905, when he fell into a bathing spring that was characterized as "one of the hottest in eastern Montana."[21] The child's father, Julius LaDuke, ran the bathing resort at Horr, Montana, and the child was buried in the Horr cemetery (the grave is unmarked today).[22] Nothing more is known about this incident, which represents an early human death from a hot spring in the Yellowstone region.

Another early fatality from a hot spring in the park occurred in 1905. There was much national newspaper coverage of this event, and it also resulted in the full-page *Washington Times* article "Dangers of the Yellowstone Park Where a Washington Woman Has Just Lost Her Life," which I discussed in the new introduction to this book. On Friday, August 18, 1905, Fannie A. Weeks, aged 51 and a clerk for the U.S. Treasury Department in Washington, DC, was traveling by Wylie stagecoach around Yellowstone's dirt road system.[23] Her stage driver, Robert Wylie, was a divinity student "whose guided trips were extremely interesting," according to park photographer Jack Haynes, who remembered him. Wylie's uncle, W. W. Wylie, owned the stagecoaches and tent camps in which Weeks was staying.

At Old Faithful, Robert Wylie walked his tour group around the geyser area. Weeks was very interested in the hot springs, and Wylie warned her at one point that she was too venturesome. The incident occurred near Grand Geyser. Standing at the edge of the crater of one of the springs there, probably Turban Geyser, Weeks "all dressed in black with a veil over her face," removed her smoked glasses to clean them of mist.[24] Haynes believed that she stepped backward without thinking and into the pool, sinking clear to her hips in water of 185–200 degrees Fahrenheit. But in a letter dictated from her hospital bed before she died, Weeks stated that "the edge of one of the geysers gave way with me and let me down into the boiling cauldron. I am terribly scalded from the elbows. Am now at Livingston in a helpless condition and under medical treatment. Do not know when I shall be able to be forwarded to Washington." She landed in the spring feet first, with the water up to her waist. Seeing and hearing her standing in the water screaming in pain until she became unconscious, Robert Wylie immediately jumped into the pool himself and pulled Weeks onto the side of its crater. She had lots of petticoats on, and these, soaked as they were with hot water, continued to inflict burns for some time afterward. Wylie was himself badly burned on his legs, arms, and hands, and according to Jack Haynes, skin grafts were required to alleviate some of his injuries.[25]

Fannie Weeks was so severely burned that little hope was held for her recovery, but she lingered on at Livingston's Ebert Hotel for three weeks, finally dying on September 4. Her companion, an Eliza Hartman, remained at her side until the end, when Weeks's remains were shipped to Washington, DC, for interment in Rock Creek Cemetery. Although newspapers, including a front-page story in the *Washington Post*, reported the incident as occurring at Grand Geyser, Jack Haynes remembered it many years later as happening at nearby Turban Geyser but did not know that the woman had died. Indeed, Turban Geyser has a much deeper and more precipitous well than Grand Geyser and would probably have more likely been the feature being looked at from close range.[26]

Confusion over which spring was the fatal one in the Weeks incident was to continue. In 1914, a Wylie Camping Company guide conducted some visitors over the formations north of Old Faithful Geyser and breathlessly whispered the horrifying story to his minions, claiming that Fannie Weeks had fallen into the Vault Spring near Giantess Geyser. "The lady was wearing glasses and taking notes," said the guide. "Absorbed in her note-taking with glasses steamed, the unfortunate woman walked straight into the pool." Even though the precise location and details of the incident had become muddled, park tour guides still told the story nine years later.[27]

It was apparent from earliest park days that the hot springs were dangerous, and various attempts were made to warn visitors. An 1883 park employee, George Thomas, cautioned travelers that walking at Norris had to be "slow and careful" because of the danger "of dropping into a hole and being scalded to death."[28] By 1888, park tour guide G. L. Henderson had apparently posted a warning sign at Norris Geyser Basin's Porcelain Terrace. Henderson noted that "Visitors ought not to cross this basin without a competent guide, and then it is at the risk of their lives. There is a [sign] board marked 'Dangerous' easily seen from the road."[29] Theodore Gerrish in 1886 commented on the "notices printed on boards in great black letters": "Do not walk on the formations."[30] Traveler Charles Gillis reported that in 1892, "we frequently saw signs put up by the Government: 'Do not drive on here,' and 'danger.'"[31]

And as one would expect, each time there was an injury or (especially) a death, it served as a new impetus to erect danger signs. Two injuries plus the 1919 death of James Hughes prompted the park superintendent to acknowledge the need for such signs:

> A small boy broke through the geyser formation near Giantess Geyser and burned his feet quite seriously. This was known to be a dangerous place, and danger signs were posted, but as is often the case, they were not heeded. With increased travel the time seems to have come when more than signs at some places in the geyser basins are needed to keep people out of trouble, as often the danger signs are not taken seriously. At this very place one lady asked if it was really dangerous or if the sign gave the name of the geyser. Another said it was not dangerous, for she walked over it and it did not break through.[32]

A photo from park archives, probably taken in the 1930s, shows Ranger Harry Trischman standing next to a sign near Giantess Geyser which reads "Dangerous."

By 1905, park photos show that narrow board planks had been laid over the ground at Norris Geyser Basin for visitors to walk on.[33] But full board walkways for visitor safety would not make their appearance in most Yellowstone thermal areas until the 1960s; indeed, blacktopped paths were in existence from the 1930s until the 1950s, paths which were very bad for the delicate ecology of the thermal areas. Thermal area walkways must, of necessity, be portable to allow for changes in the springs as well as for the protection of visitors, hence the boardwalks today.

On July 8, 1919, a 4-year-old boy named James Baxter Hughes from Gueydon, Louisiana, accidentally backed into a small hot spring at West Thumb Geyser Basin. He died the next day at Old Faithful Inn from shock caused by his burns. It is not known which spring was involved. The park superintendent attributed the boy's death to his guardians not carefully watching him.[34]

Another West Thumb–area hot spring fatality occurred on August 24, 1926. At about 8:00 p.m., the Reverend Gilbert A. Eakins, 27, pastor of the Presbyterian Church of Saratoga, Wyoming, accompanied by his wife Patti, small son, and parents from Bourbon, Indiana, were walking around the thermal area when Rev. Eakins slipped and fell into an unspecified hot spring. In attempting to get out of the pool, he backed into another one. Confused by the pain from hot water, he lost his footing and fell headlong into the first pool.

He was completely immersed but managed to crawl from the spring unaided. Eakins remained conscious to the end, but he died from shock on the way to the Mammoth hospital.

Ranger Wendell Keate, a doctor, was nearby at the road-crew bunkhouse when he heard screams and cries for help. Keate ran to the geyser basin behind Mr. Halstead, a government truck driver:

> When I arrived . . . I observed a man staggering through the trees toward the road and screaming at the top of his voice for help, that he had fallen into a pool and was burned all over.
>
> Calling to Halstead who was holding him, not to handle him roughly, I took hold of the man and asking Halstead for his knife, laid the man on his back and proceeded to cut away his clothing as carefully as possible for I could see even in that dim light that the skin had been [*sic*] slipped from large areas on his body and extremities.
>
> In two minutes a large crowd had been attracted to the scene including all the employees of the road camp and the camping company. While I was cutting away his clothing I asked for a comforter to lay him on so as not to get any foreign material into the areas which were burned. By this time my wife arrived with the car and Ranger Miller with my medicine kit. As soon as his clothing was all removed I administered one half grain of morphine. I commandeered all the olive oil and cooking oils from the delicatessen and the road camp. Mrs. Evans of the road camp had three pints of olive oil with which I covered the entire body [and] then obtained two clean sheets from the camping company. I wrapped Mr. Eakins in them so that the trunk and extremities were completely covered then soaked the sheets in oil. I gave mineral oil by mouth to relieve the burning which the esophagus and trachea had sustained when the victim had gulped hot water into his mouth and had swallowed it.[35]

The fact that Eakins's head was submerged increased his certainty of death, because his burns were then nearly as bad internally as externally due to the swallowing of hot water.

One of the scariest things about falling into a hot spring is realizing that one could indeed remain fully conscious for many painful hours while awaiting death. Following this incident, Pattie Eakins attempted to recover money from the government through congressional action but apparently failed. She stated that she believed that compensation was due because "this particular pool lies so close to a walk which is open for public use in getting onto and off a pier which appears to be used for boats and for fishermen. It seems there should be some railing or rope around this pool." The Reverend Eakins would not be the last person to experience this horror.

Rollo Gallagher of Salt Lake City, Utah, died from injuries he sustained on August 15, 1927, when he fell into a hot spring near Firehole Lake in Lower Geyser Basin. Gallagher ventured out onto a thin crust formation which failed to support his weight and he was precipitated into the hot spring. Initially, his injuries were not thought to be life-threatening, and he was advised at West Yellowstone to go to the hospital at Mammoth. Instead, Gallagher elected to drive to Salt Lake City without treatment and died shortly after he arrived there. This considerable delay in receiving medical attention was probably at least partly responsible for his death.[36]

Park visitors since earliest days have been curious about the water temperatures in thermal areas. Even today they can often be seen bending down to touch the water. The temptation to touch is almost irresistible. That temptation proved to be the undoing of George H. Brown, 52, of Lampasas, Texas, on the afternoon of August 24, 1928, the same day that Reverend Eakins had been killed two years earlier.

Brown and his party approached a hot spring "immediately east of Excelsior Geyser" at Midway Geyser Basin, probably present Indigo Spring. While bending over to stick his hand into the water, he lost his balance and toppled into the spring, which today measures around 200 degrees Fahrenheit. Brown was entirely submerged in the boiling water. His two frantic sons managed to extricate him, scalding their arms in the process. The unfortunate man was rushed toward the Mammoth hospital, but death occurred before he arrived there. Brown was conscious for the four hours prior to his death. He left a wife and nine children, and his funeral back in Lampasas was a major event.[37]

In 1929, a hot-spring death resulted in the giving of a Yellowstone place name. That year Georges Landoy, age 42, the editor of the French newspaper *Le Matin* at Antwerp, Belgium, was visiting the Old Faithful area with a party of European journalists. On July 3, at 3:45 p.m., Landoy had been watching Grand Geyser erupt when he saw Castle Geyser begin its eruption. He ran toward Castle, not watching where he was going, and fell into a "very hot" spring, apparently present Belgian Pool. About 50 percent of his body was severely burned—"both legs to the hips," the left buttock, and the left hand. Landoy was taken to Old Faithful Lodge for first aid and then to the Mammoth hospital. He died on July 5, 1929, at 5:30 p.m.[38]

There are conflicts in the accounts of this incident. Two different newspaper reports gave the location of the spring as Castle Geyser and a third one gave the location as "a discharging geyser in the Upper Basin."[39] These accounts all say that the incident happened at Castle Geyser, where its eruption hit Landoy, but I believe that the monthly superintendent's report and the Old Faithful logbook are the more reliable sources. It makes more sense for the man to have been killed falling into a pool than for him to have been killed by being splashed by an erupting geyser.[40]

Moreover, an archival letter gives the location of the pool. It states that Landoy at Grand Geyser, "with his eyes on the Castle Geyser, walked directly into this small pool . . . The pool into which he fell is one that is shallow all around its edge, and deepens to a small central throat." Horace Albright, who was superintendent of Yellowstone during the 1920s, stated in 1962 that Landoy, a "famous Belgian editor," was walking backward to photograph Grand Geyser when he fell into the spring.[41] That quiet hot spring was subsequently given the name Belgian Pool for Landoy by unknown park persons.[42]

The Landoy incident and the three other thermal deaths that occurred between 1926 and 1928 added up to four thermal deaths in four summers. These episodes stimulated safety discussions in the park. "It is remarkable that there are not more accidents," wrote park superintendent Roger Toll to the director of the National Park Service (NPS). Toll thought that if the park had more clearly defined trails through thermal areas, then "people who leave trails will do so at their own risk." A lawyer who read of the Landoy death wrote to Toll, urging him to put up fences and warning signs in thermal areas. And letters from the park landscape division make it apparent that the Landoy incident was an important event in the evolution of designated thermal area trails and log warning signs.[43]

Injury incidents no doubt contributed to the birth of those trails as well. The monthly superintendent's reports from the 1920s are loaded with instances of people being burned in the face by looking down into the cone of Old Faithful Geyser. As incredibly imprudent as this may seem, around ten persons were injured in that decade by doing it. An early instance of this happened in 1901, when a German military surgeon known only as Dr. Sellerbeck fell into the cone of a "geyser well" at Old Faithful. He was burned, but survived.[44]

During the 1930s, four persons died in Yellowstone hot springs, and numerous others were injured. The deceased victims were one adult, one child, and two teenagers. Little Joy Myrlene Hanny, age 3, of Firth, Idaho, was traveling with a group of seventeen persons who stopped at Biscuit Basin on July 13, 1932. At 1:45 p.m., while the group watched Jewel Geyser spouting its beautiful fountain twenty-five feet high, Joy was momentarily unsupervised. When the geyser erupted, Joy and her mother jumped back in surprise. The mother heard her child scream, looked down, and saw the little girl immersed all the way up to her neck. She had stepped backward into a small nearby hot spring and was scalded "very severely."

Although party members quickly pulled her out, Joy Hanny died the following night at the Mammoth hospital. The pool was measured at 150 degrees

Fahrenheit, not hot enough to cause instant death but hot enough to cause excruciating pain for thirty hours prior to death.[45] The spring into which Joy Hanny fell was described as being three feet long, two feet wide, and about two feet deep. It was located about thirty feet south of Jewel Geyser and may have been present Shell Spring.[46]

Sixteen-year-old Edgar A. Gibson of Tulsa, Oklahoma, suffered a similar fate on July 18, 1933. There are two conflicting accounts as to how this incident occurred. The superintendent's version says his party was touring the Steady Geyser area in Lower Basin when another boy dared Gibson to walk across what appeared to be a solid formation but was really hot mud. Gibson sank to his thighs, receiving severe burns from which he later died. This version is corroborated by the Old Faithful logbook that states Gibson fell through hot mud at Steady Geyser and was burned severely on his legs and thighs.[47]

The newspapers reported that Gibson's touring party of teenagers stopped at Old Faithful to walk around the geyser basin. Gibson stepped onto what he thought was a stone at the edge of a hot spring. Instead, it was a thin crust of sinter, which gave way and precipitated him into the scalding water.

Aune Frederickson, age 15, was a maid at Old Faithful Inn that summer who was pressed into emergency service to help medics minister to Edgar Gibson. "I had to help the nurse give him a hypo," she wrote. "It was pitiful to hear him groan. And I had to sit there and hold his head and hear it all. Poor kid . . . And just before he left he tried to smile to me and I just burst out and cried; I couldn't hold it back anymore."[48]

Regardless of which version of his story happened, 40 percent of Edgar Gibson's body was scalded, and that was enough to cause his death on July 25, after he lay in agony for a week at Mammoth and Livingston hospitals. The newspapers also reported that overconfidence might have played a part in Gibson's death, as he had been in the park a year earlier and "no doubt believed himself to be familiar with the section being visited." While in the hospital, he wrote several letters to Aune Frederickson. She was devastated to learn that her "cute" boy had died. "I just couldn't sleep all last night thinking of him . . . He just wrote to me Saturday & told me he was slightly better & now he is dead. I just can't write any more."[49]

Another teenager must also have suffered terribly. While fishing just north of West Thumb on August 14, 1935, Glenn LaRue Howard, 16, of Max, Nebraska, became separated from the rest of his party but continued to fish alone. Somehow he tumbled into a rather deep hot spring to a six-foot depth. It must have been difficult and painful to pull himself out, but the youth did it. He then wandered into a timbered area in search of other party members and was found half an hour after his scalding plunge. The hot spring that Howard fell into was located about two hundred yards north of King Geyser. A note in the naturalists' log stated that his skin peeled off from his neck to his toes. Given first aid at West Thumb, he was sent by ambulance to Mammoth accompanied by his parents. With burns covering 95 percent of his body, he died the next day at the Mammoth hospital.[50]

The West Thumb Geyser Basin claimed a second fisherman on July 3, 1936. At about noon on that day, James W. McFerson, 36, of Ogden, Utah, succeeded in hooking a nice trout at a location some two hundred yards north of Fishing Cone along the lakeshore. In his excitement, he failed to notice a hot spring that was four feet in diameter and three feet behind him—perhaps present Mantrap Cone. McFerson stepped backward into the hot spring, immersing himself up to his neck. His wife pulled him from the pool immediately and was herself fairly burned. Two rangers and a traveling physician gave McFerson first aid at the scene, but he died the following day at the Mammoth hospital.[51]

The West Thumb Geyser Basin seems to have been a place of many thermal injuries and deaths over the years. The numerous such incidents that occurred there finally resulted in the lakeshore being closed to fishing, probably for all time. Fishing Cone, the famous hot spring surrounded by Yellowstone Lake in which park visitors since 1870 cooked fish right on their fishing line,[52] itself injured at least one of those fishermen in 1921 when he stepped into it.[53]

The death of McFerson at West Thumb in 1936 was followed thirteen years later by that of a 5-year-old boy. Robert Kasik, his parents, and two brothers, all from Berwyn, Illinois, were visiting the West Thumb area on the evening of Thursday, July 14, 1949. At around 6:30 p.m., Robert was walking along the east side of the West Thumb cafeteria building, then located just east of the present restrooms and southeast of the ranger station. Three hot springs were all very near the foundations of the building. The ground near the edge of one of the pools was very slippery, and Robert lost his balance and tumbled into it. His 10-year-old brother Phil attempted to pull him out but could not and ran for help.

Caro Miller, a dishwasher at the cafeteria, looked out the window and saw Robert thrashing in the pool. She yelled, and her boss ran out the door to find two of Hamilton's employees pulling the boy from the spring. Robert had second- and third-degree burns from his neck to his toes. Ranger Irvin Lloyd cut the boy's pants off and wrapped him in a sheet. Six hours later, at Mammoth Hospital, Robert Kasik died. According to his father, Robert's brother Phil carried guilt about the incident for most of his life, even though the tragedy was not his fault.[54]

That same season, little Karen Lee Anderson, four and a half, of Grand Coulee Dam, Washington, was visiting Black Sand Basin near Old Faithful with her mother. At 11:30 a.m., on September 13, 1949, she pulled away from the woman who was holding her hand, ran to a hot spring near the creek, and fell into it. Karen sustained second- and third-degree burns over 90 percent of her body. She died very quickly. By coincidence, a friend of Karen's family had taken Robert Kasik to the hospital a month earlier at the time of his death. In memory of Karen and indirectly of their son, Robert Kasik's parents named their new daughter, born in 1950, after Karen.[55]

Karen Anderson was probably fortunate to succumb quickly. Danny Lewis of Austin, Minnesota, was not so lucky. The 6-year-old boy was fishing with his father, William Lewis, on the Firehole River on June 13, 1958. His misstep happened at the large hot spring named Ojo Caliente (Spanish for hot spring) in Lower Geyser Basin. Danny fell into that superheated spring and then lived for two more days. His 5-year-old sister Jean was there too. "I was holding his hand," she remembered. "He let go and just slipped into the spring. He . . . was a good patient [later]—was singing—was in no pain. We took his clothes off and wrapped him in a blanket." Danny P. Lewis died on June 15 from third-degree burns over all of his body except his head and neck. Ojo Caliente is one of the park's hottest springs at 198–202 degrees Fahrenheit.[56]

Two of Yellowstone's nineteen hot-spring deaths happened because young adults were attempting to "hot pot" (swim) in hot springs. Both were park employees. The vast majority of the park's hot springs are 50–100 degrees *too hot* for swimming.

On the evening of July 12, 1967, Brian Parsons, 20, of Nanuet, New York, an employee of the Yellowstone Park Company at Lake Lodge and a biology major at SUNY–New Paltz, decided to go on a late-night excursion with friends. It was his birthday. They drove some forty-eight miles to the Nez Perce Creek area north of Old Faithful and hiked up the creek in near darkness. The imprudent group did not secure a fire permit nor did they even have a flashlight. Parsons and his friend, Ronald May, 18, of Cheyenne, Wyoming, wandered away from the main group to go swimming illegally in one of the hot springs. In the dark of around midnight, Parsons somehow fell or dove into a hot spring of around 180 degrees Fahrenheit. May attempted to rescue him and sustained second-degree burns to both of his legs. Parsons was covered with second- and third-degree burns over 90 percent of his body. He lived for some twelve days afterward in a Salt Lake City hospital, but finally died. Because "he was greatly enamored of the outdoors and the creatures found there," friends established a biology scholarship in his name, which has ever since been awarded annually at his university.[57]

The same hot spring that killed Parsons also killed Donald Watt Cressey on the night of June 29–30, 1975. This pool on Nez Perce Creek was given the name Dead Savage Spring by the U.S. Geological Survey shortly after Cressey's death.[58] A "savage" in Yellowstone parlance is a park concessioner employee.

Cressey, age nearly 21, was a third-year Old Faithful Lodge employee from Bellevue, Washington. On the evening of Sunday, June 29, 1975, Cressey and ten to twenty other employees and visiting friends of Cressey attended a large, late-night "hot potting" party on Nez Perce Creek. Cressey somehow got into the wrong pool, the one later measured at 179 degrees Fahrenheit. When the party broke up, apparently no one missed Cressey, for the rest of the group drove home without him. This was suspicious to investigating park rangers, and the FBI was called in to investigate. Cressey, the senior cook at Old Faithful Lodge, had not been popular with everyone, and that fact, plus the group's returning home without him, made the rangers look at foul play as a possibility.

Cressey's body remained in the pool all day Monday, and when he failed to show up for work on Tuesday, a search began. On Wednesday, his body was found by a young child who was fishing with his father. Not all of it could be recovered because it had been cooking in the spring for more than two days.

Two of Cressey's visiting friends from that summer—Sandy Farncomb (Bennett) and Shannon Bruce (Wilson)—have carried the burden of Cressey's death in their heads for some forty years. Both women have wondered whether Cressey was purposely pushed into the hot spring that killed him, and both of them had been with Cressey at various times to the site of his final moments. "He wasn't the easiest person to get along with," says Shannon Wilson. "He'd worked at Yellowstone before and knew his way around, so an accident never seemed very likely to me." Sandy Bennett had worked with Cressey two years earlier. She and her friend Shannon, with two other friends, went back to visit him during the fateful summer, staying at his cabin at Old Faithful. "He was having a hard time," says Sandy, "and told us that the people working there were not very nice, that he was having problems and he seemed very worried. He talked about going home . . . We left [Yellowstone] one week before he died."

Some forty years later, the two women are still friends and agree completely with each other about what they remember. They both remain unconvinced that Cressey's death was an accident. Sandy's postscript goes back to 1973, when she first accompanied Don Cressey and others to the fateful site:

> I went with Don and a bunch of employees to the same place where he was [later] found. We all went hot potting. I remember walking down a path and Don pointing to a hot pot that was marked with a white cross. He said to "never go in that one as it was too hot" . . . Back in Seattle, I heard about Don's death on the radio and could not believe it. I wrote a lot of letters back then and remember writing to my friends that still worked in Yellowstone. They told me that Don was found fully clothed in the hot pot marked with a cross. They also told me that his car was

not at the place that he was found so that he must have rode [*sic*] with someone else . . . I have been haunted by this for years and . . . have always believed that he was murdered.

Another of their fellow employees and friends, Barbara Oxford (Bettevy), also worked with Don Cressey, and she agrees. To her the incident was not an accident. She was told by a Yellowstone Park Company insurance worker a couple of years later that there was still movement in the Cressey case. "She said she could not go into details," says Barbara, "because it was still under investigation, [and] just that it was drug related and others were involved."[59]

Exactly how Cressey fell into the pool is a mystery, but possibly it was a simple misstep in the dark. Ann Trocolli was one of the members of the actual swimming party. She stated that Cressey led the way to the pool and that "once [we were] there, someone, I think Don, dove in. Jeanne [Le Ber] was shocked that someone would dive into the pool, but Don had been there before and must have known what to expect. We all got undressed[.] There were other people, seven or so, already swimming when we got in. [After that] I never saw Don in the pool . . . There was no one left in the water when we got dressed."

Upon reading this, I assumed Cressey simply dove into the wrong spring in the darkness. But another party member, Miriam Frey, stated that Cressey undressed and was completely naked when she saw him dive into the pool. His body was found fully clothed, but nevertheless, his death was ultimately ruled accidental.[60] A plausible scenario is that Donald Cressey spent the evening swimming with other party members, got out of the 110-degree pool, put his clothes on, and then fell (or possibly, but less likely, jumped) into the other, much hotter spring while all alone. With all parties apparently assuming he rode home with someone else, no one missed him. The possibility that he was pushed into the pool is intriguing but ultimately unprovable at this point.

The sudden, searing tragedy which had perhaps the greatest impact on Yellowstone Park and the National Park Service occurred on June 28, 1970. In the middle of that afternoon, Andy C. Hecht, 9, of Williamsville, New York, was walking with his vacationing family along a boardwalk near Crested Pool in the Old Faithful area. That awesomely beautiful hot spring had so captivated early visitors to the park that it received a slough of romantic names, among them "Fire Basin," "Circe's Boudoir," and the "Devil's Well." A puff of wind apparently blew the pool's hot vapor into Andy's eyes, momentarily blinding him at a turn in the walkway. Some accounts claim Andy tripped at the edge of the boardwalk, which had no guardrail. At any rate, he plunged into the pool, where the temperature was over 200 degrees Fahrenheit. Andy tried vainly to swim a couple of strokes, then was scalded to death and sank. According to two national magazines, the last glimpse his mother had of him was seeing his

Castle Geyser and Crested Pool (hot spring where Andy Hecht died in 1970) (NPS, Yellowstone National Park)

rigid, stark-white face, the mark of his pain and apprehension of death, sinking into the boiling water.[61] Andy's father stated that they did not see him fall; he was behind them on the boardwalk when they heard a splash, turned around, and saw in horror that he had fallen into Crested Pool. Regardless, his body sank out of sight. Eight pounds of bone, flesh, and clothing were recovered the following day.[62]

The accounts of other witnesses conflict with those of the parents. Several persons, including Andy's sister, Margaret, were witnesses or near witnesses to the tragedy, and two of them say he ran into the pool. Margaret stated, "I was walking behind Andy. We were going at a pretty slow pace, and I saw him coming close to the edge, and I go 'Andy, watch out!' Then I heard this splash, and I grabbed his hand. I couldn't hold on much longer. Then I couldn't see him because of the steam; and the next thing I knew, I couldn't see him again; and he was down." Polly Eash, 15, of Greensboro, Maryland, was also a witness, and she said: "I saw him swing around and run into the pool. As he went into the pool his hands were up and his legs were in motion running. He just simply ran down the slope into the pool. Everyone was screaming and hollaring [*sic*]." Polly's friend, Amy Myers, also 15, of Denton, Maryland, corroborated Polly's account: "The boy did not trip that I noticed; he just ran right into the center of the pool . . . He just ran, actually running, right into the pool with both hands up over his head." Ron Reader of Roseville, California, was another nearby stroller. He says, "I heard some screaming and ran to [the] edge of [the] pool to see a boy with [his] arm raised sink out of sight."

Several witnesses remembered hearing the father yell "Andy!" several times. Walter Layfield of Parkersburg, West Virginia, remembered that two or three persons physically restrained the father from going into the spring after his son. And a nurse at Lake Hospital, Carol Lake, remembers overhearing Andy's father, James, saying something like, "He [Andy] was right behind us, and I heard him say, 'I wonder if this water really is hot.'"[63]

Around four the next morning, James Hecht, unable to sleep in his motel room despite heavy sedation, arose to compose a letter to Secretary of the Interior Walter Hickel about what he thought were inadequate safety procedures on the part of the National Park Service. Dr. Hecht, a chemical engineer in Richmond, Virginia, urged Hickel to take "positive action" to prevent similar future accidents.[64]

Dr. Hecht and his wife began a drive to force the National Park Service to commit to improved safety in the national parks. He testified before a senate subcommittee, accusing the NPS of failing to give adequate warnings in pamphlets and brochures about the dangers of thermal pools and of failing to erect guardrails.[65] Dr. Hecht also filed a wrongful death lawsuit against the Park Service and another suit to force the government to give him information on fatalities in the then 258 national park units.[66] An initial tort claim asked for one million dollars. Hecht's wrongful death lawsuit was eventually settled out of court for twenty thousand dollars.[67]

Other timely thermal injuries added impetus to Dr. Hecht's campaign. Shortly afterward, 14-year-old Cameron Smith slipped into a Yellowstone hot spring, suffering severe burns over 70 percent of his body.[68] Moreover, hot-spring injuries (as opposed to deaths) in general in Yellowstone during the 1960s were high, and this also added fuel to Dr. Hecht's crusade. Of course, most if not all decades between 1890 and 1970 exhibited similarly high thermal injuries. Reported injuries in Yellowstone hot springs numbered at least nine in 1961, nine in 1962, seven in 1963, seven in 1964, five in 1965, eighteen in 1966, seventeen in 1967, twelve in 1968, twelve in 1969, and ten in 1970, for a total of 106.[69] It all looked pretty dangerous to Dr. Hecht. But as usual, things were not that simple.

In all cases in the 1960s, except where a geyser erupted unexpectedly,[70] the causes were attributable to visitor carelessness. Often visitors were walking in places they were not supposed to be, were intoxicated, were traveling in darkness, lost their balance, or were looking at animals instead of watching where they were going. Additionally, at least three injuries occurred in the 1960s because visitors were trying to rescue a dog illegally off-leash. Other injuries occurred from overconfidence, disregard for signs or warnings, camping illegally, or careless running (instead of walking) in thermal areas. These still represent most of the reasons for hot-spring injuries in Yellowstone.[71]

Jim and Amy Hecht's campaign did result in increased funding for a number of regional safety officers in the NPS and more warnings in handout literature. Increased attention to safety and warnings continues in NPS ranks today, and safety is now a major concern in national parks nationwide. Angry at the NPS for what they perceived as insufficient safety precautions, the Hechts pushed for a while to have guardrails put up around every Yellowstone (or at least Old Faithful area) hot spring. Said Amy, "I don't care. I want fences around all 150 of those pools!"[72]

That was, of course, an unreasonable and illogical suggestion. Yellowstone has around ten thousand hot springs. Legally the NPS is required to give only reasonable warnings of hidden or obvious dangers. In fact, in a 1990 case which centered on the death of a climber in Grand Teton National Park, the U.S. Tenth Circuit Court of Appeals ruled that the NPS does not have to make "every possible effort" to provide protection from (backcountry) dangers.[73] But, as author Paul Schullery has noted, people react to tragedy with rage:

> They are confused and frustrated and need to strike out. They need to hate or get revenge; they need to *blame*. They need, most of all, to avoid

blaming themselves. Sometimes someone else is handy; sometimes that someone even deserves the blame . . . many dumb things have been done in the park by managers. Some of those things have hurt people. But occasional stupidity in park administrators, or occasional tragedy among park visitors, is not a good barometer of the health of the wilderness. When someone is hurt in the park, and the need to blame aches for fulfillment, you can almost count on the innocent resource getting stuck with part of the bill.[74]

While Dr. Hecht's campaign has had some arguably positive results (such as the now annual Andrew Clark Hecht Memorial Public Safety Achievement Award that the NPS director bestows upon some individual or group), it can only go so far, and then the public must take some responsibility. "I can assure you," Dr. Hecht told Congress, "that if I had only been alerted to the hazards, even if there were no fences, Andy would be alive today. Remember that very few steps have been taken to protect you [in parks]. Warnings will be understated not exaggerated."[75]

But this man was a doctor, of chemical engineering, no less. He could see the pool's bubbling water and vapor, feel its heat, and read the stay-on-walkways warning signs. The implication of statements like his is: if you want me to heed a warning, hit me over the head with it!

It is an old problem. How much warning is adequate in parks, especially when visitors are often careless and in a hurry? At the turn of the century, prior to the country's present tendency toward litigation, attitudes were different. An early Yellowstone park superintendent, in commenting on an employee being bitten while foolishly feeding a bear, stated that "he got simply what he deserved."[76] But even then, some persons harbored unrealistic expectations as to safety in Yellowstone. A woman wrote to the park in 1911 with this query: "I have been told that everyone entering the park is insured against accident. Will you kindly let me know if this is so?"[77] Needless to say, it was not.

The wilderness environment has always contained certain dangers. To remove them would require changes so sweeping as to do away with most of the reasons for having national parks. The scene would cease to be revitalizing, stimulating, and inspirational and would instead become artificial and sanitized. To develop a national park is to not have one.[78] In line with this is the problem of people who want the park wild as long as it is not too wild. Paul Schullery has discussed this in his book *Mountain Time* in the chapter entitled "A Percentage of Fools," and he says, "Some folks require the park's wildness and yet deny its right to exercise its wildness upon them." These are often the first persons to sue a park.

It is also true, however, that many people seem to have no common sense where the out-of-doors is concerned, and thus they need a few warnings. What may be natural for a ranger who grew up out of doors may also be truly strange for an average visitor. Therefore, a balance is needed between adequate warnings from a park and basic responsibility from the visitor. Perhaps there is a commentary here on where our society is heading, when so much of it seems to have no common sense about what *is* outdoors. Remember when outdoors was everywhere and indoors was unnatural? Today it is, unfortunately, just the opposite in much of the United States.

Dr. Hecht's campaign has not stopped thermal injuries and thermal deaths in Yellowstone. One cannot legislate or otherwise require reasonable care by anyone else, and warnings sometimes do no good. A very severe hot-spring injury occurred in August of 1978, when Rick Reid of Bellevue, Washington, was burned over 82 percent of his body. He somehow survived to become a ski instructor living at Redmond, Washington.[79] Other injuries occurred in 2001 and 2005. Donald E. Hansen, 39, of Shoreline, Washington, was burned on July 26, 2001, at a hot spring on Fountain Flats Drive when his dog, a chocolate Labrador, ran from their motor home unrestrained to the Firehole River and a thermal pool and jumped fatally into the two-hundred-degree spring. Hansen received burns to his arms and knees but was unable to get the dog out of the spring. On July 3, 2005, 9-year-old Matthew-Luke Hoang of Lawrenceburg, Kentucky, fell into a hot spring on the east side of Yellowstone Lake, probably one of the springs at Steamboat Point. The boy's parents entered the park's east entrance and stopped at the lake to view the springs. While Luke was playing with the family dog at the edge of the pool, he fell into it, suffering second- and third-degree burns over some 40 percent of his body. He survived in a Salt Lake City hospital.[80]

The death of David Allen Kirwan, discussed at the beginning of this chapter, was caused by his attempting to rescue his friend's dog from a hot spring. Dogs cause particular problems for park rangers in Yellowstone. They are *never* allowed to be off leash in the park and are never allowed to go on trails, including trails through thermal areas. Visitors often do not understand the prohibition, but hot springs are part of the reason. Other reasons are: dogs are predatory on small animals; dogs chase and harass large animals like elk and moose; dogs can attract bears, indeed, those two animals *hate* each other; and excrement from dogs can introduce exotic plants into an ecosystem. *Do not take your dog on trails in Yellowstone!*

On August 11, 1983, John A. Kaye, 29, of Chatsworth, California, was burned over the entire lower half of his body in trying to rescue his dog from a hot spring at Midway Geyser Basin. Including David Allen Kirwan's dog, Kaye's was the fourth dog to be injured or killed in Yellowstone hot springs that summer.[81] That dogs occasionally died in hot springs very early in Yellowstone's history was attested to some years ago by Bessie Haynes Arnold, who remembered that it happened at least once while she lived in the park (1883–1904 and 1914–1916). And at least one other such dog incident is known for that same period.[82]

Dog hot-spring incidents and most human hot-spring incidents tend to occur in summer. However, John Mark Williams's injury and subsequent death in a hot spring was not only the sole thermal death to occur in winter, but also a springboard for what was possibly the most complex winter search-and-rescue operation ever to be assembled in Yellowstone.

Williams, 24, had been a park employee pub tender at Lake, and during the winter of 1987–1988, he was an employee at Old Faithful Snow Lodge. Originally from Wetumpka, Alabama, he was the kind of person nearly everyone liked—blond, blue-eyed, intelligent, athletic, sensitive to nature, outgoing, and happy. He was in excellent physical shape and a strong skier and rock climber.

On Monday and Tuesday, February 7 and 8, 1988, a party of Snow Lodge employees winter camped near Shoshone Geyser Basin on Shoshone Lake, some eleven miles south of Old Faithful. The party consisted of Jack McConnell, Jill Fitterer, Andrea Paul, Melanie Weeks, and John Mark Williams. All were experienced Yellowstone employees of several years each, and all were excellent skiers and winter campers in good physical shape. Weeks and Paul skied in on the seventh; Fitterer and McConnell skied in together on the eighth. Williams skied in alone on the eighth and joined the others that evening. Weeks and Paul were skiing out on the eighth when they met Fitterer and McConnell heading in, heard that Williams was to join the party, and decided to go back in. Andrea Paul was to be eternally thankful that she went back.

On February 8, the group made camp at 5:00 p.m. It was not a legal camp, as they were assigned to a campsite spot but instead camped on the shore of the lake. Although rangers would later criticize them for the decision, several party members were to note later that the decision to camp there was a "common sense" one based on the incoming storm rather than any conscious disregard of park policy.

John Mark Williams had been fascinated by the beauty of the Shoshone hot springs on earlier trips and decided to go for a walk in the geyser basin while the others stayed behind to cook dinner. Perhaps John Mark wanted to see the beauty of the springs in the snow and engage in some quiet contemplation. Or perhaps he wanted to do some illegal "hot potting"—soaking in the cooler of the thermal pools (and there are not many springs that fit that description). He may have also needed some time alone to do some thinking about his prior relationship with Andrea, a relationship that had lasted several years and had ended the summer before. He invited the others to join him, and when they declined, he headed out into the geyser basin alone. It was not yet dark and was snowing only lightly at that moment, but the storm was to roll in quickly.

By 6:00 p.m., it had begun snowing a little harder, and darkness was fast approaching. Jack, Jill, Melanie, and Andrea finished eating, cleaned up their pots, and started settling into their sleeping bags. By 6:45, the visibility had grown very poor from heavy snowfall, gusty winds, and dense hot-spring vapor. Indeed, ranger Bonnie Gafney, soon to be heavily involved in the incident, would note later that while the storm was raging, "the howling wind was incredible." When Gafney opened the patrol cabin door on the shore of Shoshone Lake (where she was spending the night), she "couldn't even see the lake for the blowing and howling snow."

As time passed, the four campers grew concerned about Williams, so Melanie and Andrea set out with headlamps into the dark. Blowing snow and darkness kept them from being able to see well despite their lights, and they quickly realized that heavy snow drifting was occurring so fast that they could not figure out which way to go. Confused and disoriented, they gave up after ten minutes and returned to the tent.

"I hope John Mark is okay," Andrea commented upon their return to the tents.

"Ol' Henry (a nickname of John's) is probably loving it out there!" was McConnell's confident reply, but then he quietly noted to Jill, "Something is wrong. He should have been back by now and I've got a bad feeling."

Shortly after that, around 7:30 p.m., the four tent occupants heard screaming in the distance, then silence, punctuated only by the moaning wind and the sound of snowflakes slapping the sides of the tent. Then they heard screaming again: "Oh God, help me! Help me!" As all four scrambled to get out of their sleeping bags, the screaming grew closer.

Exiting their tents, the others saw Williams in a stumbling run, holding his arms above his head and crying, "My hands, my hands! I hurt so bad!" McConnell asked Williams what had happened, and in broken words he answered, "Oh God, I fell in a real hot one. I'm hurtin' real bad."

Moving quickly, the others stripped off Williams's wet clothes and placed him in a sleeping bag. He had been scalded from his feet to his neck. Long strips of his skin had already begun to peel off from the second- and third-degree burns which covered 90 percent of his body. The others elevated his feet in an attempt to treat him for shock, while his screams of pain filled the tent.

Jill Fitterer remembers the screams being painfully long and loud, sounds she could not get out of her head for years. She was shocked to see that his back was deep purple in color.

"I'm skiing for help," said McConnell. Jill told him that he could not go alone and that she would go, too. Jack replied that that was okay but to pack faster than she had ever packed before. Jill scrambled for anything warm she could find.

The two struck out in the darkness, hoping to find Ranger Bonnie Gafney and Steve Blakeley, who they knew were staying in the Cove patrol cabin three miles away. Unfortunately, they did not know exactly where the cabin was. Jack's headlamp bulb burned out, so he stopped to replace it with another. The second one shattered, and they had only Jill's fading light. To conserve its battery they skied in darkness, sliding backward often and falling several times while following Bonnie and Steve's dim ski tracks. Those tracks finally ended, covered by the new snow that had been long falling. They yelled for Bonnie and Steve over and over, to no avail. From a mile away John Mark's screams cut through them like a hot knife. Jill was exhausted, but kept up with Jack in terror of their being separated. In pitch darkness, she skied into low tree branches and fell again. The wind and falling snow were ruthless and unforgiving.

Unable to find the cabin, the two decided to return to Snow Lodge for help. The relatively warm temperature of twenty degrees Fahrenheit was their only relief.

Meanwhile Melanie and Andrea had begun desperate attempts to keep Williams alive. Every few minutes they gave him fruit juice or water. When that ran out they attempted to melt snow in a pan, but the wind kept blowing out the stove. They ended up melting snow in their mouths and spitting it into a cup.

Meanwhile McConnell and Jill were heading toward Grant's Pass and Old Faithful, knowing their inbound ski tracks would be long concealed by the new snow. Jack McConnell, the strongest skier in the party, went first, breaking trail. Jill followed, but three miles out lost her energy. She fell over and over, skis twisting under her, and heard herself yelling in the blackness for Jack.

Jill decided to stop and camp in order to keep from slowing Jack down. It was 10:45 p.m. The two made her a bivouac spot under a large tree. There she lay down to spend a cold, sleepless, lonely, and terrified snowbound night. The next day she skied out to Old Faithful. She wrote later that she hoped never again to feel so detached from life or to know such a great emptiness in her heart.

Through the night, Andrea and Melanie maintained their heartbreaking vigil in thick snowfall and with winds blowing so hard that the tent threatened to collapse. John Mark Williams never lost consciousness and remained coherent during the night. Between screams of pain he was able to carry on a conversation and expressed concern that McConnell would not possibly be able to return to Snow Lodge in the midst of such a fierce storm. He was alert enough to tell Andrea where his first aid kit was located, and at times, he even sat up. He stated at one point that he didn't believe a helicopter could make it to the site even if Jack were able to get help.

While the women kept busy, they were consumed by their feelings. Andrea thought to herself that she hoped never to see another person in that much pain again, but after a while she came to regard the screams as a necessary release for John. As she was later to explain, "To touch anything or to be touched by anything was excruciatingly painful for him. I remember thinking 'Oh God, just let him pass out. Let him rest.'" Melanie Weeks remembers thinking that she had "never known such a feeling of helplessness as I knew that night."

As the night stretched on, John often said he was "so tired" and continued to thank the two women for their efforts. He repeatedly apologized for the inconvenience and expressed concern about a coat he had dropped at the hot spring. "He had borrowed it from a fellow employee at Snow Lodge," Andrea remembers, "and he was quite concerned that this employee wouldn't get his coat back.

"I recall him saying that he was scared only twice, but a few times he said things like, 'I'm fighting! I'm trying!' He kept popping up and then flopping down, writhing in pain and occasionally sobbing in frustration.

"He was so good about doing what we asked," explained Andrea, "turning on his side repeatedly so we could try and get the sleeping bag zipper up around his neck, and sipping the water we gave him slowly."

The girls took turns all night long crawling out of the tent to gather snow in a small cooking pot. When the stove failed to light, they again melted small handfuls in their mouths, letting it slowly dribble back into a cup, which they handed to John every few minutes. The storm continued to rage, the walls of the tent shuddered, and the tent poles creaked, threatening to snap in two. Melanie and Andrea fought to keep snow from blowing in and kept snow-filled water bottles next to their skin in hopes that their body heat would melt more snow.

Eventually the powerful wind proved too much for the tent door zipper and it broke. The two women were then kept twice as busy keeping snow out of the tent while preparing and administering liquids to Williams.

"Not once," remembers Andrea, "I repeat, not once did he say he did not want to die, nor did he ever curse or get mad about this twist of fate. Not once did he say 'Why me?' Instead," she explained, "he kept thanking us. At one point he even reached up to barely caress a strand of my hair, and told me he loved me." Andrea remembers wondering if Jack would get through.

Meanwhile, Jack McConnell skied on alone through the night, through high winds and with no source of light, but fortunately with the blowing snow at his back. The snow was so deep, the wind so high, and the night so dark that it was very difficult to find the trail. McConnell, a longtime Yellowstone employee and very experienced in the backcountry, had the presence of mind to leave the trail in favor of the Firehole River and to ski along the river, following its sound. He skied all night long and finally made it to Old Faithful Snow Lodge at 4:00 a.m. He saw the night security guard and they dialed 911 together and informed the dispatcher of the situation. The park's chief ranger was immediately notified, and a massive search-and-rescue operation began to lurch slowly into operation. Old Faithful rangers did not want to begin the rescue until daylight because of the numerous dangers that could face the rescuers in darkness.

At 7:30 a.m., rangers Bruce Blair and Steve Sarles packed their skis and some other gear and jumped onto a double track snowmobile. Their plan was to try to drive the machine over the ski trail via Grants Pass. That would be difficult at best, as the trail crossed the Continental Divide, rising and falling through thick timber with many small streams to serve as impediments. Moreover, the weather forecast was for continued heavy snow with high winds causing blowing and drifting. A snowmobile was likely to bog down in the deep drifts of the now full-blown blizzard. Nevertheless Blair and Sarles gritted their teeth and headed into the swirling snowstorm. Skiing behind them, and at times in front of them, were two strong concessioner skiers from Snow Lodge, Curt Langer and Dave Halladay.

By 8:30 a.m., when Blair and Sarles were five miles in, other rangers heard their faint, static-filled radio reports of howling winds, low visibility, and six-foot drifts. The rescue itself was now filled with innumerable risks, and the rescuers themselves were increasingly susceptible to dangers.

Other rangers were coming from the south and west entrances to make backup attempts to reach Shoshone Lake via the DeLacy Creek trail. More than twenty people were now involved in the outdoors part of the rescue, but it was evident that it would take many hours to reach Williams. No one knew if he was even still alive.

Ranger and park medic Bonnie Gafney was spending her days off at Shoshone Lake's Cove patrol cabin. As per standard procedure, she turned her radio on that morning about 8:00 a.m., and the very first thing she heard was Shirley, the dispatcher, calling her number: "4-1-3! 4-1-3! This is 700." Gafney was shocked and responded immediately with strong apprehension. Informed of the situation by the dispatcher, she radioed that she and Steve Blakeley were packing her medical gear for a ski trip to Williams's campsite. Although the ranger staff could now breathe easier knowing that a trained medic was within striking distance of the injured man, they did not know how truly severe were his injuries.

Gafney and Blakeley struck out through the trees, wondering what horrors awaited them. Bonnie carried oxygen, first aid supplies, food, water, and all of her extra clothing. The blizzard made their travel more difficult as they tracked through unbroken snow directly across the frozen lake. Bonnie noted that their tracks from the previous day were completely obliterated:

> I was skiing faster than Steve and was also pumping on an adrenaline rush, so I pushed on ahead and left him to follow my tracks. We were skiing into the wind this time, and eyelashes quickly froze as the snow hit your face like stinging needles. You had to keep your head down, and lift it only to verify your direction of travel. We were breaking another 8–10 inches [of snow] this time. As we went I was hearing radio traffic about the incident, and could hear bits and pieces of rescue plans. I tried to talk to Steve Sarles and dispatch a number of times, but had to stop skiing to do so and didn't want to waste time. My impressions were of some thermal burns, but nothing to the extent that they were. I was thinking of foot and possibly leg burns.

At 10:03 a.m., Gafney radioed that they had reached the geyser basin and needed to know where the campsite was. Sarles replied from Grants Pass with information he had. At 10:37 the two reached a thermal pool that they believed was the site of the incident, because a water bottle was floating in it and clothing was scattered around. Bonnie recognized John Mark's clothing from the preceding day, when she and Steve had run into him on the trail. Somehow she had known it was he who had been hurt without ever having been told.

For the next nearly fifty minutes Gafney and Blakeley searched for the campsite, splitting up for efficiency but wasting precious energy floundering in deep snow. Bonnie radioed several times to report she could not find the camp in the blizzard. All ski tracks were obliterated by that time. Finally a good suggestion was radioed to her from Ranger Andy Fisher, who suspected that the group had camped on the beach.

Back at the tent, Andrea and Melanie were still trying desperately to help John Mark. Andrea was to remember it vividly:

> I was sitting by John's head and had just handed him the cup with a few sips of water. He drank them down, sat slightly up to hand me the cup and said "Thank you." As he flopped back, his eyes seemed to roll up and his jaw suddenly clenched. I feared he was going comatose and that he might swallow his tongue. I tried to pry open his mouth and force a yellow bandanna between his teeth when I heard this strange gurgling sound. I now know that his lungs were filling with fluid, but

at the time I just thought he was choking. I had his head between my hands and suddenly I knew he was no longer breathing or moving, indeed he seemed suddenly at peace. I was looking at him in total disbelief and shock. I couldn't believe he was really gone. I remember covering his nose and trying to breathe down his mouth, but nothing helped . . . Melanie and I were holding each other . . . I remember saying the words to the Lord's Prayer, crying, and lying there in disbelief. We were so totally exhausted and so in shock we didn't react for a few minutes. I remember closing his eyelids, kissing him on the forehead . . . The thought that he was really gone was totally unacceptable.

After twenty or thirty minutes a calm resolve set in. In a stupor, the two women vacillated between packing up their things or just waiting for help. Andrea found her watch and remembers thinking that it said 10:30, so John Mark must have died sometime around 9:50 a.m.

At 11:26, Bonnie Gafney topped over a small hill in thigh-deep snow to see a blue tent on the beach and notified headquarters. The two women heard her shout and crawled out of the tent, crying quietly, "Bonnie, it's too late, nothing can help him now."

Gafney and Blakeley began immediate CPR on Williams, and Melanie spelled them at intervals. At 11:54, Gafney reported via radio to a doctor that she was getting no pulse or respiration, eyes were fixed and dilated, skin blistered over 70 percent of the body, some lividity, a slight rigor in the arms, and no rectal temperature. At 12:25, the doctor ordered CPR to be stopped.

Heroic efforts by Jack McConnell and Bonnie Gafney notwithstanding, and valiant if initially delayed efforts by the other rangers (Sarles and Blair, along with Langer and Halladay, arrived shortly after Gafney), help had missed reaching Williams alive by an hour and a half. The pool he had fallen into, located immediately northeast of Black Sulphur Spring, was 187 degrees Fahrenheit and eight feet deep.

One could debate the what ifs in this incident forever. Indeed, those debates continued for some time within the Park Service, as they always do with dramatic incidents, in order to analyze the performances of both the rescuers and the rescued for the benefit of similar future incidents. Had Williams's party known where Bonnie Gafney's cabin was, or had the storm been less fierce so that her ski tracks could have been followed, Williams might (but I really don't think so!) have had a better chance for survival, for Gafney could certainly have gotten the rescue rolling before midnight, and perhaps as early as 8:15 p.m. On the other hand, getting a helicopter to the location in the storm was probably impossible, even if things had gotten rolling faster. If he had known its location, McConnell could have skied the three miles to Bonnie's cabin in perhaps half an hour. Then again, Gafney might have found the camp more quickly had the party camped in their assigned site instead of camping illegally on the beach. But would that have really mattered? What if John Mark had not gone walking that night? What if Bonnie had left her radio on all night? What if the weather had been better? What if the others had known CPR? And on and on.

Despite these questions, Andrea and Jill both argue that it is futile to debate the what ifs, that in light of John Mark's extensive injuries he had *no* chance for survival once he fell into that pool. Andrea was there. She saw the severity and enormity of his situation all night long. A fire captain later described it to her thusly: "If he were burned to that degree in the doorway of the best burn center in the country (in Salt Lake City) he still would have died."

The passage of more than fifteen hours with no medical treatment for Williams was most unfortunate, but probably could not have been helped. And one can argue, as Andrea does most convincingly, that Williams's burns were so severe that nothing could have been done regardless of time. According to the autopsy report they covered 90 percent of his body, and he died of dehydration from the burns.

According to chief ranger Dan Sholly, John Mark Williams had a reputation for pushing his limits in Yellowstone's backcountry, although Williams's compatriots certainly do *not* agree with that assessment. A park employee who was far more experienced than most visitors, Williams nevertheless became the victim of a fatal misstep, for whatever reason. In a strange coincidence, Williams's park roommate earlier had been Kent Shane Rich, a man who died falling off a mountain in the park (see chapter 11, "Fatal Attraction: Deaths from Falls"). So Williams had previously been close to a backcountry death incident and, according to Andrea, had been deeply affected by it.

Two hard-and-fast rules in Yellowstone have to be these: do not walk or ski in a thermal area in darkness or in blizzard conditions, because you cannot see the hazards, and always camp in your assigned backcountry site. One of the reasons for the camping rule here was to keep people away from the geyser basin at night. Although the Park Service, ever aware of its potential legal liability because of visitors who sue, could argue that camping illegally caused problems in this case, Andrea Paul believes that John Mark would have died regardless of where they were camped. She points out that the trip to Shoshone was Bonnie Gafney's first into the area, so Bonnie did not know the area well either. In fact, many of the party members noted that several of the rangers did not know the area well if at all, and most were unhappy with the way they were treated by the rangers. It seemed to them incongruous that their rescuers would blame them for an incident that occurred in a place the rangers themselves barely knew. On the other hand, emergency personnel are not often well received by survivors in a death incident.

Andrea Paul remembers this above all: "When Jack, Jill, Melanie, and I first reached Shoshone Geyser Basin, we heard a jubilant shout as we broke from the trees and skied into the open field which sits on the edge of the basin. John Mark was in high spirits, delighted to see us, and singing at the top of his lungs,

'My momma is a mountain lion,
My daddy is a grizzly bear,
And I'm the meanest mountain man,
This side of the Missouri River!'"

"I choose to remember him this way," wrote Andrea later, "joyful, giddy, and seemingly invincible."[83]

Williams's death brought the total of human deaths from hot springs in Yellowstone National Park to nineteen. However, the total would be twenty so far if L. R. Piper's 1900 disappearance was due to his falling into a hot spring. The possibility of that having happened is very real (see chapter 22, "Missing and Presumed Dead").

Yellowstone's twentieth documented death from thermal springs occurred in the summer of 2000, and it turned out to be the most tragic and deadly thermal accident in park history. It was a desperately sad affair that took a 20-year-old woman from the ranks of park concessioner employees and badly injured her two companions. This fatality was the result of night travel in a very dangerous area, namely the River Group of thermal springs in Lower Geyser Basin. It is a semibackcountry area where hot springs and geysers crop out all along both banks of Firehole River for dozens of yards, creating an area that is dangerous enough during daytime but many times more dangerous at night.

College students work in Yellowstone by the hundreds. It is a fabulous summer experience for most of them—one that many people remember fondly all their lives—because of reasonable working hours, room and board in dormitory style much like college, many opportunities to make lifetime friendships with people from all fifty states, and plenty of free time to hike or otherwise explore the wilderness around them in one of the world's most famous places.

Such was the case for three Old Faithful–area employees who worked for Amfac Parks and Resorts. On August 21, 2000, they decided to join a group of five other friends for an afternoon swim in Firehole River at the river's cascade near Mound Geyser. The three were Tyler Montague, 18, of Salt Lake City; Lance Buchi, 18, of Holladay, Utah; and Sara Hulphers, 20, of Oroville, Washington. The two boys had just graduated from high school. Sara was a junior at Western Washington University, studying biology. Montague worked at Old Faithful Lodge while Buchi and Hulphers were employed at Old Faithful

Inn. The three stayed with their friends all afternoon and into the evening, and by this time all eight people were somehow on the east side of the river rather than the west side, where swimming activities often began. It was between 10:00 and 11:00 p.m. when they began to walk back to their cars through an area where there was no maintained trail. Montague, Buchi, and Hulphers walked separately, behind the other five. The moon was not yet up, and the group had no flashlights, so it was quite dark for them.

With Sara in the middle holding hands with Buchi and Montague, the three began walking north along Firehole River through an area pockmarked with superheated hot springs. Whether they had been drinking at all, an investigation later showed that alcohol was not a factor. As the three walked, they reached a point where a bit of a hill partially hid a large, sunken hot spring about eighteen feet long and ten feet deep with an overhanging, earthen bank at its rear. In the dim light of night, all three thought they saw a "thin ribbon of water" in front of them, so they elected to all jump over it at once while holding hands.[84]

Instead, what they jumped over was a thin ribbon of vegetation right on the precipice of Cavern Spring, which lurked below them. Their feet landed on the edge of the earthen bank above the spring, and it crumbled. They fell directly into a deep part of the spring. The two boys were immersed up to their necks. Sara went underwater and was thus immersed 100 percent.

From a distance, the five others heard them yelling in the night and began running back to assist them. Thrashing and screaming in water that was later measured at 178 degrees, the three attempted to climb out of the spring. Buchi almost climbed out but some of the earthen bank gave way again, and he fell into the spring for a second time.[85]

The others quickly ran back and noticed that incredibly all three victims were still conscious despite being horribly injured. Buchi and Montague climbed out of the spring and then helped Sara out of it. Friends helped the two boys to vehicles and drove them back to Old Faithful Clinic. Others carried Sara, who had the worst injuries, toward the parking area and remained with her at the scene until rangers arrived some thirty minutes later and put her into an ambulance. The three victims soon lost consciousness. Eventually ambulances took them to the West Yellowstone airport, where helicopters and airplanes flew them to Idaho Falls and then on to Salt Lake City's burn center.[86]

The rangers' investigation was initially hampered because all three victims were unconscious and could not be interviewed. Never before in Yellowstone's history had three people suffered critical burn injuries all at once. Doctors speculated that the three had purposely and simultaneously jumped into the spring without realizing how hot it was. Park personnel puzzled over how three people could fall into a hot spring at the same time. With third-degree burns over 100 percent of her body, Sara Hulphers died of her injuries fourteen hours later in the Salt Lake City burn center. Her funeral in Oroville, Washington, was a major event attended by more than three hundred people, for she had been a straight-A student who had just won another scholarship. Her friend Yuvia Storm, 21, who worked with her, told friends that she and Sara were having the time of their lives working in Yellowstone. "She was so happy," said Storm. Sara's father Dan agreed. "She said it was the most wonderful experience she'd had in her whole life," he told reporters. "Everyone she worked with liked her. She said she never felt so loved."[87]

Lance Buchi and Tyler Montague suffered second- and third-degree burns over at least 90 percent of their bodies. Doctors gave little hope for their recoveries but somehow the two men held on, slipping in and out of consciousness for many days. As they gradually recovered consciousness, they were able to tell their attendants what happened. "He thought it was ground he was jumping onto," said Lance Buchi's mother later. The fact that the spring was only 178 degrees in temperature, instead of 195 like so many others, may have allowed them to survive. Forty years earlier, park geologist George Marler had ominously described Cavern Spring as shaped like a "double-bitted tomahawk" with its handle discharging into the river and its blade representing the ten-foot-deep cavern. Its undercut and overhanging ledge, wrote Marler, were "a hazard to too close an approach."[88]

On June 12, 2001, while their son was still recovering, Lance Buchi's parents filed a lawsuit in his name in the U.S. District Court in Wyoming against the Department of the Interior and the National Park Service. They sought, under the Federal Tort Claims Act (FTCA), unspecified damages for medical expenses and permanent disfigurement of Lance Buchi. (The FTCA, enacted by Congress in 1946, provides a limited waiver of the federal government's sovereign immunity for the "negligent or wrongful act or omission" of a federal employee "acting within the scope of his office or employment.") The suit alleged that "government employees were negligent in failing to warn him and to protect him from the dangers presented by the thermal feature through the use of signs, barriers, or a closure of the area." Initially the government responded with a motion to dismiss, claiming it was shielded by the Wyoming Recreational Use Act, but Judge William Downes denied that motion and the lawsuit went forward. The case of *Buchi v. United States of America* was yet another example of people wanting their wilderness wild while still wanting someone to blame when nature seemed hostile. It was complicated by the fact that Yellowstone Park posts thermal-warning signs all over the "front country" but not the backcountry. At one point, the judge himself "personally visited the site of the incident during both daylight and evening hours."

Most important to Judge Downes was the 2002 case of *Elder v. U.S.*, a Tenth Circuit case brought under the Federal Tort Claims Act following the death of a 12-year-old boy who slipped and fell over a ledge while crossing a stream in Zion National Park. In that case, the circuit court held that "the discretionary function exception [to the FTCA] . . . barred a claim of failure to adequately protect a national park visitor against a danger presented by a natural hazard."

On February 6, 2004, Judge Downes dismissed the *Buchi* lawsuit, holding that "the Zion case controls the disposition of the present case" and in fact could be applied "more forcefully to the present case because the natural feature at issue is in a backcountry location where NPS policies regarding aesthetics and natural preservation are even more important." So the circuit law, as stated by the *Elder* case, is now this: park officials have to consider a variety of interests in deciding whether or not to post warning signs "such as resource allocation, visitor safety, and scenic preservation," and under the law they are given the discretion to do so. The *Elder* court stated that "physical barriers undoubtedly spoil the view and the experience of communing with nature" in scenic parks and marveled that Zion's warning signs in place had not been enough warning for the suing plaintiffs in that case: "But what would constitute an adequate warning: Bigger signs? Signs embedded in the sandstone immediately next to each stream? Such 'solutions,' however, have an impact on park aesthetics. And even if Plaintiffs are contending only that the wording of existing signs should have been altered to mention algae specifically, such a change would necessitate a chain of further decisions. Would not Zion managers then have to decide whether it is necessary to add signs that explain how to identify algae?" The law of the Tenth Circuit now gives Yellowstone and other park managers an effective shield against such lawsuits, at least under many fact scenarios.[89]

Buchi had a tough case factually because he and his friends were walking in darkness without a flashlight and because they were park employees who arguably knew or should have known that this pockmarked area was a dangerous one, especially when they had spent many hours in the area before the incident occurred. But most importantly here, the Tenth Circuit made it clear that the exception to general liability (liability established by the FTCA) protects "those discretionary actions or decisions [of government officials] which are 'based on considerations of public policy.'" The purpose of it, said the *Elder* court, is to prevent courts from "second guessing of legislative and administrative decisions grounded in social, economic, and political policy."

Nor does public safety automatically trump other considerations by park officials. Preserving the resources is important, too, and the *Elder* court reminded both the public and park managers of this fact:

The NPS's [own] "Loss Control Management Guidelines" (NPS-50) certainly conveys the message that safety must be a priority, and it assists park management by focusing on a number of elements that should be encompassed by a safety program. But it does not dictate what actions park employees must take in response to particular problems. Indeed, the following language in the NPS-50's Introduction makes clear that safety decisions must be made in the special context of a national park and that park management retains substantial discretion:

Paradoxically, many of the natural features found in parks pose significant safety risks to the uninformed visiting public, yet those same features cannot be eliminated nor guarded against in the same manner that a prudent person would expect to find in an industrial or home setting. Therefore, NPS public safety efforts are focused on interpreting the values of the park's natural features and educating the visitor concerning the proper precautions one must take to have a safe and healthful journey at that specific park unit.[90]

Another thermal injury in the park may have occurred partly because of an employee's intoxication in darkness. Joseph Widelock, 17, was traveling off-trail in a thermal area just after midnight on July 18, 1991, when he fell into a pool of Old Faithful's Myriad Group that measured 147 degrees Fahrenheit. Climbing out of the pool, he continued on in the darkness and fell into a second (hotter) one. Climbing out of that one, he attempted to stand up and fell into the same spring again. He sustained first-, second-, and third-degree burns over 67 percent of his body.[91]

Injuries and deaths in Yellowstone's hot springs are sobering and scary. Hot-spring injuries probably number a hundred or more, and they continue to happen most summers, including a serious injury at Solitary Geyser in the summer of 2012. I cannot emphasize enough to parents that they must hold fast to their children and realize that they themselves are sometimes childlike when walking around Yellowstone's thermal areas. As a 4-year-old child, I was led around Yellowstone on a rope. I remember resenting the leash my parents put on me, but my father was very aware of hot springs and I may be still alive because of it. Visitors must never travel off-trail in thermal areas, and all persons must exercise reasonable care when traveling through any thermal area. Heart-wrenching events such as those chronicled here should teach us at least that.

2

"THESE ANIMALS ARE NOT REAL"
THE MYTH THAT CAN KILL YOU

A tame wild animal is the most dangerous of beasts. My old friend, Dick Rock . . . laughed at my advice, and got killed by one of his three-year-old bulls. I told him they knew him just well enough to kill him, and they did.

—Buffalo Jones in *Lord of Beasts*

There is perhaps not an animal that roams in this, or in the wilds of any other country, more fierce and forbidding than a buffalo . . . neither the Polar bear nor the Bengal tiger, surpass that animal in ferocity.

—Alexander Ross, fur trapper, 1825

THE BISON, OR BUFFALO, is a mythologized animal. To many Yellowstone Park visitors, it is not a genuine living, breathing creature. Instead, it is a painting, a symbol of a vanished past, a vignette of nineteenth-century America, but certainly nothing real. Many visitors want to approach it, to touch it, to somehow establish a close link with it, as if that might somehow connect them to their own frontier heritage. Having been a Yellowstone resident for more than thirty-five years, I sometimes lose sight of that simple truth. To me the animal is very real and very dangerous. But perhaps that mythologized perception of the animal is part of the reason that visitors have been injured and killed by bison in Yellowstone National Park.

As of 2013, only two human deaths from bison incidents, compared with seven from bears, have occurred in Yellowstone Park, but the continuing potential for injuries and deaths from bison in the park is much greater than it is for injuries and deaths from bears. Dr. Mary Meagher, Yellowstone's bison expert, has told us that bison numbers have continued to increase since 1978 and as the numbers increase (and visitors to Yellowstone increase) so does the potential for human injury. There are now some four thousand bison in the park compared to perhaps 750 bears, and visitors are much more likely to see and thus approach bison. Certainly park rangers are sympathetic to the power of the bison myth. But we cannot let it blind us to the danger. Considering the numbers of human injuries involving bison in recent years, it is probably only lucky that more deaths have not occurred.

Bison can weigh two thousand pounds or more, and they are unpredictable, often belligerent animals that must never be closely approached. At least one incident is known from 1890 wherein bison reportedly "attacked" and destroyed a park stagecoach in Hayden Valley, and I have personally seen them charge snowcoaches in winter in the park.

On March 22, 1902, Dick Rock, 49, a well-known Yellowstone-area poacher and animal keeper, was killed by one of his own bison near Henry's Lake, just outside the park. He was attempting to show a friend how "tame" they had become. Several people had warned Dick that the bison would kill him, but he did not listen. One Saturday morning at 7:00 a.m. when Dick was

Yellowstone bison (NPS, Yellowstone National Park)

feeding a bison, it became enraged and charged him, pinning him against the corral. His screams brought Mrs. Rock and several people from a nearby ranch. What they saw horrified them. Over and over the bison pitched Dick's body up into the air, and the bison gored him with its horns every time he hit the ground. The bison ripped all the clothes from Dick's body and left him with twenty-nine horn holes. May Garner remembered that when they got Dick out of there, "his eyelids twitched a time or two and he was gone."[1]

Before the 1990s, injuries from bison (gorings, tramplings, or strikings) numbered zero to ten per year in the park, and almost always happened because a visitor approached the animal too closely. Park bison injuries included at least eleven in 1983, six in 1984, ten in 1985, four in 1986, two in 1987, two in 1988, none in 1989–1990, four in 1991, two in 1992, two in 1993, and at least three in 1994.[2] In 1985, while I was a law enforcement ranger at Canyon, so many injuries occurred in nearby Hayden Valley from visitors foolishly approaching bison that the accompanying warning poster was created by park managers. I often spent entire eight-hour days in Hayden Valley monitoring "bison jams" and keeping people away from the animals. But the park has improved its safety record greatly, because from 1995 through 2012 human injuries from bison averaged only zero to five per year. Diane Herring, who works in the park's Law Enforcement Office, says of this, "I think we are getting better at warning people."

There is usually someone who wants to sue the park because of his or her own carelessness in being injured by a bison. True to form, a lawsuit brought by a woman who was injured in 1984 ended with the plaintiff losing the case.[3] As mentioned earlier, the park has a legal duty only to warn of hidden or obvious dangers. Park rangers do not want to seem unsympathetic to a visitor's desire to view animals, but animal warnings generally can be found everywhere: in park handout literature, on warning signs, and given verbally by ranger personnel at visitor centers or from patrol cars.

In the spring of 1992, a 70-year-old man from Pittstown, New Jersey, was tossed fifteen feet into the air by a bison at West Thumb Geyser Basin.[4] His leg was ripped open by the animal's horn when he got too close to it. My friend Leslie Quinn, a thirty-two-year Yellowstone tour guide who was present at the incident, just shakes his head whenever these incidents occur and says, "Get a clue, people. These animals are not tame!"

Indeed, even elk and moose have caused injuries in Yellowstone, but no human deaths (at least so far) have occurred that involved those two animals. Beverly Bittner, a West Yellowstone woman, was badly injured in June of 1990 while walking her three dogs in a willow thicket just north of the town of West Yellowstone, Montana, when a moose broke several of her ribs, and a moose actually killed a 71-year-old man in Anchorage, Alaska, in 1995. A 7-year-old

WARNING

MANY VISITORS HAVE BEEN GORED BY BUFFALO

**BUFFALO CAN WEIGH 2000 POUNDS
AND CAN SPRINT AT 30 MPH,
THREE TIMES FASTER THAN YOU CAN RUN**

**THESE ANIMALS MAY APPEAR TAME BUT ARE
WILD, UNPREDICTABLE, AND DANGEROUS**

DO NOT APPROACH BUFFALO

Warning poster which came into use following the many 1984 injuries to park visitors by bison (NPS, Yellowstone National Park)

girl was kicked by an elk in 1978 in the park, causing abrasions to her head and leg.[5] And a woman at Banff National Park in Canada was injured in 1991 when a pregnant elk cow kicked her in the face and arms.[6]

Coyotes have also caused a fair number of injuries to visitors in the park as they are much less reclusive than, say, wolves or mountain lions. Two coyote "attacks" occurred in 1992 (*The Buffalo Chip*, Sept.–Nov. 1992) and one during the winter of 1990–1991. Brian Dean, 27, of Oak Lawn, Illinois, an employee of Old Faithful Snow Lodge, suffered lacerations and puncture wounds to his head, face, neck, and arms. A recent letter from former ranger Norman Bishop to me detailed five coyote attacks that have occurred in the park.

Another occurred earlier. Margaret Jelinek was bitten on the hand and leg in front of the Mammoth Hotel on November 10, 1942. These incidents are a problem for park managers in that they tend to make the newspapers, causing city-living neophytes to think that coyote attacks are typical. Coyote attacks are *not* typical; they are relatively *rare*, and are often caused when the animals become habituated by humans feeding them, or by diseases in the animals.[7]

In line with other animals causing injuries, there are at least two cases on record of persons in the park being bitten by rattlesnakes. Rattlesnakes occur in Yellowstone only along its northern boundary at elevations below six thousand feet. John French, a trail laborer, was bitten in May of 1945, but fortunately the injury was not serious and he recovered.[8] One "Red River Dick" was bitten by a rattlesnake at Cinnabar, Montana (in the present park), on July 2, 1886. That the bite was not taken seriously, for whatever reason, is evident from this account of it: "A couple of gallons of snake bite juice drove all the poison out of his system. The snake is dead. Speculation is now rife as to which received the most poison from the kiss, the snake or Dick. It is the general opinion there was a mutual exchange, as there is no proof the snake was killed from any other cause."[9]

But we must take most animal-human confrontations seriously. Indeed, it never ceases to amaze me that some people just cannot seem to grasp the simple truth that animals can hurt them. While rangering in the Mammoth Visitor Center one summer, I was approached by a man with a wild look in his eyes. I have learned to recognize that confused look as a sign that a visitor wants to ask a question, so I inquired, "Yes, sir, may I help you?" Without hesitating, he said, "Can you tell me something? These animals that are just running around out here . . . they couldn't be wild, could they, or you wouldn't just have them running around loose?" I began the standard warning speech, trying very hard to be patient and not to laugh or act horrified. This man was an injury waiting to happen.

So, apparently, was Marvin Lesley Schrader, 30, of Spokane, Washington, who became Yellowstone's first bison fatality on July 12, 1971, at Fountain

Flats north of Old Faithful. Schrader and his wife and three children spotted a solitary bull buffalo lying down in a meadow just east of Rush Lake that day. Schrader walked to within twenty feet of it to take its picture. The one-ton bison stood up, charged Schrader, and tossed him more than twelve feet. The animal's horns ripped open the man's upper right abdomen and pierced his liver. With a large hole in his side, Schrader attempted unsuccessfully to rise onto one elbow and then lay on the ground groaning for a few minutes while his wife and children watched him die. Greg Barnet, first on the scene and interviewed by Ranger Chet Cantrell, said he knew instantly that Schrader was dead. Bonnie Schrader admitted later that they had been too close to the bison. In the family's possession was the park's red "Danger" pamphlet that warned of wild animals.[10]

I was a young bus tour guide in the park that summer, and I distinctly remember the stories which circulated at the time: that Schrader was throwing rocks at the animal to get it to stand up. My friend Herb Vaughan, a park bus driver at the time, also remembers hearing the rock story. A check of the case incident report reveals that the Schrader family did not throw the rocks. Rangers discovered that a group of teenagers had been throwing rocks at the bison just before Schrader arrived. "We made the buffalo get up," said a small girl who was with that party. So the bison had been provoked, but regardless, Schrader was wrong to get close.[11]

A foreign visitor was gored to death on July 31, 1983, in Hayden Valley because, according to the newspapers, he wanted to get his picture taken with a bison. Once again, the animal was a solitary bull. Alain Jean Jacques Dumont, 21, of Toulouse, France, was having his picture taken about six feet from the buffalo when it charged and gored him, tossing him ten feet into the air.

A friend of mine, tour-bus driver Leon Brunton, who served as a Yellowstone employee for more than fifteen years, has a more detailed version of this story. He was there to see it. Brunton was heading south with a busload of visitors from Canyon to Lake. Upon entering Hayden Valley, he saw a herd of bison near the first large pullout at Alum Creek. Brunton decided to allow his bus passengers a look at the animals, so he pulled into the turnout on the west side of the road, giving them the usual don't-get-too-close commentary over his headset microphone. As he pulled up to the spot, Brunton noticed a young man with a camera walking into the meadow toward the bison. The young man had just set his backpack on the ground and was already too close to the animals, so Brunton was able to conveniently add to his microphone message, "And don't do what that kid is doing!"

Brunton did not even have time to get off his bus before the bison charged. Alain Dumont had his camera up and must have seen the charge through its viewfinder. He turned abruptly to his left, and the bison's horn caught him in the right kidney, ripping him open with a vengeance. The tour-bus driver ran to the scene as Dumont hit the ground. He saw the gaping hole in Dumont. Leon Brunton remembers thinking, "Oh my God, this guy is dead."[12]

Some Japanese visitors took Dumont to Uncle Tom's parking area, where Ranger Mike Pflaum saw him. Pflaum remembers that Dumont was conscious and talking, even with a "good horn hole" in him that in fact was a partial evisceration. Dumont kept saying, "I'm dying! I'm dying!"[13]

Eventually Dumont was treated by three doctors, one of whom spoke French. Dumont sustained a torn colon, a punctured stomach, a severely damaged spleen, and four broken ribs. The spleen injury or infection was probably what killed him.[14]

Another potentially dangerous bison incident occurred in late February of 1982.[15] A party of snowmobile visitors at Fishing Bridge noticed that a bison had fallen through the ice on the Yellowstone River and was trapped. They were attempting to help it by tying ropes to it, when park ranger Bobbie Seaquist told them to leave it alone and not to approach it. That made the visitors mad, and somehow the story got into broadcaster Paul Harvey's newscast. Harvey thoroughly denounced the ranger and the Park Service in general for not helping the buffalo.

But the ranger and the Park Service were correct in my estimation. Paul Harvey was an excellent broadcaster, but he knew little about bison, about winter in Yellowstone, or about the reasons for park policies. Without getting too much into the visitors' clear violation of park philosophy by helping the bison (its falling through the ice occurred naturally and the NPS is not about to interfere with natural processes),[16] the safety consequences for the visitors here were readily apparent. No bison will take kindly to having a rope tied to it and jerked on, regardless of a visitor's good intentions. The visitors could have been badly hurt by the thrashing bison, to say nothing of the possibility of their falling through the ice themselves. Ranger Seaquist correctly saw this incident as an "accident" waiting to happen.[17]

I and others have seen people exhibit attitudes and actions around bison that are difficult to believe. In 1992, a park visitor noticed another visitor walking right up to a bison. She commented to him, "Sir, you really are too close." He replied, "Oh, they're a lot tamer than they tell you they are."[18] And Don and Joni Hofmann of Gardiner, Montana, will testify to having personally seen (in Lamar Valley in the summer of 1989) a park visitor lift his child onto the back of a bison in order to get the usual "great" photo. These two incidents illustrate how incredibly foolish some people can be, and they serve to illustrate why we will continue to have injuries and deaths from bison in Yellowstone. We must remember that when we want to make a bridge with or to touch the past, the place to do it is *not* five feet from a bison.

And, too, why should we humans do anything to an animal that might hasten that animal's having to pay for the incident with its life? The killing of an animal involved in a human injury or death incident is not automatic in national parks, but sometimes it happens.

Yellowstone visitors should never approach bison or any wild animal. All Yellowstone animals are wild and all are potentially dangerous. Even small animals can bite you, and small animals can carry diseases like rabies, tularemia, or even bubonic plague. We humans are only temporary visitors to Yellowstone; the park is the animals' home. So let's give them a break, and give ourselves one in the process . . . especially when the subject animal is a myth that can kill us.

3

HUMAN DEATHS FROM BEARS AND HOW TO KEEP THEM FROM HAPPENING

"Of the strength and ferocity of this animal the Indians had given us dreadful accounts."

—Lewis and Clark, April 29, 1805

"Again and again, the issue came back to the public and the overwhelming need to make them understand that it was unhealthy, unnatural, illegal . . . that it was wrong to do the one thing they most wanted to do in Yellowstone—feed the bears."

—Paul Schullery, *The Bears of Yellowstone*

"Carry bear spray . . . make noise . . . don't hike alone . . . play dead . . . never feed a bear."

—National Park Service advice to backpackers in Yellowstone

INJURIES TO HUMANS BY BEARS are legion throughout the history of Yellowstone. Deaths are not. Beginning in 1891, when two large park hotels opened and needed a place to throw their garbage, hotel operators created nearby garbage dumps, bears and people were thrown together in large numbers, and injuries began to occur. This lasted until around 1973, when bears no longer appeared along park roadsides as beggars due to the government's bear-transporting and dump-closing program. Thus during the period 1891–1973, one to 115 human injuries from bears occurred *each year*—mostly bitings or scratchings.

Bessie Haynes Arnold, who grew up in Yellowstone in the 1890s, recalled many years later that the problems began when the hotels got garbage dumps. She remembered that it actually became dangerous for visitors who insisted upon feeding the bears: "Some little accident would happen just about every day; someone would get bitten or scratched."[1]

Bessie Arnold was remembering correctly. From 1931 to 1969, the average yearly number of Yellowstone visitor injuries involving bears was forty-six. The high occurred during the 1930s, when 115 people were injured by bears in one year alone. Black bears were involved in almost all of these incidents (grizzly bear injury statistics are so small as to be negligible), and a high percentage of these park injuries occurred because visitors were illegally and foolishly feeding bears.[2]

Certainly one of the region's earliest bear injuries occurred in June of 1888, when George R. Dow was chased by a grizzly bear at Cinnabar Basin, just outside the park. He climbed a tree but the sow grabbed his leg and bit and clawed it badly. This injury was not related to human feeding of the bear, but probably was instead related to the female's defense of her two cubs.[3]

Another early park bear injury occurred on September 5, 1902, when R. E. Southwick of Hart, Michigan, was mauled near the Lake Hotel garbage dump while trying to pet a bear cub. Needless to say, the cub's mother was not pleased by this, and she ripped Southwick up pretty badly. Said a newspaper article at the time: "He was bitten a number of times and the flesh torn from his breast; one rib is broken and it is feared his right lung is seriously injured." Only Southwick's wife hammering the bear with a club saved his life.[4]

The first two human fatalities in Yellowstone National Park may have occurred in 1904, but so far we cannot absolutely prove that these two people died from their injuries or even that the incident happened. If it truly happened, it occurred in August and the first news of it appeared in the *Gardiner Wonderland* newspaper on August 20. "R. C. Smith," said the story, "on his arrival in town this morning reported the killing of a man and the wounding of another by a big grizzly bear near the Lake Hotel." Smith had received his information "from parties going to the scene of the killing with the hospital ambulance." Strangely, no more appeared about this story until October of that year, when an injury incident suddenly made the rounds in many newspapers as supposedly resulting in two human deaths from a bear attack at or near Lake Hotel. The story was that James Wilson and his nephew, both park visitors from Pennsylvania, came suddenly upon a bear; the boy fired a shot at it, and it charged them both. "The boy was crushed to death," said the story, "and Wilson was so badly torn and bitten that he died soon after being rescued by other travelers." The same story was soon carried by newspapers around the country in at least thirteen states. So thoroughly did ignorance come into play that one story claimed the attack was perpetuated by "tame bears" and stated that "one of the pets in Yellowstone Park" has "turned on [its] trainers." Only two of these many newspaper stories stated that the two men were in fact employees of Lake Hotel and not tourists.[5]

No follow-up stories seem to have appeared until November, when several newspapers picked up an article that appeared in *Field and Stream* magazine. Seeming to have more to say about the same incident, it stated that one Charles Wilson and his son, who were employees of Lake Hotel, were the two people so killed by two bears and that "attempts are said to have been made to suppress the news of this incident." Conspiracies or at least a belief in them seem to abound no matter what period of history may hold them, but this article certainly makes one pause to wonder whether this incident might have happened and if so whether it was lost in history. After all, in 1904 Lake Hotel was located in a very remote area, where news sometimes did not get out to the outer world. Thus I present the story's text here for posterity and consideration:

> As an animal the bear is [has] the type of rugged strength and innate ferocity [that is legendary]. For years the wild bears of the Yellowstone park, protected, fed, and petted, have done their share toward disabusing the public mind of this idea. That no one at the park has been injured by these wild bears, which feed around the hotels, is rather singular when one comes to think of the matter, for certainly liberties have been taken with these animals, tame as they have become. Perhaps in the future, people will be more careful, in view of the startling news which comes in a Gardiner, Mont. dispatch, under date of October 7. It seems that Charles Wilson and his son, who lived near the Lake Hotel, heard a noise in the meathouse and, going out to investigate the matter, found that two large cinnamon bears were in the building. Perhaps the men undertook to drive out the bears. In any case, the latter attacked them and killed them both. The two men were employees of the Lake hotel. Attempts are said to have been made to suppress the news of this incident. It would be far better to spread the news of it and to teach the people that a powerful wild animal is something not to be trifled with.[6]

While its attribution to *Field and Stream*, a magazine concerned with outdoor recreation, gives this story some credibility, three other items make me uneasy about its truth. Firstly, the story did not appear in the annual reports of the park superintendent, as later such incidents did. Secondly and thirdly, the bears involved ("cinnamon") seem to have been black bears, and two people were reported killed by two bears in the same incident. Black bears are far less likely to attack people than are grizzlies (of course here, the bears were reportedly rampaging through a "meathouse" and could thus have been protecting their food source), and two people killed simultaneously by two bears seems quite unlikely.

All together these facts (if they *are* facts) seemed to me to augur against this tale, until I examined two other newspapers. In a very long story published in the *Washington* (DC) *Post* on October 8 (p. 6) entitled "No Bear Hunting in the Park," the author editorialized against allowing bear hunting in Yellowstone because of the recent event wherein two park employees were killed by bears that were "regular habitués" of garbage at Lake Hotel. Because of its length and its inclusion of new details, this story bodes in favor of the truth of the Wilson tale. Meanwhile, the story on page 1 of the *San Francisco Call* for October 7 offered the additional details that the two men were hotel employees who were killed by "grizzlies" while traveling away from their home at the hotel. Because of this additional detail, it too militates in favor of the story's truth. In fact, the earlier story, which included the claim that one of the victims fired a shot at the bears, augurs in favor of the proposition that the two were employees rather than visitors. Soldiers at checkpoints routinely discovered the guns of visitors but might have been less likely to find an employee's gun in transported baggage.[7]

In analyzing this possible incident for truth, one immediately wonders what happened to the bodies. Treating the alleged incident as kindly as possible, I can argue that before about 1910, fewer regulations and policies with regard to bodies were in place and the park generally operated in a looser way than it did later. Issuing of death certificates was not automatic. And it was not a difficult matter, when family could not be located and when the incident occurred deep in the wilderness at Lake, to simply bury the person rather than becoming embroiled with officials at headquarters (Mammoth), sixty miles to the north. Witness what happened to Fogerty's and Parker's bodies in 1883 (buried at Lake initially), M. D. Scott's body in 1885 (buried near Lake initially), Dave Edwards's body in 1906 (buried at Lake), and even Philip Sheldon's body in 1903 (buried at Mammoth). Sheldon had just arrived for work in Yellowstone and was riding up the hill from Gardiner to Mammoth when he was thrown from the wagon and killed. The newspapers stated that no one knew where he was from or who his relatives were, so he was buried in the Fort Yellowstone cemetery. The point is that in early days all it took for this to happen was the inability to find the deceased's family or the realization that no one wanted to claim the body, and the deceased could then be simply buried. In the 1904 case of the Wilsons, what if they had no family or friends claiming their bodies? I can argue that they would possibly have been buried at Lake. On the other hand, perhaps park officials would have reburied the Wilsons at Mammoth as happened with Philip Sheldon, and thus we would have a record of it. On the other hand, Dave Edwards remained (and remains today) buried at Lake.

But as bear expert Paul Schullery points out, it is hard to believe that Park Acting Superintendent Major John Pitcher "had anything to do with such a nefarious concealment." I agree completely, and this probably tips the scales in my head in favor of the event never having happened.[8] (On the other hand, what if Pitcher simply did not know about it? Is that even possible?)

In the final analysis, I cannot say whether employees Charles (James?) Wilson and his son were killed by bears at or near Lake Hotel in October of 1904. It is fodder for further research. While I am suspicious that a covering up of this incident *may* have occurred (see note 7), I cannot prove it. My inclination is to believe that the 1904 "deaths" did not happen or else we probably would have better records about them.

There are at least two other reports of a bear-caused human death in Yellowstone Park prior to the first documented death in 1916. One supposedly occurred in 1907, as chronicled by F. Dumont Smith.[9] According to Smith, a tourist chased some grizzly cubs up a tree, poked at them with his umbrella, and then was fatally mauled by their mother. The story was obtained second-hand, always suspect to historians, but more important, there is no mention of it in any of the area newspapers of the day or in the annual reports of the park superintendent. Such an incident, if it caused death, would likely have generated much news, as happened with the Southwick injury earlier and as happened with subsequent death incidents. A second such story, probably the same incident, appeared in Clifton Johnson's *Highways and Byways of the Rocky Mountains*. Here is the account, written during a 1909 trip to the park:[10]

> There was a tourist come to the Park once makin' his brag that he was goin' to have his hands on a bear. That's a kind of hobby with some people—they want to get their hands on a bear. The men here told him he'd better not, but that didn't make any difference. So one day he and his wife saw a bear with two cubs and they gave chase. One cub ran up a tree, and the man touched it as he was climbing. He'd succeeded in his stunt, but the old bear didn't know that was the end of the game. She went for him and knocked him down. His wife drove the bear off with a club, but the man was clawed up so bad he died soon after he returned to his home in the East.

Without more specific information, I have no way of cross-checking to see if this incident actually occurred. But it sounds very much like the F. Dumont Smith story above, so perhaps they are the same story, they corroborate each other, and the death really did happen. I do not know. It is certainly possible that the incident could have gone unreported in the park if the tourist did not die until later and far away. Doubters of that possibility should read the John Graham death story below, essentially unknown in the park until the publication of this book. On the other hand, both Smith's and Johnson's stories could merely be corrupted retellings of the Southwick injury of 1902. Witness the way that story was distorted several times in the newspapers.[11]

Another example of the way that even serious maulings or possible deaths of humans by bears can be lost in history is the following story, which was unknown until the publication of this new (2014) edition of *Death in Yellowstone*. The mauling, if it actually happened, occurred in 1894, and the fact that it occurred in a wilderness area—where individual humans long traveled in remote areas by themselves—should not be a surprise. The supposed incident happened on Buffalo Fork of Snake River, just south of Yellowstone National Park and within present Grand Teton National Park (Buffalo Fork runs into Snake River near present Moran, Wyoming). One W. T. Sawyer of Cripple Creek, Colorado, told this story to Denver's *Rocky Mountain News*, and it was reprinted in the New York *Sun* in early 1895. The long account concerned the exploits of Sawyer's group of Cripple Creek men who supposedly traveled to Jackson Hole in the summer of 1894, and it contained a lot of clearly fanciful and untrue details about the country visited. But as usual with this type of story, there were enough details in it that sounded reasonable that it is possible the bear-attack portion actually occurred. Sawyer told of meeting two "hermits" who lived in primitive cabins in the Jackson Hole country named Mr. Todd and Mr. Cherry and of spending time with them. According to Sawyer, Cherry told him the following story, which, if true, must have occurred in 1894 on Buffalo Fork.

> Cherry has a comfortable cabin, with a great open fireplace, and a cooking stove for use in summer. He has cattle and horses, and is now entertaining his brother, who was maimed for life last spring in a fight with a bear. The brother is a tenderfoot, and did not notice the bear until it jumped on him from behind a fallen tree. The man was badly chewed up, but succeeded in shooting the bear. Thinking he was dying, the hunter scrawled with a lead pencil in a little book he carried in his pocket: "I met a bear, and we had a fight. I think he has finished me." Mr. Sawyer says the man fainted after writing in the book, and was found nearly dead several hours later by his brother.[12]

We must be cautioned by the secondhand nature of this story, and again we have no way of knowing whether there is any truth to it. But it is presented here as another example of how such incidents that happen in remote areas can be easily lost in history.

There is much better documentation for a human death from a grizzly bear that occurred on or about July 10, 1894, outside of the park to the north in present Gallatin National Forest. It appears to be the first documented human death from a bear mauling in the Greater Yellowstone Ecosystem, and because it occurred only about fourteen miles north of the park boundary, I am including it here.

The unfortunate incident happened to Lee Mallison, about 25 and formerly of Pennsylvania, who was residing in Livingston, Montana. Mallison had been employed as "underground foreman" for the Independence Mining Company at the head of East Boulder River until a suspension of mining operations, and he thereafter returned to prospecting. He left Livingston in early July of 1894 heading southeast through the mountains to the area of his former employment, an area then known as the Natural Bridge Mining District. In what was no doubt an imprudent move, he was attempting "to hunt a bear that had been wounded the previous day." Bear hunters from the time of Lewis and Clark knew that it was foolhardy to follow a wounded bear, and any ordinary hunter then or now could and would tell you the same thing.

Reported "mysteriously" missing about July 10, Mallison could not be found even after numerous searching parties scoured the mountains. However, they found his tracks near the mouth of Elk Creek, along with some other bad signs. "He appeared to be following a bear," said the *Minneapolis Journal*, "which was badly wounded and was bleeding freely along the route." Dreading what they might find, parties searched for several days along that creek but found nothing. Shuddering at the likelihood of his fate, Livingston residents finally concluded that Mallison "had met with some accident or that he had encountered and been killed by a bear."

He was missing for more than a year.

On September 5, 1895, prospector James Graham, exploring near the head of East Boulder River on Elk Creek—a stream high in the mountains that enters the river from the west between fourteen and fifteen miles north of the Yellowstone National Park boundary—found Lee Mallison's remains. Graham "was passing through a heavy piece of timber on the bank of Elk Creek," said the *Journal*, "when he came upon the skeleton, a gun, and a quantity of clothing." He and two others were able to identify the clothing as belonging to Mallison. "The clothing was badly torn," continued the newspaper, "and from the appearance of the surroundings, it is quite evident that Mallison came to his death through wild beasts." Graham and the two other men buried Mallison's remains there and reported the following about his body, which the *Livingston Enterprise* newspaper printed:

> Nothing remained except bones and fragments of his clothing. The head had been severed from the body and the skull was missing, indicating that wild beasts had evidently devoured the flesh from the bones and

carried away the head. The remains were found between two large fallen trees which had concealed them from view and rendered discovery impossible except by coming directly upon them. By the side of the remains was a 40-82 Winchester rifle, with the name "Chas. H. Pell" marked with tack-heads on the stock and also engraved on the wood-work encasing the magazine.

At Livingston, officials opened Mallison's rifle and found eight cartridges in the magazine and one empty shell in the chamber. This indicated that Mallison had fired the gun or that it accidentally discharged prior to his death, because otherwise he probably would have inserted a fresh cartridge into the weapon. So while it seemed possible that he had accidentally shot himself, most observers believed the other possibility, which seemed much more likely—that "coming suddenly upon a bear, he had only time to fire one shot before he was overpowered and crushed to death by the animal." The *Journal* did not accept the shooting theory at all, their newspaper having reported the blood trail found earlier along the creek. "It is now believed," wrote their editors, "that Mallison had wounded a bear and was giving chase, when it turned upon him and crushed out his life." Mallison was unmarried but had a brother in Pennsylvania, whom Livingston officials apparently contacted about his death.[13]

A supposed human death by mauling in 1935 in Yellowstone apparently never happened. Instead it appears to have been an injury to park road-crew members that occurred in 1910. Walt Stebbins, a Gardiner resident most of his life, was a small boy then, but remembers that his father, Jack Stebbins, and his uncle, Archie Stebbins, were working at a government road camp at Midway Geyser Basin when a grizzly came into the camp during the day. It got into a ruckus with a camp dog, and Jack and Archie jumped into the fray. According to Walt, the bear mauled both of the men, and Archie spent six weeks in the hospital. The local newspaper stated that Jack Stebbins died in 1935 of injuries he received in the park from the grizzly bear mauling.[14] But Walt Stebbins says his father did not die from bear injuries, and I have to believe that Walt has better information than the newspaper.[15]

Yellowstone's first documented human fatality from a bear occurred in 1916. On September 8, 1916, Frank Welch, 61, a government teamster, was killed by a grizzly bear (the one named "Old Two Toes," according to Gay Randall) while hauling a load of hay and oats to a road camp near Sylvan Pass. The incident occurred near the so-called Ten Mile Spring at Turbid Lake while Welch and two laborers were camped, Welch sleeping under the wagon with one laborer and the other laborer sleeping on top of it. The grizzly, which had already caused at least two injuries near Fishing Bridge,[16] appeared at Welch's camp about 1:00 a.m. and awakened Mr. Devlin, who was under the wagon with Welch. Devlin yelled, threw some bedding at the bear, and climbing onto the wagon, saw the bear grab Welch. The other two men threw a lunch box at the bear to divert it and it let Welch go. But when Welch tried to climb onto the wagon, the bear again rushed him and pulled him down. The two men succeeded in frightening the bear off, but when Welch attempted to again climb onto the wagon, it grabbed him for a third time. "It was probably during this last attack," wrote Major Fries of the U.S. Engineers later, "that (the bear) mangled Mr. Welch so terribly about the left shoulder, and on his side and abdomen." Two ribs on Welch's left side were broken and the muscles torn loose. His left arm was torn and badly mangled at the shoulder, there were two or three deep cuts across his right thigh, and the bear's claws punctured a lung from the rear. A newspaper account stated that the bear "dragged him from beneath the wagon and proceeded to eat him alive." Summarizing the attack, the story proclaimed that the bear "stripped the flesh from one of Welch's arms, bit into one of his lungs, and partly disemboweled him."[17]

Devlin and the other laborer flagged down a passing automobile, which took them all to the road camp on Sylvan Pass, precisely the wrong direction for Welch. The injured man was finally taken to Fort Yellowstone, where he died. Another newspaper account stated that the bear "tore large holes in Welch's stomach and nearly tore off (one of) his arms." He died on September 11 at 8:10 p.m.[18] The bear later returned to eat the hay around Welch's wagon. Fred Muse and his road camp men had rigged a trap for the grizzly. They spread garbage in front of an overturned barrel with a charge of dynamite at its opening. The dynamite was then connected by a fuse to an electric battery, and when the bear began to eat, the boys blew him up: "broke every bone in his body."[19] Historian Aubrey Haines thought that this bear had perhaps been driven to the attack by pains of arthritis or worn teeth. Major Fries thought cubs were involved, although none were in evidence. If the bear was in pain, perhaps the three missing toes it lost during its 1912 attack on John Graham (described later in this chapter) had continued to bother it.

Horace Albright, who was one of the founders of the new National Park Service in 1916, stated that Frank Welch was literally sleeping on a slab of bacon at the time of the event. Such a statement, made forty-six years after the incident, ordinarily could not be trusted. But a third newspaper account stated that one of the other men tried to distract the bear by throwing chunks of bacon at it and that it stopped its attack momentarily to eat the bacon. Thus bacon was indeed present. And naturalist Ernest Thompson Seton, certainly a trustworthy authority, confirmed that "park authorities tell me that Walsh slept with his bacon under his pillow; hence the approach of the Bear; and that the man probably provoked the Bear by striking him." So the bacon plus Welch's resistance appear to be what killed him.[20] Today Welch's grave is marked by the only wooden marker at Mammoth's army cemetery. That marker is much deteriorated and should one day be replaced, so that we do not inadvertently lose this historic gravesite.

Of course, for every fatality there were, as I have mentioned, many more injuries. The following incident probably occurred sometime in the late twenties at Tower Fall when a man and woman stopped at the Haynes store there, and the woman spied a park ranger:

"May I release my dog from his leash?" she asked. "No, ma'am," said the ranger deferentially. "It's strictly against the rules."

"There seem to be rules against everything one wants to do in this park," she said with a petulant frown. "Now what possible reason can there be for not allowing my dog a little freedom? Poor Von has been tied up all day!"

The ranger's strict training kept him from saying what he wanted to, but his face reddened at her tone. He began, "Lady, there are bears around here that might . . . "

She did not give him a chance to finish the sentence. "Oh, if that's all that worries you, Von won't hurt the bears!"

She reached for the snap on the dog's collar and unleashed him before the startled ranger could utter another word of protest.

The dog headed straight for an old black bear mother sitting at the edge of the forest some fifty yards away, her two cubs above her in a tree, lying on two large limbs. The old bear sat there calmly, her front legs braced in front of her, not seeming to notice the dog that dashed madly toward her. She even inclined her head slightly the other way as if to show just how little this canine creature interested her.

The pup charged right up to the bear, fully expecting her to run. She sat motionless and he slowed for a quick turn to keep from running into her. At exactly that instant the old bear went into action. Quicker than a cat she struck out at him and with one blow of her paw sent him spinning with a broken back. Then she called her cubs down and hurried into the woods.

It happened so quickly that not one of the spectators moved for a few seconds. Then everyone rushed to the side of the dying dog, his owner protesting tearfully, "Why didn't you *tell* me? I can't understand why such terrible beasts are allowed to run at large. Why aren't they put in cages where they can do no harm?"[21]

I reiterate the dog regulations discussed in the hot-springs chapter.

Another bear injury story illustrates not only the ignorance that park visitors exhibited for many years in feeding bears, but also how the bear would sometimes end up actually getting the blame. William Rush, the author, arrived at a park road camp one day in the 1930s to find a ranger impatiently talking to a woman visitor:

"Lady, you mustn't *do* that. You've been told time and time again not to feed that bear."

"Oh, he won't hurt me," replied the lady. "He's so cute standing there. He's the gentlest bear in the park."

"Yes, I know," assented the ranger wearily. "But even tame bears hurt people quite often. They don't mean to—it's always an accident but the injury is just as bad. It's against the rules. Why can't you obey the regulations?"

"Oh, bother the regulations!" said the lady scornfully. "You rangers are always harping on regulations. This bear is hungry. Look here, I'll show you how eager he is to get even a small morsel of bread." The ranger shook his head. "I really wish you would not feed that bear," he said and rode away without waiting for the lady to demonstrate how "hungry" her pet bear was.

Life was probably pretty dull for this woman, staying all day in a camp with nothing much to do but admire the scenery. When a car drove up a few minutes after the ranger had gone, she called to the people, "Let me show you my bear's trick. He's just too cute for anything."

They gathered around and the woman held a piece of candy at full arm's length above her head. The bear, a great black fellow, rose on his hind feet and easily reached the candy. The woman backed away a few steps and offered another piece. The bear followed, walking on his hind legs, and took the candy as before. It was fun to make such a big fellow walk around and eat candy out of her hand! Everybody laughed and applauded.

"Such quaint creatures, these bears!" exclaimed one of the ladies from the automobile party. "So tame, ever so cute and gentle!"

They watched until the woman tired of the game. She stood directly in front of the bear, facing him but offering no more candy.

"Go away now," she ordered. "No more candy for you today."

She did not move, and as the bear dropped down on all fours he put out his front feet toward her, much as he would to a tree or any other convenient object, to ease his descent. The woman screamed as his paws touched her shoulders. His claws, sharp as knives, seeking support, ripped through her clothing and skin. They tore deep cuts a foot long across her breasts and blood spurted from them. The woman fainted. The bear backed away and disappeared in the pandemonium that ensued. One of the men ordered an ambulance by telephone, then drove posthaste to the ranger station. There the apprehensive ranger heard the old familiar tale: "Something terrible happened—a bear just tore the breasts off a woman. Kill the bear! He must be killed. He is a dangerous beast. Kill the wicked bear!"

So the story went, told by the very people who had but a few minutes before thought he was "cute."[22]

A biologist from the Seattle Zoo summed it up for me this way: "On many occasions animals are not so much trying to hurt us as giving us a mere rebuke or warning. The trouble is, a mere rebuke or warning from a bear can put a human in traction."

Anyone reading the monthly park superintendent's reports from the 1920s and 1930s cannot help but be impressed by the massive numbers of bear bites and scratches to foolish visitors caused by their feeding of bears. For example, the monthly report for September of 1924 records eighty-eight bear bites at West Thumb alone. How dumb could so many be?

Sometimes, of course, injuries were not due to bear feeding. Benton Merrifield, the assistant caretaker of the Canyon Hotel, was badly injured by a grizzly defending two cubs on October 22, 1928. He probably would not have survived had he not had the good sense to play dead.[23] And even rangers were not exempt. Seasonal ranger Gunnar Fagerlund was severely bitten in the foot by a grizzly in 1934 when he unexpectedly surprised four of them. Three ran away, but one chased him up a tree, mauling his foot as he clung there.[24]

The editorial at the beginning of this book mentions people in the park putting their children on the backs of bears to have their pictures taken. I have personally heard that story so many times, indeed even had it told directly to me at visitor centers and aboard tour buses, that I am convinced it must have happened numerous times in the long history of humans and bears in Yellowstone. But I could find documentation of only one such incident. Rocco Paperiello of Billings, Montana, remembers seeing it happen near Old Faithful in late July or early August of 1970. He watched a woman trying to place her small child on the back of a bear while the husband scrambled to take a picture of the event. A similar incident—its truth I cannot confirm—was related to me by Donalene O'Neill, a teenager at the time whose relatives owned the Wilson Motel in Gardiner. She stated:

In that time frame—1949 and 1950—I helped at the Motel. My aunt and uncle, Grace and Clare Van Atta, owned a small grocery store on

Grizzly bear tracks (courtesy of Yellowstone National Park)

Main Street and Aunt Bid and Uncle Fay Horr had a bar right behind the movie theater. The point of this letter is that every afternoon I would walk uptown and visit with Aunt Grace at her store. One day I was going in and met an older couple coming out. Both the man and woman's eyes were nearly swollen shut from crying. Aunt Grace told me that they had been in visiting with her for a long time and were very upset as they had stopped at a bear jam and had watched as a young couple sat their baby on the ground in front of a bear to get a picture. The bear had taken a large bite out of the baby's head and killed the baby. Rangers came and took the baby's body into West Yellowstone and other rangers escorted the parents to the Park entrance and told them never to return to the Park. Aunt Grace cried when relating the story. I have always felt that the story was true because of the "teller's" mental condition. My folks lived in Bozeman and searched the Bozeman paper. We looked in the Billings paper and Livingston paper. Nothing was ever published [that we found]![25]

As mentioned, I cannot confirm this story either, but there are enough verifiable details in it to make one believe that the event might have happened.

The park's second human fatality involving a bear occurred August 23, 1942. On the night of August 22, Martha Hansen, 45, and four other persons were staying in cabin 381 of the Old Faithful Cabin Camp. Hansen, a nurse from Twin Falls, Idaho, left the cabin about 1:45 a.m. en route to the ladies' restroom. As she came around the corner of the cabin, she was suddenly confronted by a large brown or gray bear. Each was apparently startled by the other, and when the woman attempted to turn and run, the bear grabbed her and dragged her several feet, inflicting severe neck and head injuries. Hansen sustained a deep six-inch wound from the top of her head down over the back of her neck, another wound extending from her nose across her right eye, three other facial lacerations, and a severe bite behind her left ear. Most of the muscles at the back of her neck were torn loose.

Hansen's screams brought to the scene her roommate, Emily Heide, who immediately retreated when the bear turned on her. Several other visitors heard the screams and finally succeeded in driving the bear away by throwing sticks of wood at it. An ambulance arrived a couple of hours later to transport Hansen to the hospital at Mammoth, but she had lost a great deal of blood and died on August 27.

F. E. Milner, traveling with Hansen, claimed that the bear involved was "a large brown" that had been eating out of garbage cans near their cabin during the day. But T. R. Terry, who claimed to be a wildlife instructor at Idaho Falls, stated that the bear was a grizzly and described it in a handwritten statement.

Terry averred that he saw the bear a short distance from the spot where Hansen was injured, describing it as having a "very large bushy head, high shoulders, rather long body, [and] shaggy, grey [grizzled?] fur."[26]

No cause was ever decided upon for the bear "attack" on Martha Hansen, but it can be argued that this incident fits into the category of "sudden encounter" (surprised bear).[27] A surprised bear can be a dangerous bear, hence present-day warnings given to backcountry hikers in Yellowstone: *make noise!* And this bear, as were nearly all the bears involved in human deaths in Yellowstone, was a bear habituated to human foods. Two years later, President Franklin Roosevelt signed a bill paying $1894.95 to Christine Hansen, mother of Martha, in compensation.[28] One previous congressional bill had given money to a Yellowstone Park visitor for a bear injury, that of Margaret Constable, who received ten thousand dollars in 1929 for bear injuries.[29] And a tort claim of two thousand dollars was paid by the park for a bear bite in 1958.[30] Arguably, payment of monies through these compensation bills was bad precedent by the government, as a paper trail was thus established without necessary fact-finding litigation. Of course before Congress passed the Federal Tort Claims Act in 1946, getting the ear of a congressman was the only way an aggrieved party could get relief, because prior to that time the federal government had immunity from such lawsuits.

But after the park's third human fatality involving a bear—the Harry Walker case—this established compensation system did not work for private plaintiffs. Instead, the ensuing litigation was long, complex, and expensive, and the government won . . . sort of.

An entire book could be written on the Harry Walker case. On Friday, June 23, 1972, Harry Eugene Walker, 25, of Anniston, Alabama, and his friend Phillip Bradberry (nicknamed "Crow") hitchhiked into Yellowstone Park from the north entrance (Vikki Schlicht, an Old Faithful Inn chambermaid, gave them a ride). Because they were hitching, they did not receive the usual warning literature given to entering visitors. However, Schlicht later testified that she warned the men about bears and told them to go to the ranger station.

Arriving at Old Faithful, Walker and Bradberry did something that was truly foolish—they walked over the boardwalks of a thermal area and made an illegal camp on a wooded hillside above Grand Geyser. The nearest authorized campground was at Madison Junction, sixteen miles away. They did this despite Schlicht's warnings. Walker and Bradberry were also told by an acquaintance at Old Faithful that they were camped illegally, but they stayed there anyway Friday night and all day Saturday.

Late on Saturday night, June 24, the two men had drinks at Old Faithful Inn and then started back to their camp. Early Sunday morning at the camp, they surprised a grizzly bear that was rooting through food they had left scattered around their illegal campsite.

I was a park bus-tour guide in 1972, and I distinctly remember an investigating ranger telling me the Walker camp was as dirty as any he had ever seen. Their food served as the initial attractant, and the "sudden encounter" with the two men apparently frightened the grizzly, which decided to defend its food supply. Bradberry saw the bear charging when it was only five feet away, dove to his left, and rolled down an embankment. At the same time, Walker shined his flashlight at the bear. It charged Walker and dragged him away, while Bradberry ran screaming through the thermal area. (In retrospect, Bradberry is lucky not to have fallen into a hot spring in the darkness and in his panic.) He heard Walker cry out, "Help me, Crow, help me!" and then silence. At Old Faithful Inn, Bradberry fell to the floor shouting, "Bear! Bear! Has my friend!"

Around 5:00 a.m., rangers found Walker's body. About 25 percent of it had been eaten by the bear. Walker had died of suffocation caused by massive damage to his trachea. In addition, his entire pelvic region was missing. A grizzly bear was subsequently trapped there, killed, and examined. Human hairs were found on its claws and in its digestive system. They were identified as belonging to Walker. The bear was a 20-year-old sow that weighed 232 pounds and had a documented history of garbage feeding. Some observers thought that perhaps this old sow's injuries to her footpads and teeth might have had something to do with the attack.[31]

Walker's parents sued the NPS in U.S. district court in California, alleging that he had not been adequately warned of the danger, and won damages of $87,417.67. The NPS appealed and the decision was reversed. The family tried to recover monies through congressional action as the Hansens had done earlier, but they were unsuccessful.[32]

The Walker incident served as the final nail in the coffin of bears being allowed to feed along Yellowstone roadsides. The last open-pit garbage dump in the park had been closed in 1970 at Trout Creek,[33] and now the NPS stepped up the transporting they had begun in order to get all roadside beggar bears off their diets of human food. Normally reclusive bears can lose their fear of man when human foods are involved. A more natural bear is a less dangerous bear, and the NPS knew this. The dual attacks in Glacier National Park in 1967, as related in the book *Night of the Grizzlies*, had already cemented that fact in the minds of managers there, and now Yellowstone had its own version.

Beyond the personal tragedy of the case were and are its implications for park management. At issue is just how far the parks will be allowed to keep a natural setting. Paul Schullery has said it well: "What makes me uncomfortable about these court cases, no matter how justified any given suit may be, is that they create park policy in a judicial vacuum sometimes thousands of miles from the park. A judge with no interest in, or experience with, wilderness and national parks, can have an inordinate effect on park management, if only as managers try to anticipate where they must be most careful to avoid lawsuits."[34]

The Walker case is, of course, a perfect illustration of this. While this book is mainly about deaths in Yellowstone, I would be remiss if I did not make some comments on the impacts of these deaths upon park management, primarily because of "wrongful death" lawsuits against parks.

The judge who presided over the Harry Walker case could have had some of the very impacts that Schullery mentioned above. That he did not have more is no doubt attributable to the fact that he was reversed on appeal. But I believe it is a worthwhile exercise to examine some of this judge's comments, all made during the Walker trial. These are the types of comments that make it harder to manage parks in a natural way. They impact you, the public, by sanitizing your national parks and making them more like Disneyland than like nature preserves.

Keep in mind that the Walker trial was a judge trial (no jury). In such a trial, the judge can question witnesses in addition to letting attorneys question them. It also means the judge makes his rulings based upon his hearing of the witnesses and upon his own arguments with the attorneys. Here are some of the judge's comments:

> JUDGE: This is kind of a pre-indication of what I am thinking, but there should have been some signs down there that say to the effect, "Danger. Do not sleep or camp here. Regular campground one-half mile"—or two and a half miles, whatever it is—"Regular campsite two and a half miles northeast" . . . and then have some markers up there that would show the way to a campsite that was patrolled, that was fenced in, perhaps, from these grizzlies.

The issue here is that in a place as large as Yellowstone National Park, how many signs are we going to have and where are they going to be located? Do we really need "Danger! Grizzly Bears!" signs along geyser basin boardwalks (along with the hot-spring warnings) when they already appear at entrances and in many other places? This judge thought so. His arguments would put signs everywhere in the park because someone (somewhere, sometime) might not see them. Analogously I could ask, should New York's Central Park have signs every ten feet saying "Danger! Muggers!" just because a nonstreetwise non–New Yorker might go walking there? Analogously I could ask, should we build fences along the edge of the Grand Canyon to keep someone from falling in? Should we stretch a net across the Yellowstone River above the falls in case someone falls in?

The *Walker* judge also wanted campgrounds fenced for safety purposes. In proposing this, he gave no consideration to keeping a park natural, to the blocking of animal migration routes, to the visual ugliness of a fence, to the making of wilderness areas into places that are the same as everywhere else—in short, to the abstract and unquantifiable quality of a visitor's park experience. With fences, one gets safety, maybe, and one loses, arguably, a major thing one came to the park *for*—the very state of getting away from things like fences! As Paul Schullery says, "That may be good legal behavior, but it doesn't seem the best way to run a wilderness . . . Getting mauled by a bear in a national park is *not* the legal equivalent of slipping on an icy sidewalk. Someone else owns the sidewalk; *you* own the bear."[35]

The Walker judge was also convinced that all the park bears should be constantly tracked for safety purposes. Note how he questioned Dr. Frank Craighead, a witness for the Walkers:

> JUDGE: Let me ask you this: The thing that seems to me to be relevant here is, do you have an opinion as to whether or not this particular bear 1792, when it was tagged, should have been—how do you say it?—stuck with a beeping bug? What do you call those things that you put on them to track them?
>
> CRAIGHEAD: A radio tag or radio collar.
>
> JUDGE: All right. Do you have an opinion as to whether he should have had a radio tag or collar attached to him, so he could be trailed?
>
> CRAIGHEAD: I think that it would certainly have been helpful in following the movements of this bear when it was transplanted.
>
> JUDGE: How much does that cost to do?
>
> CRAIGHEAD: It would be in the neighborhood of several thousand dollars.
>
> JUDGE: Well, like how much, two thousand, three thousand?
>
> CRAIGHEAD: $3,000 . . .
>
> JUDGE: Let me ask you this: If you had this sort of thing put on Bear 1792, would he have been able to be tracked right up to where he attacked the Walker boy?
>
> CRAIGHEAD: [Yes.]

The judge persisted in this and included it in his ruling[36] as something the NPS *should* have done to prevent the Walker killing. And one of the judge's in-court statements bordered on a harangue:

> JUDGE: In that connection, I want to hear some arguments on whether there should have been retained this radio monitoring of these animals . . . monitoring these animals, so that at all times there could be a [display] board that somebody follows . . . [telling us] where are these grizzlies? How close are they to developed areas? Are they near Old Faithful? The Inn? Are they in the garbage dumps? Are they way back in the woods?

Are they close to the road? . . . But that is an important question. How much does it cost for them [NPS] to do that? How much would it have cost? Even today, wouldn't it be a wise thing? I do not know, but I want to hear argument on it. Wouldn't it be a wise thing for the Park Service to keep a plot like that? Wouldn't that be the best sort of patrol in the world, to bring these grizzlies [in] with these automatic transmitters?

If it can be done for three or four or five thousand dollars [then] in a sense—[and] I do not like to use the word—the hell with what the Sierra Club may say or these barefoot boys with environmental impact statements on their back. I think the big question is to protect the public, protect the public.

As the Lord said, "Use the mountains, use the land. Build upon it. Make it your home, dominate it." That is what he told human beings. He did not tell grizzlies to dominate humans. He told humans to dominate grizzlies.

I do not care about putting radio transmitters on their ears. That is not going to hurt them . . . It is ridiculous. It is a fad, all this environmentalism, a big fad. One day it is going out the window. Why? Because we can use the wilderness, whether it be skiers, whether it be backpackers and whatnot, and use it safely, if those who run the wilderness will safely control the wilderness, so it does not injure us.[37]

Of course, collaring and tracking all bears is illogical, unreasonable, and unnatural from the point of view of park managers, regardless of one judge's opinion. It can traumatize the bears, make the bears look artificial instead of natural, cost a lot of money in radios and monitoring personnel, and give the public the perception that a national park is like the movie *Westworld* (all mechanical) rather than a natural preserve.

And the idea of removing or sanitizing the grizzlies to make the park "safe" for visitors is ridiculous—as if wilderness can be totally safe and still be wilderness.

Reading the Walker transcripts, one senses that the judge's mind was made up very early in the trial. He had no feeling for the park's problems in protecting the bears (and thus part of our heritage), in giving bears a natural environment to live in, or in offering visitors the chance to see wild animals in a wild setting—all well-established, thoroughly legislated purposes of Yellowstone National Park. He had no regard for the fact that the greatest resource of Yellowstone is *its very wildness*. When you take that away by sanitizing the place—whether by radio-collaring every bear, by putting up signs every ten feet, or by otherwise overdeveloping the place—you destroy its most important element: wildness. It is not just another consumer product to be made safe. As

Schullery says, "It is no longer able to serve its function if it is paved, fenced, labeled, and regulated into a form palatable to zoo- and television-minded visitors. It cannot stimulate if it is crippled or lessened."[38]

As I have noted, this judge's decision to award the Walkers damages was reversed on appeal, and fortunately so for the national parks. But it illustrates the problems parks face in having judges make park policy based on personal injuries suffered by careless visitors. The Ninth Circuit Court of Appeals held that the park's decision to close the garbage dumps in connection with griz-zly-bear management was a "planning" or "discretionary" decision under the Federal Tort Claims Act rather than a "ministerial" one, and so the government was entirely immune from the lawsuit. But the court went further and stated that there was no evidence to support the trial judge's decision that the Park Service failed to warn Walker and Bradberry of dangerous conditions. More-over, the court stated that because the two men disregarded the advice of Vikki Schlicht to go to the ranger station or visitors' center and thereby avoided receiving bear warnings, they were comparatively negligent in the incident.[39]

Dr. Frank Craighead and others have mentioned a possible bear fatality in the Old Faithful area two years before Harry Walker was killed. It is important for us to note that this fatality has never been documented. If it happened, we cannot presently prove it, but I include it here for completeness.

The Old Faithful bear log for August 23, 1970, has the following entries:

[Time] 1651—David Hamilton, Old Faithful reports that visitors at the upper Firehole Bridge are gazing at a scalp on a blanket.
    1736—Re: 1651 [entry] It is a scalp with pieces of flesh and mag-gots, pictures taken and pieces collected and [placed] under rear of building.

Whether these were really pieces of human remains or just animal parts was never established.

A park visitor reported to Old Faithful rangers three weeks later that a bear had ransacked an abandoned illegal camp on Firehole River a half-mile south of the new highway bridge. Frank Craighead thought it to have been the same bear that eventually killed Harry Walker, but this was never proven. Rangers disassembled the camp on September 16, finding seventeen items including a tent and accessories, a fishing net, swimming mask and fins, cloth-ing, and a duffel bag that carried the name Herbert Muller and the number 37790176. In the last edition of this book I wondered whether Muller had been a bear fatality, but in 1996, I received an anonymous letter from the De-partment of Veterans Affairs confirming that Muller had died a natural death in June of 1994. "I realize," wrote the anonymous employee, "that this information does not answer the question as to whether the person who had the illegal camp was killed by a bear. However, it clearly was not Herbert Muller."[40]

Beginning in 1970, with the closure of the last Yellowstone garbage dump, the stepping up of the government's transporting program for roadside beggar bears, and the installation of "bear-proof" (odor-preventing) trash cans, the numbers of injuries to park visitors by bears began to drop dramatically.[41] But the park's fourth human fatality involving a bear occurred in 1984. The victim was a young woman from Switzerland.

On July 29, 1984, ranger Gary Youngblood was on duty at Canyon Ranger Station when a woman hiker came into that office. She had dark, shoulder-length hair, and was about five feet five inches tall and around 120 pounds. Youngblood issued the woman a backcountry permit for site 5-B-1 (north of Fern Lake) for the night of July 30. He warned her against hiking alone in Yellowstone country, and about bears particularly and foods in camp generally. Youngblood noted that the woman, Brigitta Claudia Fredenhagen, 25, of Basel, Switzerland, appeared intelligent and spoke near-perfect English.[42] District Ranger John Lounsbury, sitting in the next office, remembers that she got a good bit of bear information from Youngblood.[43]

On July 31 at 6:00 p.m., Brigitta's brother, Andreas Fredenhagen, reported to Lake Area ranger Mark Marschall that his sister had failed to meet him and his wife as scheduled at Pelican trailhead. A search was begun with two persons traveling through Pelican Valley, and the following morning Ranger Marschall began a patrol of the area on horseback.

At 10:30 a.m., Marschall found Brigitta's camp. He noted that something spooked his horse there; the horse would approach no closer than twenty yards. So Marschall walked to the green dome tent that he saw pitched some sixty feet from the shore of White Lake in campsite 5-W-1. He noticed immediately that the tent fly had rip marks in it near the door and saw a sleeping pad, parka, and other gear inside undisturbed. "As I walked up to the tent," wrote Marschall, "I noticed pieces of hair and scalp and a few small pieces of muscle, bone, and tissue." A sleeping bag lay nearby. He radioed for assistance and then continued to search for Brigitta. He could not find her but did locate her food cache thirty yards away. It had been pulled down by a bear and the food partially eaten.[44]

Sensing they had a bad incident on their hands, rangers Dave Spirtes and Tim Blank at Lake Ranger Station were helicoptered to the scene at 12:07 p.m. and began a hasty search of the area. Near the sleeping bag they found a piece of Brigitta's lip, and the rangers' faces grew grave. They searched the area between the trail and the lake. Recent thundershowers had cleansed the landscape of obvious drag trails, so the rangers swept north for about a quarter of a mile. At 12:57 they spotted a bloody article of clothing. From there a trail

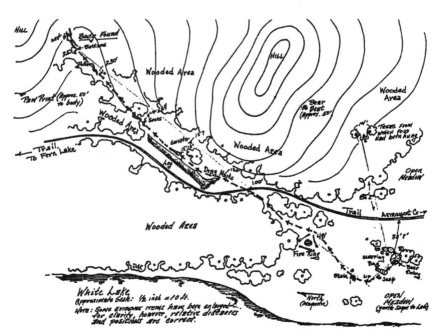

Drawings made by Ranger Dan Krapf to accompany Brigitta Fredenhagen (bear death) investigation, 1984 (Case Incident 84-2913, YNP)

of more bloody clothing and human tissue led to Brigitta Fredenhagen's body, 258 feet from her tent. Quite a lot of it had been eaten by the bear.

Shaken by their discovery, the rangers continued the investigation. From blood on and a puncture in the woman's sleeping bag, it appeared to them that the bear had ripped the tent and pulled her out either by the left side of her neck or the top of her head while she slept. There was no sign of a struggle; her hiking clothing was neatly folded inside of the tent and all other items were undisturbed. Six feet outside, she either slid out or was pulled from her sleeping bag. About twenty feet northwest of the tent, rangers found a rectangle of discolored grass where substantial blood and tissue had fallen, and this was deemed to be the site where Fredenhagen died. Because she was first attacked at her neck and face, the rangers decided she had probably died quickly, perhaps without really waking up.[45]

The bear had climbed twelve feet up a tree to get to the woman's food cache, the same way she had put the cache up—both her climbing marks and the bear's claw marks could be seen. Most of the food cache had been eaten. The tree-climbing marks and other evidence seemed to indicate a subadult male grizzly, light in color.

The rangers and autopsy people attempted to piece together what had happened. Fredenhagen had hiked 8.5 miles, camped several miles short of her permitted site, boiled water for tea, and ate precooked or cold food for dinner. She hung her food, arranged her clothing and other items neatly, crawled into her sleeping bag with her feet facing the east and her head toward the lake, and was apparently asleep when the attack occurred sometime after 10:30 p.m. on July 29. The bear was never identified or captured. It apparently left the site within twelve hours, because the woman's body was not semiburied in the fashion that feeding grizzlies often practice, and because there was no scat near the body. The rangers found scats containing human remains several miles north and again several miles east of the site, and postulated that the bear had returned once to feed on July 31. Rain had destroyed much of the evidence; in fact, it was probably raining at the time of the attack or just shortly afterward.

Rangers Mike Pflaum and Mark Marschall spent several nights in the area sleeping nervously in a bear trap made from a culvert (arguably one of the only safe places) and hoping that the bear would return. It never did.[46]

But in the final analysis no one could be sure what the reasons were. The victim was not menstruating. The tent did contain two-thirds of a one-hundred-gram chocolate bar wrapped up inside a pack. Other odorous tent items included lip salve, Micoren pills, and a butane cigarette lighter. If the bear was attracted by these items, perhaps it felt secure because Fredenhagen was hiking *alone*, a discouraged practice in Yellowstone country and probably her biggest mistake. Even the widespread thunder and lightning in the area for several days previously was suggested as somehow tying into the attack, but in the end no one knew. The woman's hanging of her food, possession of four bear-warning pamphlets given her by ranger Youngblood, bear bells in the tent, and her signature at a trail register where three bear-warning signs were posted all attested to her knowledge of and concern for precautions in bear country.[47] In fact, on August 2, while going through her belongings, Brigitta's brother and sister-in-law found a notebook in which Brigitta had made a diary-type entry, written while at the campsite. Eerily, the entry noted that she had taken "all precautions."[48]

The Fredenhagen death was partially responsible for the Pelican Valley area being restricted to day-use-only hiking (no overnight camping), a regulation that had been considered for some years before that.

Like Fredenhagen, William J. Tesinsky was alone when a Yellowstone grizzly killed him on or about October 4, 1986. Tesinsky, 38, a Great Falls, Montana, auto mechanic, was an avid wildlife photographer who was also an expert woodsman and hunter. Yellowstone's Chief Ranger Dan Sholly has described him as "cocky, confident, and used to getting what he wanted."[49] He has been characterized as able to maintain a pace in his outdoor travels that would wear out most anyone else; in fact, he usually traveled alone because he felt most people could not keep up. His attitude about hiking by himself proved to be his undoing.

Tesinsky had been somewhat successful at selling his wildlife photographs. But he had not yet photographed a grizzly bear, and he was determined to do so. Sometime on or about October 4, Tesinsky became aware that a grizzly (bear 59 in park parlance) was frequenting the Otter Creek area near its junction with the Yellowstone River. Leaving his car in a pullout on the main road, Tesinsky began to stalk the bear all by himself and carrying his camera and tripod. Just how or when he confronted the sow grizzly we will never know, but his final moments must have been frightening ones, and it is likely that he struggled, at least for a short time.

Bear 59 was a semihabituated bear; that is, a bear which had had some contacts with humans and human foods. But she had never even approached a human aggressively. She had two cubs earlier in the season when the park transported her to Cub Creek, but did not have them by October. She was also intensely hyperphagic, desperate to put on weight for the coming winter. Tesinsky apparently "crossed over that fine line between being just another pesky photographer and being a potential threat or food source competitor." Or, perhaps this was a surprised bear or even a rare instance of predation. We do not know.[50]

After Tesinsky's blue car had been parked at the Otter Creek pullout for several days, the park began checking on him. Ranger Alice Siebecker, armed with license plate information, made calls to Tesinsky's home at Great Falls and found that he had missed work. On October 6, ranger Tom Olliff scouted the area on horseback but found nothing. Then ranger Jeff Henry talked to bear researcher Steve French and discovered that bear 59 had been in the area at least since October 4. Indeed, Jeff had seen her himself at LeHardy's Rapids about October 1.[51]

Thus, on October 7, District Ranger John Lounsbury and Ranger Mona Divine, followed later by Jeff Henry, Tom Olliff, Dick Divine, and Joe Fowler, began a genuine search up Otter Creek. From the top of a small hill, Mona Divine and John Lounsbury spotted bear 59 feeding on something. Henry and Fowler walked into the old Otter Creek campground to join them. Lounsbury remembers standing on the ridge overlooking "what we call Tesinsky Meadow now" and looking through his binoculars. In the magnified scene, he suddenly saw bear 59 "with a [human] leg in her mouth and it had a tennis shoe on it." He knew at that moment that "we had probably found Tesinsky."

Through his rifle scope, Jeff Henry saw legs lying on the ground and he, too, knew that the bear was feeding on Tesinsky. Divine saw it too, and of course Lounsbury had already seen it. Because a grizzly was in the area feeding, the rangers were very nervous. Over their radios came the voice of bear specialist Gary Brown: "Are you in a position to destroy that bear?" "Yes, we are," replied Lounsbury. Brown gave the order, and Ranger Fowler shot bear 59.[52]

The rangers, still well armed with shotguns and rifles, moved into the area cautiously. Jeff Henry remembers that the scene was one of a classic carcass feeding, with coyotes, ravens, and magpies all waiting on the fringes for their turn. One of those ravens had croaked earlier, startling John Lounsbury out of a bit of a reverie and back into intensely watching his surroundings. The group walked into a small meadow about one-quarter mile from the main road and found Tesinsky's remains. And remains was what they were. All that lay on the ground were Tesinsky's legs and pelvic parts. His entire upper half was missing. Jeff remembers thinking that it looked as if someone had chainsawed him in two at the belt. Lying onsite were Tesinsky's camera and tripod. It was evident from the large amount of blood around the collars of Tesinsky's jacket and shirt, found later, that the bear had gone for his neck from the outset. In fact, Tesinsky's entire neck was missing, probably the reason for his death and an occurrence which was apparently inflicted as he ran. It probably had not taken bear 59 long to tear him apart and to subsequently bury parts of him nearby for later feeding. Tesinsky's skull was found in the burial mound.

No bear pictures were found on Tesinsky's camera film. Jeff Henry supposed that perhaps the fact that bear 59 wore a radio collar deterred Tesinsky from taking distant photos and encouraged him to try for a closer one, perhaps hoping for a turned-head photo wherein the radio collar would not show.

Moreover, his tripod was pointed down, as if the camera were aimed at something only twelve to fifteen feet away. And Tesinsky's camera had a short lens on it rather than a long lens. The last picture on his film roll has been described as "an unidentifiable dark blob, possibly an out-of-focus close-up of the ground." "Whatever he was focusing on," says Henry, an expert photographer himself, "was very close."[53]

Every bit as interesting was what the rangers found entangled on a sagebrush plant just above Tesinsky's tripod. It was a rubber, tube-type elk bugle. Rangers found blood on its cord and blood on the sagebrush on which it was snagged. Bear specialist Kerry Gunther believes that William Tesinsky may have sounded that elk bugle to get the bear to lift its head from foraging and thus may have caused the bear to charge. "Back in 1986, it was not as much in common knowledge as it is today," says Gunther, "that elk bugles can send bears (grizzly or black) into a predation mode." Thus it is certainly a possibility that the elk call might have "put the bear into a predatory mind-set."[54]

Following an autopsy of the bear and of Tesinsky, a park board of inquiry concluded that Tesinsky was killed because he was trying to photograph a grizzly bear at close range, and that the bear found near his remains was the one that killed him. We will never know what happened exactly, but the team thought Tesinsky was focusing his camera on the bear only twelve to fifteen feet away when it charged. Scott McMillion, a journalist who wrote about the attack, called it "a picture to die for." Tesinsky probably turned and ran toward the road, but the bear caught him from behind by the neck and killed him. Then, Jeff believes, the bear dragged Tesinsky back over the camera tripod (the bear's body or Tesinsky's thus bending one leg of the tripod), leaving large amounts of blood in the drag trail, to Tesinsky's final resting place. There the bear finished its job as one of nature's consummate feeding machines.[55]

The Tesinsky story and several other stories of human deaths from bears hearken us back to the idea of the buffalo as a mythical animal. We want badly to touch these animals—for reasons of affection perhaps, or domination, or whatever. But we must not. Human philosophies, literature, feelings all cry out for us to be more in touch with nature. But truly being in touch with nature includes knowing when *not* to touch. Tesinsky and some of the other bear victims here stepped over the line.

For twenty-six years following the 1986 death of William Tesinsky, Yellowstone Park saw no further human fatalities from bears, even though individual injuries occasionally occurred. Then suddenly, in 2011, two park visitors were killed by grizzlies in separate incidents. Unless the 1904 story of James Wilson and his nephew is true, never before had the park been host to two documented human deaths from bears in one summer. Officials and the public wondered whether something had changed in the park, but NPS Bear

Program Manager Kerry Gunther currently believes that fatal bear attacks will remain relatively uncommon.

Brian and Marylyn Matayoshi, of Torrance, California, entered the park's south gate on July 5, 2011, spent their first day visiting Old Faithful, and then returned to Grant Village to camp. It was their fourth trip to Yellowstone, and they had never seen a bear in the park before. On July 6, they drove to Canyon for hiking, Brian insisting that he wanted to hike on a nonpaved trail. They parked at Wapiti Trailhead near Chittenden Bridge and began hiking at about 8:30 a.m. It was a warm day—in the midseventies—with mostly clear skies. Brian, 57, and Marylyn walked past the NPS signboard there, which exhibited a sign reading "Danger, You Are Entering Bear Country" and instructions as to what to do if one encountered a bear. On the same large board was a sign that read: "Warning, July 3, 2011, Bear Frequenting Area—there is no guarantee of your safety while hiking or camping in bear country." Brian and Marylyn were not carrying bear spray.

Noticing that the Howard Eaton Trail was closed to the south (because of an active wolf den), they chose the Clear Lake Trail and walked east to the lake. They then returned to the Clear Lake/Wapiti Lake trail junction and proceeded south and east on the Wapiti Lake Trail. About 10:00 a.m. and at the Wapiti/Sour Creek trail junction, they encountered a photographer who pointed out to them a grizzly sow and her two cubs of the year, foraging in a meadow some distance to the south. He loaned them his binoculars to view the bears, but to Marylyn they seemed far away, like "boulders" in the field. They watched the bears for some minutes and even took pictures of them at 10:15 a.m., and then Brian and Marylyn hiked on. They reached a body of water that she did not know the name of and then turned around at 10:40 a.m. (shown on Marylyn's time-stamped photo) and began hiking (back) west to the trailhead. In typical Yellowstone fashion, they encountered no other hikers.

At 1.4 miles from the Wapiti Trailhead only a few minutes later and in an open spot, they saw three bears one hundred yards away. It was an area of small meadows and dry thermal areas, crisscrossed and bordered by fringes of trees. Marylyn thought Brian saw the sow first, but she could not remember later whether he saw the cubs. They instantly turned around and began walking east toward the forest, looking back often to see where the bears were. Suddenly Marylyn saw the sow's head "pop up" too near them, and she warned Brian. The sow began charging them, and Brian yelled, "Run!" Marylyn told rangers later that they shouted and yelled at this point. As they were running on the trail down a treed corridor between two small meadows, she suddenly heard Brian cry out. She turned in time to see the sow "hit him" while he was standing and knock him to the ground. The cubs were running behind their mother "growling," but she saw no more. Somehow Marylyn traveled to some downed trees with protruding branches that offered a bit of safety. She did not remember later how she ended up on the ground. Trying to get to her knees, she saw the bear at Brian's body looking at her. She dropped to the ground again and covered her head or neck with her arms or hands. Very quickly the bear was upon her, and she felt the horror of it tugging on her backpack. It lifted her off the ground by her daypack and then dropped her. Just as quickly, it was gone. The attack had occurred at between 10:45 and 10:51 a.m., had lasted no more than a minute, and the two people had run 173 yards from where they first saw the bears. (Investigators later estimated that the bear probably ran the 273 total yards in only 28 to 58 seconds.)

Marylyn stumbled to her husband, saw that he was bleeding, and attempted to use a jacket as a tourniquet for his leg. She heard a long breath escape from Brian and told investigators later that she knew at that moment that Brian was dead. She somehow found the presence to cover him with two dark-colored jackets. Now it occurred to her that the bear might still be nearby. She began yelling for help.

Other hikers in the area heard the sounds of the attack. To the west of Brian and Marylyn, four British hikers heard the bear "roar" and heard male and female voices yelling and screaming. To their east, the photographer they encountered earlier—now talking with another man and his two sons—heard a "roar" followed by a man shouting briefly and then a woman's scream. The photographer stated later that the roar, yell, and scream lasted only five to ten seconds.

Fearing for his two sons but also using them to alert rangers, the father gave them bear spray and sent them walking west toward the trailhead. He was a trauma surgeon, so he decided to stay with the photographer. Obtaining a cell signal while hiking, the two boys called 911, and the Communications Center received the call at 10:51 a.m. The boys also met the large hiking group and told them that bears were in the area. That group continued east to the father and the photographer, who confirmed to them an incident of some kind. Now it was a larger group who walked toward where the sounds had originated. Various members of the group shouted, asking if anyone needed help. Marylyn shouted back, "Help!" Obtaining a cell signal, the father called 911 at 11:15 a.m. Marylyn had also tried to reach 911 a few minutes earlier, at 11:09 a.m. and numerous times afterward, but she was unsuccessful at getting a signal. Officials at Mammoth told the father that help would soon arrive and not to enter the scene ahead of them but to wait for the rangers who were nearby, already hiking. Meanwhile Marylyn had begun hiking west, where she met the responding rangers and visitors.

Only a few minutes after Marylyn and Brian saw the bears, Ranger David Page was at the Wapiti Trailhead responding to visitor reports of hikers possibly in the closed area. He received the Communication Center's call about people screaming at 10:55 a.m. He and Ranger Brian Speeg quickly began hiking toward the fatality scene, and they were soon followed by rangers Patti Murphree and Nick Derene. Ranger Page saw Marylyn Matayoshi alone and at a distance on the trail and called out to her, asking whether she was hurt. She replied no. He asked if there were bears still in the area, and she replied no. When Page asked if anyone else was hurt, she stated that her husband was dead.

In the whirl of activity after that, Ranger Page recovered a pair of broken, black Nike sunglasses that had six to eight bear hairs stuck in the bridge of the nosepiece. As normal procedure, these hairs were retained for DNA analysis, because they could identify the individual bear. Page and his fellow rangers could not know then that these hairs would soon figure into the investigation of another human death from a bear—one that would occur only seven weeks later.

The Matayoshi bear had no previous history of encounters with humans, and it did not continue to maul Brian Matayoshi after he became quiet. Marylyn stated later that she wished they had not looked over their shoulders multiple times because that might have slowed them down and the movement might have attracted the bear. That of course was speculation. A subsequent investigative team report determined that the sow grizzly acted in a purely defensive manner in order to protect her cubs and that the bear's chase response was "likely exacerbated by their running and yelling as they fled the bear." What may have begun as merely an attempt by the bear to assess the Matayoshis' activities "became a sustained pursuit of them as they fled running and yelling on the trail," said the report.

Rangers initially called the death accidental, from "penetrating and blunt force trauma due to grizzly bear mauling." Later investigators discovered that Brian Matayoshi sustained a bite puncture to his femoral artery, a long avulsion on his forehead extending into his scalp, perhaps a fatal blunt-force injury to the chest or abdomen, and multiple biting and clawing injuries. No autopsy was performed, but a doctor told one investigator that "a person could bleed out internally from the femoral artery, the spleen or liver, or both, in 1–2 minutes." He also stated "that the blunt force of the bear hitting Matayoshi and knocking him to the ground [could have been] enough force for a fatal crushing injury to the chest or abdomen."[56]

The park's *second* human fatality in a single summer from a bear attack occurred on August 25, 2011, and it left Yellowstone officials, visitors, and supporters aghast and dispirited. The usual media scare mongering occurred, with large headlines that made environmentalists fear for both park and bears. One of those read: "Another hiker found dead in Yellowstone bear mauling, one month after park officials refused to hunt a grizzly [that] killed a California man." Media people tend to love the sensationalism of such a story and often do not understand the reasons behind such NPS or other governmental decisions.[57]

Sadly, John Lawrence Wallace, 59, of Chassell, Michigan, had been warned about the dangers presented by grizzly bears in Yellowstone but told an official who was giving him warnings at a campground that he was a grizzly "expert" who did not need the safety lecture. Wallace was a trained librarian who had spent eighteen years working at Portage Lake District Library in Houghton, Michigan, and he was also the building's superintendent there. Friends called him a "kind and gentle individual" who loved books and the outdoors. A family member stated that he told them in a voice mail left earlier that "being in Yellowstone was like being in heaven."[58]

John Wallace arrived alone in Yellowstone on August 24, 2011, and camped in the Canyon Village Campground, where he received standard bear warnings from a campground official and made the statement noted earlier. The next morning he parked his green jeep at the trailhead in Hayden Valley near Alum Creek to begin hiking on the Mary Mountain Trail. (Another visitor observed a methodical person fitting his description putting on an orange daypack and beginning a hike there at about 7:30 a.m.) A sign at the trailhead warned hikers that they were entering bear country, encouraged use of bear spray, and discouraged hiking alone. Wallace carried no bear spray and was hiking alone. He proceeded southwesterly through open meadows of grass and sagebrush with only patches of timber for about six miles. Because Hayden Valley is an area that is historically known for high numbers of grizzly bears, only day hiking is permitted there, with no overnight camping allowed.

Wallace passed an active bison carcass at Violet Creek, only 1.5 miles from the later incident site. If he saw it, it should have made him very nervous. Three days earlier, a hiker there had seen nine different grizzly bears feeding on it (but did not report it until after the Wallace incident). Rangers found a second carcass only 361 yards from the incident site along with sixteen bear daybeds around it.

John Wallace stopped to eat an energy bar, take a drink, or get something out of the pack that was later found not on his back. Probably sitting on a log in his last moments, he must have instinctively raised one or both hands, because there were bite marks on his right hand, large areas of bruising on his left arm, and scratches, lacerations, and punctures on his right forearm—all consistent with self-defense when facing a bear. But these may have occurred after the bear had already hit him, because ominously, "wounds to his neck and back suggest[ed] that the bear came from behind." It probably took very little time for Wallace to die from loss of blood. The bear then fed upon him and cached his body in a partial burial.

The following morning, another park visitor (a retired fisheries professor) and his daughter arrived at the same trailhead at 7:30 a.m. and began hiking up the same trail. At a point on the trail at nearly six miles and after three hours of hiking, the daughter saw birds circling in the air above and then observed a daypack and a water bottle containing a pinkish liquid. She walked closer to these objects and suddenly saw parts of a human body. She saw both legs below the knees with boots on the trail, and a portion of one arm nearby. The body was oriented at ninety degrees to the trail, and most of it was covered with dirt and debris. Looking at the head, she noted that "the hair stood up on the back of his neck and that it was obvious that the person was deceased." Fearing that there was a bear nearby, she and her father instantly turned around and hiked back to the trailhead. Ten minutes down the trail, they met two men in their midtwenties and told them there was a body ahead. The two hikers continued on after this warning but apparently turned around later. At the trailhead, the father and his daughter noted a green jeep parked there and then went to the canyon backcountry office at 1:30 p.m. to report the body.

A helicopter dropped five rangers two miles west of the incident site, and they began hiking east. About a mile west of the incident site, they found adult grizzly tracks and those of one yearling. At 6:00 p.m. they encountered Wallace's body lying on his left hip and back, partly buried in the manner consistent with the food-caching behavior of a bear. The body had been partially consumed. Twelve and a half meters to the southwest, the rangers found a large blood spot and a piece of boxer shorts next to the log Wallace had probably been sitting on, sans pack, when he was surprised by the bear. To the west was a bloody trail in grass with bloody footprints on logs apparently made by at least one departing bear and probably also a cub. Spookiest of all was the fact that Wallace's orange pack, rain jacket, long-sleeved shirt, and lunch container were on top of his body, apparently placed there by the bear in part of its caching activity. Two water bottles—one empty and one three-quarters full—were found nearby. The lunch had not been consumed, indicating that the attack occurred during the morning of August 25. A hard rain with hail that afternoon had obliterated many of the bear tracks on and around the trail and probably some of the DNA evidence.

The rangers collected bear hair for DNA analysis from the body, from broken branches on logs nearby, and from soil in the cache pile. They collected saliva from bite wounds on the body and collected scat from five scat piles, later identified as grizzly scat. Over the next six weeks, the NPS set bear traps in ten locations, making twenty-five captures of thirteen individual bears for examination and DNA analysis. Most telling was the fact that DNA from two scat piles a few yards from Wallace's body matched that of the female bear and one of her cubs collected on July 6 at the death site of Brian Matayoshi—only

8.1 miles to the northeast. Although Kerry Gunther has noted that he and his staff were trying right from the start to determine what bear was involved, one park official worried that the public would believe the NPS was allowing a "rogue bear" that was involved in two human killings to remain alive.

On September 28, rangers captured a bear that they called the "Wapiti sow" and captured its cubs the following day. Its DNA not only matched that from the scat pile found near John Wallace but also matched hair stuck in Brian Matayoshi's sunglasses. Although the final report concluded that the Wapiti sow and one or both of her offspring probably fed on Wallace, the bear that actually killed him may not have been that sow, because at least four different grizzly bears were in the area of the body and at least nine bears had been in the general area. Nor was there any clear evidence as to whether the bear attack was defensive or predatory in nature.

On October 2, 2011, rangers killed the 250-pound "Wapiti sow" based upon three factors: (1) DNA confirmed that she and at least one of her cubs were present at Wallace's body, (2) she may have been the bear that attacked and killed Wallace, and (3) members of this family group were very likely involved in the consumption of his body.[59]

There was no clear evidence as to what caused the bear to attack John Wallace, but this author's opinion is that he made serious mistakes, and those combined in an unfortunate manner with other intense factors. I have spent forty summers hiking in Yellowstone, and it is my opinion that hiking alone in Hayden Valley and hiking without bear spray are two of the most foolish moves anyone could make. (It is for that reason that trailheads in Yellowstone carry warning signs, and John Wallace failed to heed them.) Three other factors—a high number of bears, the presence of the cubs of the year, and the presence of active bison carcasses—together made the situation a very dangerous one. Add the possibility that John Wallace surprised an individual bear (although we do not know this for sure) and he was up against what I call the "big three" dangers (bear feeding on carcass, bear with cubs, and surprise encounter). Investigation and autopsy indicated that John Wallace died Thursday, August 25 sometime before noon of "exsanguination [loss of blood] due to multi-system trauma due to an attack by a bear."[60]

This enumeration of seven human deaths involving bears in Yellowstone Park understates the actual number of deaths in the more expansive Greater Yellowstone Ecosystem. Six other human deaths involving bears are known for the areas *around* Yellowstone Park. These incidents occurred in 1894 (the Mallison fatality, already chronicled), 1912, 1922, and 1983, and 2010 (two incidents).

The Mallison fatality is heretofore unknown, and the 1912 fatality is little known. The death of Graham, an old bear trapper near Jardine on Crevice

Mountain, occurred May 4, 1912. Stage drivers Henry "Society Red" Mallon and Herb French remembered it in 1961 while talking with park photographer Jack Haynes and historian Aubrey Haines.[61] Gardiner resident Edith Ritchie[62] remembered that his name was John Graham, and Aubrey Haines recalled that park ranger Lee Coleman picked up Graham's skis sometime after the incident and donated them to the park museum collection.[63]

According to Mallon and Jack Haynes, the incident occurred on or near Crevice Mountain. Graham, 63, had his usual bear trap baited and ready, this time inside a fenced pen. He was planning to use the bear for target practice after it was in the trap but instead, while Graham was standing there, rifle or shotgun in hand or nearly so, the bear got out of the trap and killed him. From the note in the park museum file (see note 63), it would appear to have been poetic justice.[64]

The John Graham story has been chronicled slightly differently by Gay Randall, a longtime Gardiner resident. According to Randall, Graham saw the tracks of a large bear near his mining claim on Crevice Mountain, so he returned to his cabin to get his rifle. He soon found that the bear had been feeding on the carcass of a dead horse, so he decided to trap the bear on its return to the carcass. He lugged his sixty-pound bear trap over to the site and then stopped off to mention his activities to a neighbor named Adolph Hageman.

Randall's account, as told to him by Hageman, differs from those of the newspapers and the doctor who saw Graham. According to Randall, the next morning Hageman heard two loud shots from Graham's .45-90-gauge rifle, so he started for Graham's trap site. When he arrived a half hour later, there was no answer to his calls. Hageman followed the drag marks of the trap down the hill a couple of hundred yards to find John Graham gasping his last. The bear was gone.

Hageman surveyed the scene. Graham's gun was leaning against a far tree while a nearby tree was scarred by claw and teeth marks. The trap lay wedged between two logs. Between its jaws were three bloody toes with four-inch-long claws of the grizzly that had done Graham in. Hageman believed that Graham had followed the bear down the hill where it dragged the trap and had fired two shots at it when he saw it tangled in deadfall. Believing it dead, Graham apparently set his rifle down and walked to the bear to skin it. Only stunned, the bear must have come to, jerked free of the trap leaving three toes, and torn Graham up.

The doctor's story was different. Dr. W. B. Shore of Gardiner, Montana, went to the scene soon after the event and found that the bear had first given Graham a blow that sent him reeling, then had torn his throat and face open, which loosened the teeth on one side of his head. The bear also lacerated Graham's windpipe, exposing it. He says Hageman heard the initial shot and ran to help skin the bear but met Graham coming toward the cabin. Seeing that Graham was badly wounded, Hageman ran to town to get the doctor. Graham died in the cabin.

Gay Randall remembered riding with his father and other men to the trap site the next day, after Graham's body had been packed down by Hageman and others. They spent the day searching for the grizzly to no avail. Randall stated that from that day on the bear was known as "Old Two Toes."[65]

The John Graham death story was carried twice in the local newspaper,[66] which gave us still a third version of the affair. The newspaper claimed that Graham was merely walking through the forest when he suddenly encountered the bear and it attacked, Adolph Hageman running to Graham's assistance upon hearing his cries. The newspaper claimed Hageman shot the bear, which "broke Graham's jaw and chewed terrible gashes in his head and arms." Except for Hageman shooting the bear, the newspaper account jibes reasonably with the other two. Historian Jeremy Johnston has pointed out that it is remarkable that this killing of John Graham by a bear was not splashed all over the nation's newspapers and remained essentially unknown in history until the first edition of this book was published in 1995.

The death of Joseph B. "Frenchy" Duret is a story that has fewer variations, but it made the newspapers in large style. Duret was a Frenchman, alleged to be a deserter from the French army. He had settled on Slough Creek, just north of the park boundary, in the 1890s, later marrying Jennie McWilliams, a mail-order bride. According to Horace Albright, Duret trapped animals and poached in the park for years but was never caught. He is known to have supplied meat early for the Fort Yellowstone army garrison, and in 1899, he had been arrested in the park for running a pack string without permission. Interestingly, in 1902, Frenchy was charged with stealing elk meat from John Graham, who would later be killed by a grizzly on Crevice Mountain. Because of earlier testimony by Frenchy, Graham had served some jail time for illegally selling elk meat, so no doubt Graham saw his chance in the 1902 charge to get revenge against Frenchy.[67]

Duret routinely had traps out for bears. On Monday, June 12, 1922, he found a large grizzly caught in one of his traps. He returned to his ranch, informed his wife, picked up his rifle, and left about 10:00 a.m. Said one newspaper account, "Mrs. Duret never saw him again."

On the morning of the fourteenth, park superintendent Horace Albright, chief ranger Sam Woodring, and chief buffalo keeper Bob Lacombe were on horseback up Slough Creek when they met assistant buffalo keeper Peck Hutchings, who told them of Frenchy's death. Hutchings and ranger William Denhoff had found Duret's body at 8:00 p.m. on June 13. It was badly torn and mangled, and the two noted that Frenchy had crawled a mile and a half after

Photo of Joseph "Frenchy" Duret, wife, and friends at his cabin about 1920, north of bound-ary of Yellowstone National Park, before he was killed by a grizzly bear. Frenchy stands by his horse in the center of photo (photo 32162, YNP Collections).

escaping from the bear. At the trap site were signs of a severe struggle, and one cartridge had been fired from Frenchy's rifle. The ground near the scene was blood soaked, and the rifle was found with the stock chewed half off and the barrel bearing deep scratches, as if Duret had used it as a club. Pieces of griz-zly fur, strands of Duret's hair, and torn bits of flesh lay all around. Moreover, Frenchy's dogs bore marks of having attacked the bear as it finished its work. "It is assumed," wrote Albright, "that the enraged bear made a lunge, either before or after the shot, broke the chain of the trap, sprang on Duret, and mangled him badly." The bear escaped, wounded or not, carrying the heavy trap along with it and was never found. The trap was found a year later along Slough Creek. At least since 1922, the meadows just north of Silvertip Ranch have been known as Frenchy's Meadows.[68]

As often happens with bear attacks, Frenchy Duret's death in early June made newspapers in large and garish fashion, some of them even running the gruesome story months later. The *Bourbon News* of Paris, Kentucky, carried it in August, and the New Orleans *Herald* carried it in mid-September. "Huge Bear Devours Trapper in Montana" read the page 1 headline in the *Ogden* (UT) *Standard Examiner*. The *Anaconda Standard*'s front-page story was head-lined "Trapper Loses Terrific Death Battle with Huge Grizzly Bear." Its first s: "With one arm and a leg partially chewed off and the head and ¦ and lacerated, the body of Joseph Duret, aged 60, was found early today on Slough Creek." In New Orleans, the *Herald's* story was quite detailed. It stated that Duret "was well aware of the danger of encountering a vicious bear, and yet he appears to have flirted with death in trying to kill alone a huge grizzly, and to have lost." The story stated that Duret caught the bear in his trap, hastily returned home to tell his wife of his catch, and then returned to the trap. The bear then jerked the chain loose from the trap and jumped upon Duret. "It was apparent," continued the *Herald*, "that Duret had tried to defend himself by using his gun as a club but his fight was useless." Local observers believed that Duret lost consciousness and the bear then dragged him to another location. He apparently awoke and was staggering-and crawling toward his cabin in a fairly straight line when death overtook him. "One arm and a leg were torn off and the body was mangled," said the newspaper, which added that Jennie Duret searched the hills for him all day long on Tuesday after Duret did not come home Monday night.[69]

Fascinatingly, the *Herald* stated (and at least two other newspapers also ran it) that Ranger Denhoff "found Duret's mangled body nearly two miles from where he had engaged in a life and death struggle with the beast [in a] wild, desolate place not ten feet from where Duret in 1910 was introduced to and warmly greeted by President Roosevelt." The problem with that statement was that Roosevelt never visited Yellowstone in 1910. Two other historians with whom I consulted—both of them experts on Theodore Roosevelt—believe that this was a local piece of malarkey making the rounds in 1922.[70]

Frenchy Duret was buried at nearby "Frenchy's Meadows." "A park ranger read a few words from the Bible," stated a newspaper, "and Duret's wife placed a bouquet of wild flowers over the rude mound hastily constructed to shield the remains of the bear's victim."[71]

A 1983 death that occurred four miles west of the park boundary at Rainbow Point on Hebgen Lake involved an habituated grizzly and two men in a campsite who had apparently taken all recommended measures for careful camping in bear country. On June 24, 1983, Ted Moore and Roger May, both from Sturgeon Bay, Wisconsin, cooked a meal of steak and corn on a portable grill, cleaned their dishes, and put things away. They drove to West Yellowstone, where they had a few beers and returned to their tent at about 11:00 p.m. The two were camped in loop A, number 17, at Rainbow Point on Hebgen Lake, a Gallatin National Forest campground, some nine miles northwest of the town of West Yellowstone, Montana.

At 2:30 a.m., the men were awakened by the shaking of their tent, as if, according to Moore, someone were playing a Boy Scout prank on them. The aluminum tent poles rattled loudly and suddenly the tent collapsed. The

two murmured something to each other, and then Roger May began screaming and was pulled through a hole in the tent. The bear's first bite apparently
caught him in the upper part of his body. As Moore exited through the same
hole, he saw a large bear only ten feet away standing over his companion. He
heard his companion's terrified screams.

On seeing Moore, the bear reacted by grabbing May by an ankle and
dragging him thirty feet at a run. Moore was astounded at the speed of the
movement. Picking up a tent pole, Moore charged at the bear and threw the
pole at it. The bear seemed to him to back away from May. Moore yelled, "Are
you all right?" From the darkness, he heard his friend say, "I'm okay, but I'm
not doing so good."

Moore then ran to the tent, looking for his glasses, car keys, and a flashlight. The car was locked, and because Moore could not see well, he had
trouble finding anything. He is not sure how much time elapsed as he fumbled
in the darkness, searching especially for the flashlight, but it was a few minutes
according to him. Then Moore suddenly heard renewed screams from May, and
after a short time silence.

At this point, several other campground occupants began to appear, flashlights and car lights coming on, but the bear remained at the edge of the forest
feeding on May's body. The sheriff, summoned by campers, arrived ten minutes
later, and the grizzly picked that moment to drag the body across the sheriff's
tire tracks on the main road. The sheriff and others began a search. At 3:30 a.m.,
May's body was found some fifty feet from the road. About seventy pounds of
it had been eaten by the bear.

The investigation team was unable to find any overt explanation for the
attack on Roger May. The U.S. Forest Service had provided signs discourag-
ing tent camping in the area, and all human foods had been secured. However,
there were some odor-causing substances in the tent. Campho-Phenique had
been applied to the victim's foot, and this odor was quite strong. May's sleeping bag was not his own and had not been cleaned in a long time. And neither
man had showered in forty-eight hours. Just as important, private residences in
the area were not securing garbage and dog foods from bears. There was strong
evidence that the bear involved obtained human-related foods from private
residences within twenty-four hours of the incident. Roger May could have
been a victim of this carelessness by local residents. Bear 15, a large male grizzly,
was subsequently trapped in the area. Analysis of fecal materials showed hairs
from Roger May's head, and the bear was thereafter destroyed.[72]

Even a scientist can become a bear victim if he does not use due care or
breaks the established rules. Botanist Erwin Frank Evert, 70, of Park Ridge,
Illinois, had spent forty summers at his cabin on Kitty Creek in Shoshone National Forest, only seven miles east of Yellowstone National Park, and he often

hiked alone in the area to research animals as well as plants. He had discovered five different previously undescribed plants in the region and one of them, the Evert Desert Parsley (*Cymopterus evertii*), had been named for him. His book entitled *Vascular Plants of the Greater Yellowstone Ecosystem* had just been published. On June 17, 2010, he hiked into a site where a grizzly had been captured and released earlier that very day. There he encountered bear 646, and it killed him with puncturing bites to the face and back of the head. He also suffered deep puncture wounds covering his entire body, but otherwise was not fed upon by the bear.

When Evert did not return to his cabin later that afternoon, his wife Yolanda went looking for him and ran into a member of the Interagency Grizzly Bear Study Team, whom she told. The researcher returned to their capture site on Kitty Creek and found Evert's body at that site. Like John Wallace would do two years later in Hayden Valley, Erwin Evert was hiking alone and not carrying bear spray. Bear 646 was located two days later by its radio-collar signal and shot to death from a helicopter two miles from the site where Evert was killed. Laboratory analysis showed it was the bear that killed him.

"We try to do everything we can to minimize the risks [of hiking]," said Chris Servheen, grizzly bear coordinator for the U.S. Fish and Wildlife Service. "But we can't protect ourselves against people that ignore every warning we give, and we can't protect people against themselves." Servheen authorized killing of bear 646 because "experts could not definitively determine whether the animal's actions were natural and defensive or aberrant and unusually aggressive." Evert's friend and professional colleague Chuck Neal, a professional ecologist and author of *Grizzlies in the Mist*, stated that he spoke with Evert a few days before his death and that Evert was "absolutely aware" of the risks of hiking in the area. Neal thought that the attack might have been occasioned by a "close-range, surprise encounter," but of course no one knew for sure. "He was an extraordinary man who made a very ordinary mistake."[73]

Yolanda Evert filed a wrongful-death lawsuit in Wyoming U.S. District Court alleging that the two government trappers' decision to remove warning signs on July 17 caused her husband's death. But a judge ruled in 2012 that Wyoming's Recreational Use statute immunized the land owner (here the government) from any duty to warn. Under that statute, any property owner, including the government, who allows their land to be used for recreational purposes free of charge generally has no duty to keep an area safe or warn of a dangerous condition. Additionally, according to the *Powell Tribune*, the judge stated that it was not obvious to the researchers that Mr. Evert would follow their footsteps and enter the trap site.[74]

Only five weeks later in a campground just outside of Yellowstone, a grizzly bear killed one person and injured two others. This incident confounded officials because it seemed not to relate to bears attacking lone hikers, bears in a surprise encounter, or bears protecting cubs. Nor were carcasses or other natural foods present. There were and are abundant natural foods around this campground and, although bears were seen or heard by at least two parties during three previous days, there were no reports of aggression by these bears or conflicts associated with them. The campground contained many warning signs that grizzlies frequented the area. Investigators at first thought the bear's poor condition was a factor in the attack but later stated that the cause of the attacks "cannot be clearly explained or understood."

The three attacks were separate and occurred early in the morning. At about 2:00 a.m. on July 28, 2010, Ronald Singer, 21, of Alamosa, Colorado, was sleeping in his tent just outside Yellowstone National Park's northeast entrance at the U.S. Forest Service's Soda Butte Campground east of Cooke City, Montana. Sleeping in the same tent in campsite 16 were his girlfriend (Maria Flemming) and their dog, a young puppy. The campground is a small one, with only twenty-seven sites, and on this night all but three of them were occupied. Singer was awakened by his tent moving "several feet." An adult female grizzly bear whose three yearling cubs were probably nearby bit Singer's lower left leg through his tent. He punched the bear through the tent several times and it left. His girlfriend screamed, awoke, and ran to a nearby tent where her father and sister were sleeping and woke them. The three were applying first aid to Singer's leg when they heard a woman scream from a nearby campsite. Now thoroughly frightened, the four drove to Cooke City, where they called emergency responders.

At about 2:15 a.m., the same bear accosted Deborah Freele, 48, of London, Ontario, who was sleeping alone in a tent in campsite 11. She awoke and felt a bite to her upper left arm. "I screamed, he bit harder, I screamed harder, he continued to bite," she said later. "I went totally limp, [and] as soon as I went limp, I could feel his jaws get loose and he let me go . . . It was very quiet; it never made any noise." Next door, her neighbors heard her yelling, "Stop, no!" and heard a bear "huffing or woofing" nearby. While dressing hurriedly, they heard Deborah shout, "Help! I've been attacked by a bear!" They drove to Deborah's site but were afraid to leave their car, so instead yelled to her that they were going to get help and drove around the campground honking the vehicle's horn. Left alone for five to fifteen minutes, Deborah wrapped her arm in a shirt to stop its bleeding. The first party returned to find others parked at Deborah's site, so all exited their cars and administered aid to her. Alerted by emergency calls, the Park County Sheriff's Department and the National Park Service responded to the campground and began to move everyone out of the area. A piece of the bear's upper right canine tooth was found in Deborah's tent.

Perhaps emboldened by its first two experiences, the bear then attacked Kevin R. Kammer, 48, of Grand Rapids, Michigan, who was alone in his tent at campsite 26, some six hundred yards west of Deborah Freele. Kammer was not so lucky, and no one heard or saw the attack. He was sleeping in a small, one-man tent with insect screen and full weather fly stretched over it. The bear ripped open the screen and pulled Kammer out by his head and shoulders. She dragged him ten yards toward the creek and—with her offspring—consumed a significant part of his torso. He died of blood loss. Neighbors who were sleeping sixty yards from Kammer's camp heard nothing—the sounds perhaps being covered by noisy Soda Butte Creek at the south—and were only awakened when officials drove through the campground to clear it of campers. That was at 4:21 a.m., and that was when Kammer's body was discovered by Park County Sheriff's Department deputy Justin Chaffins and NPS ranger Brian Chan.

Because it involved three attacks, this event received great attention in southwest Montana and northern Wyoming and set residents and visitors on edge. Sales of bear spray immediately increased, and people talked widely about the incidents. A public meeting was convened in Cooke City. Officials involved included Montana Fish, Wildlife, and Parks (the lead agency); the Park County (Montana) Sheriff's Office; the U.S. Forest Service; the National Park Service; the U.S. Fish and Wildlife Service; and later the Wyoming Game and Fish Department. Most observers agreed that the bear's behavior was odd and not typical. Kerry Gunther, who has headed or worked for Yellowstone's bear program for twenty-seven years, stated that such predatory events—if this were one of those—were "the exception rather than the norm." Gunther called such events "extremely rare."[75]

Subsequent DNA analysis confirmed that the bear that killed Kevin Kammer was the same bear that attacked Deborah Freele. Officials believed without absolute proof that it was also the bear that attacked Ronald Singer. The sow and its three yearlings had been seen in the park at Barronette Peak on July 6 and it had bluff-charged jogger Elaine Sabo at 9:00 a.m. on July 21 between the northeast entrance and Silver Gate, but ran off when Sabo yelled at it. Scientific analyses showed that the bear had consumed almost exclusively a plant-based diet over the previous two years. There was no evidence of food-storage problems or other food attractants in the area or that bears in the region had obtained human foods. The sow was captured on July 29 and her three cubs shortly thereafter. She had never been captured before, was ten to fifteen years old, and was underweight, only 216 pounds—low but not outside normal range. The cubs were also in poorer than usual physical condition. Steven Herrero's bear studies have shown that poor body condition may be a contributing factor to a predatory attack but is not by itself enough to explain such behavior.

The bear lived without incident in the area of Soda Butte Campground her entire life, so her behavior remains strange and unexplained. But one cannot help wondering whether she was simply hungry and that this was therefore one of those extremely rare, predatory attacks. This bear was euthanized by lethal injection on July 30 and her cubs given to Zoo Montana at Billings.[76]

Human injuries from bears have continued to occasionally happen in Yellowstone. Of the three bear maulings that occurred in 1994, two of them happened to hikers who were hiking alone and the third victim had only one other person with him. In 2007, Yellowstone's safety officer was alone when he surprised a sow grizzly with cubs in the Little Trail Creek area. Ken Meyer was hunting black bears just outside the park in Gallatin National Forest near Beattie Gulch on September 9, 2007. "The sow came out of nowhere," stated the park's news release, "launched at him and knocked him to the ground." They wrestled momentarily and then the cubs made a noise, so the bear left him to check on her cubs. He crawled to his rifle and she came back, stopped five feet in front of him, and charged him again. Meyer fired three shots at the bear, and she rolled into the creek and was later found dead. He managed to walk back to his vehicle and drive to his residence at Mammoth, where his wife called for medical help. In only seconds, the bear had inflicted "deep injuries," including bites to his back and other injuries to his left leg, stomach, and both forearms. He learned later that the sow was also protecting an elk carcass. In Meyer's case, the bear's charge was so quick and unexpected that his rifle did not keep him from being injured even though the bear was later found dead. Bear spray might have been preferable.[77]

Two bow hunters in the Beattie Gulch area were mauled in separate incidents by a grizzly with three cubs very soon after Ken Meyer's injury—on September 14 and October 7, 2007. Dustin Flack tried to climb a tree but could not get up it before the sow snapped the tree in half and pulled him to the ground. He played dead and survived. Roman Morris saw the sow with cubs and hid behind big sagebrush, but the bear saw him and attacked. He fought the bear at first but then played dead and survived. These two hunters probably encountered the same bear.[78] Hiking alone in the Yellowstone region, even when armed, continues to be an unwise thing to do.

My friend Randy Ingersoll, then 37, was mauled by a grizzly bear on June 20, 1994.[79] Randy has been working in Yellowstone for more than thirty years today, and I have known him for a good percentage of that time. I have hiked and skied with Randy on a couple of occasions, and on one of those trips we even discussed the fact that he often hiked alone. Randy is an expert on Yellowstone's backcountry and a very experienced hiker and backpacker, but even the experienced should not hike alone in Yellowstone. At about 3:00 p.m. on June 20, Randy was hiking off-trail about four miles in on the Thunderer

Cutoff trail near the park's northeast entrance. He was wearing stereo head-phones, listening to music, as well as hiking alone. As he entered a grove of trees, he noticed a sow grizzly with two yearlings at a distance of only thirty feet.

Randy was standing right next to a large whitebark pine when he saw the bears. They were standing up, standing still, and looking at him. He immedi-ately decided to shinny up the whitebark pine. As soon as he started to climb, the bears dropped down, and all three made a definite move to leave. The sow apparently changed her mind about leaving, turned around, and charged. Randy had only climbed about two or three feet up the tree when the sow reached him, pulled him off the tree, threw him to the ground, and began to maul him. She bit and scratched his left shoulder and raked his forehead and upper arm. Instinctively, Randy raised his arms to protect himself, but then remembered to "play dead." "Playing dead," or remaining perfectly still, is one action recommended in an attack initiated by surprising a grizzly sow with cubs, because playing dead may signal to the sow that the person being attacked is no longer a threat to her cubs. The moment he "played dead," the bear broke off the attack, huffed, and ran back to her yearlings and out of sight into the forest. Randy believes the attack lasted about ten seconds.

Randy says he felt no pain during the attack itself. He lay there bleed-ing for "only about a minute," hoping to give the bears enough time to leave the area, and then got to his feet. Concerned about losing blood, and feeling increasing pain in his left shoulder, his foremost thought was to "be steady and get to the road." He paused several times to drink from streams that crossed the trail, and most important he kept his focus.

Park visitors took Randy to Lamar Ranger Station, and rangers then conveyed him by ambulance to the hospital at Yellowstone Lake where X-rays revealed a fractured left shoulder. Transferred to Deaconess Hospital in Boze-man, Montana, he spent three and a half days there, undergoing two operations to repair the damage. In retrospect, Randy believes that his frantic effort to climb the tree was a mistake that caused the bear to perceive him as a threat. He thinks a better alternative would have been to back away slowly and calmly and then find an alternate route out of the area. He regrets not having bear spray but always carries it with him when he hikes today.

More recent advice from the National Park Service discourages hikers from climbing trees to avoid bears, partly because many people cannot get up trees quickly enough. While I have twice used that old advice to my own advantage, I did that back in my twenties when I was young, nimble, and a fast tree climber. Three people in this book (Randy Ingersoll, Dustin Flack, and George Dow) failed to get up the tree before a bear pulled them down, and the NPS also warns that climbing one may provoke an unaggressive bear to attack you. I particularly like this sentence from the NPS's "Encountering a Bear at Close Range"—"Remember, you have probably not climbed a tree since you were ten years old; it is harder than you remember."

Randy Ingersoll's experience and that of John Wallace both illustrate the precept that even very experienced Yellowstone hikers must obey the rules of bear country. Don't hike alone and don't hike silently; make noise to avoid surprising a bear. Carry bear spray. Be sure that *you* can hear what is going on around you, that is, no headphones. And of course avoid the "big three" dangers—a bear with cubs, a bear eating on a food source, and a bear that has been suddenly startled by your presence.

Of Yellowstone Park's seven bear-involved fatalities, four victims were alone when the incidents occurred. Five out of the six fatalities that occurred just outside the park also fit into this category. Thus nine of thirteen human fatalities involving bears in the Greater Yellowstone Ecosystem occurred when the victims were *alone*. Of the others, three victims had only one other person with them, and only one (Welch) was with more than one other person. I reiterate: never hike alone in Yellowstone country. This points up the wisdom of the National Park Service's regulations requiring parties of three or more in some backcountry areas of the park (I personally prefer four people). One simply has better chances with more people along.

Even when carrying bear spray, small parties in a hiking group can be attacked by bears. On August 15, 2013, two hikers on the Cygnet Lakes Trail (one of them was an NPS interpretive ranger) encountered what seemed to be a solitary bear cub. That raised (or should have raised) an immediate "red flag" for the group, and sure enough, a surprised mother bear was lurking nearby and charged them. The two hikers fired off their bear spray, and the bears ran away but not before the sow had inflicted bites and scratches upon them. Another party of two hiking in the area joined them, and all four people hiked out together. Carrying bear spray is a basic safety procedure for hiking in Yellowstone.[80]

Of the park's seven bear-involved fatalities, five probably involved bears that were habituated to humans or human foods. At least one of the five fatalities that occurred just outside the park also fit into this category. Thus six of thirteen fatalities involving bears in the Greater Yellowstone Ecosystem involved habituated bears. (The habituation status of the Duret bear is unknown.) Truly wild bears appear less likely to attack.[81] Therefore, the NPS's post-1970 attempts to wean bears away from human foods and return them to wild foods make great sense. Again, a more natural bear is generally a less dangerous bear.

It is probable that all thirteen fatalities in the Greater Yellowstone Ecosystem involved grizzly bears, although technically we do not know for certain the types of bears involved in the Mallison, Hansen, and Duret incidents. Black bears are statistically less likely to attack.[82]

The reasons (so far as we can truly know the reasons) for the incidents are complex and overlapping, but hard rules do indeed emerge from these events. Three of them (Hansen, Walker, partially Matayoshi, and perhaps Wallace) involved surprising the bear (causing a "sudden encounter"), at least one incident involved getting too close and thus becoming a perceived threat (Tesinsky and perhaps Wallace), three—maybe four—involved provocation (attempts to trap or shoot bears—Mallison, Duret, Graham, and perhaps Evert), and five were probably related to bears conditioned to human foods (Welch, Hansen, Fredenhagen, May, and Walker). The Fredenhagen incident is difficult to assess for causation, but possibly involved a habituated bear, some odors, and hiking alone. The cause of the Walker incident may also have been partially rooted in a bear protecting a food source, and the Welch and Walker bears may have been partially reacting to old injuries. The Matayoshi incident involved not only a surprised bear but also a bear protecting her cubs. The Wallace incident involved two if not all three of the "big three" dangers plus hiking alone. The Evert incident involved hiking alone and may have involved a sudden encounter and/or a bear that was recovering from a drug-and-capture. The Kammer incident involved being alone plus a bear with cubs and may have been a rare predation event.

We see here the reasons for the NPS's warnings to backpackers about making noise (don't hike silently!), about never approaching bears (or any animals) closely, about never hiking alone, and about never feeding bears. Additionally, when cubs or food sources are present, one must be even more vigilant. The worst possible situation is a person hiking alone who surprises a bear that is feeding (as on a carcass) and also has cubs. If this last situation happens to you, we will not expect to see you back at the trailhead.

How can one keep from being the next human fatality in bear country? By obeying all of these rules.

4

"DON'T EAT WILD PARSNIPS"
DEATHS FROM POISONOUS PLANTS

We were cautioned by our Indians during the march, to prevent our horses feeding by the way, in consequence of a poisonous herb, resembling a parsnip, which abounds there, and causes death shortly after being eaten.

—fur trapper Warren Ferris on Henry's Fork, 1834

We have to admit the existence of some absolutely bad plants, created perhaps solely to point out the merit of those plants that are useful to us, but these absolutely bad plants fortunately are quite rare.

—Pierre Joigneaux, 1865

ORTUNATELY FOR US, that French scientist's assessment remains correct. Of the approximately three hundred thousand species of plants on earth, records indicate that only about seven hundred have caused death or serious illness in man or animals in the Western Hemisphere.

Of plants that grow in Yellowstone only two, other than several mushrooms, are considered virulent enough to cause human death: the water hemlock (*Cicuta douglasii*) and the death camas (*Zigadenus venenosus*). No known deaths or even nonfatal poisonings have occurred in Yellowstone National Park from death camas, but two, perhaps three, fatalities have occurred from water hemlock.

As many as six of the deadly poisonous mushrooms probably grow in Yellowstone, and many other Yellowstone mushrooms are considered poisonous but not deadly. Deadly poisonous ones are the death cap (*Amanita phalloides*), the destroying angel (*Amanita virosa*), the deadly conocybe (*Conocybe filaris*), the deadly cort (*Cortinarius gentilis*), the deadly galerina (*Galerina autumnalis*), and the conifer false morel (*Gyromitra esculenta*). All occur throughout North

91

America in conifer forests, and all can kill. (90 percent of fatal mushroom poisonings in the U.S. have been caused by the two *Amanitas*.) Death from most of these mushrooms occurs because of kidney and/or liver failure. All six types have caused fatalities. Morel gatherers should be careful to recognize *Gyromitra esculenta*, although in fairness it should be noted that people do eat this one. Although it has caused acute illness, has been fatal in a few cases, and produces tumors in laboratory animals, some persons nevertheless eat it after drying it or cooking it to remove the toxins.[1]

I have been unable to find instances of mushroom fatalities in Yellowstone Park. One newspaper article gives us the impression that there were two in 1947,[2] but a check of other relevant sources, including two other newspapers of that time period and the monthly and annual reports of the park superintendent, fails to turn up the information. Probably the "fatalities" were only illnesses.

Water hemlock is arguably the most dangerous of Yellowstone plants because of its similarity to several edible wild parsnips or carrots. (In fact, it is a member of the parsley/carrot family.) It is considered by many authorities to be the most virulently poisonous plant in the earth's north temperate zone. The toxin affects the nervous system, causing severe convulsions and usually death. The plant is easily recognizable because its leaf veins proceed to the notches of the leaves rather than out to the points of the leaves. Children have been fatally poisoned by blowing whistles made from its hollow stems, and one mouthful of the root is enough to kill an adult male. An extract from a similar plant is probably what killed Socrates in ancient times.

Water hemlock gets its reputation as our most toxic plant more from the violence of the symptoms it produces than from its degree of toxicity, which is matched or exceeded by several other plants. There is a vivid description of a case of water hemlock poisoning that occurred in England in 1670. Six children found the plant growing along a stream and ate "greedily" of it, thinking it a parsnip. Jacob Maeder, a blond boy of age 6, returned home "happy and smiling":

A little while afterwards he complained of pain in his abdomen, and, scarcely uttering a word, fell prostrate on the ground . . . Presently he was a terrible sight to see, being seized with convulsions, with the loss of all his senses. His mouth was shut most tightly so that it could not be opened by any means. He grated his teeth; he twisted his eyes about strangely and blood flowed from his ears. In the region of his abdomen a certain swollen body of the size of a man's fist struck the hand of the afflicted father [*sic*] with the greatest force, particularly in the neighborhood of the ensiform cartilage. He frequently hiccupped; at times he seemed to be about to vomit, but he could force nothing from his mouth, which was most tightly closed. He tossed his limbs about marvelously and twisted them; frequently his head was drawn backward and his whole back was curved in the form of a bow, so that a small child could have crept beneath him in the space between his back and the bed without touching him. When the convulsions ceased momentarily, he implored the assistance of his mother. Presently, when they returned with equal violence, he could be aroused by no pinching, by no talking, or by no other means, until his strength failed and he grew pale; and when a hand was placed on his breast he breathed his last. These symptoms continued scarcely beyond a half hour. After his death, his abdomen and face swelled without lividness except that a little was noticeable about the eyes. From the mouth of the corpse even to the hour of his burial green froth flowed very abundantly, and although it was wiped away frequently by his grieving father, nevertheless new froth soon took its place.[3]

The death of park ranger naturalist Charles Phillips (1890–1927) is attributable to water hemlock. On April 11, 1927, Mr. Bauer, the winter keeper at Old Faithful, went to springs above the hotel reservoir to clean out the growing vegetation along the stream that emptied into the reservoir. He collected some roots of plants that were growing there and took the plants to Phillips for identification. Phillips announced that they were good to eat, thinking them roots of the camas plant eaten commonly by the Indians. So the two men and Mrs. Bauer ate them sometime between eight and ten that night. Phillips ate two of the roots and the Bauers ate a part of one each. The only reason all did not eat more was that only three roots had been brought down. Later on that evening, Phillips picked up the top of one of the plants and began to look at it more closely. The Bauers stated that he had kind of an undecided look on his face, and then he commented, "Some of these [herbs] should be cooked but I like them raw."

About two in the morning, the Bauers were awakened by waves of nausea and vomiting, which made them so sick they stayed indoors until the next night. Mrs. Bauer was practically a "raving maniac" until four in the morning, vomiting continually and having convulsions just before daylight. Mr. Bauer had smothering spells and was intensely sick to his stomach but could not vomit.

The next day, Mr. Bauer went to his chicken coop and became very ill with chills. Both of the Bauers rested until 1:00 p.m., at which time they had cold sweats.

It was Phillips's habit to come to the Bauers' home each night at about 8:00 p.m. to talk and listen to the radio. On the night of the twelfth, Bauer wondered why he had heard nothing from Phillips, so he crossed the several hundred yards of deep snow to the ranger station. He found the building dark and cold and Ranger Phillips dead on the kitchen floor. The ranger had apparently died sometime very early that morning.

Phillips was lying on his back with one shoe unlaced and his clothing partly open. He apparently had had his bed slippers in his hand when the attack occurred, because they lay on the kitchen floor. Investigators found that he had apparently come out of the bedroom into the kitchen and fell forward, striking his head above his left eye on the table. Dirt on his hands indicated he had crawled on the floor for a while, probably in agony, and he exhibited the vomiting and frothing at the mouth which are characteristic of hemlock poisoning.

Bauer immediately laid the blame for their illness on the roots they had eaten, because Mr. Phillips had not eaten with the Bauers that day. Why Phillips did not call them during the night was not known, unless it was because the poison acted too quickly.[4]

The hauling of Phillips's body over deep snows by sled to West Yellowstone became a winter adventure story for rangers Harry Trischman and Joe Douglas.[5]

Charles Phillips was widely read, educated, cheerful, and well liked by all in the park. He had a keen sense of humor and was an excellent writer and observer of the park's thermal features, having written pieces for the park's *Ranger Naturalists' Manual*. Had he not died, he probably would have written a book on Yellowstone's hot springs and geysers. A hot spring at Norris Geyser Basin was subsequently named for him as Phillips Caldron.

On Saturday, August 3, 1985, Keith Marsh, 25, of Norfolk, Nebraska, and two companions hiked to Heart Lake and camped in a backcountry campsite. Marsh sampled parts of a plant he picked, as did one of his friends. But the friend spit it out because "he didn't like the taste."

Marsh apparently mistook the plant for edible yampa root. During the evening, he went into violent convulsions. Rangers Brian O'Dea and Pat Ozment rode bicycles into Heart Lake just before midnight and found Ranger Ann Marie Chytra with Marsh at Sheridan Creek. The rangers finally got an IV going, but it was too late for Marsh. He suffered at least seventeen seizures while rangers Chytra and Wes Miles gave him CPR and rescue breathing for many hours. "It was the most violent death I've seen," said Brian O'Dea later, acknowledging that it had taken Marsh eight painful hours to die.[6]

There is a third possible fatality from water hemlock in Yellowstone. On September 5, 1971, 26-year-old Virginia Hall of Golden, Colorado, was brought to the Lake hospital having convulsions. She was dead on arrival. The doctor who performed her autopsy stated that her predeath symptoms and postmortem bodily condition were completely consistent with water–hemlock poisoning. He also stated that four days before the autopsy was performed, she and her companions were known to have eaten "wild carrots" in Yellowstone. Unfortunately, the doctor could not be certain of the cause of death.[7]

The obvious cardinal rule about plants is do not eat them unless you are certain of what you are eating. Even mushroom experts can make mistakes with regard to them. My own rules for eating plants in Yellowstone are three-fold: never eat wild mushrooms, never eat plants that resemble wild carrots or parsnips, and more generally, never eat any plant unless you are positive of what it is by virtue of specific training. Obeying these rules will reduce your chances of contact with the French scientist's "absolutely bad plants."

5

NOXIOUS FUMES AND A
DEATH FROM POISONOUS GAS

Why, it appears no other thing to me than a foul and pestilent congregation of vapours.

—*Hamlet*, act 1, scene 5

S O SPOKE THE BROODING Hamlet about his outlook upon the world, and so have spoken generations of Yellowstone visitors about the smell of park thermal areas. Early visitors wondered if the smelly gases could harm them. At least two naturally occurring gases in Yellowstone Park can be deadly: hydrogen sulfide (H_2S) and carbon dioxide (CO_2). One has odor and the other does not. Both occur in the park's thermal areas and in caves in the Mammoth area. Decomposing organic material in vats, tanks, and manholes can also produce poisonous gas, but so far Yellowstone has not been home to such a fatality.

Hydrogen sulfide occurs, in most places in Yellowstone, in such low quantities as to be harmless. It is such a strong gas that one can smell it at concentrations of only 0.13 parts per million. But it takes a whole lot more than that to cause illness or death. Death Gulch, a place in northeast Yellowstone, is historically noteworthy for H_2S concentrations that kill animals, including grizzly bears.[1]

Carbon dioxide, which is odorless, occurs in many of the small thermal caves in the Mammoth area, including the Devil's Kitchen and McCartney's Cave. CO_2 concentrations in those places and at Poison Spring, Poison Cave, and in the Stygian Caves have a long history of killing birds, insects, and small animals in great numbers.[2] For some reason, bats do not seem to be affected by the gas and live in the caves apparently without harm.

At least one near death is known from these gases. In the summer of 1883, Barbara Henderson (known to her family as "Lillie"), the daughter of park assistant superintendent G. L. Henderson, descended the steps into the basement portion of her family's residence near Mammoth Hot Springs. Before she knew it, Lillie was overcome by seeping gases and passed out. Fortunately she was missed, and a family member carried her up to fresh air in time.[3] The gas responsible here was probably carbon dioxide. No human deaths are known from it in Yellowstone, unless Bill Nelson's was partially caused by it.

Another gas death involved hot-spring bathing and it occurred very early, just outside the park to the east, in the Cody country, where later oil drilling would contribute to hydrogen sulfide deaths. It was January 27, 1885, and Thomas Hefron was riding his horse and pulling a packhorse along the North Fork of Shoshone River, west of present-day Cody, Wyoming. The town of Cody would not exist for more than ten more years, so Hefron was a long way from civilization. Hefron worked at the ranch of Compte du Dore at Corbett, Wyoming (between Cody and Red Lodge, Montana). A few other ranches existed on Pat O'Hara Creek north of today's Cody, and Meeteetse, Wyoming, had a post office, but the closest town of any size was Billings, Montana. Located far to the north, it was only three or four years old.

Thomas Hefron rode along the North Fork, known at that time as the Stinkingwater River from the smell of hot springs along it. Whether he was in the canyon of the stream west of present Cody or farther west at the junction of the north and south forks (the place the fur trappers called the Tar Spring) is not known, but he stopped at the hot springs to soak. Two days later his packhorse returned to Dore's ranch without him. His fellow cowboys went searching, and Hefron's "saddle horse was found tied to a large rock about 100 yards from the hot springs. On close examination his dead body was found in the hot water, where it had evidently been lying from the morning of the 17th until the morning of the 29th. It is supposed that he had gone in to bathe and was suffocated by the gas from the springs."[4] The whereabouts of Thomas Hefron's relatives were unknown, so the newspaper asked the public for information. His death was a strange and early one in a remote region.

On June 26, 1939, three Bureau of Public Roads employees were driven to a worksite at the bridge across the Yellowstone River just east of Tower Junction. They were Bill L. Nelson, 20, Vaughn H. Roley, 21, and Earl A. Johnson, 18. Nelson was a new employee who had been working only thirteen days for the government. They were to perform some work in a twenty-six-foot-deep pit that had been dug by the Bureau of Public Roads. The bureau routinely dug these types of holes when building roads and bridges in order to accrue information about ground formations before building. When supervisor Bill Whitmore drove away from the site, leaving the men there at 8:30 a.m., he noticed nothing unusual.

Johnson and Nelson lowered Vaughn Roley in a bucket into the test pit that measured five by six feet at the bottom. In descending, Roley noticed a slight sulfur odor when he was eight feet from the bottom, but rode on down and got out of the bucket. At that point, hydrogen sulfide gas had begun to cut his throat and lungs and haze his vision, so he got back into the bucket and called for the other two men to pull him up.

Suddenly Roley lost consciousness. He fell out of the bucket, leaving only his feet in it. Nelson immediately began sliding down the rope in an attempt to get Roley back into the bucket. But partway down the rope Nelson, too, was overcome by the gas.

Earl Johnson then began to operate the hoist. Seeing that Roley's feet were still in the bucket, Johnson pulled him to the surface. Fifty-five years later, Johnson still remembered the "terrible yellow foam" which came out of Roley's mouth and nostrils. When Roley regained consciousness, Johnson ran to the Tower ranger station for help.

During the interim, Roley again lost and regained consciousness. Then he began attempts to use the hoist rope as a lasso, trying to catch Nelson by his feet or hands in order to lift him to the surface. "I could see Bill Nelson sprawled on his stomach in the corner of the test pit," Roley wrote later, "and could hear his deep, harsh breathing." Roley was still trying to lasso Nelson when Johnson returned with park ranger William Bugas and some other persons.

Bugas had brought ropes and used one to lower Gabby Johnson (carrying the hoist rope to slip over Nelson's foot) into the pit. But Johnson, too, was overcome by the gas and soon was hoisted from the pit unconscious. It took him about half an hour to fully recover, even though he had been in the pit only sixty seconds or less.

Finally, holding his breath, Roley was lowered into the pit by a rope tied around his chest. He was forced to take a breath at the bottom of the pit and immediately felt himself blacking out. But he was able to slip the hoist rope around Nelson's foot before the gas caused Roley to lose consciousness. Then both men were pulled to the surface. Earl Johnson, who wrote me from Roundup, Montana, says that Nelson was unconscious in the pit for forty-five minutes to an hour. Again Johnson saw the hideous yellow foam all over Nelson's mouth and nostrils, and some of it was still on Roley.

Both men were taken to the hospital. Roley survived, but Nelson died the following day. More than a year later, the Gardiner newspaper reported that the "Carnegie Hero Fund Commission" presented a bronze medal to Bill Nelson's mother, Mrs. L. A. Crew, for his sacrifice.[5]

Many of the death incidents described in this book were caused by negligence, but Nelson's was a freak accident. Strangely, another pit had been dug three years earlier just ten feet from the death pit, and no gas had been found in it. Moreover, a third pit had been simultaneously dug just across the river from the death pit, and no gas had been found in it, either.

U.S. Bureau of Mines engineers subsequently tested the death pit for gases and issued a report. At the request of the park superintendent, they also tested Devil's Kitchen and a number of caves in the Mammoth area for the presence of gases. Their reports emphasized the danger in both places.

The engineers found fatal concentrations of hydrogen sulfide gas in the bottom of the death pit, as well as a good deal of carbon dioxide. At that time, it was known that even concentrations of .01 percent hydrogen sulfide could cause death after some time. At the bottom of the well were found concentrations of .02 to .04 percent hydrogen sulfide, as well as over 20 percent carbon dioxide. Despite the high concentration of CO_2, the engineers seemed certain that the hydrogen sulfide was the gas responsible for Nelson's death.

Reporting on gases in Mammoth's Devil's Kitchen, the engineers noted that 7 percent carbon dioxide had been found there and recommended that no visitors be allowed to enter the cave, a place that park visitors had been climbing into since its discovery in 1872. From that time on, the Devil's Kitchen and all caves in the Mammoth area have been closed to visitors because of noxious fumes. The essential impetus for those closures was the 1939 death of William Nelson, who succumbed to a "pestilent congregation of vapors."[6]

6

FREAK FATALITIES
DEATHS FROM LIGHTNING

It is vain to look for a defense against lightning.

—Publilius Syrus, 42 BC

AT LEAST FIVE PERSONS HAVE DIED from being hit by lightning
during the recorded history of Yellowstone National Park. That this has
been a much more common occurrence in the history of at least the state of
Montana than one would think is evident from a reading of the *Livingston
Enterprise*, *Livingston Post*, Bozeman *Avant Courier*, and other area newspapers.
There are numerous references in these newspapers to lightning fatalities in
Montana. I have no information on lightning fatalities in Wyoming or Idaho,
but I suspect that similar numerous instances exist for those states.

In general, Yellowstone Park officials do not find it necessary to stress
lightning warnings for the tops of mountain ridges as park officials do in, say,
Rocky Mountain National Park, Colorado. Perhaps they should, if the experiences of several park visitors and employees and the U.S. Geological Survey
are any yardstick. In fact, the case law in this area has evolved a bit since 1995.
Those readers interested in it should see "Original Introduction and Recent
Additions."

This fascinating park lightning (or perhaps static electricity) incident
occurred in 1872. Members of the second Hayden survey climbed a peak in
northern Yellowstone and, with a storm coming in, experienced minor shocks
and the hair on their bodies standing painfully on end. They attributed the
crackling noises and shocking feelings to electrical charges building up; perhaps lightning was playing a role. Because of the experience, they named the
mountain Electric Peak. At least one subsequent hiker experienced the same
thing there in recent years.[1]

It was not the last lightning event to imperil U.S. Geological Survey members. In 1885, Arnold Hague's U.S. Geological Survey parties were exploring Yellowstone Park. On Sunday morning, September 5, one party under topographer John H. Renshawe put out into Yellowstone Lake in an old sailboat which they had found. The party of four set sail for Mary Bay from the Yellowstone River outlet on this unusually warm day. Renshawe sat in the bow managing the sail; M. D. Scott took the seat near the mast to handle the oars, and the other two men sat in the stern. The sun was out and no threatening clouds were present, although the day was somewhat sultry. The men were about one hundred yards from the shore.

Suddenly, the men back on the beach heard a crashing thunderclap that stampeded their horses. The four men on the lake were rendered unconscious by a bolt of lightning that knocked down the mast of their boat. Renshawe gradually awoke in a dazed condition to find that neither of his legs worked, nor did his right arm. On his wrist was a severe burn.[2]

Looking around, Renshawe saw that Scott was bent over his knees, dead; the "bolt from the blue" had struck him in the head, causing a large burn mark. A long, dark streak ran the entire length of Scott's body, showing where the lightning had run, and a hole in the bottom of the boat showed where it had exited the craft. Fortunately, the boat was close to shore and drifted in.[3] The third man was relatively unharmed but the fourth was "out of his head all night."[4] Renshawe gradually recovered the use of his legs, but his arm remained paralyzed for two weeks, and the burn on his wrist left a lifetime scar.

We have John Renshawe's personal description of the incident, and it is dramatic. He says that the dead man, Scott, was

[O]ne of those wandering spirits we used to meet in the old west, chiefly employed in prospecting or such other congenial opportunities as might furnish occupation between times. Scott was an unusually high class man, and while, as was natural in such a wandering life, he carried all his worldly goods in his pack ... [We] started across the lake to storm point to make a "station" using a small home-made boat with a square sail and oars. In the party, besides myself, [were] Scott and two other men. We started out using the sail, but when about half way across the wind gathered too much force for the rude sail so we resorted to the oars. I sat at the bow holding a corner of the sail which I had wrapped around the mast. Scott sat on the seat in front of me, which also served as a base for the mast. The other two men sat one on the next seat and the other at the stern. As Scott pulled at the oar his back and head would bump against the mast, and evidently the lightning bolt after striking the mast switched to his head at the moment of contact, down the left side of his body and out through the bottom of the boat. All of us were left unconscious. I was the first to wake up as from a sound sleep and found Scott lying across my lap, having fallen backwards from the seat in front of me, and apparently having died instantly—the other two men were lying in the bottom of the boat which was then half full of water—but after a time both revived, and applying the oars soon pulled in to the shore. Fortunately for all of us the boat had been made of new lumber, and as the bolt passed through the bottom the broken fibers fell back and to a great extent stopped the inflow of water. The bolt of lightning that wrecked us apparently came from a clear sky and when I waked up the sun was shining and the air was quite still.[5]

M. D. Scott, 46, was an employee of the U.S. Geological Survey and had been in the region for a long time at Bozeman, Livingston, and Yellowstone Park. Renshawe took charge of his effects and buried Scott temporarily near the site of present Lake Hotel. The topographer then set out with a horse party for Mammoth Hot Springs to report the incident and to notify Scott's relatives. As the party was crossing Tower Creek, an unusual discovery was made. After a stampeding mule dropped a pack into the creek and it was opened to be dried out, M. D. Scott's wallet was curiously discovered to contain some sixteen thousand dollars in cash and certificates. This, of itself, stated Renshawe, "shows that he was above the usual class of wanderers."

Nothing else was determined, but Scott's father and his two brothers, all from Alexis, Illinois, showed up two weeks later. They traveled to Yellowstone Lake where they disinterred Scott's body, already buried for seventeen days, and returned with it to Illinois.[6] Granville Turner of Montana accompanied the body to Livingston. He had been a "friend and inseparable companion" of Scott's for several years. Considering that the lightning that killed Scott came from a clear blue sky, it appears that the Roman philosopher Publilius Syrus was correct. One might as well attempt to fly to the moon as to look for a defense against lightning.[7]

Another park lightning incident occurred in September of 1887 near Norris Geyser Basin, although no one was killed. Ed Lamartine (a road crew boss) and his men had pitched their tents around a large tree. According to Lamartine, lightning struck the tree, shattering it into slivers. All in camp were prostrated (knocked out) by the shock and rendered unconscious for a time. When one of the men, "Pete," came to, he noticed near the tree thirty-two sticks of dynamite in a sack, which fortunately did not explode.[8]

A well-known area hunter, trapper, and guide was killed by lightning "in the park" on August 27, 1894. He was Bayard T. "Curley" Rogers, whose grave today in the Livingston, Montana, cemetery is marked with the note that he died "on Rogers Peak." At the time of his death, Curley Rogers, his wife, his son, and his friend John Walker all were accompanying the party of H. B. Claflin, a New York hunter, to the mountains near the head of the Gallatin River. It is not known precisely where the party was when the accident occurred. The description, "on the high divide between the Yellowstone and Gallatin valleys not many miles from (the town of) Horr," probably places it somewhere in the Sheep Mountain–Big Horn Peak area, in the present northwest corner of the national park. (That area did not become a part of the park until around 1930.)

While camped on Gallatin River, the party went into the high country to the east to hunt bighorn sheep. Rogers started for the top of a ridge to scare down a band of sheep so Claflin could get a shot at them. Near the summit, lightning struck Rogers in his left shoulder, ran all the way through his body, and exited through his left leg. Probably dead at that point, Rogers fell some two hundred feet into a chasm and onto a protruding ledge.

Twenty-four hours later, a recovery party saw his body through field glasses from where he had fallen. His rifle lay thirty feet from the edge. On recovery, the entire left side of Rogers's body was seen to be seared by the lightning.

Unfortunately for the writers of Rogers's tombstone, not a good enough location of this place, which they called Rogers Peak, was given for us to retain that place-name. One wonders, however, just how much influence, if any, this incident had in the giving of names to Sheep Mountain and Big Horn Peak. Big Horn Peak did, after all, receive its name around 1895.[9]

Eleven years later, Rogers's brother came to the Gardiner–Livingston area hoping to locate Curley's grave in order to return him to Michigan. Apparently he did not, for Rogers is still in the Livingston cemetery.[10]

A sheepherder was the park's next lightning victim, on Monday, June 19, 1899. That day, Isaac Rowe went up to Swan Lake to tend some of the Van Dyck and Deever sheep herd that was kept there to supply the abattoirs (slaughterhouses) from which fresh mutton was delivered to park hotels. While standing on the margin of the lake at 6:00 p.m., Rowe was struck by lightning and instantly killed. His body was found by John Cramer (Klamer?) of the relief party that went looking for him. Rowe was a young, single man with no relatives in the area. He was buried in the army cemetery at Mammoth in grave 16. Nothing else could be learned about him.[11]

In another freak incident, a park visitor, Ed Robinson, was struck by lightning at the auto camp at Tower Fall on August 10, 1926. He recovered after being unconscious for about ten minutes.[12]

Robert S. Wright, 21, of Gardiner, Montana, was not so lucky. An employee of the Yellowstone Park Transportation Company, he was driving on the

Mammoth–Tower road in a company truck on July 18, 1929, when his truck broke down near Oxbow Creek. Simultaneously it began to rain, so Wright sat down under a large tree. Lightning struck the tree, killing him instantly. He was buried in the Gardiner Cemetery in his family's plot.[13]

A young canoeist was killed by lightning on Lewis Lake on Thursday, August 7, 1975. Brenton Kirk Jr., 21, of New Philadelphia, Ohio, was canoeing with his 19-year-old brother, Philip, when witnesses on shore saw lightning strike Brenton. Both men were thrown into the water; Philip was rescued but Brenton was lost. The two had not checked in with park rangers and had no boating permit or life preservers.[14]

Several scary lightning incidents have occurred in the park that injured but did not kill their victims. Ranger James V. Court was involved in an incident at Old Faithful Geyser in early June of 1966. A terrific thunderstorm rolled in about noon one day, just as the geyser was predicted to erupt. Just before the eruption, a bolt of lightning struck the cone of the geyser. In a freaky manner, the charge traveled "down from the cone toward the visitor center along a wire which was connected to a recording device in the visitor center that sensed eruptions of Old Faithful." "When the charge passed under the boardwalk," stated Court, "it jumped to the wet boardwalk and struck a number of people in the immediate vicinity." Several people were injured. One lady was badly burned and taken to Lake Hospital. "The clothes on her were almost burned off," said Ranger Court.[15]

A double lightning incident occurred on Yellowstone's Specimen Ridge on July 9, 1986. Charlotte Zappala, 36, and Vincent Zappala, 49, both of Anaheim, California, were struck simultaneously by lightning. They were standing under a tree in a storm. The tree took the main hit, and the two were blown some distance by the lightning. Near Glacial Boulder, some miles to the southwest, photographer Lee Silliman was terrified "by the darkness of the cloud formation and the number of lightning bolts issuing from it." Ranger Brian O'Dea remembers seeing the Zappalas' clothes badly ripped and smelling ozone everywhere. Another ranger, Mike Pflaum, heard a radio transmission from the site, so he grabbed his medical gear, including a defibrillator, jumped into a helicopter, and flew into the storm. Several hikers in the area had seen the Zappalas get struck, and they and O'Dea were taking turns giving two-person CPR on both victims when Pflaum arrived. That is what saved the Zappalas, according to him. "We helped," Pflaum says, "but they really did it. Had the lightning strike occurred unwitnessed, I am relatively certain that the two would have died." Pflaum called it "one of the most dramatic incidents I've been involved with, because lives were actually saved!"[16] For a while Charlotte Zappala was in critical condition and Vincent was in serious condition at area hospitals. They eventually recovered.[17]

My friends Paul Rubinstein and Mike Stevens—former park employees for Hamilton Stores and Xanterra, respectively, and with whom I wrote the book *Guide to Yellowstone Waterfalls*—are convinced that they attract lightning, as on five different occasions in 1990 to 1992, while hiking in the Yellowstone backcountry, it struck very near them. They narrowly missed death on all these occasions.

Lightning incidents killed one man just north of the park in 1997 and injured eleven at Old Faithful in 2005. On September 8, 1997, Christian David Bowers, 23, was struck near Pray, Montana, while riding his motorcycle north toward U.S. Highway 89 at a point two-tenths of a mile beyond Mill Creek Road. The Gardiner man, originally from Mississippi, was taken to Livingston Hospital, where he died four hours later. Nearly eight years later, an incident at Old Faithful on June 21, 2005, was particularly dramatic because it involved so many people. More than two hundred park visitors had gathered that day around 3:15 p.m. to watch an impending eruption of the famous geyser, when a "very intense, fast-moving storm cell" suddenly rolled in. Lightning struck about fifteen yards in front of the geyser's boardwalk, causing pandemonium in the crowd. Twelve-year-old John Hughes of Maryville, Tennessee, was the most seriously injured, but ten other people were also hurt. The boy was life-flighted to Idaho Falls, while the others were treated at Old Faithful Clinic.[18]

Deaths and injuries from lightning are genuinely in the realm of true accidents, freak fatalities sometimes called "acts of God" in legal parlance, and thus cannot generally be attributed to anyone's negligence. While the stories are interesting, it is difficult to draw rules, morals, or theses from them. Hikers should avoid the tops of ridges and never stand under solitary trees when thunderstorms or threatening clouds are present. Gretel Ehrlich, a writer who authored the Wyoming book *The Solace of Open Spaces*, was herself struck by lightning and has published a book about the experience.

7

LYING IN THE SNOW
DEATHS FROM AVALANCHES AND FREEZING

Oh, the cold and cruel winter!

—Longfellow, *Song of Hiawatha*

AT LEAST FIVE (perhaps six) persons have died in avalanches inside the Yellowstone National Park and at least twelve by freezing ("exposure"). But these figures do not include at least nine by avalanches and five by freezing at locations just outside the park. (For example, we now know of four avalanche fatalities at Emigrant Gulch in 1872–1873, per the Bozeman *Avant Courier*, May 30, 1873.) Nor do those statistics include complete information on Cooke City fatalities, which are not thoroughly researched. Some of the incidents occurred in early park days, long before there was a winter season for visitors in Yellowstone (see also chapter 22, "Missing and Presumed Dead"). But today we continue to experience both avalanching and freezing incidents in the park.

Many of the twenty-seven winters I have spent in Yellowstone have been relatively mild ones, but occasionally temperatures drop to lethal levels: fifteen to sixty degrees below zero. On any given winter night, temperatures will usually be below twenty degrees Fahrenheit, with daytime temperatures usually ranging from twenty above zero to twenty below. Snowfall varies with the elevation, but usually averages one hundred to four hundred inches annually. Avalanche danger is routinely at least moderate during Yellowstone winters.

People who live in Montana, Wyoming, and Idaho are used to cold temperatures, but even those of us who live here can become complacent. Many of us sometimes walk out the door at night without a coat in order to retrieve something that we have left in our car or to run a quick errand while thinking, "I'll only be out for a moment." It is easy for a door to accidentally slam shut, thus locking us in the cold without proper protection. When one lives "out in the country" and no one else is around to help, that hasty decision can be a lethal one, especially at night. Likewise a suddenly disabled car can become a life-threatening emergency when one is inadequately prepared for lethally cold weather (again, especially at night). Carry extra clothes and supplies in your car in winter and do not become complacent just because you live in a cold climate.

Beginning in the winter of 1971–1972, one hotel was kept open in Yellowstone National Park. Since then, the winter season has so grown in popularity that today the park receives more than one hundred thousand visitors who travel its roads on snowmobiles, snowcoaches, and cross-country skis. Cross-country skiers should avoid skiing at the bases of steep or vertical slopes or onto cornices, and winter backcountry users should have proper equipment. As always, everyone should avoid skiing or snowshoeing alone. Safety warnings notwithstanding, Yellowstone's increasing winter visitation virtually guarantees that more persons will perish from freezing or from avalanches and will be found, like the subjects of the stories presented here, lying in the snow.

The name of the earliest known freezing (exposure) victim is unknown. The Butte (Montana) newspaper reported on January 20, 1881: "A dead man was brought into town on Friday, from the park. It is supposed that he froze to death, but the particulars are wanting." Probably more than one person died alone in the park or near it in early days without anyone knowing about them, for those days were full of solitary travelers and local residents who risked much to travel alone in winter.[1]

Another example of a death in solitude is the case of Fred Heckman, who reportedly died alone in a snowslide above Cave Falls in the park's southwest corner. Old-timer Ernest Murri, who was in that country as early as 1902, recalled this story and the victim's name in a 1968 interview. He stated that Heckman was listed as a missing person, but nothing else is known, including the year that it happened.[2]

The first completely documented avalanche victim in Yellowstone Park was Jacob Hess on February 21, 1884. Hess was a Finlander who worked on one of Oscar Swanson's park road crews. That night, Hess and a party of six friends were returning by sleigh to Mammoth Hot Springs from Gardiner, where they had spent the evening drinking in one of that raucous town's many saloons. In those days, the present road through Gardner Canyon did not yet exist, so the men were sleighing on what is today known as the Old Gardiner Road, a much higher route located near many steep slopes. J. C. Vilas passed their sleigh at one point and stated that the men were "noisy and badly intoxicated." About halfway between the two places, a snowslide occurred, which threw the seven men and their single team of horses one hundred yards down the mountainside. A James Wrist helped four men to get out, and two more were saved by digging, but Hess was buried in the snow and suffocated. The local newspaper noted that "the party had been drinking heavily at Gardiner and were not in condition to manage the team."[3] Hess was interred in the Mammoth civilian cemetery. His grave today is one of the unmarked (and thus unknown) ones. A newspaper item on the affair stated: "The deceased was a Russian Finlander and leaves a wife and family in Finland. When in drink he was quarrelsome and dangerous. It is said that he had killed one of his companions while under the influence of drink and had served a term of years imprisonment for that offense. When sober he was a good workman and was well liked by his comrades."[4]

We know of the freezing death at Mammoth of Sarry E. Bolding in early 1886—if that is indeed how she died—only because of family stories handed down. Mira (Myra) Adeline Robison Tuck (1896–1990) told her granddaughter Janice Weekley a story that apparently her parents told to her. Her parents, Martha Elizabeth Teel and William Addington Robison, lived in the Gardiner–Mammoth area at that time, and they told their daughter that Sarry Bolding did not come home one cold night. The men who went looking for her found her sitting under a tree frozen to death. Those men thought that she might have fallen into a stream, for she was wet, but nothing further is known. Sarry Bolding was buried in the Mammoth civilian cemetery (see appendix A).[5]

The following winter—that of 1886–1887—was the legendary "hard" winter all over the Rocky Mountains. Temperatures plunged to fifty degrees below Fahrenheit in places, cattle by the thousands starved to death on the prairies of Montana, and the snow accumulated to amazing depths in the mountains. Two miners, Anthony Wise and Clarence Martin, were killed at Cooke City (just northeast of Yellowstone Park) in an avalanche on New Year's Day that was a mile long and half a mile wide. Old-timers were stating by January 15 that the amount of snow was "already far in excess of the usual," with five feet of it in Cooke City and eight feet in the mountains.[6]

The dangerous cold of that legendary winter also froze Alexander "Mormon" Brown to death. Brown, about 35 and formerly of Ogden, Utah, left Gardiner with Thomas Garfield on January 2, 1887, intending to stay at a cabin five miles away. He had been drinking heavily for some time and got delirium tremens upon reaching the cabin. The two stayed there for two nights, and on the third evening, January 4, they again fell asleep. Garfield awoke to find Brown gone. He attempted pursuit but gave up because of darkness. The following morning, Garfield again followed Brown's trail, but it soon petered out, and he returned to Gardiner.

A search party of eleven men began looking for Brown. He had left the cabin in his stocking feet without much cold-weather clothing. The party found the place where Brown had tried to wrap his feet in his shirt and another place where he had torn evergreen limbs from trees, apparently to keep his feet from touching the snow. They found the places in the deep snow where Brown had lost his footing on a slope and slid about sixty feet, regained his footing, and continued sliding to the Yellowstone River. His body was found lying there in the snow, partially covered with water. The final portion of his trail was marked with blood from his torn and naked feet. The recovery team was forced to carry Brown's body one and a half miles through waist-deep snow to the Gardiner cemetery, where he was interred.[7] The Brown and Hess incidents are relevant to us today because of their commentary on mixing alcohol with Yellowstone winters.

John W. Nunley, the park's second documented avalanche victim, died on January 12, 1894. His death on the north slopes of Electric Peak not far from his home at Cinnabar probably served for many years as a warning to other residents to stay away from those steep gulches on one of the park's premier mountains. Nunley, who was about 30, and John Mantle, both of them residents of Cinnabar, went hunting on Friday, January 12, "in the mountains north of the National Park." At that time the area along Reese Creek below Electric Peak's summit was not yet part of the park, and the men wanted to set a trap just north of the boundary. Electric Peak was and is a spectacular mountain that rises steeply to 10,992 feet.

It was after dark when they finished the trap and headed down a gulch traveling north. The two were wearing "snowshoes," but whether they were skis or web snowshoes is not known. Nunley was traveling a bit in advance of Mantle and "when near the foot of the mountain an avalanche of snow came thundering down and buried him [Nunley] 15 or 20 feet deep. He saw the slide coming down and yelled to his companion, who was above the spot where the snow had parted, and said, 'I'm gone!' He had scarcely uttered these words when he was entombed beneath a mountain of snow."[8]

The slide carried Nunley to the foot of the mountain, and John Mantle thought that Nunley had been buried anywhere from fifteen to forty feet deep. Mantle tried digging, but it was to no avail in the dark. He had no shovel, so hurried on to Cinnabar to get help. Hampered by darkness, the rescue party did not leave until the next morning.

Five men, including John Mantle and George Reese, left Cinnabar on Saturday morning to look for John Nunley. Unfortunately Mantle was not able to locate the exact spot of the avalanche, so all parties were convinced that Nunley's body would not be found until spring. The team went back to the perceived location later and continued digging. Within a week they located John Nunley's body, buried not as deeply as all had thought. "The body lay face down under about two feet of snow," said the *Livingston Post*, "with one hand up to the face," as if Nunley had attempted to create airspace for himself. "One of Nunley's snowshoes was still on and his gun and knapsack were strapped to his back." It was evident to all of the searchers that "he had smothered to death" in a snow that "had packed amost as hard as ice." Friends buried John Nunley, who was single, at nearby Horr, Montana, as his relatives at Virginia City, Montana, waited to hear more.[9]

A well-heeled if apparently demented park employee managed to freeze to death in the springtime rather than the winter and near Mammoth Hot Springs, supposedly one of the warmer places in Yellowstone. Joseph Mullery had come west from Saint Paul, where he worked for the Northern Pacific Railroad. Hired as the stenographer at Mammoth Hot Springs Hotel and newly arrived, he became despondent on the night of April 30, 1896, and began drinking. Other hotel employees tried hard to keep him from going out into the night, but Mullery sneaked away and was soon missing. Shortly after he disappeared, the valley received heavy rains accompanied by snow. The hotel conducted a search to no avail, and a week later Mullery's brother came to the park to do his own search. He enlisted the aid of a famous old mountaineer, Jack Baronett, who was quickly given the help of two troops of soldiers by park superintendent George Anderson. On May 11, Baronett deployed his troops at intervals of fifty yards per man to comb the country south of Mammoth. He found Mullery near Golden Gate in less than two hours, lying on a log with his coat and vest off. Mullery had frozen to death some five days earlier after trying to live off of aspen tree bark. Slivers of aspen were found in his teeth, and pieces had been cut from nearby trees. In his dementia he had apparently believed himself at home safe in bed.[10]

Seven park victims of winter freezings and avalanches were all army soldiers from Fort Yellowstone at Mammoth Hot Springs. We know little of the circumstances surrounding the freezing death of Private Andrew Preiber, 25, of Company I, Sixth Cavalry. A German from Saint Louis, Missouri, Preiber was found comatose on the road between Mammoth and Gardiner on March 14, 1893. Taken to Gardiner, he died before medical aid could arrive and was buried in grave 5 at Mammoth army cemetery.[11]

Likewise, the circumstances surrounding the apparent exposure death of Private David J. Mathews are somewhat mysterious. Mathews, of Company D, Sixth Cavalry, was stationed at Riverside Soldier Station near the park west entrance and set out alone on skis on March 14, 1894, intending to pick up mail from the station at Lower Geyser Basin. He evidently became lost and froze to death; his body was found more than a year later, on June 9, 1895.[12]

There was much talk at the time, and apparent conviction on the part of a number of people, that Mathews had been shot by poachers. Charley Marble, an old-time trapper and guide, even so stated in a "badly garbled" reminiscence.[13] And according to park photographer Jack Haynes, many other folks, including later assistant superintendent Chet Lindsley, also believed this. Haynes stated that Mathews's remains were found on the south side of Gibbon River about three miles above Madison Junction.[14]

These rumors of Mathews's death by poachers probably originated with the park superintendent himself, for Captain George S. Anderson wrote the following about the incident:

> In March, 1894, a private of "D" Troop, Sixth Cavalry, left Riverside for the Lower Basin, for the mail. The sergeant in charge of the station went about six or eight miles on the road with him, and he was then over the half of his journey. He was never seen or heard of after, until his remains were found a year and a half later, ten miles or more from where he was last seen, entirely out of his proper direction and in a place where he must have forded at least one large stream to reach. He either became lost and wandered about until he perished from cold or he met with some of our good neighbors, the poachers, and they gave him his quietus. The latter theory is not at all unlikely.[15]

But for all this talk of poachers, no one ever mentioned finding bullet holes or other obvious wounds in Mathews's skull or clothing.

As a result of Mathews's death, soldiers in the park were ordered never to travel alone in winter; but in disobeying that order another soldier froze to death in late 1897. Private John W. H. Davis of Company D, Fourth Cavalry, and a man known only as Private Murphy left the soldiers' station near Mud Geyser on Monday, December 13, 1897, skiing toward West Thumb. They were to meet two south-entrance soldiers there to exchange mail and reports.

The weather was mild when the two men left the station, so they did not wear much heavy clothing, depending on the exertion of skiing to keep them warm. They reached the lake that night and camped at the hotel, but overnight the weather turned frigid, falling to sixteen below zero by the time the two continued on Tuesday morning along the lakeshore. About seven miles out, Murphy decided he could not endure the cold and turned back. But Davis was determined to press on, disregarding the order not to travel alone.

After spending the night at a cabin on the lakeshore, Murphy returned to Lake Hotel on December 16 with frostbitten fingers, ears, and toes. Davis's failure to return plus the lowering temperatures caused concern. A telephone call was placed to headquarters at Mammoth and a rescue party was sent out late on the sixteenth. It took rescuers a couple of days to ski from Mammoth to Lake. On the morning of the eighteenth, two miles beyond the place where the two men had split up, the party found the frozen body of John Davis. The

Soldier who froze to death, probably John W. H. Davis in December of 1897, being taken home on his ski (from Lewis R. Freeman, "Ski-Runners of the Yellowstone," *National Magazine*, February 1904, p. 613)

mercury had dropped to minus thirty-five degrees Fahrenheit at Norris on Tuesday morning and probably lower at Lake on Tuesday night. Sergeant Max R. Welch skied 132 miles over eight days to transport Davis's body from the place he died to the cemetery at Mammoth.[16]

Davis was a Kentuckian and apparently very experienced in winter activities in the park. Possibly he became overconfident as to his abilities and stamina. Scout Hofer was incredulous, finding it "almost impossible for a man to lose his life in such a way in that country as there is any quantity of dry wood and timber all along the road. He could not have been so careless as to be without matches." Lieutenant Elmer Lindsley was even less charitable. He attributed Davis's death to disobedience of orders, not being properly clothed (Davis wore summer underwear and only a campaign-type hat), and resting while perspiring freely. As a result of Davis's death, army regulations were strengthened again, forbidding soldiers from traveling alone in winter and even prescribing clothing to be worn on ski patrols.[17]

Another soldier from Fort Yellowstone became an avalanche victim on February 17, 1904, and his death was probably the impetus for a park placename. He was Corporal Christ H. Martin, 38, a career soldier with more than twenty years military experience in places like the Arizona Apache wars and the Philippines.

During the winter of 1903–1904, Martin was stationed in the northwest corner of the park. The soldiers stationed at an early soldier station on Wickiup Creek (the later station on Specimen Creek was not yet built) had been told by a local prospector never to travel close to the foot of a steep mountain located just west of the Gallatin River at a point about one-half mile south of the station.[18] On or about February 17, 1904, Corporal Martin and Private Charles Nelson, both of Troop C, Third Cavalry, started skiing south along the Gallatin River heading for the station at Riverside. They crossed to the west side of the river and unwisely decided to travel below the precipitous slope above the river bench. The local newspaper reported the accident, which occurred around 3:30 p.m.:

> While they were traveling carefully in order to avoid disturbing the tons of snow and ice, some movement loosened the mountain of snow above them and it started toward the two soldiers, pigmies [*sic*] in the path of the slow moving, but irresistible avalanche. Martin and Nelson saw their peril in a flash, and they began a mad race against death. The avalanche gained speed with each second of time and soon it was roaring down the precipitous side of the mountain with the velocity of a railroad train. Nelson, being the younger man, was able to move faster than his companion, and he managed, by the dint of almost superhuman effort to reach a large tree, which he grasped and held himself fast, while the edge of [the] death dealing slide passed over the heels of his snow shoes. When the slide had passed, Nelson looked for Martin, but no trace of him was to be seen. Nothing greeted the eye of the survivor of the tragedy but a broad expanse of snow and ice, silent, cruel, murderous.[19]

Charles Nelson immediately began to ski for help. Three-quarters of a mile north he ran into scout R. A. Waagner and, after informing him of the incident, skied two more miles to Jim Trail's cabin. There he found Jim and Ed Moorman, who had just returned from a hunting trip. Nelson and the others went to the avalanche site with shovels and dug unsuccessfully for the rest of the day.[20]

The next day, Waagner skied down along the Gallatin River to Bozeman and caught the train to Livingston and Gardiner. At Mammoth, he reported the accident, and a detail of soldiers was sent to the site. They, too, were unsuccessful. Not until April 16, after six men shoveled for many days, was Christ Martin's body recovered. He was buried in the Mammoth army cemetery in grave 21.[21]

The name Snowslide Creek was given sometime after this incident to the stream near the avalanche site that enters Gallatin River from the west. Other soldiers and civilian scouts at Gallatin station were apparently commemorating the Martin incident with the new place-name by 1907–1909.[22]

There is a conflict as to whether a soldier at south entrance froze to death or died en route to Mammoth of illness, but regardless, the moving of his body sparked a park legend. According to two letters in the park archives, Private Richard R. Hurley of Company F, Third Cavalry, was taken ill with dysentery at Snake River Soldier Station near the park's south entrance on April 15, 1904. The illness got progressively worse with Hurley becoming "nothing but" a skeleton, until Sergeant Samuel Martin decided to send him to Mammoth for treatment, Hurley being transported by Private James McBride and a Private Tuberville. He died on May 3 at West Thumb while en route. This version of the story probably explains why the park internment record says Hurley died "at West Thumb Emergency cabin" and why the Lake Soldier Station report for that day states that Hurley died at West Thumb while being taken "to the hospital at Fort Yellowstone."[23] Civilian scout Ray Little recalled the story differently, however. According to him, Hurley's illness did not appear to be serious, so his comrades left him well supplied with wood and went on a ski patrol. When they returned, they found Hurley dead of exposure where he had been trying to build a fire in the cabin. Ray Little remembered burying Hurley at the south entrance and then moving him to Mammoth, where he buried Hurley again.[24]

Unless he was remembering a completely different incident, the records indicate that Little recalled the affair incorrectly. Regardless, there is less chance that four other men remembered subsequent events wrongly. Old-timers Bill Wiggins, Ted Ogston, Scotty Bauman, and Harry Liek all recall that the transporting of Hurley's body to Mammoth was grist for the mill of Yellowstone legend. Ogston thought he remembered, as many did, that the story happened at Norris,[25] but Liek, Bauman, and Wiggins all placed it at Fountain station. While transporting the body, the soldiers stopped for the night at Fountain, where a poker game generated. According to Wiggins, after a little whiskey had been drunk, Harry Liek said, "We better let old Joe (the dead soldier) play a hand." So they stood him up by the window, dealt him a hand of cards, and left him there all night. Ogston claims the veteran scout and ranger Harry Trischman told him that he (Trischman) personally set up the frozen body and that it scared the others silly.[26]

We know little about the death of Private Presley H. Vance of Company H, Eighth Cavalry, because it failed to make the local newspaper, but apparently it was due to liquor. Vance died of exposure in Elk Park, where his body was found sometime just before October 16, 1908. William Nichols, head of the Yellowstone Park Association, stated that Vance got drunk and fell off his horse. "I believe there were two or three men with him at the time," said Nichols, "but they were all drunk too." Apparently Vance was well liked, however, for his funeral was an event at Fort Yellowstone that included a corporal and eight privates, pallbearers wearing dress uniforms, the flag at half-mast, firing of guns, taps, and work canceled for the rest of the day.[27]

Not much is known about the last moments of Bill "Scout" Jones, who disappeared above Jardine, Montana, in October of 1910. Jones, formerly the sheriff at Medora, North Dakota, and an "old time scout and hunter," left Gardiner with a load of supplies and became lost in a snowstorm. He tied his team to a tree and wandered off in an apparent epileptic fit. Nine months later, Jones's body was found on the North Fork of Bear Creek about three miles from Jardine, where he had seemingly died of exposure. No one knew anything else.[28]

That is what the rough Yellowstone country can do to the unprepared or even to anyone who is stuck "out in it" for an extended period of time—namely, kill you. It happened in late November of 1910 to Ora Tuttle, whose family ran businesses in Whitehall, Butte, and Anaconda, Montana. He went hunting and then missing along the west side of the park near Tepee Creek and Madison River. A month later, his brother E. U. Tuttle was writing to Yellowstone's acting superintendent Colonel Lloyd Brett, who wrote back on December 21. "Since your brother has, I understand, been lost for about a month," said Brett, "I fear there is little if any likelihood of finding him alive." Brett was right, for Ora Tuttle remained missing for nearly three years, notwithstanding the five-hundred-dollar reward offered by his family. In October of 1913, another hunter found his skeletal remains near Lyons, Montana, downstream from today's Quake Lake. His body had been "torn to pieces by wild animals" after Tuttle died of exposure when he apparently could not find his own camp.[29]

At almost the same time that Ora Tuttle went hunting and disappeared, a wealthy Idaho banker did the same thing. In mid-November of 1910, a prominent businessman from Boise named Bert E. Corbin, 41, traveled east to Fremont County, which borders on Yellowstone Park's Bechler region, with the idea of shooting some elk. Enlisting local guides Harry Lamberton and Fred Coleman, he accompanied them on an initial hunt that was successful in bagging a number of animals. Then riding horses, he and Lamberton left Big Springs camp near Warm River, Idaho, on November 19, heading into the country southwest of Yellowstone. In hopes of scaring up a bull elk, Corbin elected to spend that night out alone near Rea's Pass[30] while Lamberton returned to Big Springs. When Corbin failed to check in on Sunday morning, the twentieth, there was no initial concern because he was an experienced woodsman. But after two more days passed, a posse of ten men began combing the hills north of Big Springs, between it and the national-park boundary. They built numerous fires on hilltops, hoping he would see the flames and smoke.

When he still was not found three days later, another posse made plans to leave Saint Anthony, Idaho, on the twenty-sixth. The country had been inundated by two feet of snow, and clear weather made continuing cold temperatures likely. Locals well knew that drifting in the mountains made the snow much deeper than the mere two feet in valleys.

Concerns for Corbin's safety mounted as time passed. Mrs. Corbin hired more search parties and began to hope that her husband had wandered into Yellowstone Park to be arrested by soldiers for poaching. The Bechler Soldier Station, built in the summer of 1910, was brand-new at this time and the manning of it by U.S. Army soldiers had just begun on a year-round basis. Recent storms in the park had knocked down the telegraph wires, so Mrs. Corbin hoped that Bert had been taken to Mammoth for trial and that communications were merely delayed. "My husband is a man who could not stand to see another hunter beat him," she noted. "In the event one of the men got an elk and he did not he would not stop until he had made a killing," she continued, adding that his determination might have taken him into the park. Corbin was brash and a bit of a braggadocio, so some believed that his tendency toward overconfidence might have led to disaster. The failure of his horse to return to Big Springs seemed to be another negative portent.

Harry Lamberton and his searching posse came into Big Springs on the twenty-seventh, a week after Corbin's disappearance, with no leads. They restocked their supplies and went out again. On the twenty-eighth, soldiers from Yellowstone joined in the search. "Gravest doubts are entertained by his friends for his safety," stated the Boise newspaper, which noted that Corbin's business partner E. H. Lee, with yet another posse, was heading toward Saint Anthony soon. Locals there thought that Corbin had met with some kind of winter accident after perhaps tying his horse to a tree and pursuing an elk on foot. Many hoped that he was merely lost, but almost everyone now believed that his death was a certainty. No one thought he had starved to death because he had plenty of ammunition and there was game in the country. Instead, most thought he had met with an accident or frozen to death or both. Considering snow depths in the area, some must have wondered whether discovery of Corbin's body would have to wait until the spring thaw.

Late on Friday, December 9, nearly three weeks to the day after Bert Corbin's disappearance, U.S. Forest Ranger Ralph Stevens and local guide George Wilcox—traveling on snowshoes—chanced upon his body "lying in deep snow" near Rea's Pass. Corbin had somehow wandered to a point only six miles west of the park boundary and only a bit farther from the very remote place in deep timber where Idaho, Montana, and Wyoming all come together. "Wolves and other animals of the woods," stated a reporter, "have eaten nearly all of the flesh from the bones of the unfortunate man."

There was no obvious clue as to how Corbin died, although freezing seemed the most likely reason. Beyond that possibility, many questions persisted. A couple of reports stated that his horse was found nearby, but a bit later John Blevins of Big Springs became convinced that the horse that came in a week earlier was the one ridden by Corbin, so by December 13 it appeared that his horse was not with him at death. Writers of that report thought that Corbin had died of heart failure, touting his "often remarked" statement to friends that he could not tramp far on foot. Another story stated that he was found near his old camp. If that were true, perhaps he lingered there, hoping that Lamberton would return to the spot. Yet another story placed the location as a mile and a half from the old camp. Perhaps Corbin fell from his horse or was thrown or dragged. Or perhaps, as one writer suggested, he did not recognize the camp and was merely wandering disoriented or lost about the mountains "until the snow became too deep to travel further, when his horse fell and died." In a snowy world where visibility may have been limited, as many skiers can attest, all kinds of dangers can lurk—falling over a precipice, becoming trapped in deep snow, or meeting with an avalanche. And there was no doubt that Corbin encountered wolves and/or other predators, whether before or after his death. Regardless, all of these variables probably paled in the face of the overwhelming cold that accompanies Yellowstone winters.

Like the earlier tale of Ora Tuttle, Bert Corbin's story remains for us today an unfinished mystery. Adding to it is the intriguing statement of E. H. Lee, one of the men who went hunting with Bert Corbin at Big Springs. Following the finding of Corbin's body, the *Statesman* reported on December 12 Lee's statement that two other men had been simultaneously lost in the same locale as Corbin:

> They disappeared about the same time that Corbin dropped from sight and not far from the point where he was last seen. "I do not know the names of the men from Butte and Bozeman," said Mr. Lee last night. "There is a reward of $500 for the recovery of the Bozeman man, dead or alive. He was lost on the other side of the divide in the Henry's Lake country." Jay Whitman, one of the best scouts of the district, and who is located at Henry's Lake, was on his trail for five days. The man threw away his gun, which was found, and he was headed north. It is believed that he has gone crazy. His traveling in the water was much faster than the scouts could make through the timber on snowshoes, and after five days' time, during which it was evident that they were losing ground, they gave up the search and returned. I heard about the Butte man's disappearance from J[esse R.] Brown, chief scout of Yellowstone.

Whether these two men were found or not and what happened to them are facts and events that are unknown at this time, but they point to the possibility that in more cases than we know, such unknown persons have become lost through the years in winter in the vast Yellowstone country. Many of those unfortunates may have died alone and unchronicled.[31]

Similarly, little is known about the circumstances surrounding the freezing death of Edna Durrel, age 29. She was a schoolteacher, "whose frozen body was found" on March 22, 1914, by park soldiers between the east entrance Soldier Station and Pahaska Tepee, advertised as "Buffalo Bill's hotel in the Rockies." Sergeant James P. Brooks at Sylvan Pass Soldier Station noted that she was a "guest of Pahaska Tepee" who was "found frozen to death" on the main road. This kind of death reminds those of us who live in winter climes not to venture outdoors in winter without adequate clothing or at night when one may become lost. Being a bit complacent can cause a winter tragedy.[32]

And then there are those who are simply reckless. Occasionally we see an instance where someone's thirst for adventure overwhelms his common sense, but in this case a hired newspaper reporter seems to have been reckless if not somewhat demented. He did not die, but could have. He was Max Haw, a visitor from Germany in 1906 who decided to go skiing (and later hiking) into the park in winter—and alone at that. Hired by the *Berlin Illustrated News* and "a number of other German papers" to make sketches and write a story on Yellowstone in winter, Haw met with the commandant at Fort Yellowstone, who tried to dissuade him from the assignment. Persevering, Haw set out on skis in early March with two soldiers named Reinholtz and "Graham," who was probably Samuel D. Graham. It is not known how far into the park they went, but when they returned to Mammoth, Haw noticed that his notes, purse, and sketches were missing. He immediately set out to retrace his steps—this time by himself and without proper equipment—and got into trouble. "He soon discovered that he had lost every idea of the way he had come," said a newspaper article, "and was hopelessly lost."

Haw's situation was horrible, and to make matters worse he could not speak good English. The temperature was ranging from zero to minus ten, and there was a great deal of snow. For twenty-four straight hours he went without food and feared for his life. One of the newspapers got this much of his earlier story from him at what was apparently Norris Geyser Basin, although with the translation difficulties we must wonder exactly what Haw told them and what they made up on their own:

> I was up to my neck in snow at times, and blood came from my nose
> and mouth. I was almost famished and could go but little further when
> I discovered tracks we had made during the forenoon. Reaching one of

the geysers I began washing my hands and face in hot water, when suddenly I heard a rumbling sound, and there was a big eruption of all the geysers in the vicinity. Frightened, I rushed away with all speed possible, and from a distance beheld one of the most wonderful sights man ever saw—an eruption of geysers in the dead of winter.

Somehow finding his way back to Mammoth, Haw skied and walked the fifty-five miles to Livingston, Montana, where he pawned his gloves and other articles for four dollars that he used to buy food. He then skied and walked more than seventy-five more miles to Helena, arriving there on March 13, where a local German society gave him aid and newspapers picked up his tale. His story makes us shake our heads in disbelief at his recklessness and wonder how he survived.[33]

We know a lot more about the avalanche death at Mammoth Hot Springs of Lieutenant Joseph McDonald, an event that was so terribly sad that Bessie Haynes Arnold remembered it vividly fifty-four years later at the age of ninety-two.[34] The sudden snowslide that took his life on January 9, 1916, apparently occurred in a very strange place—in the narrow and steep-sided defile north and west of Cleopatra Terrace.

Joe McDonald, 25, was an unusually popular officer whose engaging personality had won the admiration of everyone at Fort Yellowstone. Raised at Havre, Montana, he was a West Point graduate with two brothers and a father all in the military. McDonald had been at his post for a little less than a year.

On Sunday afternoon, January 9, McDonald went skiing with captain and medical doctor Jacob M. Coffin, a Lieutenant Patterson, and 12-year-old John Sparrenberger. As the party passed in single file about 3:45 p.m. below a cliff near Cleopatra Terrace, the avalanche occurred. Joe stated that he wanted to turn back and Coffin replied, "Don't be a quitter!" just as Joe shouted his last words, "Look what's coming!"

The two accounts differ as to what happened next. One says that Captain Coffin was able to extricate himself, pulled the young boy out by the hand, and then worked with him to free Patterson.[35] A later version says that the snowslide buried everyone but Patterson. Patterson then located the young boy by a faint sound under the snow and went to help Captain Coffin, "whose shouts could be heard where he had been able to tunnel an opening above his head." Coffin was rescued, but the three could not find Joe McDonald. They rushed to the fort, and scores of soldiers ran to the spot to find the buried man.

Forty-five minutes after the avalanche, the shovelers located McDonald. Teenager Marguerite Lindsley remembered that it took an entire troop of soldiers almost an hour to dig him out from a depth of six feet because the snow was "deep and icy and very hard packed." Conveyed to the hospital, McDonald died two hours later, never regaining consciousness.

Bessie Arnold was so saddened by the affair that she pasted several newspaper clippings about it into her diary with these notes: "Joe McDonald was with us, playing cards the night before [he died]. Showed us the diamond engagement ring he had purchased for his fiancée . . . We women waited at the McLaurins' till Lt. McLaurin came from the hospital to tell us that Joe had not recovered! He was gone!"[36]

The Mammoth area is not noted for great amounts of snow, so the McDonald incident points up the danger of skiing below vertical cliffs, even relatively small ones.

An unknown man froze to death on Hellroaring Creek about one and one-half miles inside the park north boundary sometime in January, February, March, or April of 1920. His body was found April 21, 1920, by U.S. Forest Service ranger W. R. Johns. Park rangers Winn and Harr buried the man in a grave located on the "right" (west) bank of Hellroaring Creek near where he was found. Due to the severe weather at the time, it was deemed impractical to move the body, and it was buried in a grave marked with stakes at the head and foot and with a blaze mark cut on a nearby tree.[37]

This unknown man was five feet and five inches tall and 120 pounds, age about 40 and had long black hair and a black mustache. Park officials thought him to be a foreigner whose feet had apparently been frozen, leaving him badly crippled. Superintendent Albright noted that the finding of his body probably explained a report made by C. O. Davis of Gardiner, Montana, to park rangers on January 31, that he had seen the bloody tracks of a man leading into the park while trapping north of the park line on Hellroaring Creek. Davis stated that he knew the man had been living for about a month at the U.S. Forest Service cabin on Hellroaring Creek, because the man consumed all of the rations in the cabin.[38]

More recent years in Yellowstone brought an inevitable tragedy involving snowmobiles. Remarkably only one man died in the freezing incident involving sixteen snowmobilers on Beartooth Pass (outside of the park to the northeast), but he was a well-known Montanan and someone important in the history of Yellowstone National Park. He was Hugh D. Galusha Jr., 51, who had been lawyer and accountant to the famous Frank and Jack Haynes family of Yellowstone photographers. His journal article entitled "Yellowstone Years" remains today one of the most important historical writings on the renowned Haynes family. Hugh Galusha had spent years supporting and defending the Grand Old Park. The tale of his tragic trip has become perhaps *the* premier cautionary story of winter in Yellowstone, even though its location was technically outside the park.

A party of sixteen people, which included park Assistant Superintendent Vern Hennesay and one woman, left Red Lodge on Saturday afternoon, January 30, 1971, driving snowmobiles over Beartooth Pass in an attempt to reach

Cooke City and then tour Yellowstone. Neither of those plans worked out. One Cooke City resident later called the decision to make the trip "very poor judgment" on account of approaching bad weather plus a lack of experience by some persons with their snowmobiles. "We've had people make it over the pass [uneventfully] in four hours," he said, "but it's a bad place." Another town resident affirmed that the trip "never should have begun in such weather."

Hugh Galusha seemed no worse for the wear after he hit a snow ridge at nearly ten thousand feet and spilled himself and snowmobile over the guardrail. Together they lodged twenty feet down against a fir tree, with Hugh "lightly reproving himself" while others roped and towed them back up.

The blizzard struck them at twilight. Freezing rain at Red Lodge became hard-packed ice and snow at the higher elevations, and the elevation at the "West Summit" was 10,936 feet. "High winds blowing the freezing rain," said the newspaper later, "quickly coated all exposed parts [of the machines] with ice. Carburetors and the machines' tracks simply became inoperable." The party was soon fighting winds of seventy miles per hour (with some gusts to near ninety), which combined with subzero temperatures to produce a windchill temperature of eighty below zero. "You couldn't really stand up, up there," said party member Dee Street. At one point, the wind snapped a windshield off a snowmobile and those standing there watched it spiral into the darkening cloudiness, presumably into a canyon somewhere. No one had to tell them that gusts able to break off a machine's windshield could easily kill them.

One by one the snowmobiles sputtered and stopped after crossing the west summit, so party members began doubling up on the few that worked. In the high winds and blowing snow, those soon gave out, too. Now they were trapped on the summit in a blinding blizzard, and it was already dark. Even if the snowmobiles had suddenly worked, turning around and going down the almost vertical slopes without being able to see was so dangerous as to be hopeless. Writer Jim Klobuchar described it well: "Somewhere in the impenetrable night the canyon walls fell away thousands of feet." Everything back toward Red Lodge was essentially vertical.

They decided to try to walk west toward the closed but shelter-offering Top of the World store. Vern Hennesay encouraged all to eat what snacks and supplies they had, which was not much. Many were experienced in mountain survival but some were not, and those included two members of the Minnesota Vikings football team—Jim Marshall and Paul Dickson. The parties split into several groups and hiked in the dark the rest of the evening in knee-deep snow while wearing the thick, heavy snowmobile suits that slowed their movements and greatly fatigued them but kept them at least somewhat warm. All experienced the terror of watching their strength deteriorate in the face of cold, wind, hunger, and thirst. They fought the deepening lethargy in their bodies and the creeping disorganization in their minds. Cold, wind, and hunger made their bodies begin to shut down. Dehydration stole their heat. Fatigue muddled their minds. At times they did not know whether to cry, pray, or retch, so they did all three.

Many stopped to rest about 2:00 a.m., and they built snow caves. Marshall, Dickson, Street, Bobby Waples, and Marilyn Waples did not stop, instead hiking all night and somehow building a fire. Two others reached the Top of the World store, but most did not. Minnesota newspaperman Klobuchar, in one of the other parties, said some members spent the night literally sleeping in each other's arms and getting up every forty-five minutes to get blood circulating and to keep warm. In another snow cave near Long Lake, to which he had walked many miles alone, guide Vern Waples arose early. He continued walking to a mountain ranch to call local guide Ralph Huckaba, who rescued ten people at Top of the World on Sunday with a large wide-tracked snow machine. Waples later partially blamed himself for allowing the group to split up, thus depriving many of the knowledge of how to build a good snow cave. He possessed that knowledge and knew that a snow cave, properly built, could raise the temperature to twenty-five degrees Fahrenheit—enough for life.

Hugh D. Galusha died of exposure about 6:45 a.m. Sunday morning in a poorly built snow cave near the summit with Bob Leiviska and Monte Later. Later, 39, was an experienced mountaineer from Saint Anthony, Idaho, and a longtime Yellowstone guide. Jim Klobuchar, whose moving and information-packed account of this tragedy was published in his book *Where the Wind Blows Bittersweet*, wrote that Galusha's "heart and deepest urges were in the sweep of the prairie and the mountain wilderness . . . Yellowstone was a spiritual trust of his . . . He loved the country where he died and he understood people who got there for the pure joy of it, because he was one of them."[39]

Twenty-one years after those terrors on Beartooth Pass, a park researcher died in an avalanche. Gregory Felzien, 26, of Bellbrook, Ohio, was a mountain lion researcher, conducting independent research for the Wildlife Research Institute at the University of Idaho. Mountain lions are few in Yellowstone, but Felzien knew that there were some twenty to thirty-five of the big cats in the northern part of the Greater Yellowstone Ecosystem. He had been tracking one large, radio-collared male in particular.

Felzien was one of the best of field researchers. His friend Dr. Bob Crabtree says, "I never knew anyone as good as he was in the backcountry." Ironically, Felzien had told Crabtree, "If I ever have to die, I want it to be here in Yellowstone tracking cats." Felzien enjoyed traveling alone in Yellowstone's backcountry, something that is not encouraged. He decided to snowshoe into the base of Mount Norris in the Lamar portion of the park to follow his big cat by radio transmitter. For someone experienced in the backcountry, Felzien's actions on this day were not prudent.[40]

The day Felzien chose—Saturday, February 22, 1992—was not a good one for snow conditions. Park employees Diane Ihle and Roy Renkin were skiing on the nearby Lamar River trail to Calfee Creek that day. Diane remembers remarking to Roy that the snow seemed avalanche-prone. They both noticed that the snow made loud, slumping noises and would ripple and collapse for fifty to one hundred feet ahead of them with every plant of their skis. Diane, who had been in Yellowstone for nearly fifteen years, had not seen that phenomenon before.[41]

Greg Felzien stopped on his snowshoes near the base of Mount Norris in a very steep drainage, wondering where his big cougar was. Whether he knew what was coming and tried to run away from it or whether he was buried by surprise, we will never know. The avalanche—one hundred yards long, ten yards wide, and five feet deep—was upon him before he knew it. He must have made feeble or perhaps even valiant last efforts to escape it. But Felzien was dead. Seven rescue workers found his body not completely covered by snow. Eerily, his mother had dreamed only two nights earlier that her son would be killed in an avalanche.[42]

Exactly one year later, an avalanche killed a snowmobiler. On February 22, 1993, 17-year-old Robbie Rudy, a teenager from Cut Bank, Montana, died in an avalanche on Two Top Mountain, four miles southwest of West Yellowstone, Montana, and just outside the park. While snowmobiling in the Cornice Gateway area at about 11:00 a.m., he got off his machine and walked onto a cornice to admire the view. He was unaware that he was walking out over nothing but the sky below, all of it hidden by a crusty but thin layer of snow. The resulting avalanche was three hundred yards wide and a quarter of a mile long and could be seen from the town of West Yellowstone. Rudy was found face-up lying in snow about fifty inches deep.[43]

In 1999, an elderly park visitor strangely froze to death in late May. He was Paul Hudson, age 66, of Orlando, Florida, who died on May 26. Hudson and his wife Phyllis arrived that day at Artist Point, elevation more than 7,900 feet, late in the afternoon. They hiked up the Artist Point trail, but how far is not known, and around 5:00 p.m. they were hiking back to their car. Phyllis Hudson was a short distance ahead of her husband and noted that he stopped to talk with some other park visitors. She slowed her pace to allow him to catch up, but when she arrived at the parking area he was no longer behind her. She turned back to look for him and enlisted the aid of others when she could not locate him. Contacted by cell phone, NPS rangers searched until midnight without success and resumed the search at daylight. At 8:30 a.m. one of their dog teams located his body near Point Sublime, about a mile to the east. Perhaps Mr. Hudson became confused as to his directions and walked east into the woods rather than west back to the parking lot. He died of exposure due to hypothermia.[44]

A recent death from freezing (exposure) occurred north of Gardiner, Montana, in the Big Creek area. James E. Burns, 62, of Gardiner crashed his truck very early on December 8, 2009, somehow got wet in Big Creek, and tried to walk through the night to a residence. He was found dead from exposure the following morning a mile and a half from his vehicle. That evening the *Livingston Enterprise* ran the story of his death right next to its main headline about the temperature having reached twenty-three below zero.[45]

Before we chronicle one final avalanche death in Yellowstone National Park, it is well to note that we do not have complete statistics or stories for the avalanches and freezings that have occurred in the Cooke City, Montana, area outside of the park. There have been many of these, including the deaths in separate avalanches on December 31, 2011, of well-known wilderness advocate David Lee Gaillard, 44, of Bozeman, Montana, and Jody Ray Verhasselt, 46, of Sidney, Montana. Gaillard was killed while climbing near the base of Pilot Peak in the Hayden Creek drainage, and Verhasselt died while snowmobiling in an avalanche in the Fisher Creek drainage north of Cooke City that was three hundred to four hundred feet wide and six hundred to eight hundred feet long. These avalanches were the first two of that winter and occurred "not long after three feet of heavy, dense snow fell on the Cooke City area's extremely weak snowpack." Official warnings had been issued the previous day stating that snow conditions in all of southwest Montana were "highly unstable."[46]

For employees of Yellowstone National Park, no death was sadder than that of park geologist Rick Hutchinson, who died in an avalanche while cross-country skiing in early 1997. So sad was it to this author personally that I put off chronicling it until the very last bit of writing for this book.

Roderick A. "Rick" Hutchinson, originally from Iowa, arrived in Yellowstone in 1970 and within three years ascended to the position of geothermal specialist. It was a prestigious job because it involved studying and interpreting the park's geysers, hot springs, mudpots, and steam vents—the spectacular geologic features that Congress had sought to protect by establishing Yellowstone National Park in 1872. I was a step-on bus tour guide in the early 1970s who held a tremendous interest in the park's thermal features, and I immediately strove to make friends with Rick. I saw him as a person who could help me learn about those features, for he seemed as enthralled by them as I was. For the next twenty years or so, as I worked in numerous Yellowstone jobs, I shadowed Rick around the geyser basins, peppering him with questions and probably making a nuisance of myself in my zeal to learn about the geysers. At times, I was fortunate enough to hike into the backcountry with him to observe remote thermal features, such as Rainbow Springs and Hot Spring Basin Group on Mirror Plateau. Rick was a gentle soul who could be depended upon to be seen wearing his trademark plaid shirt with NPS green jeans. He wore this outfit virtually everywhere he went, and I became so used to it that after a while I did not even notice it.

By the 1990s, park geologist Rick Hutchinson was one of perhaps two foremost authorities on Yellowstone's geysers and hot springs. His knowledge of those features bordered on encyclopedic and for it he was known and sought after by scientists around the world. Married to Jennifer Whipple, the park botanist, Rick seemed to have the happiest of lives. The winter of 1996–1997 began no differently from any other time in the park for Rick. On Saturday, March 1, 1997, he began one of his winter ski trips into a backcountry thermal area, intending to spend his fiftieth birthday (March 5) engaged in the activity he loved most. It was Hutchinson's twenty-first winter trip into Heart Lake.

Rick Hutchinson and his ski mate—fellow geologist Diane Dustman, 37, of Jamaica Plain, Massachusetts—snowmobiled many miles to the Heart Lake Trailhead in the southern part of the park and then cross-country skied the eight miles into Heart Lake Geyser Basin, where they were planning on studying the features there. Diane, who was employed by Boston Dynamics in Cambridge, had an MBA as well as a geology degree and had worked with Rick on several computer projects involving Yellowstone's geothermal features. As Rick's official VIP (volunteer in park), she was a trusted assistant who had taken a month off to help Hutchinson in one of the earth's great geologic places.

When they arrived at Heart Lake Patrol Cabin, Rick Hutchinson unlocked the door and the two of them took off their packs and built a fire in the stove. As the cabin warmed, they put together a meal and planned their next few days of observing and monitoring spectacular thermal features such as Columbia Spring, Rustic Geyser, and the five hot-spring groups up Witch Creek. They spent March 2 monitoring thermal features in the area and staying warm in the cabin.

On Monday morning, March 3, the two again set out on skis. About 8:00 a.m., Rick took a few moments to comply with the usual procedure for NPS staff traveling in the backcountry (the NPS is an agency that is rightfully and constantly concerned about the safety of its employees). By radio, he called the Mammoth Communications Center and checked in with them. He arranged to meet two other rangers halfway between Heart Lake and the trailhead on Tuesday morning. Then Rick and Diane began skiing northwest up Witch Creek and along the east side of Factory Hill to explore the five different groups of thermal features in the area. At the northeast side of the big hill, a small avalanche must have frightened them momentarily, for their ski tracks showed that they skied into it (or near it) and out of it. The time was between 9:00 and 10:00 a.m.

The huge avalanche rushing down the northeast face of Factory Hill from eight hundred feet above them—at least sixty yards wide, two hundred yards long, and four to twelve feet deep—must have been a complete surprise to them.

The following morning Hutchinson did not check in by radio. Nor did the two rangers skiing into Heart Lake encounter Rick and Diane during the eight miles to the lake. Descending Paycheck Pass, the rangers twice reported "collapsing and whomping" of snow. They observed recent avalanche debris at the base of Factory Hill at about 2:30 p.m. and saw ski tracks, but skied on to Heart Lake Patrol Cabin to see whether Rick and Diane were there. At the cabin the rangers found most of Rick's and Diane's personal items with other evidence that the two had last been there on Monday.

Now on rescue alert, the rangers called headquarters by radio to report what they had found and began a cursory ski-and-search in the area. They returned to the avalanche debris zone to look more carefully at it. Most disturbing was their observation of ski tracks going in and out of the first avalanche and entering but not exiting the second avalanche. The weather was deteriorating by this time, so they decided to continue the search at first light the following morning with others that they knew would be coming to the scene.

The search resumed on Wednesday morning. The overhead team and ground searchers, consisting of more than thirty people, began to arrive by helicopter. Now dangerous avalanche conditions prevented access to the site where they had seen the last ski tracks. Ranger Renny Jackson from Grand Teton National Park set explosives to decrease avalanche danger, and four search-dog teams arrived to aid the search. That afternoon probe teams, directed by site commander Les Inafuku, began walking and skiing over the site. They searched unsuccessfully until dark and abandoned the hill that night. Helicopters landed carrying more personnel and one additional dog team.

On Thursday, March 6, around fifty people were involved—fifteen for overhead support, thirty-four ground searchers, five to eight dog teams, and the helicopter. They covered the base of Factory Hill and searched for the entire day. At 4:30 p.m., they found a ski pole belonging to Rick Hutchinson and shortly after that found his body with a probe line. He was lying under four feet of snow.

The helicopter evacuated Hutchinson's body the following morning, and the entire team resumed the search. At around 11:40 a.m., the team found Diane Dustman's body about fifty feet upslope of where Hutchinson had been located. She was lying under seven feet of snow.

Investigators believed that Rick and Diane triggered the avalanche when they skied across the toe of the avalanche area. The starting zone of the avalanche (eight hundred feet up) measured forty degrees in slope, while at the toe, where the two had been buried, it was only sixteen degrees. Once again, skiing at the base of a hill—even in an area that seemed relatively flat—had proven fatal.

Two weeks later, I opened a letter from Jeff Koechling of Boston. He wrote that a year and a half earlier he had received a birthday gift from a friend of his that was a copy of this very book—*Death in Yellowstone*. His friend had visited Yellowstone on a cross-country drive and had "fallen completely in love with the place." The two of them discussed the book, said Koechling, and his friend returned to the park for a longer vacation and then made plans to do so again. "The story has a sad ending," wrote Koechling. "My friend's name was Diane Dustman."

Instantly my eyes filled with tears. Hardly able to read any more, I made plans to place Jeff Koechling's letter in the park archives. "I'm still in shock over the loss," he continued. "It helps a little to know that Diane was having the time of her life, skiing in a beautiful area."

Only a few days after the park's terrible loss, Park Superintendent Mike Finley issued the following statement. Before Finley officially released it, the statement was read aloud over the park radio station to park employees by Assistant Superintendent Marvin Jensen:

> For more than a quarter of a century, Rick Hutchinson has been a Yellowstone institution, one of those rare, authentic experts who can be counted on to help the many people, visitors, and researchers alike, who come and go in a place like Yellowstone. It was almost as if he was a part of the park itself, a gentle presence that had always been here and would go on forever. Nobody loved Yellowstone more, or was more wholly devoted to embracing its spirit and caring for its wonders. Rick touched many lives here, and will not be forgotten.[47]

The NPS held Rick Hutchinson's memorial service at Old Faithful Lodge some days later. As a final salute to him, the entire park staff, including Superintendent Finley, wore plaid shirts along with our green NPS jeans. I cried like a baby.

8

A YELLOWSTONE MYSTERY
DEATH BY CAVE-IN

I T IS SOMETHING OF A MYSTERY as to exactly what happened to Peter Hanson, a civilian employee of the park engineering department, on May 13, 1907. All we know is that he was on Capitol Hill at Mammoth Hot Springs, or perhaps at its base, when an embankment broke free and buried him. Hanson died of asphyxia and was buried in the Mammoth army cemetery on May 15. For some reason, his death was not reported in local newspapers.[1]

9

MISSILES FROM ABOVE
DEATHS FROM FALLING ROCKS

I wish I were a little rock,
A-sitting on a hill,
A-doing nothing, all day long,
But just a-sitting still.

—Frederick Latimer, 1875–1940

IN THAT DITTY, a weary poet longed to lounge like a stone, forever resting on a hillside. But as we know, stones on hillsides do not always remain stationary. Three, perhaps four, deaths are known to have occurred in Yellowstone National Park from falling rocks. They often occur when rocks are dislodged by people, animals, or geologic forces. The missiles often gather momentum over a great distance before striking their unfortunate victims.

In early Yellowstone days, before laws existed prohibiting such things, visitors did not think about the ramifications of actions such as throwing stones into canyons. The account of 1885 traveler George Wingate is one example:

> After fully enjoying the scene, we amused ourselves by rolling large rocks over the cliff. It was wonderful to see a stone the size of a trunk leap into the air in a plunge of 200 or 300 feet, strike the shelf below as if thrown by a catapult, and with such tremendous force as to rebound twenty feet, and after a series of such terrific bounds, make another tremendous leap to the slope below, continuing in bound after bound until it reached the creek . . . While indulging in this boyish sport a faint shout came up from below signifying that there was some one down in the cañon. It is unnecessary to say that we at once stopped the stone rolling.[1]

131

One wonders if anyone was injured by Wingate's thoughtlessness, for certainly people would later be both injured and killed in Yellowstone by these types of capricious activities.

Civilian scout Raymond Little remembered an incident (or perhaps remembered hearing of it) wherein a rock bounded down the mountainside in Gardner Canyon and into a stagecoach, killing a lady passenger. Historian Aubrey Haines reported this incident, but unfortunately Little did not give a date or any other details. Little's wife thought the incident was connected to the Gardner Canyon road being moved to the west side of the canyon. That occurred in 1902, so if she was right, the accident happened that year or before. But newspaper research has so far failed to turn up information on the incident. If she was mistaken and it was instead related to the road being moved from the west side back to the east side, it may well have happened during the period 1913 to 1918.[2]

Another early death of this type occurred in 1917. The trail to the base of Lower Falls is Uncle Tom's Trail, a stairway which leads to a very rocky and unstable area in the Grand Canyon of the Yellowstone River. On August 7, 1917, 20-year-old John Havekost of Coleridge, Nebraska, and a chance acquaintance named Perry Norris hiked down Uncle Tom's Trail. Leaving the trail, they walked along the river near thermal springs that were then known as the pencil geysers. Suddenly, a rockslide above the two men sent many rocks hurtling downward. A small rock struck Havekost in the head, rendering him unconscious and knocking him into the river. Norris dragged him out of the river and yelled for help. A number of visitors including two doctors were close enough to give aid, but Havekost died the following day at the Mammoth hospital of "a very bad compound fracture of the skull." Ironically, the two men had been warned by trail maintenance workers that they could be injured by falling rocks. Park superintendent Chester Lindsley noted that danger signs were posted on the trail and that others would soon be posted, but that "these will not deter tourists from making this most wonderful trip which they have for years been making over a trail that [is] really dangerous."[3]

In two such other cases, deaths can be attributed to persons on the rim of the Grand Canyon of the Yellowstone purposefully throwing or accidentally dislodging rocks that fell onto persons below.

Lorrie Grewe, 11, of Portland, Oregon, was the victim of such carelessness on July 11, 1972. On that day Lorrie, her father, and other family members were standing on the brink of the Upper Falls platform looking at the falls. Suddenly a rock the size of a football struck her in the head. Lorrie suffered a skull fracture and a concussion. Her father, neurosurgeon Ray Grewe, was on hand at the time and gave her emergency treatment, but she died later. An unidentified boy about 14 years old was seen throwing the boulder into the canyon above the trail where Lorrie Grewe was walking.

What was doubly sad about this incident was the attitude of the boy's parents. The boy had climbed illegally onto a ledge some twenty-five feet above the Grewe family and had thrown the rock in an apparent attempt to hit the river. Angry words passed between the Grewes and the boy and his family. The Grewes asked them to remain, but they hurriedly left the scene before rangers arrived. One of Lorrie's brothers took a picture of the boy as he stood or sat in front of his family car, but his parents refused to provide any information. According to a witness, they even coached him to "just tell them you slipped" and dislodged the rock if anyone asked. These parents, who were no doubt worried about their own potential criminal and civil liability, left the area refusing to even identify themselves or concern themselves in any way with the injured girl.[4]

Another child died in similar fashion. On August 6, 1983, Tom Pearse, 10, and his parents, all from Ottawa, Illinois, were walking down Uncle Tom's Trail into the Grand Canyon of the Yellowstone below Lower Falls. Unfortunately for him, four concessioner employees from Grand Teton National Park had chosen that day to climb illegally in the canyon. They dislodged several rocks, including one that weighed about thirty-five pounds. It gathered momentum by falling a great distance before it struck Tom Pearse on the left side of his head.

Ranger Mike Pflaum arrived just as someone was carrying the child into the Uncle Tom's parking area. Pflaum, a park medic, immediately saw that the head injury was a bad one. "I remember feeling just terrible," says Pflaum. Tom Pearse was evacuated by helicopter and died of massive head injuries en route to the Lake Hospital.[5]

Following a search for the four men and accompanying press coverage of it, the men turned themselves in to Yellowstone rangers. They were fined twenty-five dollars each for traveling off-trail. There were no witnesses to their climbing and no apparent malicious intent, so no criminal charges were filed. (A civil lawsuit was possible, however.) The men were Richard Benedix, 19, of New Brighton, Minnesota; Greg Riddell, 19, of Denver, Colorado; Robert Johnston, 19, of Logan, Utah; and Joe Wirthlin, 19, of Sandy, Utah.[6]

A federal statute, 36 CFR 2.1(3), prohibits the throwing of rocks into canyons, valleys, or caves or off precipices in national parks. The prevention of injuries and deaths and the protection of natural resources are the good reasons for that law. Moreover, climbing in the Grand Canyon of the Yellowstone is specifically prohibited (closed area) to protect delicate rock formations there, and to prevent persons from dislodging missiles onto other persons below. Even a little rock can kill.

10

"I Think That I Shall Never See . . ."
Yellowstone's Deaths from Falling Trees

Only God can make a tree.

—Joyce Kilmer

TREES ARE LOVELY THINGS THAT remind us of the poetry of Joyce Kilmer. Certainly no one thinks of them as killers, especially while one travels through the wonderland of Yellowstone. But four, perhaps five, deaths from falling trees have occurred in the park, and at least one more occurred just outside. The incidents happened from windstorms, logging/cutting incidents, or rotting of trees.

In mentioning logging, I should say that Yellowstone has never been extensively logged for timber, because it was declared a national park by Congress before settlers arrived to begin timbering. But early in its history, limited tree cutting was allowed in places like Mammoth Hot Springs, Sepulcher Mountain, and Mount Everts to support small sawmill operations that provided lumber to build park buildings.

Little is known of the earliest death from a falling tree because we know of it only from an offhand mention in a newspaper article. It occurred in the autumn of 1893; the victim, Ike Barrows, was apparently killed by a falling tree while engaged in park road work. Prior to his death he had testified in the murder trial of Charles Northrup at Livingston, Montana (see chapter 20). When Northrup's third trial came up, Barrows was suddenly not available as a witness. The newspaper stated only that Ike Barrows "is dead, having been killed in the park last fall by a falling tree while engaged in government road work."

Also spooky was the death of Patrick Sheahan, age about 60 and a resident of Gardiner, because it, too, involved a witness in the same murder trial. Like Ike Barrows, Sheahan had testified in the first and second murder trials of Charles Northrup. Sheahan died in the same manner as Barrows and only a few months earlier. On May 13, 1893, wood contractor Frank Phiscator and his men were felling timber in a special cutting area at Mammoth above Fort Yellowstone. Sheahan and his partner Myers were cutting a tree that, in falling, struck another tree, and its course changed. As the tree hit the ground, one of its larger limbs struck Sheahan on the head, producing a concussion of the brain. At first it was believed that he was not seriously hurt, but for the next few days he grew worse and on May 20, he died. Like Barrows, he would not be available as a witness for Charles Northrup's third trial.[1]

At the turn of the century, R. N. Adams was employed by Reese Tunnel to chop timber for Tunnel's sawmill. On December 18, 1900, Adams was attempting to cut down a tree (in Tom Miner Basin outside the park, according to one report, but inside the park according to two other reports). The tree, having been once cut, was lodged against another tree as a "leaner." In axing it down, Adams miscalculated and the tree fell, catching him across his back and bearing him frightfully hard and fast to the ground. The large tree had to be chopped in two before he could be removed.[2]

Adams was taken to Livingston and then on to a hospital at Helena, Montana. He lingered there in poor health for almost a year before being taken to Oberlin, Kansas, the residence of his sister. He died there on January 23, 1902, his death being "directly traceable to the injury he received while working in the Park."[3]

Technically there was an earlier death from a falling tree, but it occurred just outside the park at Cooke City, Montana. That small town saw its origin in 1870 from a gold strike made by four prospectors, including A. Bart Henderson. The town was tiny then and remains tiny today. In 1883, George H. Eaton (whom everyone called "Major Eaton") and his assistant Selleck M. Fitzgerald were running a sawmill there in connection with Eaton's mining operation. One of Fitzgerald's teamsters, Chancey Butler, age about 21 and from Topeka, Kansas, was driving a wagon full of logs to the mill one day. One of the rear wheels struck a standing dead tree, and it fell and struck Butler on the head. A colleague reported:

> There was another man on the wagon, who, seeing the tree falling, jumped and called to Butler to look out. Butler looked up just as the tree struck him, and as his skull was not broken it is generally believed his neck was broken, as his head was bent back when the tree struck him. He was buried at 2 o'clock yesterday. There being no minister here Major Eaton officiated.[4]

Windstorms in Yellowstone Park commonly occur, usually once or twice per summer. Because 80 percent of the trees in the park are lodgepole pine, a very shallow-rooted tree, a windstorm is a major and sometimes dangerous, but completely natural, event. Trees fall over routinely in windstorms, often by the hundreds.

Robert R. Walker, 6, his parents, and two sisters of Billings, Montana, were staying in the Fishing Bridge cabins on the evening of July 7, 1936, when one of the park's windstorms struck. Robert was playing outside of their cabin when the first gusts hit about 8:00 p.m. Deafening thunder and dazzling lightning accompanied the winds, which uprooted at least 176 lodgepole pines in the nearby campground. Nineteen tents, trailers, and cartop outfits were damaged and three persons were injured.

The Walker family became alarmed at the storm and ran from their cabin only to find Robert lying outside. He had been instantly killed when a large tree came crashing to the ground and pinned him beneath it.[5]

Another park windstorm occurred four years earlier, in July of 1932, and, strangely, a windstorm occurred at Fishing Bridge almost exactly a year after Robert Walker's death, injuring two children.[6]

A third major windstorm that blew down thousands of trees and cost the park thousands of dollars occurred June 29, 1970.[7]

Yet another windstorm, in fact a rare tornado, occurred on July 12, 1984, at Elk Park and Norris. As a law enforcement ranger stationed at Norris that summer, I personally saw the funnel cloud and worked this windstorm, and I recall that it blew down hundreds of trees and blocked traffic for hours, creating a jackstraw situation east of Virginia Cascade that was later wrongly blamed on the forest fires of 1988.[8]

On September 12, 1992, a fifteen-minute windstorm toppled at least 194 lodgepole pines in the Norris Campground.[9]

While no one died in any of those storms, falling trees caused by other storms have claimed park victims. The employee of a park road contractor became another casualty of a falling tree on October 30, 1953. George R. Anderson, 36, of Saint Paul, Minnesota, died on the Norris–Canyon road while he was engaged in a road-clearing operation for the Peter Kiewit Sons Company. Anderson was assisting a crew in clearing trees from the route of a new park road, probably the Blanding Hill rerouting, when a large tree fell on him. He suffered a basal skull fracture, a crushed chest, internal injuries, and a fracture of the left leg and died instantly.[10]

The death of Carol Ann Keller from a falling tree was desperately sad. On July 29, 1984, Carol, 11, and her father Bill, the photographer for Yellowstone National Park, were gathering firewood on Daisy Pass, just outside the park to the northeast. Bill was cutting down a tree, and Carol was sitting in his truck. He called out to warn her that the tree was falling the wrong way, and Carol got out of the truck and ran. But the top fifteen feet of the large tree broke off and struck her in the head. She died very quickly.[11]

The Stephen Athan case greatly influenced the National Park Service's policies on trees in campgrounds. Park visitor Athan, 39, accompanied by his wife and 3-year-old daughter, all from California, entered Yellowstone's south entrance in the late afternoon of July 2, 1966. He was directed to the Lewis Lake Campground, where he camped in site number W-9. At 5:30 p.m., Athan erected his tent there and was standing inside when a huge lodgepole pine tree fell onto the tent and bore him to the ground. He was taken to Lake Hospital, where he died a few hours later. The tree was seventy feet long, thirteen inches in diameter, and about three hundred years old.

Stephen Athan's estate sued the government in wrongful death and won $43,750 in damages. The court ruled that the tree contained a rust canker which extended some fifty inches above the ground and which had resulted in about 70 percent of the tree rotting away. A large basal hole below the canker was clearly visible and should have been discovered by the NPS upon routine inspection. In short, the court said the tree was clearly a "hazard" tree.[12]

Regardless of how meritorious the Athan case may have been, hazard tree cases are a huge headache for the National Park Service. The NPS is caught between its and the public's desire to keep things natural and beautiful and the long-established legal duty of landowners and occupiers to inspect for dangerous conditions (primarily in campgrounds and other inhabited areas), including dangerous trees. Falling trees in city, state, and federal parks have a long history in American law. Cases are legion and go both for plaintiffs and defendants, but plaintiffs often win where they can show that a tree was in a dangerous condition for a long time and that the park had notice of it or reasonable opportunity to discover it. Landowners, including governments, have well-established duties to inspect for hidden or obvious dangers to visitors, although in some cases the Park Service can establish some kind of governmental immunity.[13]

The problem is exacerbated in campgrounds by sheer numbers of people, whose constant tramping around the trees compresses the earth unnaturally and makes the lodgepole pines even more likely to fall. Frustrated by these potential legal problems, the NPS in 1984 solved the problem at Bridge Bay by simply cutting down all of the trees in the campground.[14] Thus those persons prone to bringing meritless lawsuits have only themselves to blame if a campground is not quite as pretty as they might like. The rest of us get to suffer because of them.[15]

If, in the future, you find yourself camping in Yellowstone in a campground with no trees, you now know one possible reason. Sadly, the object of Joyce Kilmer's famous poem can be a mixed message in city, state, and national parks. To paraphrase:

I think that I shall never see,
A thing more dangerous than a tree.

A tree that may in summer wear,
A nest of lawyers in her hair.

Upon whose bosom the park can cause pain,
With great bulldozer and with crane.

Poems are made by fools like me,
But only plaintiffs can take away a tree.

11

FATAL ATTRACTION
DEATHS FROM FALLS

Fain would I climb, yet fear I to fall.

—Thomas Fuller, *Worthies of England*, 1662

It don't hurt you when you fall, only when you land!

—Michelle Shocked, from her song "Over the Waterfall"

THE TERROR OF HURTLING DOWNWARD uncontrolled through space is a bad dream that many of us have experienced in sleep. When it happens in real life, moments of gaiety become moments of catastrophe. Most of the persons who have died from falls in Yellowstone have been fatally attracted by the panoramic vista of a high and beautiful overlook only to suddenly experience a real-life nightmare. As of 2013, there have been at least thirty-six deaths from falls in Yellowstone National Park, plus a few more just outside the park. At least four persons fell from manmade structures (these could arguably be placed in the "Death by Man" section, but they are falls, so I have placed them here), five from mountain peaks, and most of the rest from heights into canyons.

Then there is the special case of a man and his wife who backed their car off the rim of the Yellowstone Grand Canyon in *Thelma and Louise* style. This one is truly hard to believe and defies categorization—is it an auto wreck or a fall? I am pronouncing it a fall, so I will start with it.

Mr. and Mrs. Earl J. Dunn of Minneapolis were visiting the canyon area on Sunday, July 13, 1924. He was aged 34 and she, the former Miss Louise Thill, was 29. At 3:30 p.m., after obtaining a grand view of the canyon at Grand View, the pair returned to their Ford coupe and started it up. They were parked at a spot about fifty feet north of Grand View, and there Mr. Dunn apparently had some difficulty turning the car around. Disaster struck in an instant. Mrs. Dunn must have screamed as she realized he had backed them off the edge of the canyon and they were falling vertically. The car fell one hundred feet and bounced mercilessly for another nearly vertical one hundred feet, finally lodging at the foot of a ledge. The two bodies continued downward, rolling and bouncing off numerous pinnacles and rock outcrops, and landing some eight hundred feet below Grand View and two hundred feet from the river. Mr. and Mrs. Dunn were mangled and broken and quite dead.[1]

Ranger Quentin Wert and Fred Hudson, a bus driver with the Yellowstone Park Transportation Company, were first on the scene, climbing into the canyon and directing the recovery work from the bottom. Wendall McLean (another YPT bus driver) and Ray Mann, the superintendent of the canyon transportation garage, both also helped in this recovery operation. The bodies were described as horribly mangled and bloody, and the Ford was barely recognizable as a car.

This truly strange occurrence not only made a front-page headline in the local newspaper, but also a prominent editorial as well. No one could figure out how it happened. An eyewitness pronounced it due to "inexperience and carelessness." The final consensus was that Mr. Dunn was simultaneously attempting to turn around in a dangerous place while backing riskily toward the canyon. An editorial written at the time was prescient when it stated that "tragedies of this sort are too soon forgotten, and too soon some other person with a venturesome spirit is likely to duplicate the terrible story told concerning the unhappy ending of a Park vacation trip."[2]

The earliest recorded instance of death from a fall in Yellowstone occurred on July 3, 1883, while the National Hotel at Mammoth Hot Springs was under construction. Two unnamed workmen there fell from a staging scaffold fifty-four feet to the floor. The hotel owners immediately sent a man fifty-seven miles north to Livingston, Montana, to engage Dr. R. D. Alton, who set out for the springs carrying his medical supplies. One of the workmen died on July 7, but the other was able to return to work after a couple of weeks of painful convalescence.[3] The dead workman would have been an excellent candidate for the first burial in the Mammoth civilian cemetery, except that Mary Foster's gravestone states that she was first to be buried at Mammoth. If the workman was buried in the cemetery later, he is in one of the unmarked and unknown graves today (see appendix A sidebar on Mammoth civilian cemetery).

Jack Davis, 48, of Daniel, Wyoming, met his death in a similar sort of incident. Davis was working on the high scaffolding of Lowdermilk Construction Company's bridge project over Lamar River at the crossing six miles east of Tower Junction. At 10:30 a.m. on Thursday, August 29, 1940, Davis stepped on a weak spot on the scaffolding, felt a bolt pull through one of the supporting timbers, and yelled as the scaffold collapsed under his weight. He plunged forty-five feet to the ground. Davis died two hours and fifteen minutes later at the Livingston Hospital.[4]

Another workman fell from a building at Mammoth. George Pugh, 23, died July 22, 1916, at 6:15 p.m. from a concussion caused by falling from a roof.[5]

On July 14, 1953, a park insurance adjuster fell from a ramp. George Ross Miller of the Yellowstone Park Company somehow managed to fall off a ramp at the Canyon Hotel. He struck the pavement twelve feet below and died on July 17.[6]

All the foregoing were accidents involving workmen, but two incidents in the Yellowstone country involved high bridges and people walking across them. Visitors and residents at Gardiner, Montana, near the park's north entrance as well as visitors at the Sheepeater Canyon Bridge just east of Mammoth often wonder as they walk across these bridges whether anyone has ever fallen from them. And indeed they have. The bridge over Yellowstone River at Gardiner is *in* town, technically outside the park, but only about a hundred yards from the park boundary. At least one person has survived a fall from this bridge, but James Byrd, 24, formerly of Lincoln, Nebraska, was not so lucky in early 2006. He and a female friend were walking home from a bar at about 2:30 a.m. on February 14, 2006, and were crossing the bridge. They split up for a minute, the woman walking ahead. She heard Byrd yell for help, ran back, and found him hanging over the railing of the bridge. She grabbed for him to try to pull him back up, and he tried to swing his leg up twice, failed both times, and fell eighty-five feet onto the rocks below. No one saw why he was hanging from the railing or how it happened, so his friend thought it a complete accident.[7]

The incident that killed a father and son at Sheepeater Canyon Bridge south of Mammoth on September 16, 2005, remains a mystery. The bridge is sometimes called the Gardner High Bridge by locals because it spans a two-hundred-foot-deep cavity over Gardner River at this point. Around 9:30 a.m. that day, park visitors Drew Webster Speedie, 50, and his 13-year-old son Brent Quinn Speedie, both of Scottsdale, Arizona, stopped at the bridge to take pictures. At about noon a visitor who could not speak English well contacted a park ranger in a patrol car to report that some sort of incident had occurred or was occurring at the bridge. Not completely understanding the visitor's report, the ranger hurriedly drove to the bridge and encountered a woman there who stated that her husband and teenaged son had gone to take a picture two and a half hours earlier and had not returned. She said she hiked a short distance looking for them but without success. The ranger began searching the area and soon discovered two bodies two hundred feet below near the river embankment.

How they died remains a mystery. The visitor who made the initial report could not be relocated, nor were there any other apparent witnesses. Park officials released statements asking anyone who might have witnessed the fall to come forward, but no one ever did. The driver of a dark-colored van seen in the area was also sought, as officials believed its driver might have information, but that person was never found either. "We just don't know what happened," said Public Affairs Officer Cheryl Matthews. "When you have something like this happen, you don't rule anything out." The possibilities that the incident was a murder-suicide, a double murder perpetrated by other passersby, a double suicide, an accident followed by a suicide, a double accident that occurred during an argument, or a double accident that happened as one person tried to rescue the other were all discussed. It seems completely bizarre not to know the answer, but that is the case for this unfortunate incident.[8]

As one might imagine, the Grand Canyon of the Yellowstone River has been the scene of many fatal falls, both at Canyon and at Tower. Early Yellowstone visitors certainly thought about falling into the canyon. Prospector A. Bart Henderson opined that it was a view to "cause anyone to shudder."[9] Another writer averred that when looking into the canyon, "an almost uncontrollable impulse comes over you to cast yourself into it."[10] Herman Haupt noted in his 1883 book of "shuddering at the prospect of a fall into such a terrible chasm."[11] And an 1897 visitor gushed shamelessly about his feelings there: "I couldn't help thinking what a thoroughly elegant place this is to commit suicide. Jump and your family would have ample time to forget you while you were reaching the bottom."[12]

Indeed, one marvels at the canyon's beauty while simultaneously being terrified of it. But this, as Phillip Terrie has told us in his *Forever Wild*, is a main characteristic of our response to wilderness—ambivalence. According to him, our reaction to wilderness is "an endlessly interesting mixture of sympathy and fear, of love and hostility, of the impulse to embrace and the equally powerful urge to flee." This is the fatal attraction.[13]

The earliest fall at the canyon (apparently a side canyon of Grand Canyon below the first road up Mount Washburn) that I have been able to find is one that occurred in 1904. In the original interment book for the Mammoth army cemetery is a notation that for some reason does not appear in the very similar book that is merely a handwritten *copy* of the original book.[14] The notation in the original book says that one John Murphy died from a fall eight hundred feet into a canyon on August 10, 1904, while working for the U.S. Engineers. The book says that the body was taken to Chicago, Illinois, probably where Murphy was from. Although John Murphy's death from this fall did not appear in local newspapers, it did appear in those farther away. A Salt Lake City newspaper carried the story five days later. Murphy had charge of a government crew working on the new park road over Dunraven Pass. "While giving directions," stated the story, "he lost his balance and fell, dropping more than 200 feet, lighting on his head on the jagged rocks below." Murphy's body was recovered with considerable difficulty.[15]

With regard to falls, naturally there were close calls at the canyon. A few made it into the local or national press, as was the case of two hikers in 1910. In that incident, college student Eli Taylor saved fellow student Erastus Borgquist from certain death on July 7. On Uncle Tom's Trail, Borgquist lost his footing when a rock gave way and rapidly slid down a steep embankment only a few feet from a five-hundred-foot precipice. Taylor grabbed his hand at the last second as he went rushing by, thus saving his life, but it still took them two more hours to climb out of the canyon.[16]

The next actual death was that of a woman. Around 1:30 p.m. on August 17, 1926, Grace Crans, 31, of Denver, Colorado, and Dr. Erhard Fuss of Windsor attempted to descend to the bottom of the canyon from a point on the south rim opposite Red Rock, which sounds like it, too, was near Uncle Tom's Trail. Park officials were later to state that descent from this point was impossible. The two proceeded down a wooded ravine for about two hundred feet below the rim and were then confronted with a vertical drop. Exploring to their left, Crans became frightened, saying she was afraid of falling, and found a seat while Dr. Fuss explored further. He abandoned the attempt upon reaching a spot some seventy-five feet below her, and was headed back up to her when he heard her cry out that she was falling. Almost instantly she hurtled past him, sliding, and then over the precipice in a vertical fall of nearly one thousand feet.

Ranger Ted Ogston and others recovered Grace Crans's body using seven hundred feet of rope. She was found to have sustained a fractured skull, the left side of her chest was entirely caved in, and she had lacerations and bruises all over her body. Her clothing was nearly abraded away.[17]

A teenager was another canyon-area victim. Sixteen-year-old Steven Robert Bailey of Tujunga, California, was exploring the area between Grand View and Inspiration Point at noon on August 14, 1964, when he fell backward and plummeted six hundred feet to his death. Two witnesses said the youth walked past car barriers over to the rim to take a picture, slipped from the edge for ten to fifteen feet, fell another fifty to sixty feet, and then tumbled hundreds of feet to the bottom of the canyon.[18]

A German woman fell from the Red Rock trail. At about 2:30 p.m. on November 8, 1965, three young female German exchange students were hiking down the Red Rock trail on the north rim of the canyon. Marita Eilers, 22, and her friends, Renate Salge and Angelika Meyers, had saved their money for this tour of the United States from their university at Hartford, Connecticut. Marita was curious, so much so that she and Salge left the established walk, disregarding signs that warned them to stay on maintained trails in order to photograph the Lower Falls. Marita lost her footing and in front of the horrified eyes of her companion she fell two hundred feet to a rock ledge. Rangers recovered her body several hours later.[19]

Another foreign woman managed to do what no one else has ever done—fall over *both* the Upper and the Lower Falls of the Yellowstone River. On June 30, 1973, Christiane (Mrs. Jean-Claude) Chabanis, 29, a resident of both Raleigh, North Carolina, and France, did the unthinkable: she fell into the Yellowstone River above the Upper Falls and was swept over its 109-foot drop.

At 10:40 a.m. that day, park visitor Lawrence Shypherd of Somerville, New Jersey, was walking down the trail to the brink of Upper Falls when he was passed by a woman going the other way. When he reached the point where the trail met the river he saw the same woman now behind him. He stated: "I saw this girl remove one sneaker. My attention was drawn elsewhere. Suddenly I heard a short scream . . . My wife said, 'There's a girl in the water.' I turned and saw a person floating in the river. By this time she was downstream toward the falls. I watched as she kept going downstream with head and one arm above water until she disappeared in the rapids."

At 10:50 a.m., Frederick Bahr of Oakdale, New York, and other witnesses were on the brink of the Lower Falls trail. Bahr reported seeing a woman with long black hair and white slacks floating face down in the river. His party saw the body float to the brink of Lower Falls and fall over its 308-foot drop. Technically it is not known whether Chabanis died of drowning or the fall. Regardless, she was probably dead by the time she hit the bottom of the first waterfall. Of course, her death might have been caused by drowning, but the drop alone could have killed her.[20]

Another north-rim fall occurred at the brink of Upper Falls, and it was a desperately sad affair. Corey L., 22, and Laurie Miller, 20, of Murray, Utah, were newlyweds five days into their marriage and on their honeymoon. At about 4:45 p.m. on September 1, 1983, they arrived at the brink of the Upper Falls parking area. Laurie went to the edge of the canyon about one hundred yards from the parking lot. She climbed over or around several large boulders, skirted a live tree, and ducked under a fallen tree to reach a sloping rock on the very edge of the canyon. Laurie directed Corey to get on a rock so she could take his picture, and to do that she had to have her back to the canyon. Corey stated later that he was facing away from her, and as he turned toward her he heard her say "Corey!" She was not there when he finished turning. Racing to the edge he looked down and saw her lying one hundred feet below and not moving. Laurie had apparently backed up to get a better view and did not see the edge of the canyon. She died the next night of massive head injuries.[21]

Laurie Miller was unconscious but still alive when rangers Mike Pflaum and John Osgood arrived on the scene. Pflaum recalls the affair as a "strange incident." It was one that "we never could figure out just how it happened." A board of inquiry determined that Laurie Miller had drunk some whiskey and had taken some Valium just prior to the incident and that she had been wearing thong sandals. Her judgment and coordination may have been impaired by the alcohol and the medicine, and her footing may have been impaired by the sandals.[22]

Two young boys died from falling into the Grand Canyon of the Yellowstone in 1988 and 1990 incidents. On August 6, 1988, at 5:30 p.m., Dennis B. Rumple, 7, of Scottsberg, Indiana, was hiking on Uncle Tom's Trail on the canyon's south rim with his parents and grandparents. Dennis was excited to have his grandparents giving him this tour because they were park employees at Grant Village. The party had stopped at a rest platform halfway up the metal walkway's steps, and Dennis's older brother had gone on ahead. Dennis was playing, standing on a bench to get his brother's attention. During a moment when his parents were not watching, he slipped through or over the bars of the railing. He plunged into a gully on the side of the canyon, bouncing some 220 feet nearly to the bottom. Dennis Rumple sustained a broken arm, a broken leg, serious head injuries, and internal bleeding.

The recovery effort was elaborate and stunning. Ranger Stephen Dobert remembers that the helicopter stopped abruptly in midair in order for the litter ropes to swing into position for the rangers to grab them in the difficult gully where David had fallen. But it was to no avail. David died the next evening in an Idaho Falls hospital.[23]

One and one-half years later, 11-year-old David Childers became Yellowstone's first fall death to occur in winter. He, his parents, and his younger brother, all from nearby Livingston, Montana, took a late winter outing in February of 1990. They snowmobiled to the canyon on February 25, and David and his brother raced down the snow-covered trail to the brink of Lower Falls. The route was slippery and rutted, full of the snow holes of previous walkers. Unsupervised, David and his brother ran on far ahead of their party, their father having gone to Fishing Bridge to get fuel for their snowmobiles. David was exhilarated by the frosty air, the deep snow, and the natural beauty all around him. He had been on this same trail the previous summer, so perhaps he was overconfident and could not wait to view the spectacular canyon, where the falls plunge 308 feet into the hazy color of the majestic yet sobering abyss. David slipped and fell once, got to his feet, and continued running. He ran to the viewpoint platform just above the brink of one of America's tallest waterfalls. He slipped again. But this time there was no recovery. David was falling through hundreds of feet of cold air. If he had time to see the huge ice cone rushing up to meet him, it was the last thing he ever saw.

Ranger Andy Fisher hung from a line attached to a helicopter, the winds whipping all around him. It was his job to recover David's body, and it was not fun that day to be a ranger in Yellowstone.[24]

David's parents, Robert and Mary Beth Childers, filed a ten-million-dollar lawsuit against Yellowstone National Park. They alleged that the park was negligent in failing to post warning signs at the trailhead. In July of 1993, following a trial, U.S. District Court judge Jack Shanstrom at Billings, Montana, rejected every legal claim of the Childers family. Shanstrom found that the Park Service decision not to place warning signs was made by employees exercising their "discretionary function" and thus the government was immune from the lawsuit. Shanstrom also ruled that Wyoming's recreational use statute barred the lawsuit as well, as it states that plaintiffs cannot make claims for injuries when a landowner does not charge the person who enters his land for recreational purposes (the park does not charge persons under the age of 16 to enter).

But Shanstrom went further than merely granting the government immunity. He stated that the NPS's admonitions in handout literature and maps as well as from rangers stationed in the area provided adequate warnings to the public. The judge found that the Park Service was not required to give warnings about common snow and ice, and he castigated the boy's parents:

> Mrs. Childers . . . negligently permitted the boys to get out of her sight. While it is not reasonable to expect that 11 and 13-year-old boys would hold their mother's hand while walking down a trail, common sense dictates that youngsters in Yellowstone should be kept within sight. This basic precaution was not followed in this case. Indeed, the evidence indicates that the boys were fully 467.5 feet, or approximately three switchbacks in front of the mother while they were on the observation deck. [This caused them to] feel more secure at a time when common sense indicated that caution was appropriate. The actions of the Childers were all the more unreasonable [because] they understood that the trail to the Brink of the Lower Falls was steep, and that there was a sharp drop off from the observation decks, since they had hiked down it the year before.

And significantly for the park, Judge Shanstrom added a statement about visitor responsibility: "Courts have uniformly required visitors to Yellowstone to exercise common sense when dealing with natural conditions."[25] One, of course, instinctively feels terribly sorry for the Childerses' loss. But the park was not at fault.

The death of Isadore Morris Kisber occurred in a climbing accident. On July 7, 1925, at about 5:30 p.m., the 18-year-old Kisber, of Jackson, Tennessee, and his friend K. V. Jenkins were climbing in the canyon of Tower Creek just below Tower Fall and above the place where Tower Creek enters Yellowstone River. In attempting to ascend the south wall from a point just below the falls,

Kisber dislodged a boulder that he was holding onto for support and fell fifty feet onto rocks. Taken to Mammoth Hospital for treatment of a fractured skull, Kisber lingered nine days before finally dying on July 16.[26]

Visitors in 1995 and 1999 died near Grand View when they stepped over warning barriers or ignored warning signs. Three men from Slovakia hired a translator from Bozeman to guide them through the park in September of 1995 to celebrate the fiftieth birthdays of all three. At around 5:00 p.m. on September 17, the translator dropped them off at Grand View intending to pick them back up at Lookout Point. While the three were walking along the road, 50-year-old Milan Kapusta of Banska Stiavnica approached the canyon's edge to take pictures with a video camera. He stepped over a log barrier, slipped, lost his balance, and fell some four hundred feet into the canyon. His companions, who witnessed the incident, stated "that he had been filming with a video camera at the time of the incident and might have been trying to get a better picture" when he "walked beyond warning signs." He was fluent in English, which suggests that he was able to read the sign.[27]

Four years later, on September 4, 1999, 74-year-old Norma Norton Vaughn of Billings, Montana, left her husband in the car when they parked at Grand View overlook at 1:30 p.m. and walked directly from the vehicle to the canyon. She walked past a warning sign, slipped on loose rock and dirt at the edge of the canyon, and fell eighty feet to a stop. She then continued rolling another 420 feet on into the canyon. Helicopter occupants spotted the victim at about 4:00 p.m. lying five hundred feet below the overlook. Recovery was delayed until the following morning due to lateness of the hour and high winds in the canyon. No one had seen her fall.[28]

A recent falling fatality broke the hearts of many park employees, because the girl was one of us and had just arrived to work in the park. Eighteen-year-old Maria "Masha" Sergeyevna Rumyantseva of Kaliningrad, Russia, was hiking with three friends near Inspiration Point just before 6:00 p.m. on June 7, 2012, when she ventured off-trail onto a rock ledge. It broke loose under her, and she fell four hundred feet into the canyon. It was her very first day in Yellowstone.[29]

Another recent falling fatality took the life of a young Cornell graduate who was working in Gardiner, Montana, at a local business. Twenty-three-year-old Joseph Austin Parker of Valdosta, Georgia, made the mistake of hiking alone in Yellowstone, and one wonders whether anyone cautioned him against doing that. He picked a monstrous hike for his first one, namely the ascent of nearby Electric Peak (elevation 10,992 feet) on July 16, 2013. Parker called some friends at 2:30 p.m. via cell phone to tell them that he was just below the summit of the mountain and that because of nearby lightning, he was starting to descend. Instead, it appears that he fell and suffered fatal head injuries.

Rangers found him two days later while on an aerial search. His chances of surviving might have been better if he had not been alone.[30]

Six persons (including Isadore Kisber, already mentioned) have met their deaths in the park by hurtling into the Grand Canyon of the Yellowstone River (or into side canyons) about twenty miles downstream from Lower Falls. The Tower area, with its beautiful columns, spires, pinnacles, and scree slopes that captivate viewers, has probably hypnotized several persons into not watching their footsteps and thus becoming the victims of a fatal attraction. Robert L. Landram, 31, of Salt Lake City was one of these who fell into the canyon just north of Overhanging Cliff while trying to get a better view of the high, panoramic overlook there. Landram died on July 19, 1955, at about 7:30 p.m., when he fell about 490 feet from a ledge at the stone wall near the tall spire known as the Needle. Two companions, William Brown and R. C. Corr, said Landram missed a tree while descending to a clump of trees at the edge of the precipice. He went over the ledge, fell 130 feet and hit another ledge, and then fell the remaining 360 feet into the Yellowstone River. His body washed downstream and was never recovered. A photo of the spot reveals it as one that no prudent person should have approached.[31]

Others could not resist it either. An 18-year-old Naples, Florida, youth actually climbed over a retaining wall near the same spot where Landram fell. On June 28, 1973, Victor Ivan Songer succumbed to the temptation of getting a better picture and stepped over the stone wall at the roadside to stand on the slippery rock slope above the canyon. He lost his footing and plunged 350 feet into the Yellowstone River. His body was recovered eleven days later.[32]

Nearly the same thing happened to 54-year-old Lois J. Mayer on August 15, 1978. At 10:50 a.m., the Dayton, Ohio, woman climbed over the stone retainer wall at Overhanging Cliff to get a better view, and apparently slipped in loose ground. She fell about 150 feet and then slid an additional 150 feet on a steep slope into the Yellowstone River. Her body was not recovered until weeks later.[33]

This precipitous spot that some visitors cannot resist was the site of two more deaths, both of them women, in 2006 and 2007. Deborah Chamberlin, 52, of Rockford, Michigan, stepped over the rock retaining wall to look at the canyon at about 10:00 a.m. and fell five hundred feet to her death on June 17, 2006. Her husband flagged down a passing motorist, who called 911. The other incident happened late Friday afternoon, September 28, 2007, when 32-year-old Charlotte Harrison of Beverly Hills, California, who was traveling with a 39-year-old boyfriend from Los Angeles, stopped to take pictures at a pullout near Calcite Springs. She fell from the cliff. Rangers received the report about 6:30 p.m., and when they arrived they could see her lying motionless on the canyon floor. Due to darkness, steep terrain, and the complex nature of this

The Grand Canyon of the Yellowstone (courtesy of Yellowstone National Park)

type of operation, park staff had to wait until the following morning to recover Harrison's body. Family and friends soon flew in to retrieve the deceased and console her male friend. The established lesson for this spot and for any comparable place in Yellowstone is this one—*do not climb over any retaining wall . . . ever!*[34]

A Colorado man was killed at Lewis River Canyon. On September 14, 1974, at 11:00 a.m., Anthony Joseph Haschke, 51, of Inglewood, Colorado, stopped on the main park road 6.6 miles north of the south entrance to view the canyon with his wife, Corine. He climbed over a guardrail and walked out onto a pinnacle. Wanting a better view, Haschke jumped to another rock, lost his balance, and fell backward. His wife watched him plummet three hundred feet to an instant death.[35]

A fall occurred at Kepler Cascades on May 17, 1976. Lawrence Crawford, 19, of Concord, California, and two companions, all employees of the Yellowstone Park Company, were climbing the steep walls of the canyon known as Devil's Gate below those cascades. While momentarily out of the sight of his friends, Crawford apparently slipped and fell sixty feet to his death.[36]

Raymond Guntz's death happened at Undine Falls near Mammoth Hot Springs. On August 16, 1980, Guntz, 37, from Indiana, and his wife Suzanne, stopped at Undine Falls overlook and began a short hike to take pictures of the sixty-foot waterfall. At about 3:00 p.m., Guntz slipped and fell 150 feet into the canyon of Lava Creek. Another visitor, Robert Bower of Idaho Falls, by chance an expert climber, immediately climbed down the steep, grassy slope to the stream to help Guntz, who was still alive. Bower found him lying partially in the creek unconscious, gave him mouth-to-mouth resuscitation, and decided he had severe internal injuries.

"He was the classic tourist out of his element," remembers Bower. "He had smooth street shoes and polyester on. There wasn't much else I could do." Guntz died at 6:50 p.m., during the evacuation.[37]

There were no witnesses to the death of David Haller, 11, on July 25, 1984. David, of Grand Island, New York, and nine other boys were visiting Yellowstone on a vacation tour. The group stopped at 7:15 p.m. at Firehole Falls in Firehole Canyon to view the place. No one is quite sure what happened, but apparently David was climbing a rock wall when he fell.[38] Helicoptered to a hospital at Idaho Falls, David Haller died a few hours later.

At least five young men have died climbing Yellowstone's mountains. Three were park visitors and two were park employees. David Rasmussen, 18, a visitor from Miami, Florida, went hiking with his friend Stuart Rucker, 23, of Norman, Oklahoma, on July 30, 1969. The two were in the northwestern corner of the park between 5:00 and 6:00 p.m. on Big Horn Peak when Rasmussen fell from a cliff. Rucker hiked out alone to get help. Nightfall and remoteness of the area precluded recovery until the following afternoon, when park ranger Floyd Klang reached Rasmussen's body.[39]

Albert Paul Knight, called Paul by his parents and friends, was a young man who loved nature and the environment. He spent hours planning his backpacking trips into Yellowstone from his faraway Warren, New Jersey, home. Paul and a single male companion hiked into the Slough Creek country on June 19, 1985, heading toward a 10,691-foot peak on the park north boundary called Cutoff Peak. For unknown reasons, Paul and his friend split up at some point, apparently intending to meet when they both reached the summit. When Paul's friend reached the summit, Paul was not there. His friend waited and waited. Paul did not show up. His friend found Paul's tracks in a snowfield on a spur of Cutoff Mountain, but no Paul, so he hiked out and contacted the rangers.

Rangers Mike Robinson and Jeff Henry were helicoptered in with Jeff's tracking dog, Hoss, on June 21. Paul had been missing for two days. They began searching, along with some two dozen other park personnel. Jeff remembers having to lift his dog from one ledge to another, so rough was the country. But on Friday, June 21, Jeff's dog found Paul's body at the foot of a vertical ridge. The crumpled position of his body told Jeff at once that Paul was dead. He had fallen about 110 feet, apparently landing on his head and neck. He probably died instantly. Jeff remembers feeling extremely badly for Paul's parents, because he knew Paul was the only child of a close family.[40]

Almost exactly a month later, Kent Shane Rich, 22, of Muscle Shoals, Alabama, a park employee at Lake Lodge, began a solitary hiking trip into Yellowstone's backcountry. Interestingly, one of Shane's roommates at Lake was John Mark Williams, who would later die from hot-spring burns at Shoshone Geyser Basin. Another of Shane's roommates, this one at Mallard Dorm, was Kyle Hannon. Both Hannon and friend Brian Kruse remember Shane as a great guy. "He was a born-again Christian Southern redneck who loved Copenhagen and country music," says Kyle. "I was a hard-drinking Midwestern agnostic who preferred Duran Duran. Nevertheless we got along fine . . . He was funny, outspoken and confident." Kyle says Shane loved the adventure of gaining summits and then choosing a more direct way down.

Perhaps that habit did him in. Shane, against the standard warnings of the park and other employees, elected to hike alone into the northeast country near the Thunderer, a peak with an elevation of 10,554 feet. No one knows exactly what happened to Shane Rich, but this author can personally testify from years of looking for waterfalls on the Thunderer that the rock up there is a nightmarish, crumbly, andesitic talus. When he failed to return, a search was instituted. A helicopter crew spotted his body on a north slope of the mountain at 7:00 p.m. on June 22, 1985, probably the day he died. Shane had made it to the very top of the mountain. For some reason he fell from the summit, in a plunge of about six hundred feet. Both Kyle and Brian vividly remember being with him the day before Shane went to the Thunderer. Driving a car containing the two others, Brian slammed on his brakes in Hayden Valley to avoid rear-ending a buffalo-gazing tourist. "When the truck stopped, just shy of someone's bumper," said Kyle, "Shane turned to Brian and said, in his heavy southern drawl, 'Brian, if I die out here I want it to be from falling off a cliff, not from some car wreck.'" Following Shane's death, it took Kyle several days to ask Brian whether he remembered what Shane had said. "It was too painful," recalled Kyle. But Brian *did* remember.[41]

Brendan O'Connor's death fall happened just outside of the park in the Beartooth Range. O'Connor, 22, a T. W. Services employee at Old Faithful, went hiking in July of 1988 in an apparent attempt to scale Fox Peak, elevation 11,245 feet. When he failed to return to work, a search was begun, but searchers could not find him. A year later, on July 21, 1989, a hiker found a body near a trail below Fox Peak. Investigators identified it as O'Connor through dental records, and postulated that he had scaled the mountain. He apparently fell from the summit in a two-hundred-foot drop onto a ledge, dying instantly from massive head injuries. His body was lodged there until spring freshets washed it down a slope nearly a year later. A footprint on the summit attested to his having gained the top.[42]

Gary Lee Brockway, 43, a visitor from Maplewood, Minnesota, decided to climb Tuff Cliff near Madison Junction on September 8, 1995. He was free climbing without ropes or a helmet late in the afternoon when suddenly he lost his footing and fell vertically about one hundred feet. Sustaining massive and multiple head, chest, and extremity injuries, Brockway was pronounced dead by rangers at the scene at 5:30 p.m.[43]

The winter sport of ice climbing took two climbers' lives on Saturday, May 23, 2010. Mark William Ehrich, 28, and Michael Alan Kellch, 29, both of Bozeman, Montana, were experienced ice climbers who arrived in the park that day and hiked into Surface Creek from Artist Point with their equipment. Intending to climb the ice on the twelve-hundred-foot-tall Silver Cord Cascade, the two appear to have begun descending into the Grand Canyon of the Yellowstone. The end of May is quite late in Yellowstone's winter, and the ice was apparently weakened by melting. Ehrich and Kellch were climbing the frozen waterfall when its ice crumbled and they fell. When the men failed to return on Monday, friends reported them missing and park rangers began a search. Spotting an immobile person and climbing gear from a north-rim viewpoint, rescuers rappelled into the canyon from the south rim and found the two men dead on a rock ledge about three hundred feet below the rim. Darkness fell, impeding the rescuers, and the climbers' bodies were not recovered until the following day (Tuesday).[44]

Even a park ranger died in a fall in the Yellowstone region, although it technically did not happen in the park. Park ranger Charles C. White, 27, was killed in a fall on Cinnabar Mountain, just north of the park boundary, while deer hunting on November 13, 1945.[45] Aubrey Haines was a park ranger at that time, and he remembered that White was hiking down the Devil's Slide. "That was a miserable, mean place to get a body out of," said Aubrey, "but he shouldn't have been out there anyhow" because "he had a trick knee" that made him "not really fit for outdoor work." White was a wartime fill-in for the rangers. Haines was the first ranger back from the war, and he says that at that time "Charley already had his termination notice; he was going back to New York."[46] Perhaps White's bad knee was the cause of his fall.

A final death from a fall (if it was from a fall) is bound up in an unsolved mystery that happened just north of Yellowstone National Park. In the early 1890s, Maggie and Morgan T. "Bud" Williams lived at Horr, Montana, where they fought with each other constantly. When Bud, a raucous rounder, disappeared in 1895, Maggie was relieved and turned her attentions to the village blacksmith, Frank Holem. Two years later, 11-year-old Ida Miller and her mother moved into the Williams's little house at the foot of Cinnabar Mountain. Walking around the house one day, little Ida fell into a deep hole nearby.

Another ranger shown standing where ranger Charles White suffered a fatal fall at Cinnabar Mountain north of the park on November 13, 1945 (NPS photo #27047, YNP Archives)

The hole, filled with brush and dead leaves, scared Ida silly, but she decided to explore it further. In the bottom of the hole Ida found a side tunnel, which led to a door. Prying it open, the little girl found that it led into a cellar. She saw a human bone and then another and then the entire skeleton. Ida took bones up to her mother, who became fearful. When their neighbors, Mr. and Mrs. Allen, visited them that night and were shown the bones, Mr. Allen proclaimed knowingly, "Everybody wondered what became of Bud Williams." Pointing to the ceiling, Mr. Allen showed Ida and her mother the many bullet holes there. "Those," said he, "is where Bud used to shoot at Maggie when she was up there and he was down here. Used to keep her dodging pretty fast to miss them." Did Maggie Williams kill Bud Williams? Or did he simply suffer a fall into the cellar when she was away? Or did one of his own shots ricochet and kill him?[47]

It is a great story with a fascinating cliffhanger. The problem with it is that Morgan T. "Bud" Williams's disappearance has now been linked to moving elsewhere rather than death. The *Livingston Enterprise* for August 7, 1897 (p. 2) noted that he was involved in copper mining at Castle, Montana. So whose skeleton did little Ida Miller find? We may never know.

Falls generally are true accidents, or are caused by negligence. They often occur unexpectedly due to a moment of carelessness or inattention. The deaths of Knight, Rich, White, and O'Connor occurred when the parties were alone, three choosing that status and one splitting up from his companion. Obviously, there is no chance of help when one is alone. And two persons can look out for each other more efficiently than one can. I reiterate: never hike alone in Yellowstone country. On the other hand, hiking in pairs cannot by itself prevent tragedy, as the Rasmussen death and the more recent deaths of the two ice climbers make clear.

Sudden plunges can happen to anyone while looking at a waterfall, staring into a canyon, or climbing a height. And there are plenty of places in Yellowstone where one can become the victim of this kind of fatal attraction.

12

DEATHS FROM FOREST FIRES
SMOKE CHASING CAN KILL

Fire is an event, not an element.

—Stephen Pyne, *Fire in America*

His eyes are bloodshot, his back near broke,
For he has been chasing a distant smoke.

—Charles Scribner, "A Smoke Chaser," 1929

CONSIDERING THE EXTENT AND POWER of the 1988 forest fires in Yellowstone National Park, it is amazing that no one died in the park from them. A fire-related airplane crash on September 11, just south of the park at Jackson, killed pilot Don Kuykendall. And Clover Mist firefighter Ed Hutton, 26, of Casper, Wyoming, a Bureau of Land Management employee, died on October 11, 1988, when a seventy-two-foot burning snag fell and hit him during mop-up operations in Shoshone National Forest. Firefighters were injured in Yellowstone, but no one died.[1]

A 1940 fire, however, did take a life. Civilian Conservation Corps (CCC) worker James Hester, 19, of Norwood, Ohio, lost his life while fighting the Chipmunk Creek fire on June 22, 1940. Hester was killed eight miles south of Yellowstone Lake when a blazing snag fell and hit him. His fellow firefighter, Clifford Otey of Akron, Ohio, was simultaneously injured. Some four hundred men under chief park ranger Francis LaNoue were battling that fire, which at the time was considered "one of the worst in the history of Wonderland."[2]

Another horrible fire incident took the lives of fifteen firefighters and injured thirty-nine others of the CCC and U.S. Forest Service on August 21, 1937, at a place on Blackwater Creek just outside the park to the east. The

Blackwater Fire deaths are today commemorated by a firefighters' memorial located about fifteen miles east of the park's east entrance. A sudden windstorm whipped up that fire, killing eight men at Clayton Gulch and seven more along the stream. Signs and monuments now mark the important locations along the Blackwater Creek trail where the incidents occurred. Technician Rex A. Hale Jr. was one of those killed, and a Forest Service campground near there today bears his name. Updrafts from that fire were so powerful that Yellowstone Park Transportation Company bus driver Gerry Pesman found charred spruce needles on the hood of his bus in Cody, Wyoming, some thirty-six miles away.[3]

Following the fires of 1988, park rangers warned visitors constantly about the dangers of entering freshly burned areas. Standing burned trees can fall without a sound. And of course, staying out of a burning area is self-evident.

Andrew Mitchell, a Yellowstone fire supervisor who was present at many of 1988's most severe fire incidents, states: "It is a tribute to the fire managers' organizational skills and to the woodsmanship and training of individual firefighters that during the 1988 fire season only one death occurred and it was outside the park. The thousands of firefighters and hundreds of vehicles and aircraft plus park visitors created an extremely high potential for tragedy."

There have been numerous forest fires in Yellowstone since 1988, but so far there have been no human fatalities caused by them.

13

THE GLOOM OF EARTHQUAKES
SHAKY BREAKY PARK

. . . the gloom of earthquake.

—Shelley, "The Revolt of Islam"

EARTHQUAKES OCCUR IN Yellowstone National Park nearly every day. The area is so seismically active that on an earthquake map of the United States where quakes are represented as hundreds of tiny black dots, Yellowstone Park is represented as a huge black square. Newspapers like the *Livingston Enterprise* are loaded with references to earthquakes in the park even as early as the 1880s.

No deaths from earthquakes have as yet occurred in Yellowstone. However, the largest known quake in the Yellowstone region, which occurred at 11:37 p.m. on August 17, 1959, and measured 7.5 on the Richter scale, killed twenty-eight people in the Madison Canyon just northwest of the park. Those stories have been well told in Edmund Christopherson's *The Night the Mountain Fell* (1960), in William Fischer's *Earthquake: Yellowstone's Living Geology* (1960), and in Richard Bartlett's *Nature's Yellowstone* (1974).

14

DANGER IN THE WATER
DEATHS FROM DROWNING

Lord, Lord! methought, what pain it was to drown;
What dreadful noise of waters in mine ears!
What ugly sights of death within mine eyes!

—Shakespeare, *King Richard III*

THERE ARE MORE DEATHS in this category than for any other in Yellowstone National Park, except for auto/snowmobile wrecks and illness, neither of which is included in this book. More than one hundred persons have heard Shakespeare's "dreadful noise of waters" in their ears before they drowned in Yellowstone.

The earliest known drowning in Yellowstone was that of Matthew J. Carey on August 22, 1880. Called by the Bozeman newspaper an "estimable young man" from Adobe Town (near Virginia City), Montana, he drowned in Firehole River, exact location unknown, while "making a tour of the National Park" with others, probably on horseback. He "went into a deep hole in the river to swim," stated the newspaper. "Suddenly he sank in about twelve feet of water, and although he was taken out soon after, his comrades found it impossible to resuscitate him." Three years later, friends or relatives disinterred his body and moved it to the Catholic cemetery in Dillon, Montana.[1]

Two more early drownings in Yellowstone happened in a single incident in 1883. John H. Fogerty and Thomas P. Parker, ages unknown, were traveling together in the park. At Excelsior Geyser they met Franklin Bauers and Amos Fisher, and the four men traveled together for several days. On August 15, 1883, according to Fisher and Bauers, the four men were attempting to cross the Yellowstone River from the east side to the west side at a point just below Yellowstone Lake. Bauers stated that Fogerty and Parker (must have) disappeared just before he looked up and noticed they were gone. Their horses turned and swam back to shore, said Bauers, looking "as if they had been in deep water, as the saddles were wet on top." Fisher stated that he heard no outcry from the drowning men.[2]

Fisher and Bauers took the two men's horses and returned to Livingston, Montana, where they told the story. Local law enforcement officers at first did not believe the men and so arrested them on suspicion of murder charges. But as no case could be made, they were eventually set free.

When their bodies were found, Fogerty and Parker were hastily buried near present Fishing Bridge. A year later Dan Parker, a relative of one of the deceased, traveled to the lake to exhume the bodies and rebury them at Mammoth in the civilian cemetery. There they were interred in the only grave with a footstone. The footstone today still bears the initials "J. F." and "T.P.P.," but the headstone, which was there in 1947, is gone today. Little is known about either of the men except that Parker's family owned a boardinghouse at Gardiner, Montana, and later a ranch on Eagle Creek.[3]

As one might expect, a number of drownings have occurred in the park from swimming accidents, in both natural bodies of water and park swimming pools (during the days when the park had swimming pools).[4] Thomas Brennan, a stock herder for the hotel company at Mammoth Hot Springs, drowned in Bath Lake on the afternoon of June 24, 1889. His body was found floating about two hours after he went for a bath.[5] Private Harry E. Donaldson, a soldier at Fort Yellowstone, also drowned in Mammoth's Bath Lake, on April 10, 1898. He had gone swimming alone in an attempt to treat his rheumatism.[6] Another park employee, Louis Jongenel, drowned on or about August 27, 1899, in a different Bath Lake. That body of water at Lower Geyser Basin is today known also as Ranger Pool, and Jongenel, of Washburn, Wisconsin, was an employee of the nearby Fountain Hotel.[7] Ed W. Davies, 18, of Sheridan, Montana, lost his life on September 2, 1905, while swimming with two companions in the Madison River at Riverside near the park west entrance.[8] A really unusual drowning involved an infant—probably the area's youngest drowning victim ever—and an irrigation ditch. The *Gardiner Wonderland* newspaper reported that it occurred in Jardine, Montana (just above Gardiner) on July 24, 1905, "in a large irrigating ditch that runs through Jardine." Fifteen-month-old Vera Downs—daughter of Mr. and Mrs. Elmer Downs—was being supervised by her older sister when the girl set the baby down so that the sitter could pick up stones along the stream. When she returned, the baby was gone, and a subsequent search revealed her body about one hundred feet from where she had fallen into the ditch.[9]

Whether or not Oliver Adkins's death and that of Peter S. Christensen were swimming fatalities is not certain, but probably they were. Adkins, age about 23, disappeared from Gardiner, Montana, on March 20, 1905, and was missing for more than two months. His large family there merely thought he had gone somewhere else for employment. However, in late May, Adkins's body was found floating in "Lake Cinnabar," probably one of the small lakes on Landslide Creek south of Gardiner. An inquest determined that he had drowned there. His brothers Melvin and Ernest believed ever after that Oliver was somehow murdered by the bad crowd with whom he ran, but that was never proven. Peter Christensen, a park employee from York, Nebraska, drowned in the park in an unknown location on or about June 6, 1906. His body was not immediately recovered. Only three months earlier, he had been sworn in as a U.S. citizen.[10]

At least four persons have drowned in park swimming pools—three at Old Faithful and one at Mammoth. Ernest Hansen, 22, of Brown Valley, Minnesota, an employee of the Jardine Mining Company, drowned in the Mammoth swimming pool on August 16, 1925, sometime between 5:00 p.m. and 7:00 p.m. while he was swimming alone. Wilfred Karls, 20, of Molt, Montana, drowned in the Old Faithful pool on July 7, 1937. Unable to swim, Karls was hanging onto the side of the pool, and his subsequent shouts for help were misinterpreted by others as being part of a water polo game in progress. Kenneth Chandler, 12, of West Yellowstone, Montana, drowned in the Old Faithful pool on August 25, 1937, when he apparently fainted (he was subject to fainting spells and his mother had thus asked him not to go into the water). And Lois Pallesen, 11, of Neligh, Nebraska, drowned in the Old Faithful pool at 6:45 p.m. on July 28, 1947. No one saw her go under, and when she was pulled from the water artificial resuscitation was attempted for four hours, to no avail.[11]

Swimming, of course, was not the only way people could drown. A total of three soldiers from Fort Yellowstone were drowning victims in 1910 and 1918. Private Frank F. Monaghan of Company H, First Cavalry, was reported as a deserter on December 1, 1910, after he disappeared from the post. His body, clothed in army khaki, was found by Gardiner resident Albert Spiker on January 8, 1911, who encountered it while fishing on Gardner River about a mile above its mouth. Monaghan's drowning was attributed to intoxication on or about November 22, 1910.[12] And a double tragedy occurred on July 21, 1918, ironically just when the army was leaving Yellowstone at the very end of its long tenure. Sergeant Arthur S. Brewer, 29, of Philadelphia, Pennsylvania, and Private Victor Manterfield, 19, of Maryland, both of Troop C, were drowned when their boat overturned on Trout Lake (then sometimes called Fish Lake) near the Soda Butte Soldier Station. The men were fishing with two other soldiers, and apparently the boat was in very poor condition. The other two men managed to swim to shore when it capsized.[13]

A very sad drowning occurred in 1899. Mrs. Louis Helbut was returning on June 26 from Gardiner to Cooke City, where her husband worked for a mine. Because one span of Baronett's Bridge was out, she, J. P. Allen, and Frank Lynch crossed the river successfully on a log they found for a footbridge. According to the newspaper, they continued east to "Tate Creek" (probably the first creek south of Pebble Creek, near J. B. Tate's squatting site five miles above Soda Butte), described as "a small stream which is readily forded at all seasons of the year." There they found another log to use as a footbridge. Mrs. Helbut had been subject to fainting spells, and she apparently swooned and fell into the stream. She was washed down under the willows that skirted both banks of the creek and could not be found. Allen and Lynch went on to Cooke City and reported the sad incident. Mrs. Helbut's husband went to the scene much bereaved and recovered her body, burying it temporarily on the banks of the stream. He then went to Livingston, secured a casket, returned for her body, and brought it back to Livingston, where she was buried in Mountain View Cemetery. The soldier who made the entry in the Soda Butte station log believed that the stream involved was Pebble Creek.[14]

So important and touching was the drowning of the socially prominent Walter Shaw of Gardiner, Montana, that several hardened stagecoach drivers remembered it vividly thirty-six years later. Walter Shaw, age about 46, was the son of Amos Shaw, president of the Shaw and Powell Camping Company in Yellowstone Park. Raised in that environment, Walter followed in his father's footsteps, and was himself operating a camp for tourists at Grasshopper Glacier near Cooke City, Montana, while he simultaneously ran the Shaw Hotel at Gardiner. During the off season, he promoted his family's enterprise by speaking in the East. Walter Shaw was drowned in a horse accident at the "Turkey Pen crossing" of Gardner River, also known as Soldiers' Ford.

On the morning of June 19, 1925, Walter Shaw, his daughter Louise Shaw, Grace Johnson, and three other men left Gardiner heading into the park, driving twenty-four horses and bound for the Shaw's Camp near Cooke City, Montana. After passing through the new ranger check station near the arch, they proceeded to the ford of the Gardner River about one mile south, near the present Rescue Creek footbridge. Before driving the horses across, Shaw assisted the girls in crossing on their horses and then started back across the stream to help the men. According to Herb French, Shaw's horse slipped, threw its head back, and clipped Walter, throwing him into the stream. Stage driver Johnny McPherson saw the incident and said Walter tried to grab for a tree branch but missed, and the stream was running very high.[15]

There was considerable uncertainty as to exactly how the incident occurred. The local newspaper stated that Shaw "was swept from his mount when the horse stumbled and was either stunned when he struck a rock or the horse trampled him as it attempted to regain its feet." Regardless, he appeared to have been riding the horse without a saddle. Shaw's body was quickly carried downstream into the Yellowstone River and was found several days later some thirty miles north near Emigrant, Montana. He left a large family, including a wife and three daughters, two parents, and four siblings, most of them in the town of Gardiner.[16]

At least seven persons have drowned in Yellowstone National Park because of car wrecks, and six of those wrecks occurred in Gardner River between Mammoth Hot Springs and Gardiner, Montana. Gertrude L. Tomasko, 24, a park employee of Mammoth Hotel from Minneapolis (September 19, 1925);[17] Albert Collins, a park electrician of Mammoth (December 22, 1926);[18] Charles E. Strombaugh, 27, of Buhl, Idaho (July 20, 1935);[19] Ralph L. Johnson, 39, a park employee from Los Angeles (June 24–25, 1952);[20] Mark Dallas Swift, 19, a park employee from Great Falls, Montana (June 28, 1974);[21] and Lisa Cavagnaro, 20, a park employee from Berlin, New Hampshire (June 27, 1982) all were in cars that ran into the Gardner River. Ironically, the last of these, Lisa Cavagnaro, was always afraid to drive in Gardner Canyon, as she told people on numerous occasions that she was afraid of the river.[22] Additionally, Charles Stewart, 22, and Thomas A. Cavenaugh, 30, both of Livingston, Montana, drowned near Norris Campground on October 11, 1936, when their car plunged into the Gibbon River.[23]

Yellowstone's Gardner River has taken at least three lives by drowning in scenarios other than auto accidents, again mainly in the stretch between Mammoth and Gardiner, Montana. A seemingly small river, its current and depth are deceptive, especially during the high water season of May and June.

Preparing to remove drowning victim Charles Stewart's body from Gibbon River on October 1, 1936 (NPS Photo 27024, YNP Archives)

Joseph P. Speitel Jr., 20, a park employee from Newton Square, Pennsylvania, drowned on June 17, 1963, following a series of strange events that made park rangers initially believe his death was caused by foul play. Speitel and a friend, Jeff Jennemann, both park concessioner employees at Mammoth Hot Springs, went hiking up nearby Mount Everts on June 16, 1963. The two separated, and Jennemann attained the summit without Speitel. When Speitel did not show up, Jennemann reported him missing, and park rangers initiated a search. Ranger Ted Weight found Speitel's body from a helicopter; it was partly floating in a beaver pond on Bluff Creek below the Mammoth incinerator. Because there were no marks on his body to indicate a fall, Speitel's friend, Jennemann, was at first investigated for suspicion of murder. But ultimately it was determined that Speitel attempted to ford Lava Creek at its mouth and was swept into Gardner River, probably drowning in its high water, with fatigue possibly playing a role.[24]

Scott Allen Olson, 16, and William A. Frank, 22, both drowned in 1982 when they went soaking in the warm water at Boiling River. Olson, from Livingston, Montana, went swimming with friends on the evening of February 12, 1982. He was last seen at 12:30 a.m. on February 13, and apparently was caught in the swift current of Gardner River, on the outer fringes of the Boiling River area, and swept downstream. His body was recovered several hours later. A board of inquiry determined that intoxication might have played a role.[25] William Frank, a student at Montana State University from Bellmore, New York, went with four companions to Boiling River to soak on the evening of May 30, 1982. Friends lost sight of him at 2:30 a.m. and his body was found at 5:00 a.m. one mile downstream.[26] Partly as a result of these two drownings, the Boiling River swimming area was totally closed to night swimming, and an additional annual closure was instituted in May and June of each year during high water times.[27]

At least six persons drowned in relatively unusual places in Yellowstone Park: Gallatin Lake, Soda Butte Creek, Indian Pond, Slide Lake, Tower Creek, Hellroaring Creek, and Bechler River. Harry Asche, 17, of New York City, was drowned in Gallatin Lake, some ten miles in the backcountry, on or about August 12, 1928, when he attempted to swim out to recover a girl's hat that blew into the lake. Harry attempted to swim for it in spite of his group leader's protests. He almost reached the hat, then suddenly turned back in distress and was not seen again. Ranger Cottrell worked "night and day" to recover his body.[28] Fred W. Gonder, 26, of Livingston, Montana, drowned in Soda Butte Creek while fishing with two other men on August 28, 1937.[29] James Walker, 24, of Wheeless, Oklahoma, drowned in Indian Pond (then called Squaw Lake) on June 5, 1938, when his canoe overturned while he and another man were fishing.[30] Lee Monson, 18, a park camp worker from Glenwood, Minnesota, drowned July 6, 1947, in Slide Lake north of Mammoth. Monson fell from a raft while swimming on the lake, and heavy plant growth impeded both his rescue and the later body recovery.[31] Major John P. Adams, 67, of Burlingame, California, died on July 15, 1947, in Tower Creek while fishing about two miles above Tower Campground.[32]

Park concessioner employee James Brent Wilkerson, 19, was drowned on Hellroaring Creek near its mouth on July 18, 1982. Wilkerson, of Centerville, Tennessee, was attempting to ford the creek (a known nearly unfordable stream) to aid a female companion struggling in the water when he was swept into the nearby Yellowstone River.[33] A fellow employee, Todd Wilkinson, remembers him as a "mild-mannered, well liked guy." It had been a wet winter and the stream was running very high. Rather than use the footbridge a mile farther upstream, they decided to ford. The woman was swept to safety, but James Wilkerson was flushed from Hellroaring Creek into the Yellowstone River. Todd remembers that Wilkerson looked back at his companions with a bewildered expression, and that was the last they ever saw of him. His body was never recovered.[34] Hellroaring Creek has been known to be dangerous since the 1860s. Prospector A. Bart Henderson wrote on May 18, 1871, about "Hell Roaring river": "This stream is 80 feet wide, rapid and deep, with large boulders in it—very dangerous fording."[35]

The only known drowning in the park's southwest (Bechler) corner occurred on September 10, 2009. Heidi Llewellyn Smith of Jackson, Wyoming, was enjoying hiking and camping in the backcountry with three friends at a campsite near Bechler Ford on the Bechler River. The 30-year-old woman stated that she felt ill but went swimming in the river anyway. One of her friends discovered her under four feet of water against a log and found that she was not breathing and had no pulse. Her friend ran five miles to Bechler Ranger Station to report the incident, and park rangers who responded declared her dead at the scene.[36]

At least eight persons have drowned in Yellowstone's Shoshone Lake, which is 7,791 feet in elevation and 212 feet deep. As early as 1890, esteemed park guide Billy Hofer knew that this lake was dangerous, for one of his guidees noted that year as they were attempting to boat across it: "less than half way across, opposite camp, a breeze sprung up; Hofer, who knows the treacherous character of [these] mountain lakes advised rowing to shore . . . Before we reached shore the water was quite rough . . . This [phenomenon] makes the lakes very unsafe for small craft and inexperienced persons."

One drowning story is that of Lee Burrows, 32, of Casper, Wyoming, who drowned on June 12, 1958. Bill Keating, a survivor, remembered that a windstorm kicked up five-foot waves south of Grizzly Beach. At 4:50 p.m. a big wave crashed over their fourteen-foot boat. The boat went down, stern first, and then surfaced upside down. Burrows yelled for help from forty feet behind the boat. Keating tried to throw him a rope but was too cold to do so. Burrows's body was never recovered.[37]

Another Shoshone Lake story involved a troop of Boy Scouts from Saint Anthony, Idaho, and should not be confused with the Explorer Scout incident that happened on Yellowstone Lake five years earlier. The Shoshone Lake drownings of two scouts occurred at least partially due to improperly loaded canoes, but also because of a sudden killer windstorm. On July 20, 1978, back-country travelers Rodney Plimpton and his family saw a troop of eight Boy Scouts and two leaders in five colored canoes paddling up the Lewis River channel toward Shoshone Lake. Plimpton remembered later that the group was "an accident waiting to happen." "I couldn't believe them," he said later. "They were a ragtag bunch that seemed to have no organization." Plimpton remembered seeing two boys about 12 years old in a terribly overloaded canoe that seemed to him to be ready to tip over.[38]

Two high school teachers from Saint Anthony, Idaho, were fishing near the outlet of Shoshone Lake around 4:00 p.m. when they heard the noisy scout group splashing up the channel. The two teachers, Sam Christiansen and Darrel Gibbons, continued fishing, not realizing that those scouts were from their hometown.

The scouts of Troop 63 stopped at the outlet of the lake in order that leaders Layne Reynolds and John Bishoff could locate their assigned campsite. Imprudently, the party had not brought a map along, but they nevertheless decided that their camp lay directly across Shoshone Lake, probably an hour's paddling.

The group struck out across the lake, the six most experienced scouts in the three lead canoes and the two leaders and two remaining scouts in the two trailing canoes. By 5:00 p.m. all were halfway across the lake. But the weather in Yellowstone can change very suddenly. The blue sky grew black. A ferocious wind hit them with no warning. In the lead canoe, scout Kim Bishoff's hat was blown off his head, and he yelled at his companion, Brant Kerbs, to stop. The wind was hitting them head-on and whitecaps were already apparent all around them. A huge black cloud rolled in from their left, and suddenly Shoshone Lake seemed to erupt in waves and wind.

The new lead canoe suddenly tipped over, pounded by four- and five-foot waves, and scouts Dayton and Williams found themselves holding onto it in frigid, forty-five-degree water. Kim Bishoff and Kerbs fought the waves nearby, wishing they could take on passengers but knowing they could not. Their canoe had no built-in air pockets; if it capsized, they would sink. They decided to head for shore to get help. For nearly forty-five minutes, Kim Bishoff and Brant Kerbs paddled furiously, eventually getting within a few rods of shore. Thirty feet away they saw the canoe with the party's two strongest scouts, Van Hansen and Lane Potter. The two were almost to shore and Kim figured they would make it, but his canoe began to slip backward. With the waves now against them, they were forced to paddle the opposite direction, heading for the mouth of Moose Creek on the south shore. Landing there, Kim was amazed to see two high school teachers from his school, who were apparently camping. He began to tell Sam Christiansen and Darrel Gibbons what was happening to his friends.

Meanwhile, scout leaders Layne Reynolds and John Bishoff had been swamped. They weighed four hundred pounds together, so their canoe had been riding low in the water. Now they were immersed in the icy lake. Scouts David Bischoff and Wade Singleton managed to pull close to them, and Layne somehow was able to roll himself into their canoe without tipping it, but John was lost in the process. The three paddled for about an hour but made little progress.

A huge wave suddenly swamped their canoe. Large waves and roiling water threatened to suck them under. Layne grabbed David's belt and lifted him onto the upside-down canoe. He and Wade noticed that John was still missing. All of them were growing relaxed and sleepy as hypothermia set in.

Back on shore, Kim Bishoff had convinced teachers Sam Christiansen and Darrel Gibbons that a rescue was necessary. They lashed two canoes together for stability and launched them into the freezing and treacherous waves. The two teachers pulled alongside Layne and the others and loaded them into their rig. "Where's John Bishoff?" Darrel asked. "Dead," whispered Layne Reynolds. "Been in the water over two hours." Arriving at shore, Sam and Darrel began to scrutinize the lake for a glimpse of Daren, Darris, or John. Spotting a gleam of orange color, Sam yelled and the two teachers again jumped into their double canoe. It took half an hour to paddle to John Bishoff, who could not talk or move. They dragged him aboard and returned with difficulty to shore.

While resuscitation and warming efforts were underway for Bishoff, Darrel, Layne, and Ray Gibbons fearfully scanned the tempestuous lake for the others. The survival prospects for Daren and Darris in the freezing water seemed low. Van Hansen and Lane Potter were presumed to have made it. Suddenly they spotted dots in the water. Four of them raced for the double canoe and began paddling again. When almost to the site, they saw another canoeist, who yelled to them, "I'm a registered nurse; bring the boys to our campsite." The canoeist had Daren and Darris aboard, both only semiconscious. Daren would later go into convulsions at the campsite, but both would survive.

With all seemingly safe on the south shore, the united parties slept soundly that night after regaling each other with their adventures. The following morning the bad news hit them. As Darrel Gibbons and his father walked along the shoreline, they ran into the washed-up canoe that had been piloted by Van Hansen and Lane Potter. It was badly battered, and the two scouts were nowhere to be found. How could they have not made it when Kim Bishoff had seen them only about one hundred yards from the north shore?

Van Lyle Hansen, 17, and Lane Potter, 16, were the two oldest and strongest scouts. They had been trapped in a whirlpool of wind and waves, some of which were six feet high. Their boat apparently capsized just short of shore, and the frigid water of Shoshone Lake was probably what ultimately killed them. Lane Potter's body was spotted that morning by helicopter crews; Van Hansen's body was found the next day, several miles from Lane's. Thus ended tragically the ordeal of the Idaho scouts. A park review team concluded that the party's boats were spread out for a mile and the boaters were unable to help each other.[39]

A young and popular park ranger was killed at Shoshone Lake on July 3, 1994. Ryan Francis Weltman, 22, was, to hear his boss Michael Ross tell it, "energetic and devoted to his job." Weltman was "very conscientious, safety-wise, and experienced." He was an emergency medical technician who was also dive certified with advanced lifesaving training. Weltman's sister Ursula was a park naturalist at Norris Geyser Basin, and the two, from Andover, Minnesota, were very close.

Ryan loved his new job at Shoshone Lake, which required him to kayak around the lake virtually every day. In fact, he told friend Smokey Sturtevant, "Smokey, I think I've found heaven."

Conscientious to a fault, Ryan sometimes hiked great distances to help park visitors before reboarding his kayak. Ironically, his very conscientiousness may have cost him his life. On July 3, Ryan checked a campsite near Windy Point and then for some reason reentered the lake. The wind was blowing at least thirty-five miles per hour and waves three or four feet high whitecapped across from west to east. Some Utah campers at site 8-R-1 saw Ryan in trouble on the lake. For about two hours they watched him trying to get back into his kayak in high waves. The campers attempted at one point to paddle out to him but capsized in waves twenty feet offshore. They made no further attempts to help him. Strangely, they did not report what they saw to anyone, instead electing to remain in the backcountry for two days. "How smart do you have to be," said one south entrance ranger angrily, "to figure out that when someone is in trouble you call for assistance?"[40]

In the final analysis, no one knows why Ryan Weltman went back onto the freezing Shoshone Lake during a storm, but probably he simply made a fatal mistake in trying to be a good ranger. High waves and hypothermia had taken another good life on one of Yellowstone's very cold lakes.

It would not be the last death on Shoshone Lake. Drowning because of hypothermia took the lives of David Graham, 39, and his 12-year-old son

Quinn Graham, both of Chubbock, Idaho, probably on June 7, 2002. The two obtained backcountry campsite permits on the lake's south shore for the nights of June 6–7. Apparently seen early on June 7, they probably got into trouble in their canoe later that day from high winds and waves. At about 6:30 p.m., another group of boaters noticed an overturned canoe along the east shore of the lake. After leaving the area, they contacted rangers at Grant Village, who located the canoe late on June 8 and spotted the body of Quinn Graham wearing his partially attached flotation device a quarter mile north of the canoe. David Graham's body was recovered on June 16 in Moose Bay after helicopter teams saw it from the air. Water temperature during this period was measured at thirty-eight to forty-two degrees Fahrenheit. Both probably died from drowning or hypothermia. Rain and snow all weekend hampered the search.[41]

Two other drownings at Shoshone Lake occurred two years later. On Friday, September 7, 2007, two elderly fishermen named Fred Kisabeth, 74, and Charles Peters, 80, both from Boise, Idaho, paddled their red canoe out into Shoshone Lake. Both were experienced canoeists and both were wearing life jackets. They had fishing permits and a backcountry permit for three different campsites. It was a windy day, and moving between their campsites required the pair to make several open-water crossings. What happened to them is unknown, but just before 7:00 p.m. on Friday night another camping group found their overturned canoe and, discovering that a cell phone somehow worked, reported it to the National Park Service. Rangers responded from Grant, Old Faithful, and South Entrance. The next day they found one man in the water near the lake's eastern shore and the other a bit farther out. Both died of drowning, and as usual hypothermia may have played a role.[42]

If only a few persons have lost their lives in Shoshone Lake, at least eight persons have drowned in Yellowstone's Lewis Lake. Most of the drownings were caused by the combination of sudden storms that capsized their boats and the very cold water of the 7,779-foot-high lake, which is 110 feet deep. Gerry Monihan, 45, of Moose, Wyoming; Jacob W. Gotwals, 64, of Los Angeles; and Howard Schroeder, 37, went fishing on Lewis Lake on August 3, 1947. A sudden windstorm that evening caused high waves to swamp their boat, and only Schroeder survived, by hanging onto the boat. Fortunately for him, help came fairly quickly. The bodies of Monihan and Gotwals were recovered on August 11.[43] Interestingly, the year 1947 holds the record for most drownings in Yellowstone Park in one year, with thirteen.

Bad weather at Lewis Lake was not the reason for the mishap that drowned Leo Wester and Henry Thomas on September 10, 1950, but cold water apparently was. The two men and a third, William Anderson, were fishing about noon on Lewis Lake when one man caught a fish and stood up in their light aluminum rowboat. The boat tipped over at a point about two hundred yards from shore. The three men attempted to hold onto the boat in the icy water, but it began to sink. Wester could not swim, so Anderson and Thomas started to swim for shore. Anderson soon became exhausted and was about to give up when he heard Thomas, who was swimming about thirty feet behind him, encouraging him to "keep going." Thomas continued to shout encouragement as they battled their way through the icy water. When only a short distance from shore, said Anderson later, he became too exhausted to go on and went down. His feet touched the bottom and he took four or five steps underwater. Suddenly, he stepped on rocks and his head came out of the water. He stumbled on, then fell on his hands and knees and crawled to shore, gasping. The bodies of Wester, 39, and Thomas, 27, both from Livingston, Montana, were recovered the following day.[44]

Lewis Lake took others. Charles M. Brower, 47, and his son Philip, 12, of Encino, California, died when their seven-and-one-half-foot boat capsized in a sudden storm on August 13, 1955. Their bodies were apparently never found.[45] And Billy B. Arnold, 36, a park fisheries biologist from Fort Collins, Colorado, drowned there on July 2, 1967, when rough water overturned his boat. Two other men survived that affair.[46]

A recent death in Lewis Lake occurred in 2005. On July 2, visitor Joseph R. Miller, 59, of Seattle, Washington, was seen launching his canoe from the dock at Lewis Lake Campground between 2:00 and 2:30 p.m. A storm was approaching and the lake was rough in appearance. "He was alone, had camping equipment and did not appear to be wearing a life jacket," stated the park press release. Miller was last seen in his canoe in the northern part of the lake in two- to four-foot waves. At the time, winds were blowing twenty-five to thirty-five miles per hour and the water temperature was fifty-four degrees Fahrenheit. He was not seen again, but a backpack, life jacket, canoe, and several other items identified as belonging to him were found much later that day. Missing for twelve days, Miller's body was recovered by rangers on July 14.[47]

The park's Firehole River has claimed far fewer lives than one would think given its substantial size; in fact, I can find only five deaths, including that of Matthew Carey, the very first drowning in this chapter. Gary Steven Chase, 21, of San Francisco, drowned at the Firehole swimming area on August 3, 1974. Friends noticed that he was floating underwater and could not revive him.[48] James M. Thompson, 17, of Bozeman, Montana, drowned in the same place on the evening of August 9, 1975, while swimming with a friend. Thompson was floating in rapids, went down, and failed to come up.[49] Near the same place, 15-year-old Lisbeth Clair Skollingsberg of Boise, Idaho, was swimming on August 6, 2003, without a life preserver in the rushing channel that runs through the gorge when she "pinched her nose and ducked under the water but failed to resurface." The family searched for her for ten minutes and then asked for help from other swimmers. One of them found her underwater about ten minutes later trapped under a ledge, but it was too late.[50]

Finally, 22-year-old Lin Ching-Ling, a Taiwanese visitor, died on July 28, 2010, when she fell into the Firehole River near Old Faithful. Another park visitor saw the woman on the bottom of the river ten feet below the surface and dove down to retrieve her. He called for help and began giving her CPR. Although he and park rangers recovered a pulse for her, she died in an Idaho Falls hospital after transport there by helicopter.[51]

In the park, the Yellowstone River is second only to Yellowstone Lake in the number of lives it has claimed. Of the minimum twenty-seven persons who so died, at least eighteen were fishermen, two were crossing the river, one died due to alcohol, two were engaged in illegal activities when the drownings occurred, one died of unknown circumstances, one drove into the river, one was on a commercial raft trip, and one person merely fell into the river at a turmoiling location.

I have already discussed the 1883 drownings in Yellowstone River of Fogerty and Parker, the second known drownings in park history. A Yellowstone River drowning that occurred on September 17, 1933, was due to illegal activity. Christopher D. Gray and Knute Hansston, workers for a park construction contractor at Yellowstone Lake, were passing through Hayden Valley early one Sunday morning. Gray, 21, of Creston, Montana, saw a Canada goose on the river and illegally shot it, intending to take it home. In attempting to retrieve the poached, floating bird, Gray was swept downstream. His body was recovered the following day.[52]

George Palermo of Gardiner, Montana, drowned in 1982 while trying to illegally smuggle elk antlers out of the park. Palermo, 27, hiked into the northern end of the park and gathered cached antlers. He loaded 250 pounds of them onto a raft, which he then tied to a one-man raft that he was to ride in. While running the river, Palermo's raft apparently overturned about one and one-half miles above the mouth of Gardner River early on September 1 or late on August 31. His body was found washed up at the mouth of Gardner River on September 6, and his raft was found near where it probably overturned. A second raft carrying the elk antlers was found near Palermo's body.[53]

I will enumerate the fishermen who drowned on Yellowstone River. Typically enough, one of the river's earliest victims was a fisherman. Gus Nelson, a Swede from Gardiner, attempted to swim the river near Cinnabar while fishing during the week of July 7–12, 1889. A stock tender for the Yellowstone Park Transportation Company saw Nelson go under, and his body was found floating near Emigrant a week later.[54] Wesley Hunt, 35, of Dacoma, Oklahoma, drowned on August 22, 1939, when he stepped into a deep hole while fishing in Yellowstone River near Mud Geyser.[55] Arnold Van Heuvelen, 44, of Fallon, Nevada, the janitor at the Mammoth Visitor Center, was fishing with park naturalist Frank Rentchler above the mouth of Deep Creek on August 10, 1951, when he slipped on a rock and fell into the swift river.[56] David Gaskell,

12, of Ypsilanti, Michigan, drowned on July 30, 1955, while fishing with his father near Mud Volcano.[57] Terry Lee Prince, 7, of Norwalk, California, died when he slipped from a rock while fishing near the bridge at Tower Junction on August 15, 1955.[58] Idahoan Paul Ray Ingebretson, 16, drowned near Mud Volcano on August 21, 1961, when he tried to wade to an island in the river while fishing.[59]

Another drowned fisherman, a park employee, was a last-minute hero. Clark M. House, 53, of Davenport, Iowa, worked on a park road crew, and his wife was a seasonal payroll clerk. On July 8, 1961, House was fishing in the Yellowstone River at a point about one and one-half miles below the "gravel pit" suspension bridge, or about halfway between it and the mouth of Hellroaring Creek. He was accompanied by 8-year-old Edward Hudgens and two other men. When young Hudgens slipped into the rushing stream, House jumped in and pushed the boy to safety before being swept away himself by the swift water. Clark House's body was never recovered.[60]

We do not know the circumstances or location of the drowning of Roy Milton Barth, 39, of Los Angeles, who died July 17, 1965, except that it was in the park and in Yellowstone River.[61]

Eleven-year-old Leonard Szuberla of Morton Grove, Illinois, died on July 29, 1968, while on a fishing trip on the Yellowstone River some four miles north of Fishing Bridge. In the excitement of seeing his 15-year-old brother catch a fish, Leonard rushed into the water to see it and was swept off his feet. His hip waders probably contributed to his inability to regain his balance.[62]

And at least nine other fishermen drowned on the Yellowstone River due to swift currents or waders filling with water, or both. Keith Alfred Jensen, 34, of Salt Lake City drowned while fishing near Seven Mile Hole on June 27, 1970. His body was found three miles north of Gardiner, Montana, after having been swept some thirty miles downstream.[63] James H. Hambrick, 49, of Lakewood, Colorado, drowned on August 17, 1971, near Mud Volcano when his waders apparently filled with water.[64] Louis Stephen Majosy, 68, of Cedartown, Georgia, died on September 5, 1975, four miles downstream from the lake outlet.[65] Kenneth Gilbert Fullerton, 68, of Wichita, Nebraska, slipped on a wet rock just south of the mouth of Lamar River and was swept away at noon on July 20, 1981.[66] Matthew Tighe, 25, of Cincinnati, Ohio, died on September 7, 1984, when he stepped into a hole in the river just south of Mud Volcano and his waders filled with water.[67] LeRoy Stuppy, 42, of New London, Pennsylvania, drowned near the mouth of Hellroaring Creek on July 1, 1985.[68]

Mr. Stuppy's story is fascinating because of his wife's separate story. On the day he was missing, she went to the Tower Ranger Station to report it, where she encountered Ranger Dan Krapf and his wife Barb. Dan assured Mrs. Stuppy that fishermen were often late in returning, and Mrs. Stuppy countered with the fact that the two of them had dinner reservations that evening, be-cause "today is our anniversary and I'm sure he wouldn't miss it." As the con-versation continued, Mrs. Stuppy suddenly looked down at her hand and let out a little scream. When Dan and Barb asked what was wrong, she exclaimed, "My wedding ring!" She then noted that she had had a ruby inserted in it to represent their son and a sapphire inserted in it to represent LeRoy Stuppy, and that the sapphire was suddenly missing. Trying to comfort her, Dan said something like, "Well, such stones routinely fall out of rings." She replied, "No, I just had it cleaned," and the prongs were tested for strength, so "something's happened and he's gone!" LeRoy Stuppy's body, missing for several weeks, was eventually found more than five miles downstream. Ranger Krapf found the spot near the Hellroaring Bridge, north shore of the river, where Stuppy had apparently attempted to descend and had slid fifty or sixty feet down the steep canyon wall into the raging Yellowstone River. His glasses, hat, and fishing tackle were found scattered at the bottom of the track of his slide.[69]

Both the missing Boy Scout in 2005 and the long-missing female em-ployee from Roosevelt Lodge that same year remain strong on the minds of local people around the park, but both drowned in Yellowstone River. Six Boy Scouts from Helena, Montana, and three leaders backpacked into the Black Canyon in late June of 2005, intending to camp. On June 24, 13-year-old Luke Sanburg, a math whiz who loved to hunt and fish, was pushing logs into the river with other scouts in the turbulent rapids below Knowles Falls. One of the logs clipped Luke, sweeping him off his feet and into rapids. He was last seen floating downstream with his head above water level as the river curved out of sight. More than 250 people, including about one hundred of Luke's friends and family, searched the river downstream to Corwin Springs, Montana, for two weeks. For days, many people stood on the highway bridge at Gardiner looking east at the river hoping for a sign of him, but only his white tennis shoe was found. The search was scaled back on July 8, and he has never been found.[70]

Only five days later, 19-year-old Xanterra employee Candace May Kel-lie of Belgrade, Montana—a wrangler at Roosevelt Lodge—drove away from there after midnight on June 29, 2005, in her green Ford Explorer. Heading toward Cooke City and just east of Tower Junction, she hit an embankment on the right side of the road, crossed to the left side, and went over an embank-ment one hundred feet into Yellowstone River, where she was swept away. Her car was removed from the river, but she was missing for more than two years. In September 2007, anglers upstream from Gardiner, Montana discovered a hu-man skull in the river. DNA testing confirmed that it was part of the remains of Candace Kellie, and park officials announced it in June of 2008.[71]

A double tragedy occurred on August 6, 1979, involving a Texas man and his wife. Orville Sigrist, 60, and his wife Pearl, both of Houston, were fishing in the Yellowstone River near Tower when Pearl fell into the river. Orville dove in to rescue her and both were carried away. Their son, Gregory, unsuccessfully attempted to rescue his parents and then went for help.

My brother, Curtis Whittlesey, was working for the National Park Service at Tower when this incident occurred. He remembers leading a packhorse from Tower to Garnet Hill to meet rangers Bill Foreman and Dan Krapf, who were just pulling Sigrist's body from the river. Curtis packed Orville Sigrist's body out, noting that Pearl Sigrist had not been found. Her body was found six miles downstream on August 12.[72]

The most recent angler was 70-year-old Ernest Trim of Ennis, Montana, who was fishing near Nez Perce Ford on July 17, 2013, when he lost his footing and was carried two hundred yards downstream. A witness ran downstream and pulled him from the river, but it was too late.[73] Sixty-five-year-old Frank Jaszcz (pronunciation uncertain) of Cedar Rapids, Iowa, drowned in Yellowstone River in 2010 while fishing near Mud Volcano when he attempted to walk out to a small island and lost his footing. The strong current carried him six miles downstream to the river bank just north of Elk Antler Creek.[74]

A 1990 drowning in the Yellowstone River involved alcohol. Charles Tom, 21, of Crownpoint, New Mexico, an employee of Hamilton Stores at Fishing Bridge, walked home at 2:00 a.m. on August 8, 1990, after drinking heavily at the Lake employee pub. Fellow employee Michael Squires was with him. In the center of Fishing Bridge, Tom asked Squires if he wanted to see "something funny." Squires said no, but Charles Tom "did the Nestea plunge" anyway into the water. Caught in the current, Tom kept yelling for Michael to help him, and Michael yelled directions. But after a while Michael did not hear anything more from Tom. Charles Tom's body was recovered several hours later.[75]

As Montanans can testify, the Yellowstone River drowns numerous people each year below Yellowstone National Park as it wends its way to North Dakota. As early as 1884, the *Livingston Enterprise* cynically, or perhaps realistically, reported: "At noon today a man was seen to start down the river on a little raft on which were his bedding and food supplies. There is a prospect of another job for the coroner."[76]

Such a drowning occurred on the park boundary on June 16, 2011, and it involved a commercial raft trip floating north from Gardiner, Montana. The center of the river is the actual park boundary for about five miles northwest of Gardiner, and on this day the river was running deep and fast in the high water of spring snowmelt. Thirty-three-year-old Christopher Johnson, a native of Indiana who was stationed with the U.S. Navy in Virginia, was somehow knocked from the raft in which he was riding. Although wearing a life jacket, Johnson was swept away and pulled from the river deceased near LaDuke Springs, some miles to the north.[77]

The most drownings in Yellowstone Park (about forty) have occurred in Yellowstone Lake. All things considered, no body of water in Yellowstone Park and probably in all of the United States is more potentially dangerous. The lake is 136 square miles in size with 110 miles of shoreline. It is 450 feet deep in places with an average year-round temperature of forty-three degrees Fahrenheit, due primarily to the fact that its elevation is 7,731 feet above sea level, and because it is fed most of the year by melting snow and ice. Prevailing southwesterly winds each afternoon can produce waves five to six feet high when they combine with the very deep water. In short, the lake is a huge inland sea that is potentially very dangerous to boaters because of its low temperature and high waves. Even early explorers noticed this, for Dr. Hayden stated in 1871 that "the most accomplished swimmer could live but a short time in it,"[78] and Captain W. A. Jones reported in 1873 that Yellowstone Lake "at any time is cold enough to break down the constitution of the strongest bather."[79] Occasionally, a brazen visitor of today will question why no one is swimming, put on his bathing suit, and jump rashly into the water. This person soon discovers why no one is swimming in Yellowstone Lake.

Boating incidents on Yellowstone Lake are the most common types of drownings in the park. Often the victims drown when their boat capsizes during one of the lake's all-too-frequent windstorms or thunderstorms. Waves on Yellowstone Lake sometimes reach six feet high, and the water is so cold one cannot generally hold onto a capsized boat and wait for help. Instead, hypothermia sets in after only about twenty minutes. Signs today at Bridge Bay alert boaters: "Warning—water extremely cold. Survival time limited to twenty minutes." Small boats are particularly vulnerable because they can become easily swamped in high waves.

I believe that generally a capsized boater must strike out swimming for shore if he is to have any hope of surviving. Rick Fey, long a boat ranger on Yellowstone Lake, tells me he sees it as a *Catch-22* situation: the victim will surely freeze if he waits with the overturned boat, but a swimmer will use much more energy swimming in cold water than he would if he simply waited with the boat and might thus freeze anyway, especially if shore is a long distance away. Rick certainly has a point. But the number of persons who died waiting in the water for help far outnumbers those who survived by such waiting, and a fair number of persons did survive drowning on Yellowstone Lake by swimming for shore and making it. In this debate one simply has to hope that if a boat turns over the person is not too far from shore, for the Hobson's choice is bad either way. Rick Fey acknowledges that sometimes waiting with the boat can buy a person time if the water is not too cold, but he notes that water takes heat from a person's body twenty-five times faster than air and recommends swimming for the shore "only when you absolutely know you can make it."[80]

Most Yellowstone Lake drownings occurred after 1930, but the first such incident happened in 1894. Three wagon drivers for Frank Phiscator's wood concession at Yellowstone Lake were involved. Henry Hubbard, James Wilder, and Ed Vinage secured a rowboat on July 4 of that year, along with a quantity of beer, and started for Stevenson Island. They failed to return that night, so a search party was sent out the following day. Their boat was found floating bottom side up, close to the shore of the island, and the men were gone. It was supposed that they were intoxicated, but nothing else is known.[81]

Another early Yellowstone Lake drowning was apparently attributable to overloading a small boat and the lake's cold water. On the evening of August 26, 1906, W. B. Taylor, A. D. Taylor (both from Bozeman, Montana), Private Harry E. Allen from Fort Yellowstone, a fourth man, and two ladies all got into a small rowboat at West Thumb. They intended to go for a pleasant evening row, but when only about one hundred yards out, the boat filled with water and capsized. One lady swam ashore, and A. D. Taylor with the fourth man was able to help the other lady, but Harry Allen and W. B. Taylor drowned in the near darkness as they tried to swim to the beach. The night was described as "very cold," so perhaps the victims died from hypothermia, if not drowning. Their bodies were not recovered.

This incident spawned, or perhaps merely perpetuated, a legend about Yellowstone Lake. In an eerie letter to the acting park superintendent, the father of the still-missing Taylor stated that he had heard that Yellowstone Lake "never gives up its dead" and wanted to know if it was true. The park superintendent did not quite know how to respond to that statement, but certainly it is true that at least eleven and perhaps as many as seventeen bodies of drowned persons were never recovered from Yellowstone Lake. Moreover, the propensity of very cold water for preserving bodies is well known. Perhaps it is farfetched, but lake rangers have imagined bodies floating to the surface or being swept onto a beach of Yellowstone Lake, dressed in the clothing of an earlier era.[82]

That very thing happened, at least in a small way, when a remnant of one of the 1906 drownees was recovered. Nearly a year later, an employee of the Yellowstone Lake Boat Company found a human skull washed onto the west side of Stevenson Island. A soldier who saw the skull noted: "There was some flesh left on the jaws and some skin on the head. The left ear was also remaining. Two teeth were missing from the front of the lower jaw. The skull was that of a young man, and must have been in the water a long time—at least 9 or 10 months."

The skull was shown to two of W. B. Taylor's relatives, who could not identify it as Taylor. But the consensus was that this skull belonged to Taylor or Allen and that it had been carried by prevailing currents to Stevenson Island from West Thumb.[83] Just as interesting was the burial of parts of Private Allen, which occurred a year and four days after the drownings. Soldiers at West

Thumb Soldier Station reported that "one arm and one leg of Private Allen who was drowned" were buried just north of West Thumb "between the road and the lake." It is not known why or how only pieces of Allen were found, but two trees were marked with crosses near Allen's grave.[84]

The era of drownings on Yellowstone Lake really began in the 1930s, once the numbers of private boats and boat rentals began to be fairly high. Boats, of course, had been operated (mostly by concessioners) on Yellowstone Lake since the *Anna* in 1871, the *Topping* and the *Sallie* in 1874–1875, the *Explorer* in 1880, the *Pinafore* in 1885, and the *Zillah* from 1889 to about 1916. But there were not significant numbers of private boats on Yellowstone Lake until the 1930s.

Including the three 1894 drownings, at least forty-one persons are known to have drowned in Yellowstone Lake and, as mentioned, at least eleven (if not seventeen) of those bodies were never recovered. Nearly all of these drownings involved a boat or canoe which overturned in one of the sudden windstorms and/or thunderstorms for which Yellowstone Lake is well known. Single drownings are the rule, with the most in one incident being four. At least eight victims have been park employees (one of whom was a park ranger), and the rest were park visitors.

A triple drowning on August 31, 1933, began Yellowstone Lake's modern drowning history. Dr. Shaen S. Magan, 35, his son Bobby, 7, and George Steckel, 25, all of Covina, California, were in a sixteen-foot metal rowboat on the lake near Lake Lodge, at a point about five hundred yards east of the ranger barn. A sudden windstorm raised large waves on the lake, and the three were bailing water from their boat within five minutes of leaving shore. The boat apparently capsized, and all three bodies were eventually recovered.[85]

A military officer, Major Julius T. Flock, 35, of Fort Douglas, Utah, drowned in West Thumb bay on July 23, 1941, after an amazing exhibition of physical strength. Flock and Captain R. H. Carmichael, 28, both of the Ninth Bombardment Squadron, were in a boat that overturned during a severe storm at about 1:30 p.m. The two men held onto the boat for hours, Flock finally succumbing to the cold water at around 5:00 p.m. Carmichael was rescued about 7:30 p.m. after an amazing six hours in the freezing water! Apparently sheer physical strength saved him, and this is one of the few instances where a potential victim survived drowning on Yellowstone Lake by holding onto a boat. Ironically, the two had earlier beached the boat to wait out a different storm. Major Flock's body was never recovered.[86]

An evening windstorm and drowning took the life of C. L. Anderson, 49, of Long Beach, California, on August 21, 1942. Anderson and R. C. Crawford of Greenville, Texas, were boating near Dot Island about 8:00 p.m. when high winds capsized their boat. Crawford was rescued about 2:30 a.m. after other fishermen heard the two calling for help.[87]

Yellowstone Park Company rowboat number 78, in which J. T. Flock drowned, taken July 25, 1941, a typical type of small boat in which many people drowned on Yellowstone Lake (NPS Photo 29078, YNP Archives)

Attempted recovery of J. T. Flock, who drowned July 23, 1941, on Yellowstone Lake (NPS Photo 29077, YNP Archives)

As mentioned earlier, 1947 was and is the record year for drownings in Yellowstone National Park. In addition to the five victims already enumerated at Slide Lake, Tower Creek, Old Faithful swimming pool, and Lewis Lake, eight persons drowned in Yellowstone Lake that summer for a total of thirteen persons, all in July and August. On July 28, 1947, three men from Elk Basin, Wyoming, rented a small metal outboard motorboat intending to go fishing on the lake. Gene Reidiman, 30, Robert A. Clark, 30, and Herman H. Hutton, 25, told the boat rental people that they were headed for Stevenson Island. A storm with high winds on the same day capsized and sank their boat, and the men were drowned. Lee Deming of Anaheim, California, saw the three men from his boat during the storm, battling waves. Deming had all he could do to keep his own boat from turning over and stated that the three men were "being tossed pretty high with the heavy waves" when he lost sight of them. Their bodies were not recovered.[88]

Only a few days later, on August 1, nearly the same thing happened to Herbert J. Kleine and M. C. Baldwin. Kleine, 47, of Altoona, Pennsylvania, and Baldwin, 57, owner of the Ne-Hi Bottling Company at Lawton, Oklahoma, left the docks at Fishing Bridge in a small boat at around 10:00 a.m. Kleine's 16-year-old son Richard accompanied them. At around 3:45 p.m., one of the season's most severe storms struck Yellowstone Lake just south of Crystal Beach. A large wave broke over the boat, filling it nearly full of water. The next large wave turned the boat over. Young Richard said later, "it started to sink and we all jumped out." The three began holding onto the boat. Richard remembered that Baldwin became very frightened and cold and had to be helped in holding onto the boat. Finally, Kleine advised his son to swim to shore. The youth desperately battled high winds and waves for one and a half miles to the beach near Fishing Bridge Museum and then stumbled to there for help. But his father and Baldwin were dead. Hypothermia killed them if drowning did not.[89]

Three weeks later, another triple tragedy occurred, bringing the park drowning total for 1947 to thirteen. On Friday, August 22, a party of six persons from Cody and Powell, Wyoming, including the owner of the *Cody Enterprise* newspaper, came into the park bringing two boats. A storm was raging on Yellowstone Lake for much of the day, but in the evening it seemed to lift, and they launched the sixteen-foot boats from the docks in front of Lake Hotel. Ernest F. Shaw, 57 (owner of the *Cody Enterprise*); Dr. Karl G. Avery, 33, of Powell, Wyoming; and Jack Metzler, 12, of Powell all boarded Shaw's outboard motorboat. Jeff Metzler, Wesley Metzler, and O. L. Casinger, all of Powell, boarded Metzler's boat. The six headed for Dot Island.[90]

A sudden squall, probably a spinoff from the earlier storms, caught the two boats about 8:30 p.m. one-quarter mile east of Rock Point. The Metzler boat was able to make a safe landing, but the Shaw party's boat was driven in high winds toward Rock Point. The high waves capsized the boat, which sank, and all three were drowned, or more probably died of exposure, as all were wearing life jackets. The bodies of Avery and Shaw were recovered August 23 and that of Metzler on August 25, 1947.[91]

The number of drownings in the Park during 1947—the most in any year—rises to fourteen if we count what may be Yellowstone's strangest case—Henrietta Ross Bailey's death from cold water immersion that apparently resulted in hypothermia, complicated by other elements including the possibility of murder. It is difficult to categorize and I've placed it elsewhere (see chapter 20, "Malice in Wonderland"), but it strongly involved Yellowstone Lake.

A double drowning in 1950 on Yellowstone Lake brought great sorrow to the Yellowstone Park Company employees of Old Faithful Inn. On July 6, Oliver Schmoker, 37, of Oklahoma City, the bell captain at the inn, and Zellar Ellen Hensley, 36, of Los Angeles, a waitress at the inn dining room, were both killed when a sudden windstorm overturned their rented boat in West Thumb bay. A third member of their party, Victor J. Nelson (the chief clerk at Old Faithful Inn), was rescued while hanging onto the boat, after a boathouse employee saw their overturned craft while scanning the lake through binoculars. Schmoker and Hensley died of exposure in the frigid water. Nelson, too, would no doubt have died had help not arrived.

The Schmoker–Hensley case began as a joyous employee outing. They had been fishing all afternoon. Joseph Gentry, Fred Fleming, and Joan Folsom were in boat 32 and Oliver Schmoker, Victor Nelson, and "Billie" Hensley were in boat 13, both rented from the West Thumb dock. Nelson had to return early, so the boats began heading back. Gentry remembered that as the boathouse was getting closer, Oliver Schmoker's boat drove close enough for Schmoker to shout, "When you get near the boathouse shut down your motor. They don't like you to come gunning in." Those were the last words Schmoker ever spoke to him.

At 5:15 p.m., the storm came up so suddenly that it caught them all off guard. Gentry recalled, "I had never seen such a savage wind. It was so strong that it blew spray in the boat and started to fill it up. That was the first time I had ever really seen death staring at me." Gentry and his party soon had too much to do to watch the Schmoker craft. Battling the waves toward the south shore, they were carried to the beach.

In the other boat, disaster was striking. Victor Nelson said later that big waves filled the three-person craft with water faster than they could bail it out. The boat capsized, and Nelson could not remember anything after that. Nearly two hours later, rescuer Julian Novak spotted something floating about one-quarter mile from the boat that he and the dock manager had hastily manned. As they arrived, Nelson, nearly unconscious from the icy water, groggily asked them, "Where are the others?" Nearby, Oliver Schmoker and "Billie" Hensley were floating face down. Schmoker's watch had stopped at 5:35 p.m., probably the time the boat capsized. Schmoker had been wearing a life preserver; Hensley had not. But life preservers did not always matter on frigid Yellowstone Lake.[92]

Several persons have simply vanished on Yellowstone Lake. An El Dorado, Kansas, man, Lloyd J. Weikel, rented a sixteen-foot boat at Fishing Bridge on August 16, 1945, and started off to fish between Stevenson and Dot Islands. It is assumed he drowned, but no trace of him or the boat was ever recovered.[93] Carl George Mihlberger also simply disappeared on Yellowstone Lake. Mihlberger, 64, of Salt Lake City, took a fourteen-foot rowboat from Fishing Bridge out onto Yellowstone Lake to fish on July 8, 1953. He had been drinking but was "not overtly intoxicated." His boat was found that evening just north of Stevenson Island still right side up but with three inches of water in the bottom. He apparently fell overboard while attempting to free fishing line which was wrapped around the motor propeller or perhaps while trying to start a stalled motor. The body was never found. Mihlberger and Lloyd Weikel represented two of only three known drowning victims on Yellowstone Lake whose deaths were not the result of a sudden storm and/or boats capsizing.[94]

Like Carl Mihlberger and Lloyd Weikel, Duane McClure vanished without a trace. A park ranger from Grant Village, he apparently drowned on May 22, 1980, in West Thumb bay. McClure, 35, had been in Yellowstone for over six years and was a "very precise and cautious person." He left Grant that day on a canoe trip to the south shore of West Thumb in good weather. What happened to him is a mystery, as his body was never recovered. His canoe was found swamped on the south shore of West Thumb about one mile from his destination site. Although some of his fellow rangers always believed that he had been the victim of foul play, a board of inquiry determined that he had probably drowned in a storm on the lake that occurred at around 1:00 p.m.[95]

Thomas Hughes, 66, of Salt Lake City was trapped in the cabin of an eighteen-foot cabin cruiser when it overturned in a snowstorm and high winds. He drowned on September 11, 1961, at 7:50 p.m. about three-quarters of a mile from Fishing Bridge while accompanied by four other persons. Two of them swam to shore and two clung to the boat. Fortunately for the clinging pair, help arrived quickly. The bow of the boat was found sticking up, the craft hanging vertically with its cabin and two large motors down. One of the party members stated that between Stevenson Island and Lake Dock, the boat inexplicably filled with water. Even an eighteen-foot boat could be vulnerable on Yellowstone Lake.[96]

Small boats or canoes, both of which overturn easily, have been involved in most drownings on Yellowstone Lake. A canoe trip on West Thumb ended in death for two employees of the West Thumb service station (YPSS) on July 19–20, 1967. When Steve Smith, 21, of Dallas, Texas, and Kenneth Ables, 19, of San Marino, California, failed to return from their canoe trip on West Thumb bay, a search was instituted. Park rangers found two life jackets, a canoe paddle, and Smith's ice chest floating between Breeze Point and Dot Island. The men had been headed for Peale Island in the lake's South Arm but did not make it. Their bodies were not recovered.[97]

Two Yellowstone Lake drownings in 1971 and 1972 were attributable to failure to wear a life preserver and hypothermia. On August 9, 1971, Laura E. (Mrs. Thomas) Ward, 58, of Stockton, California, fell from a fishing boat near Gull Point when her husband stood up to land a fish and the boat tipped both of them out. He was not wearing a life preserver, and she was using only a cushion.[98] And Charles F. Wright, 56, of Las Vegas, Nevada, fell from his aluminum rowboat on July 23, 1972. Other visitors saw Wright trying to swim ashore, and he was apparently overcome by the lake's cold water and/or fatigue. His boat was found upside down with both oars inside.[99]

Another man, Lloyd V. Ryan Jr., 25, of San Antonio, Texas, was drowned on June 14, 1972, while trying to swim ashore. His gamble did not work, thus giving some credence to ranger Rick Fey's argument for staying with the boat. At around 2:00 p.m. that day, Ryan, his brother Gentry, and his small son Chris put into Yellowstone Lake at Mary Bay in a small plastic raft. When out some distance, high winds blew them east to a large boulder some two hundred feet off Steamboat Point. Lloyd and Chris climbed onto the rock to eat lunch, but Gentry rode on to Steamboat Point on the raft. Waves on the lake had become too high for Gentry to return, so Lloyd attempted to swim the two hundred feet to shore. The cold water killed him, and rangers had to rescue his son Chris.[100]

Yellowstone Lake's worst multiple drowning occurred in the Southeast Arm of the lake, killing two Explorer Scouts and two scout leaders. Once again, the dramatic cold of the lake was to blame, as all but one of the victims were wearing life preservers. On July 18, 1973, seven Explorer Scouts and their two leaders, all of Explorer Chapter 406 from Albuquerque, New Mexico, launched their five canoes and two kayaks from Sedge Bay on the east side of Yellowstone Lake. All were excited to begin the six-day canoe and camping trip for which they had planned so long. The boys, ages 14 to 17, had earned the money to build their own canoes and kayaks, and some had studied water safety.[101]

Paddling along the east shore of the lake, the party stopped for lunch at Park Point, and then proceeded into the Southeast Arm. They were crossing the Arm to its west shore in their homemade crafts and were about in the middle of it when the thunderstorm struck them very suddenly at 4:00 p.m. "It just hit like a bomb," 14-year-old Harlan Kim Jones recalled later. "The storm scattered us all over the lake." His general comment is one for today's boaters to remember: "It was so strange to see the lake change as rapidly as it did, and it became terrifying."[102]

Traumatized by extremely high waves, wind, and rain, the occupants of four canoes and two kayaks turned around and headed for the east shore. The fifth canoe, in which 15-year-old Ken Foley was paddling desperately, made it safely to the west shore.[103] But two of the canoes capsized and one filled with water in the waves and high winds. Several were too heavily loaded and were therefore riding low in the water.

Kim Jones and 16-year-old Bob Safran, manning one of the only two-person canoes, began to take on water. Kim remembers being very scared, and then suddenly he and Safran were thrashing about in the icy water.

"Bob made a mistake," said Kim later. "He insisted on floating on his back and let [*sic*] the waves carry him in but the waves kept hitting him in the face. I told him you have to keep moving or you'll die. Bob started turning real purple after about thirty minutes and couldn't get his breath. He said 'Buddy, don't leave me,' and I said, 'I won't.' I turned around and he was gone."[104]

The two scout leaders were Darwin Seamons, 47, and Burris Wollsieffer, 26, paddling furiously in the same canoe. They were in trouble too, along with

NPS investigation into Burris Wollsieffer drowning on Yellowstone Lake, which occurred July 18, 1973, showing weight and gear distribution in canoe (NPS photo #29084, YNP Archives)

16-year-old Tom Gower. Their two crafts capsized and, although they were wearing life jackets like everyone else, they could not survive the lake's freezing water. Seamons, Wollsieffer, and Gower all died as Safran had, with their core temperatures reaching points too low to allow them to keep swimming.[105]

Meanwhile Kim Jones was swimming frantically. Every time he would stop moving his arms in the water, they would freeze up. "I figured," said Kim later, "Old Buddy, you'd better keep moving because if you don't, you're dead."[106] For more than an hour he kept fighting the cold water until at last, exhausted, he fell headlong onto the east shore of Yellowstone Lake. For a while he just lay there, thanking God. Then, rising slowly, he realized he was barefooted and alone in the dark. Kim began walking north on the east shore trail. He had seen a cabin earlier and thought it to be a ranger station. All night long he walked, falling down several times, his feet badly beaten by rocks and downed timber.

A bear surprised him all of a sudden, and Kim climbed a tree, hurting his bare feet more. He stayed in the tree for an hour until the bear got tired of slapping it, and then resumed his hike in the dark, trying to stay near shore to attract the attention of any boater. Kim prayed constantly and kept thinking, "Some of my buddies are in trouble and I've got to get help for them." But there were no boaters until 10:00 a.m. the next morning, when the youth flagged one down from shore. He had walked about seventeen miles.

Park rangers found the other four teenage survivors—Paul Porter, Kevin Seamons, Russ Hallett, and Ken Foley—and took them all to Lake Hospital, where Kim Jones was recovering. Ranger Jerry Ryder remembers interviewing Jones in his hospital bed. Jones told the rangers that his father had always told him if he ever fell into cold water to swim, swim, swim.[107] When he first arrived at the hospital, Jones said he felt that he had abandoned Bob Safran in the water, but later he decided, "if I had tried to pull him in, we both might have been dead."[108]

Three of the bodies were found initially, but Wollsieffer's was never found.[109] The tragedy haunted John Dracon and his friend Richard of White Sulphur Springs, Montana, for thirty-five years. Dracon was then superintendent of schools in that town. He was canoeing on Yellowstone Lake that day and, before the incident, exchanged pleasantries with the Explorer Scouts near Park Point.

> While I cannot recall their faces, I do recall their equipment and their eagerness to get down the lake. What struck me then was the size of their canoes, which I felt were undersized and looked homemade. Talking with the leaders, we learned that they were going to camp in a variety of sites, beginning with Columbine Creek that evening. Since their

next site was going to be on the east side of the Promontory, we cautioned them not to attempt a crossing unless it was early in the morning
and the water was calm. We in fact were emphatic in our recommendations. . . . Much to our surprise and sorrow, we read several days later in
the *Billings Gazette* an accounting of the tragedy. Both Richard and I
were sick at heart. Being fathers we understood the grief of the parents
and loved ones, and we knew what happened and why, but the fact that
we had tried to warn them to no avail became a special burden for us.[110]

This quadruple drowning of scouts and their leaders stimulated much dis-
cussion in the park as to lake safety. Rangers agreed that the one-quarter-mile
travel limit was fruitless—it was hard to enforce and created resentment—and
that boat inspections were unrealistic. They also agreed that the park lake patrol
was terribly understaffed (it still is today) but that visitors had to be warned
about overloading of small boats, the water temperature of Yellowstone Lake,
and the potential for sudden storms.[111]

Yet another storm on the lake took two park construction workers. On
the evening of June 20, 1980, at about 7:30 p.m., William Bo Bess, 26, of
Caldwell, Idaho, and Michael Dale Bitterli, 22, of Wendall, Idaho, left the Lake
Village area in a canoe with their dog and only one life jacket. Within an hour
of their departure, the area began to experience severe lightning, thunder, and
high winds. Park employee Ron Jones reported seeing the canoe "in trouble"
at 8:30 p.m. near Stevenson Island, and by 8:45 p.m. it was no longer visible.
Bess and Bitterli were drowned. Bess's body and that of the dog were found
the next day.[112]

Another multiple drowning on Yellowstone Lake involved a father, his
two sons, and their grandfather. On the evening of June 20, 1985, David
Carter, 33, his sons Dustin, 9, and Caleb, 7, and his father Jack Warren Carter,
all from Palm Desert, California, were plying the waters of Yellowstone Lake
in their seventeen-foot boat. A sudden storm kicked up the usual five- to six-
foot waves, and their boat was swamped near Park Point. All four were thrown
into the icy lake. Jack Carter attempted to help the others swim to shore, but
lost contact with them due to high waves. Bear biologist Dan Reinhart was
camped at Park Point when Jack walked into his camp, told him the story, and
broke down. The two boys and their father had all died, said Jack, even though
the boys were wearing life jackets. The bodies of the boys were found soon
after. Rangers Mike Pflaum and Nick Herring found their father's body about
a month later, washed up on the east shore of Yellowstone Lake.[113]

Christopher Lee Quintana drowned in Yellowstone Lake in one of only
three incidents that did not involve a boat or a storm. Quintana, 20, of Worland,
Wyoming, was fishing alone in front of Lake Hotel on the morning of June 18,

1987, when he apparently had a seizure of some type and fell into the shallow water along the lakeshore. Rangers performed CPR on him and restored his breathing, but Quintana died anyway on June 19.[114]

Yellowstone Lake claimed two more victims in 1997, and the deaths may have been the result of afternoon thunderstorms. On June 11 of that year, Michael D. Divine, 49, and Steven A. Divine, 41, were apparently attempting to end their extended backcountry canoeing trip early when their canoe capsized, probably during an afternoon thunderstorm. On the following morning at about 10:30 a.m., park concessioners operating an Amfac Parks and Resorts boat found one body floating about one-quarter mile from Rock Point with the overturned canoe. After notifying rangers, boatmen found the other body within ten minutes, also floating. Investigations indicated the victims had been in the water for an extended period of time and died of hypothermia; water temperature at the location was thirty-eight degrees Fahrenheit.[115]

So what lessons are we to glean from all of these Yellowstone Park drownings? If you must go boating on Yellowstone Lake in a small, short boat, stay reasonably close to shore. Make sure the boat is in good shape. Get off the lake when storms are looming. Do not overload canoes. Do not stand up in small fishing boats. I personally would not even consider sailboating on Yellowstone Lake unless it was in early morning or late at night, times when high winds are not as likely. Remember that storms are most likely to occur between 1:00 p.m. and 6:00 p.m. And above all, respect the fact that the high, deep lakes in Yellowstone Park are extremely cold. Life jackets are not enough; one must get *out* of the water if a boat turns over, *unless* time in the water will be short.

The safety rules for waters other than Yellowstone Lake are the ones our mothers always told us about. Do not swim or fish alone. Wear a life jacket. Do not combine water activities with alcohol. Beware of fording even smaller streams, as they are often deceptively swift and deep. Realize that waders worn by fishermen can fill up with water and pull one under. All of these things have contributed to danger in the water.

Above all, respect the wild nature of Yellowstone.

II

DEATH BY MAN

15

CLASH OF CULTURES
DEATHS FROM INDIAN BATTLES

War is hell.

—William Tecumseh Sherman, 1879

THAT FAMOUS ASSESSMENT OF human conflict was written by an army general experienced in warfare, who traveled through Yellowstone in 1877. Sherman's association with Yellowstone National Park was limited to laying out the first road from the south entrance and having his name placed for a time on the Washburn Range as "Sherman Volcano." But he knew war, and condemned it in his 1879 address to a military academy graduating class: "It is only those who have neither fired a shot nor heard the shrieks and groans of the wounded who cry aloud for blood, more vengeance, [and] more desolation."

Sherman's summation applied to all wars, including Yellowstone conflicts. There have not been many deaths in Yellowstone National Park from battles involving Native Americans, at least that are known. Five fur trappers were killed in 1839, two park visitors in 1877, and two men just outside the park in a skirmish in 1869. And there were at least three other possible battles wherein human beings were probably killed. Of course, we know far less about the Native American side of the story than we do about the Euro-American side. Native Americans no doubt were killed in these and probably other skirmishes at various times in the Yellowstone country. Unfortunately, we do not know their names or much about the events. Perhaps future archaeology will shed light on those shadowy encounters.

Yellowstone National Park was never prime country for Native Americans, at least in historic times. While the Shoshones and Bannocks lived to the west and south of the park, the Blackfeet to the north, and the Crows to the northeast, only the small Sheepeater tribe actually inhabited areas inside the present park. Although at least twenty-six tribes claim some homeland connections to Yellowstone over the long period that represents unrecorded history, many Indians during the period 1730–1889 traveled through Yellowstone only in summer months, rather than living there permanently.[1] The following stories represent essentially all that is known about Indian-related deaths of Euro-Americans in Yellowstone.

William T. "Uncle Billy" Hamilton's account is the only one in existence that chronicles the 1839 affair. It was a battle that occurred near present Indian Pond between fur trappers and Piegan Indians, an offshoot tribe of the constantly warring Blackfeet to the north. Hamilton stated that in 1839, a party of forty fur trappers that included Baptiste Ducharme, Lou Anderson, Jim and John Baker, Joe Power, L'Humphrie, and others crossed Two Ocean Pass to Yellowstone Lake and traveled down to the meadow east of the outlet of the lake. Hamilton says:

> They also described a fight that they had with a large party of Piegan Indians at the lower end of the lake on the north side, and on a prairie of about half a mile in length. The trappers built a corral at the upper end of the prairie and fought desperately for two days, losing five men besides having many wounded. The trappers finally compelled the Piegans to leave, with the loss of many of their bravest warriors. After the wounded were able to travel, they took an Indian trail and struck a warm-spring creek. This they followed to the Madison River.[2]

Of course, the names of the trappers killed are not known, nor is the exact location, but probably this skirmish happened near Indian Pond.

Considerably more is known about the deaths of Charles Kenck and Richard Dietrich, two park visitors who were killed by Nez Perce Indians in 1877. The foray by those Indians across the Northwest in their attempt to escape from the U.S. Army into Canada is well known and documented. Although General William Sherman would later decry war as hell, in 1877 he, like many other army generals, was in the West because of the Nez Perce situation and because the Indian scene in general was still unsettled from the preceding "summer of Custer." Sherman decided on a side trip to Yellowstone National Park that summer while overseeing the Indian situation from the sidelines. While he did not propose to interfere with the strategies of his subordinate generals ("Too many heads are worse than *one*"), Sherman nevertheless held a vigorous opinion about Nez Perce affairs. As head of the army, he articulated its formal position, albeit weakly:

The time has come when these restless Indians . . . should not be allowed to traverse the scattered and exposed settlements of Montana,
where hunger will sooner or later, compel them to kill tame cattle and
steal horses, thus leading to murder and war. Besides, these Nez Perces
should be made to answer for the murders they committed in Idaho,
and also be punished as a tribe, for going to war without any just cause
or provocation.[3]

Correct in his later assessment of war in general, Sherman was decidedly
incorrect in this statement. The Nez Perce had both just cause and provocation for going to war. The whites were in the process of stealing their ancestral
lands and had cheated, robbed, and killed some of them. Thus the Nez Perce
left their home in Wallowa Valley, Oregon, that spring of 1877 on a flight to
avoid being placed on a reservation when gold miners and settlers coveted
their home. After a series of skirmishes with the army in Idaho and western
Montana, about seven hundred men, women, and children and two thousand
horses under chiefs Joseph and Looking Glass headed southeast and east along
the Bitterroot Range, entering Yellowstone National Park, then only five years
old, just north of the present town of West Yellowstone, Montana. The Nez
Perce arrived eight days after General Sherman's party left the park.

With General O. O. Howard chasing them from the west, the Indians traveled up the stream known today as Nez Perce Creek after forcibly impressing
a white man named Shively into service as their guide. They captured a party
of tourists in Lower Geyser Basin, shot and wounded two of them, and carried the others across Mary Mountain to Yellowstone River. There, the tourists
were released and told to ride hard for Mammoth Hot Springs while the main
body of Indians forded the river at Nez Perce Ford and continued east.

The Nez Perce left several small groups of warriors behind to cover their
flank and to try to slow the army. A party of tourists from Helena, Montana,
was then camped near the Upper Falls. On August 25, during a side trip to see
the wonders at Crater Hills, the party spotted the Indians from the top of one
of the hills and decided to move their camp to Otter Creek. Charles Kenck,
a German immigrant and proprietor of the Washington Brewery at Helena,
made it known that he would rather ride straight to Mammoth. He set off on
his own, but soon gave it up. Unbeknownst to the party, the Indians had already
been informed of their presence by James Irwin, a solitary sightseer whom the
Nez Perce found hiding in a ravine.

The Helena party consisted of Andrew Weikert, Richard Dietrich (who
himself would soon be killed at Mammoth), Fred Pfister, Joe Roberts, Charles
Kenck, Leslie Wilke, Leonard Duncan, John Stewart, Ben Stone, and August

Foller. They camped about a mile and a half above the Upper Falls near the forks of Otter Creek, and near the place where William Tesinsky would be killed by a grizzly bear 109 years later. The site was about a mile west of the present main park road and overlooking the place where later generations of visitors would park their cars to watch bear feedings. On the morning of August 26, Weikert and Wilke rode south to scout for Indians while the rest of the party lounged in camp. Full of foreboding, Charles Kenck remarked to Ben Stone, their black cook, "Stone, what would you do if the Indians should jump us?" Stone replied, "You take care of yourself and I'll take care of mine."

When the party of Indians hit them, the men were completely surprised. Ben Stone was just starting to prepare lunch when the shots rang out. He thought it was Weikert and Wilke funning them, so he called out for them to stop their foolishness, adding, "You can't scare us." But at the second volley, the men all began to run for cover.

Pfister, Dietrich, and Stone ran for the Yellowstone River. Roberts and Foller did some "tall running" and got away too, as did Duncan, but Stewart and Kenck did not manage as well.

Stewart had been asleep when the attack began, but quickly awoke and, with Kenck, ran for the timber on the opposite side of the creek. Just after Stewart crossed the stream, a bullet hit him in the leg, causing him to fall. About that time, he heard Kenck cry out, "Oh, my God!" Then two more shots and Stewart heard, "I'm murdered!" A ball had struck him in the back of the neck, breaking it instantly. Kenck was dead. The Indians rifled his pockets, and then returned for Stewart, who begged them to spare his life. When they asked for money, Stewart gave them 263 dollars and a watch, and was amazed when the Indians left.

After the Indians took his money, Stewart said, "I tried to make my way up the hill to see whether Kenck was dead or alive. I was too weak and had to abandon the trip. I then called him at the top of my voice, but could receive no answer." He was washing his wounds in the creek when Stone hobbled up. The two were commiserating when Weikert and Wilke rode back into camp, so all decided to ride back to Mammoth.

Fred Pfister's account says: "I was busy getting wood when all of a sudden, pop, pop, went the guns and I heard the Indians' yip! yip! I looked around and saw the camp full of Indians with the boys jumping and going in every direction. I saw two of the boys coming towards me and I lit out for the river. I reached the river and on looking back heard two shots and [heard] some one exclaim, 'O, my God!'"[4]

On the thirtieth, Weikert and James McCartney arrived back at Otter Creek after traveling from Mammoth. They found Kenck's body three hundred yards from camp and buried it, and then hunted without success for Roberts and Foller, who would be found later. McCartney later disinterred Kenck's body and took it to Helena, where it was finally laid to permanent rest.

Richard Dietrich apparently walked (perhaps rode part of the way) back to Mammoth Hot Springs, a distance of about fifty miles, for on August 27, Leonard Duncan brought the news into the springs that Dietrich was about two miles out at Gardner River but completely exhausted. Weikert took an extra horse and rode out after him.

Dietrich was a Helena music teacher and probably the least rugged member of the party. As a young man, he had gone with his sister by wagon to California to find gold so that the two of them could return to Germany to study music. Finding no gold, the pair wrangled passage anyway. After graduation, Richard returned to Helena, where he set up vocal and instrumental music classes. He was an unlikely figure to be killed in an Indian attack.

An ambulance was traveling to Mammoth to take Stewart back to Bozeman, and Weikert thought Dietrich should go on it, too. But Dietrich refused to go, saying, "My God! What will Mrs. Roberts say if I go away and leave Joe? Through my inducement he came. What shall I say when I meet his mother, when she asks me where is Joe?" That Dietrich was still quite afraid of Indian attacks, however, is evident from his remark to Andrew Weikert just before Weikert headed to Otter Creek to bury Kenck: "Andy, you will give me a decent burial, won't you?"

On August 30, Jake Stoner, having seen an Indian party on Lava Creek, hastened back to Mammoth to warn Dietrich and Stone. Dietrich hid in the woods behind McCartney's hotel and shortly after that was joined by Ben Stone. The two men spent the night in the brush on Clematis Creek. When they saw a party of eighteen Indians approaching, they climbed a tree and watched them loot the place and head north toward Henderson's ranch.

On August 31, a Nez Perce party attacked James Henderson's ranch on present Stephens Creek and spent two hours fighting with several white defenders over it and some horses before finally setting the place on fire. There were no casualties at the ranch, but on the way back through Mammoth the Indians caught Richard Dietrich returning to the hotel to get something to eat.

Dietrich at one point apparently got hungry and/or tired of waiting in the tree, so he climbed down and went to the hotel, leaving Stone in the tree. It has been speculated that he possibly failed to connect the sound of horses' hooves coming from that direction with Indians and carelessly walked out the front door. Dietrich was shot down there at the entrance to McCartney's hotel and thus became the second Yellowstone Park fatality in the Nez Perce war.

Lieutenant Hugh L. Scott passed by the spot shortly after that, chasing the small Nez Perce party south from Henderson's, and found Dietrich's body still warm on the porch. He said: "We rounded a point and at McCartney's cabin in a side gulch found a white man lying dead at the door, not yet cold. He had been standing in the doorway, looking out, when one of the Indians we were chasing rounded the point and shot him. He had plunged forward on his face, and been shot again, the (second) bullet going the length of his body."[5]

Apparently the first bullet was enough to kill Dietrich, hitting his heart.[6] When Weikert and McCartney returned the next night, they lit a candle to see and found Dietrich's body lying on the floor. The next day they buried him in an "old bathtub." As late as 1882, the grave was still there near Clematis Creek, for traveler Mary Richards wrote the following confusing lines about it: "His body lies on the other side of the brook, and is marked by a rough wooden bath tub in which he was placed for burial. Finding the improvised coffin too large, and the grave too small, they took out the corpse and placed it uncovered in the ground. The bath tub [is] awaiting removal."[7]

Those two killings of whites and the five in 1839 are the only ones known to have happened during Euro-Americans' encounters with Native Americans inside Yellowstone National Park. But at least one more may have occurred in the shadowy era of prediscovery Yellowstone. Park gamekeeper Harry Yount found a human skull in 1878 on the Yellowstone River above Yellowstone Lake. The chronicler of this event, park superintendent P. W. Norris, thought it represented the killing of a white man by Indians within park boundaries. That was never proved.[8]

Additionally, "two prospectors who have never since been heard of," as chronicled by Hiram Chittenden, may also have been killed by Nez Perce during the 1877 foray. This information came from the Radersburg party, who, as they were being marched east of Mary Lake, "heard considerable firing in the timber to their right."[9]

Finally, Indians killed some of their own traditional enemies within Yellowstone National Park during the Nez Perce foray, and two of those victims are known. At her own request, the Nez Perce abandoned one of their very old women at their camp near Mud Volcano at Nez Perce Ford. Lieutenant S. G. Fisher's Bannock scouts, who came through shortly afterward in pursuit of them, killed and scalped her.[10] And a Nez Perce Indian boy who was probably no more than 15 years old was killed at the head of "Little Blacktail Deer Creek," although this was probably Blacktail Deer Creek proper. E. S. Topping chronicled the account in the 1880s. From east of the park, Colonel Samuel Sturgis sent three couriers—J. S. Leonard, John J. Groff (perhaps Goff or Gough), and an Indian boy—into the park with a message to General O. O. Howard, who was chasing the Nez Perce through the park. The three couriers crossed Baronett's Bridge heading west, and

[a]s they were passing around the head of Little Blacktail creek they were saluted by a volley from concealed Indians, who had seen them

coming and hid. The Indian boy fell, and Gough, who was wounded in the neck, ran with Le[o]nard to a point of rocks near the trail, but out of sight of the boy. After a few shots had been exchanged, the Indians went on. Night soon came and the two scouts went on afoot without looking for the boy. About noon of the next day, Jack Baronett and John Werks [Work], who were scouting with Lieut. Doane, came to where the fight had occurred, and finding a trail of blood leading toward the Little Blacktail, followed it. The Indian boy had recovered consciousness and crawled a half mile. Near the creek the trail was lost and his body was never found.[11]

The killings of Jack Crandall and another man in 1869 occurred outside of the park on present Crandall Creek near Cooke City, Montana. The incident is a fascinating part of Yellowstone country history, so I include it here. In the fall of 1867, three miners (Arch Graham, Jack Crandall, and a man known only as Dougherty or Finley)[12] began working a prospecting claim at the mouth of Crevice Creek on the Yellowstone River inside present Yellowstone National Park. They continued it in 1868. In August of 1869, the three decided they were not doing well, so they took off to join Bob Anderson and Jim Lee on a prospecting trip into the country northeast of the present park. There Crandall and Dougherty stayed to prospect while the others returned to the Yellowstone River.

A week later, a party of about twenty men, including Frederick Bottler and Adam Horn Miller, went to Clark's Fork. They were supposed to meet Crandall and Dougherty on the upper river. When the two men did not show, the others concluded something had happened to them, so Bottler began a search. What he found was truly horrible. Killed by Crow Indians,[13] the two men's heads had been cut off and stuck on the points of their picks, with the other points stuck into the ground. Their tin cups had been placed in front of their heads, apparently to tell others that the two had been surprised while eating. Their headless bodies lay nearby.[14] The coyotes and probably other animals had eaten the flesh from their bones, but Crandall was recognizable by his teeth—he wore a plate—and by his long black beard. The Indians had taken the hardwood handles from their picks to make handles for their quirts. Bottler's party buried the two, but coyotes kept digging up their bones, so in the fall of 1871, Jim Gourley and Bill Cameron buried them again, piling rocks onto the graves and marking them with hewn pine headboards.[15]

Adam Horn Miller stated that later he was riding across the Crow Reservation when he saw an Indian wearing a "plug hat" which he knew to be Dougherty's. The sight gave Miller "an itchy trigger finger," but he did not dare to shoot the Indian on the reservation.[16]

There are at least three other possible battles in Yellowstone National Park involving Indians wherein humans could have been killed. They are shadowy stories told by trappers and none are strictly verifiable, but neither can I dismiss them entirely.

The three stories all come from Thomas Michener, a settler in the Gallatin Canyon who arrived there in 1889. His account says that Native Americans in the Yellowstone country told stories "many times" to trappers about a "fierce battle that was fought perhaps several generations ago" between the park Sheepeaters and bands of several other tribes. The battle supposedly lasted several weeks among the peaks of the Gallatin Range and finally ended on Three Rivers Peak, where the Sheepeaters made their last stand: "They made a large stone fort, which can still be seen, but they were wiped out to the last man. Jim Bridger and other trappers of that day had heard of this battle as it was described by the Indians." Michener claims that he himself saw the stone structure in 1891 built by the defenders on Three Rivers Peak.

Michener also related an account of two white trappers who were supposedly involved in an affray with some Blackfeet Indians on Porcupine Creek (just north of the park boundary) in the early 1860s. He says one trapper and one Indian were killed and the other trapper got away.

Michener's final story concerned Nels Murray and his brother Andy, two early-day settlers in Gallatin Canyon. Michener says the two were camped on the present site of the 320 Ranch with about sixty horses. Some Indians that were camped near the mouth of Cinnamon Creek were agitating to steal the horses, so, according to Nels, the two supposedly stole up and killed every one of them and threw their bodies into the Gallatin River.[17]

These last three incidents, if they occurred, are fascinating as possibilities, but as of now they cannot be verified. A total of seven persons are known to have died in Yellowstone National Park from Indian fights and two others just outside the park. Even the ancient battles that probably occurred in Yellowstone between tribes of Native Americans, the battles about which we know almost nothing, can be characterized as clashes of cultures. And all certainly were part of Sherman's hell.

16

A KNOCKOUT AT BACON RIND
DEATHS FROM FIGHTS

Men must fight.

—Euripides, 430 BC

ONLY ONE DEATH FROM A fight is known to have occurred in Yellowstone National Park, with another occurring just outside the park. The one inside occurred in 1933 in one of the park's Civilian Conservations Corps camps due to a discipline problem.

The Civilian Conservation Corps (CCC) was a part of the Yellowstone scene from 1933 to 1941, building trails, cleaning up debris, erecting some buildings, and providing employment for many young men and women. On July 13, 1933, 18-year-old camps worker Abraham Yancovitch of the Bronx, New York, ate breakfast at the CCC camp on Bacon Rind Creek near the park northwest boundary. He and his friends usually washed their breakfast dishes below a small dam on the creek, but on this morning Abe decided to wash them above the dam. That was a violation of drinking-water regulations, but Yancovitch did not care.

When Yancovitch's superior, regular army first sergeant George Satriano, ordered him to obey the regulations, Yancovitch refused and cussed out the sergeant. Thereupon Satriano suggested that the two of them settle the matter with fists, which they soon did.

During the fight Satriano hit Yancovitch "on the left side of his head" with a right-handed blow. The youth fell, rolling on the ground and holding both his hands over his left eye. An observer picked him up, and then Yancovitch apparently walked to his tent under his own power. But several hours later he died of a fractured skull and a cerebral hemorrhage. The camp superintendent wrote that Yancovitch died "due to his own misconduct in the deliberate and direct disobedience of a lawful order given by a lawfully appointed superior."[1]

For a while, as one might imagine, conditions at the CCC camp at Bacon Rind Creek were tense. One of Yancovitch's friends, a youth named Singer, caused some trouble and was arrested. Another youth named Bressler said he was getting a lawyer from New York. Both men were fired and sent home. Sergeant Satriano was cleared in the official investigation and continued in his duties.[2]

A fight killed Frank Cheplak in May of 1903 at Aldridge, Montana, just north of Yellowstone Park. He stumbled into John Yonskovitch's saloon at Happy Hollow on the night of May 7. He wanted to fight someone, and he did not much care who it was. One witness said he threatened everyone. So Anton Krumparichnick, John Stanfield, and John Rakoon "pitched into him and warmed him soundly with chairs." No one was convicted for his murder. Euripides had been proven right again.[3]

17

A DEATH FROM DIVING

Or dive into the bottom of the deep,
Where fathom-line could never touch the ground,
And pluck up drowned honor by the locks.

—William Shakespeare, *King Henry IV*

MANY HAVE WISHED THAT it were that simple to recover lost honor, dignity, health, or life. But it is usually not. With regard to diving incidents, a moment of bravado can translate into a lifetime of pain or paralysis. Fortunately, only one known death of this type has happened in Yellowstone.

On August 15, 1919, Louis D. Boatman of Morrill, Nebraska, was touring the park with his aunt and sister. The cold temperature of Yellowstone River notwithstanding, he decided to go swimming in it at Fishing Bridge. Boatman dove from the bridge, struck his head on the bottom, and died instantly from a skull fracture.[1]

Another diving incident caused injury rather than death. On July 5, 1940, Thomas Cole Wright, a park employee at Old Faithful Inn, dove into Firehole River some fifty yards northeast of the Old Faithful sewage disposal plant. He hit his head on the bottom, crushed a vertebra, and was paralyzed from his neck down for the rest of his life.[2]

Considering the penchant that park visitors have today for diving and jumping off the high cliffs in Firehole Canyon, it is amazing that there have not been more injuries of this type. Signs there warn visitors of the danger, and rangers regularly issue citations for doing it, but fools continue to jump into the Firehole Canyon. It is a safe bet that someone will be injured or killed there while disregarding the rules.

18

WILD HORSES

DEATHS FROM HORSE, WAGON, AND STAGECOACH INCIDENTS

It seemed like the wilder the team acted, the more people wanted to ride with 'em!

—Henry Del Jenkins, Yellowstone Park stagecoach driver,
1897–1914

WILD HORSES AND SAVAGE DRIVERS were the stars of what one historian has called the "best of all possible worlds" in early Yellowstone. Hundreds of drivers and thousands of horses occupied the park during that time of the "Grand Tour." A traveler to Yellowstone in those days usually came to the park by train (to the north or west entrances) and then spent five to ten days doing the park in a stagecoach. Well-heeled railroad visitors shared the narrow roads of Yellowstone with Montana cowboys and schoolteachers who stayed in tent camps. Stage drivers, called "savages," "popped the silk" over their tackies, which hurtled down the dusty roads at six miles per hour. Certainly there were moments of danger with horses and wagons. At least nine horse, thirteen wagon, and four stagecoach fatalities are known to have happened in and near Yellowstone National Park during those halcyon days.

The horse and stagecoach era in Yellowstone lasted from 1872 through 1915, with both horses and autos present in 1916. From 1880, when the first commercial stagecoach carried visitors through the park, through 1916 visitors to Yellowstone utilized stagecoaches and were part of what was called "the carriage trade." Yellowstone Park had forty-five years of horse-traveling visitors before it ever saw an automobile and before most national parks in the United States were ever born.

Horses, of course, had to be dealt with carefully. Incidents, often called "runaways," were fairly common, as auto accidents are today. Stagecoach companies usually reported up to four stage wrecks per year, 1880–1916. Huntley

Child, who grew up in Yellowstone to eventually manage the Yellowstone Park Transportation Company, remembered many years later that during his tenure the company experienced "about one accident per year."[1] Indeed, statistics in 1909 indicated that there were thirty fatalities for every one hundred million horse-traveled miles in the United States, compared to about one-sixth that today for automobiles.[2] The park stagecoach companies tended to be close-mouthed about stage wrecks because few or none of them carried liability insurance. Thus they often attempted to "settle" quickly with an injured passenger. Causes of accidents tended to be inept drivers, sudden wild flights of teams, mechanical failures of equipment, or intoxication.

The first known horse-and-wagon accident in the park resulted in the first burial at the Camp Sheridan (later Fort Yellowstone) cemetery. Thomas Horton, a private who was in the infantry, fell from a wagon in late September of 1888 near Norris Geyser Basin. The wagon rode "over his body injuring him very severely." He was placed in the wagon and brought to Norris. Later an army ambulance took him to Camp Sheridan at Mammoth, where he died on October 1.[3]

The runaway accident suffered by J. L. Sanborn at Cinnabar (inside of the present park) probably illustrates something that happened fairly often in

1895 photo of stagecoach at the Hoodoos, near Mammoth Hot Springs, where the road caved in at least twice, causing stagecoach wrecks (NPS Scrapbook photo 7-JN, YNP Archives)

horse-drawn America. Sanborn, who resided for many years at Bozeman and who was described as "one of the pioneers of Montana," was mining at Cooke City with his wife and son in 1890. On August 12, during a visit to the ranch of H. J. Hoppe of Cinnabar, Sanborn got into a playful mood and, after loosening the picket rope from his saddle, attempted to lasso E. J. Keeney's horse. That movement started both horses on the run, and in the excitement, Sanborn's horse rode him against the side of a building. Sanborn's head struck the building with such force that his neck was instantly broken.[4]

A soldier at Fort Yellowstone was kicked by his horse. This type of injury, too, occurred fairly commonly in horse-drawn America, if Montana newspapers are any indication. Sergeant James P. Pruitt of Company E, First Cavalry, was instantly killed at Mammoth on September 11, 1891, when his horse kicked him in the stomach. He was buried in the Fort Yellowstone cemetery. He was probably the same soldier that the Livingston newspaper referred to as "Sgt. Trint" a week later.[5]

Similarly, First Lieutenant Lunsford Daniel of Company I, Sixth Cavalry, was thrown from his horse on May 27, 1894, on the Mammoth–Gardiner road near Gardiner. He left Gardiner that night about 11:00 p.m. riding toward Fort Yellowstone. Scout Felix Burgess found Daniel lying unconscious by the roadside about one mile south of Gardiner, where he had evidently been thrown from his horse and probably dragged some distance when his foot was caught in the stirrup. He died on May 31 without ever having regained consciousness.[6]

Likewise, a horseback incident killed W. A. Babcock, president and general manager of Bishop and Babcock Company of Cleveland, Ohio, on Slough Creek on September 23, 1895. Babcock was hunting with seven other men "in the neighborhood of Slough Creek" and "40 miles from Mammoth." The exact location was "on the divide between Slough Creek and Buffalo Creek, a very dangerous place," at Bull Pass and north of the park boundary. His party was a large one, with thirty-two horses, several guides, and seven hunters. The Cleveland *Plain Dealer* stated that the party reached a narrow pass on a high precipice. "Our guides ordered us to dismount and proceed with care," said C. B. Stowe, who was in the party.

> Everyone did so, except Mr. Babcock, who persisted in keeping his saddle, and just as we were going through one of the most dangerous points of the pass his horse slipped and rider and animal were precipitated down the steep bank, a distance of about forty feet. In falling the horse fell directly on Mr. Babcock and that caused his death. When we reached him Dr. Buell made an examination and found besides scalp and head wounds that his right lung had been crushed by the fall and

that recovery was impossible . . . He was conscious to the last and bid us all goodbye.

"My God, Babcock is dead!" yelled Dr. Buell as the party looked down upon him. Babcock lived for two and a half hours after the incident, saying "Good-bye, boys" several times and blaming himself for it. His horse survived. The party took his body to Uncle John Yancey's hotel and then on to the train at Cinnabar.[7]

A bicycle and a horse killed Ellis Lingard. Private Lingard of Company D, Sixth Cavalry, was intoxicated and riding his horse on a park road on August 2, 1893, when he encountered a tourist named Parkhurst from Michigan riding a bicycle directly toward him. When Lingard had nearly reached Parkhurst, the latter, fearing he would be run down by the horse, jumped from his bicycle onto the roadside. Lingard directed his horse directly at the bicycle and attempted to jump the horse over it. The horse's legs became entangled in the spokes, throwing it and Lingard to the ground. Lingard never regained consciousness, and the bicycle was totally wrecked.[8]

Dick Hull was probably killed when his horse threw him. A stock tender who worked at Soda Butte for the park mail carrier, Hull left there on Saturday, September 17, 1910, to look for some other horses. His horse returned alone to the Soda Butte Soldier Station on Tuesday. Scout James McBride found Hull's body high in the mountains on September 23, and he was buried at the spot where he was found. His skull was crushed in front, and the soldiers believed that he had been killed by being thrown from his horse and striking his head on a large rock nearby.[9]

A boisterous steeplechase killed a Fort Yellowstone soldier in 1912. Lieutenant Robert Launsberry, of Lake Mills, Wisconsin, aged 28 and the quartermaster of the First Cavalry, was engaged in horse festivities with a good crowd on the Gardiner target range (east of Gardner River between it and Turkey Pen Peak) on October 1. His horse collided with one ridden by a Miss Chase, he was pitched into a mound of boulders, and he died the following day from his injuries.[10]

Until 2012, the most recent park fatality involving only a horse and no wagon occurred August 29, 1956, on a concession horse ride from Canyon Village. Diana Alberta Parks Schramm, 27, of New Milford, New Jersey, was enjoying a Yellowstone Park Company trail ride to Clear Lake about 3:00 p.m. with her husband when her horse stumbled and fell, throwing her into a tree. Wrangler Robert Myers stated that her horse was running to catch up with the string and "she hit a tree with her head and left shoulder [which knocked] her off the horse." Schramm suffered a fractured skull, a broken neck, and internal injuries, and died about forty-five minutes later. Her death was reminiscent of

Visitors' view out of the window of a stagecoach toward two horsemen in the Hoodoos (where several stagecoach wrecks occurred), n.d., circa 1904 (author's collection)

a vanished Yellowstone era.[11] So was the death of 56-year-old Carl Dullmaier of Gernsheim, Germany, on July 30, 2012, in a freak accident. Park officials stated that some birds flew up from a bridge just as his horseback party was getting ready to cross it on a concessioner horse ride near Tower Junction. The horses spooked, throwing Dullmaier from his saddle. Life-flighted to a Billings hospital, he died there of head injuries.[12]

Horses combined with wagons have killed at least thirteen persons in Yellowstone Park. Alexander Deckard, about 59, was a freighter engaged to drive teams from Cooke City to Cinnabar. On September 5, 1895, he had just left Cooke City and was heading "down the mountain" with a six-horse team and a heavy load of ore when he was thrown from his wagon and "crushed under its wheels." Ironically, a fellow employee who would die in the same manner the following week was the person who found Deckard. Aaron P. Bliss reported that Deckard was "lying on the mountain roadside dead with his ribs broken."[13] Only a week later in that same fashion and on that same road, Aaron P. Bliss, about 50, a teamster who hauled ore from Cooke City to Cinnabar, was thrown from his wagon and instantly killed just before September 14, 1895. And a driver for independent tour operator F. M. Scott was killed in a wagon wreck at Virginia Cascades on July 23, 1897. George Williams was whipping his team near the steep curve known as Devil's Elbow when the wagon struck

YELLOWSTONE PARK   June 29, 1903.

File C-131

Major John Pitcher,

    Acting Superintendent,

        Yellowstone Park.

Dear Sir:-

      The drivers for this Company are making daily complaints to our Superintendent about the location of the camps of camping parties throughout the Park. In many instances they are located directly alongside of the road, and with blankets, washing and tents flapping in their faces, the horses get almost beyond control, and it is extremely difficult to pass many of the camps.

      Wont you kindly look into the matter, and have the campers and road crews follow the regulations with regard to the location of camps.

               Yours truly,

                      President.

Archive document 5479, dated June 29, 1903, wherein president of Yellowstone Park Transportation asked for help to prevent scaring of the horses, which causes wrecks

a rock, throwing him from his seat and under the wheels. Lieutenant G. O. Cress and Sergeant Driscoll turned Williams's body over to his employer and telegraphed headquarters about the fatality.[14]

    L. V. Brigham, a civilian teamster of the Quarter Master Division at Fort Yellowstone, was killed on December 28, 1897, at Mammoth, "from injuries sustained by [being thrown?] from a wagon." Brigham was 72 years old. He was "a well known character at Fort Yellowstone" who "had been employed in the National park for many years" and who simply fell from his wagon while hauling supplies from Cinnabar to Mammoth. It is not known whether the wagon ran over him or the fall alone killed him.[15]

Another wagon wreck that apparently did not make the papers killed muleskinner Hi Jehnsen. Jehnsen had come to Yellowstone in 1884, and everyone liked him. He was a colorful character whose joshing yarns "were to a dull hour what spice is to a Christmas pudding." The details and location of his wagon wreck in 1896 seem to be lost, known to us only because 10-year-old Ida Miller remembered him well. While "coming down the mountain road from Cooke City," Jehnsen got into trouble. For some reason he was unable to manipulate the foot brake on his wagon with the necessary agility. The wagon turned over onto both him and his team, killing all.[16]

Another teamster was run over by his wagon. Charles Baldwin, age about 35 and single, had just begun driving for the government after working for two years for the Yellowstone Park Transportation Company. On October 19, 1900, Baldwin went to Cinnabar to pick up a load of beer, returned to Fort Yellowstone, and unloaded the beer at the canteen. He had just started driving toward the government stables when something frightened the team and it took off in a high-speed run. The wagon struck the stump of a tree and Baldwin was thrown from it, the wheels passing over his body, breaking several ribs and driving one of them through a lung. At the hospital, Baldwin lingered five hours before he died.[17]

Philip Sheldon was new at Fort Yellowstone. Sheldon, 25, had just arrived and was riding from Mammoth to Gardiner on July 13, 1903, in a wagon driven by a man named Knutson. On "Soldiers' Garden Hill" (today called Soap Hill) about one and one-half miles north of Mammoth, the team became frightened and ran away. One horse fell and Sheldon was thrown between the wheels, one of them crushing his head. No one knew where he was from or who his relatives were, so he was buried in the Mammoth army cemetery. Perhaps his faraway relatives and friends, wherever they were, forever wondered what had happened to him.[18]

On December 23, 1895, Harry Brown was driving a team of six mules hauling hay for the Hoppe brothers. Two miles above town in Gardner Canyon, Brown got too close to the river and tipped over his load into the stream and fell under it. Observers were not sure whether he had been held underwater by the load of hay he was hauling or whether his neck was broken on rocks in the river. Brown was "an old-timer on the upper Yellowstone" who had worked a number of years for the Yellowstone Association.[19]

Emil "Swede" Johnson, a farmer on Montana's Shields River, died while drinking and driving. On the evening of October 6, 1903, Johnson, a teamster who was about 60 years old, was simultaneously drunk and hauling a load of large sewer pipes on his wagon from Gardiner to Mammoth. Just south of Gardiner, Johnson's wagon struck a culvert that was twenty to thirty inches deep. The wagon and all of its pipes turned over on him, crushing him instantly.[20]

Likewise, one of the "old time freighters of Gardiner" was a victim of drinking and driving. Frank Rose, age about 50 and described as sandy-haired with a sandy mustache, had a few Halloween drinks on October 31, 1905, and then drove his eight-horse team from Mammoth to Indian Creek. At the "seven mile post," about the same place where the road bridge today crosses Gardner River, Rose apparently lost control of his team and fell from his wagon, and the wagon wheels passed over and crushed his chest. "Horribly mangled," said the newspapers, he died at the site and laid there until he was found by park stagecoach drivers. His team was found three-quarters of a mile beyond his body, loose in the road but still hitched up.[21]

We know little about the circumstances surrounding the death of civilian William Eaton on May 30, 1904, because for some reason it did not make the newspapers. He was killed when he fell from his wagon during a runaway at Mammoth. A fracture at the base of his skull attested to the accident, and he was buried in the army cemetery there.[22]

Of course, many wild runaways involving both wagons and single horses occurred outside the park, and two of them are of interest here—M. A. Bucke's because he was socially prominent and John Hartz's because he was possibly the first burial in the Gardiner cemetery. Maurice A. Bucke, 31, was a mining engineer and the general manager of the Bear Gulch mining company. He was an educated geologist who was well liked by his Jardine employees. On December 8, 1899, he left Jardine in a buggy heading for Cinnabar and riding with Alfred Blair. On the so-called Z hill above Gardiner, the horses ran away, the buggy overturned, and Bucke jumped from the carriage. He struck a granite boulder, which crushed his head and also broke his neck. Alfred C. Blair was so badly injured that he had to crawl for help.[23] John Hartz, age about 60 and a tinner (tinker) employed by P. H. Tooley, got on a fractious horse on October 3, 1886, at Gardiner. The horse reared on its hind legs, throwing both horse and rider backward. In attempting to keep from being smashed beneath the horse, Hartz struck his head on a rock so forcibly that it crushed his skull. He died without regaining consciousness. Interestingly, he had injured himself a year earlier while drunk and employed as a tinner or tinker for Babcock and Miles in Livingston. Hartz was very possibly the person for whom the Gardiner cemetery hill was named Tinker's Hill, and he was probably the first burial there.[24]

Stagecoach wrecks are probably the most interesting of the horse-related episodes from Yellowstone's past. Although wrecks usually occurred in the park one or more times per summer, amazingly only four fatalities are known—

three inside the park and one just outside. A wreck involving a Monida and Yellowstone Company stagecoach killed a woman passenger in 1899. Mrs. Joseph Lippman, age about 30, and her husband, an attorney from Salt Lake City, were traveling from Monida, Montana, to the park and had not even reached Dwelle's (eight miles west of the park) when the accident occurred. At 10:00 p.m. on Friday night, August 26, when the coach was about three miles west of Dwelle's and coming down Targhee Pass, it struck a large rock in the road and began to overturn. Perhaps attempting to escape, Mrs. Lippman stuck her head out of the careening stage and a tree struck her head, breaking her neck and killing her instantly. The wheels turned and tipped the stage partly onto its side, and the horses continued to pull it for a short distance over Mrs. Lippman. Mr. Lippmann was thrown violently from the coach and lost consciousness. At least four other persons, including Mr. Lippman, were injured simultaneously.

The wreck happened because of darkness. The Monida and Yellowstone Stage Company—just organized the preceding year by W. W. Humphreys and F. Jay Haynes—had consented to drive the group after dark because they desired to make a hurried trip. But according to Livingston newspapers, the company had "admonished all that they accepted such transportation at their own risk." The accident occurred "on a divide" of sorts, and the driver could not see the obstacle in the road.[25]

The role of the park's Fountain Hotel in the incident is a bit confusing, and its part in the story probably caused some newspapers' misreporting of the wreck itself as having occurred inside of Yellowstone Park. Following the incident, Mr. Lippman was taken on to Fountain Hotel (an additional distance of about thirty miles) rather than being put up for the night at Dwelle's—probably because Fountain Hotel could provide medical treatment, better facilities for the stage company, and better general communications. We know this because the newspapers reported that the surviving Mr. Lippman dictated a telegram to his children from there the following day. It read as follows: "Fountain Hotel, Wyo., August 27, 4:29pm. Am seventy-five miles from nearest telegraph station, and in bed. Doctor gives me no hope of getting away today. Will come as quickly as doctor permits. Am not seriously injured, but doctor insists upon my keeping quiet. Be of good cheer. PAPA."

First report of the wreck occurred on August 27, and its particulars were given in the follow-up story as printed by the *Salt Lake Herald* on August 28. The account provides a dramatic glimpse of stagecoach travel in and around Yellowstone during those primitive days:

> The stage left Monida behind schedule time Friday morning. The journey continued all day and far into the night, and but three miles more were to be traveled, when Fountain Hotel, at Dwelle's, Wyo.

[*sic*—Dwelle's hotel, in Montana], the party's destination, would have been reached. Mr. and Mrs. Lippman had been riding on the boot of the coach during the day, but towards evening it grew cooler, and they were seated inside. The stage went on its course through the dark canyons and over steep inclines, lurching from side to side [o]n the miserable roads until the occupants were well nigh prostrated with nervousness. They had just traversed a level plat of 100 rods, as described by Agent McKenzie, and entered upon a road cut through masses of tall pines, which only made the darkness more impenetrable. Suddenly the wheel of the coach struck a large boulder that had rolled down from the mountain side, and the conveyance was heaved to a dangerous angle, when a piece of the harness broke, and the horses started to rear and plunge. The wheel at one side got off the road, and slewed [caromed tipsily] down the mountain side a few inches, and Mrs. Lippman, terribly excited, struggled to escape. She put her head out of the window or upper part of the door, just as the horses gave another plunge forward. It was then the fatality occurred, though not until later was it known. The driver succeeded in stopping the horses before they had run over thirty-five feet, but for that distance Mrs. Lippman was dragged and the other occupants thrown from side to side and out of the coach. Mr. Lippman was unconscious when his wife's body was picked up and tenderly laid across a seat in the coach by the other members of the party. The drive was resumed in all haste to the Dwelle's hotel.[26]

According to his boss, the very experienced driver of the coach—Roger Sherman—was consumed with grief over this incident. He requested that he be relieved from further duty, saying that "he could not drive a team over that road again after the death of that beautiful Salt Lake lady."

Another stagecoach wreck involved the Yellowstone Park Transportation Company, and it indirectly killed Dr. Charles J. Blank, a Buffalo, New York, veterinarian. The wreck occurred sometime between September 26 and 30, 1904. One of the last stage runs of the season had just reached a point four hundred yards north of Golden Gate Bridge when the incident happened. Dr. Blank's left leg was badly injured, and he was taken to a hospital, where he lay for a week. Surgeon M. C. Usher noticed that gangrene had set into his leg and amputated it, but Blank died about an hour later on October 3, 1904. Captain Usher listed Dr. Blank's cause of death as "shock and septicemia following gangrenous left-leg amputation."[27]

Typical of noninjury stagecoach wrecks in the park was one that occurred on October 1, 1907. The stage, which ran from Cooke City to Gardiner, was heavily loaded with fourteen passengers. Just before crossing the Yellowstone

River near Tower Junction, its front axle broke and the right front wheel came off, overturning the stage. The driver, Rollo Weingarten, apparently showed considerable presence of mind in keeping the coach from falling into the river, and one small girl was rescued just before she fell into the swirling waters. All passengers walked to nearby Yancey's Hotel after the wreck to secure another coach. F. C. Byrne, manager of the mine at Cooke City, suffered a broken collarbone, a bruised arm, and internal injuries.[28]

Another stagecoach wreck happened on August 10, 1907, on Blanding Hill, between Canyon and Norris, and in it the driver and seven passengers were seriously injured. The driver, in his "overweening zeal" to get ahead of the other coaches, turned onto the old road on Blanding Hill, it being shorter than the regular, newer road. But coming down the steep hill, the team got away from him. At the junction of the two roads was a ditch, which the coach struck with such a vengeance that it broke the safety strap and separated the team from the coach. The whole rig then came down hard onto the road and broke completely in two, injuring eight of the nine people on board. Some of the horses ran off with the front running gear, but one of the wheeler horses fell down and was dragged quite a distance, losing most of the skin from its body.[29]

Two stagecoach fatalities occurred in 1910, in the same week. On August 13, 1910, a YPT Company stagecoach was traveling through the fallen limestone formations known as the Hoodoos, just south of Mammoth Hot Springs. Fifty yards south of Silver Gate, the road suddenly gave way under the wheels of the third coach from the last in a string of thirty, the entire roadbed falling into one of the many caverns that honeycomb the limestone-clad Mammoth area. When the coach's forward wheels suddenly sank into the formation, falling ten feet into a cavern, W. Lewis, the driver, was thrown out and the horses ran away toward the mountain embankment. Daniel E. MacKay, a sixtyish gentleman from New York City, jumped from the careening vehicle at the first hint of danger. Unfortunately for him, he landed hard with his feet far apart, and the force drove the bones of his legs up into his body and lacerated his bladder. Then the caroming coach fell foursquare upon him. MacKay died soon after at the Fort Yellowstone hospital. Four others were also injured, including Mrs. MacKay. Postwreck investigators thought perhaps that the road had been undermined by heavy rains.[30] Huntley Child Sr., one of the heads of the YPT Company, recalled this incident vividly many years later. He remembered that Mr. MacKay "telescoped against the rocks."[31]

Apparently, this collapsing of the roadbed through the Hoodoos happened more than once, for Aubrey Haines has chronicled an incident involving a stagecoach falling into a cavern at that location. The two incidents must be different ones, however, for in the Haines incident no passenger was injured, but the team and coach were.[32]

Another fatality occurred the very same week as MacKay's and even in a similar location, but it involved a woman passenger. Ross Bodge, who had been living with her aunt and uncle in Livingston, Montana, for a couple of years,[33] was traveling in a stagecoach south of Mammoth Hot Springs on August 7, 1910. At 2:00 in the afternoon, the horses became so frightened that driver Roy Armstrong, a "very competent and careful driver" according to the local newspaper, could barely control them.[34] Believing that the horses were out of control, Bodge jumped from her high seat next to the driver and was instantly killed.[35] Another stage driver, Herb French, remembered many years later that her neck was broken.[36]

What was probably the last stagecoach transportation wreck to happen in Yellowstone during the stagecoach era appears to have had a big influence on the ultimate removal of all horses from the park. It happened at about 3:30 p.m. on July 24, 1916, the only year that Yellowstone had both horses and cars on its roads. Four-horse coach 26 of the Wylie Camping Company, driven by H. E. Thompson and headed from Mammoth toward Gardiner, was one mile out when the team was suddenly confronted with a stalled automobile. The horses bolted in fright, and the coach careened wildly down the road, narrowly missing going over an embankment. However, it turned onto its side, throwing all nine passengers out and crushing many of them between it and a rocky wall.

A Wylie stagecoach in 1910 (courtesy of Yellowstone National Park)

The injuries were severe, with three persons suffering painful fractures. This wreck was big enough to warrant a huge, front-page headline in the *Livingston Enterprise*. It was obvious that horses and automobiles did not mix, so the following summer, all horse-drawn vehicles were removed from the park.[37]

Apparently there was a stage wreck that killed two persons just outside the park, but we currently know nothing about the date or circumstances. YPT Company manager Huntley Child recalled a runaway stage accident involving a Monida and Yellowstone coach that killed two persons just west of the park. If this happened, it probably occurred between 1898 and 1913, the years that company was operating.[38]

The era of wild horses was over when the "infernal internal" combustion engine made its rattling, popping, sputtering appearance on the Yellowstone scene. "Here's luck to all you spark-plug cleaners," wrote one old stage driver poetically. "You have gasolined in here at last; may you have the success in the future that I and my tackies have had in the past." But motorization was to produce wild horses of a different kind.

19

DEATHS FROM ACCIDENTAL AND SELF-DEFENSE SHOOTINGS

THERE ARE AT LEAST TEN DEATHS from accidental and self-defense shootings in the history of Yellowstone. All were tragic, but of course the self-defense ones were arguably less so.

What was called an accidental shooting occurred at Mammoth Hot Springs on November 15, 1938, but a classmate of the boy involved has always believed it was a suicide. Robert Leroy "Pud" Robinson, the 13-year-old son of the park's master mechanic, was playing with a loaded .22-caliber rifle in his home. At 5:15 p.m., his mother heard a thump and went upstairs to investigate. Tragically, she found that her son had shot himself through the head.[1]

This was naturally a very sad incident for the park community at Mammoth Hot Springs, because it involved one of their own and a child at that. Pud's classmate Bill Kearns, son of one of the park's ranger-naturalists, believed it a suicide, which he thought happened because Pud's father was "so severe" in the punishment he gave to his children that Pud "committed suicide to keep from getting what he knew was coming." "I think his father really loved him," wrote Kearns, "but couldn't control his anger at times." Kearns kept that disturbing news to himself, but believed it all his life.[2]

A self-defense shooting occurred at Gardiner in 1886. Alex Ferguson, 20, and Charles Carpenter, 40, were both stockmen who had had a previous row about Ferguson's cattle being on Carpenter's place. On June 21, 1886, Ferguson was on horseback and driving his employer's cattle from Gardiner to a ranch on Eagle Creek when he met Carpenter, also driving some cattle. The cattle became intermixed, and in separating them there was a fracas. Carpenter threw rocks at Ferguson and then grabbed Ferguson's horse by the bridle, threatening him with a rock in a way that seemed sure to throw both horse and rider down the embankment. Ferguson drew his gun and warned Carpenter to desist or he would shoot, but Carpenter refused and tried to hit Ferguson. Ferguson shot him in the left side through the ribs, and the bullet coursed downward to the right hip. Carpenter died within a few minutes. A jury found Ferguson not guilty on grounds of self-defense.[3]

Liquor seems to have been behind an 1892 shooting at Cooke City that involved William Chick, 50, an old-timer there, and James Malloy, a new prospector from Fort Dodge, Iowa. On the morning of September 21, 1892, there were already drinkers in R. B. Emison's saloon. A squabble arose between Malloy and a man named Allen. William Chick, a bit drunk already, interfered by slashing at Malloy with a knife. His blow fell short, and Malloy knocked Chick down with a chair.

Chick then went to his cabin and got his rifle. Later he met Malloy in front of the saloon, and the argument began again. Witnesses testified that Chick brandished a butcher knife and threatened to "cut out Malloy's liver and feed it to the buzzards." Malloy started to back away; Chick switched the knife to his other hand and drew a revolver. Malloy then picked up a .45-caliber rifle standing near an oil can and stepped out into the street, ready to use it. At almost the same instant that Chick's revolver discharged, Malloy raised his weapon to his hip and fired. Chick missed, but Malloy's "leaden missile" entered Chick's left side and passed through his body to exit at his backbone. Malloy then said, "Somebody take his gun away from him and I'll give mine up." William Chick died two hours later. Malloy was acquitted at trial on grounds of self-defense.[4]

We know little about the accidental event that killed Jessie Lane other than what appeared in a brief newspaper article. On or about August 31, 1899, he was killed at C. B. Scott's saloon in Gardiner, Montana. William Thomas accidentally dropped his gun, it discharged, and the bullet struck Lane.[5]

That incident was probably not the same as the incident told by Jack Ellis Haynes about an event that happened when he was a teenager, but the two occurred at about the same time. Born in 1884, Jack grew up in Yellowstone and was fifteen in 1899. His father was park photographer F. Jay Haynes, who founded the Monida and Yellowstone Transportation Company in 1898. Jack told historian Aubrey Haines that his father employed "a man to wash the stage-coaches and one day the fellow didn't show for work," so his father asked Jack to go to Gardiner and check the saloons. Aubrey wrote:

> The first one he entered had a narrow door, bar down one side and card
> tables in the center of the floor. As Jack was entering, a man facing him
> at a table stood up suddenly, pulled out a pistol and fired point-blank
> into the man who had his back to Jack (he claims that the pistol was
> looking right at *him*, except for the man in between). As the wounded
> man slumped to the floor, his assailant ran toward Jack, who put his

arms across the doorway to bar it. The fellow stopped in front of him, gave him a long look and then ran out the back door. Jack says he, the denizens of the bar and many townspeople pursued the assailant down to the old bridge (about opposite the depot), where the man jumped into the river from mid-span. The body washed up at Emigrant Bar several days later. The man shot in the saloon was the missing coach-washer. He died.[6]

The incident undoubtedly occurred, but has not yet been confirmed through research in the local newspapers, because we do not know exactly when it occurred.

A 1907 shooting at Gardiner involved the cranky and somewhat shady Robert "Buckskin Jim" Cutler, who for once was not at fault. Cutler had contracted with Axel Hill for Hill to construct an irrigation ditch for him. Hill demanded the 108 dollars for the ditch, and Cutler claimed that the specifications they had agreed upon had not been followed, pointing out where the deficiencies lay with William Jones and James Cutler present. A fight ensued among the four in which Hill and Jones got the worst of it, so Hill went home to brood about it. The next day, Hill and Jones drove up to Cutler's and again demanded the money; Cutler again said the work would have to be completed. Hill then called Cutler a "dirty son of a bitch" and said that he would fight him a duel right there. Hill fired once and missed; then Cutler fired once and missed. Cutler then fired a second and third time, the second bullet hitting Hill in the chest and the third shot severing an artery in Hill's leg. Hill bled to death in about ten minutes. Cutler turned himself in to the sheriff, and in a subsequent trial he was acquitted of murder on self-defense grounds.[7]

The very next year an accidental shooting near the park's south entrance made big news in the town of Pocatello to the southwest of Yellowstone National Park, as "one of the saddest things that ever occurred in Idaho." On the evening of September 1, 1908, W. L. Escher of Pocatello (a young bookkeeper for Kane's Grocery), his wife Georgia, Mamie Taylor (a student at the Academy of Idaho), and the little son of Claim Agent Edginton of the Oregon Short Line Railroad were driving in a mountain wagon with camp outfit from Jackson, Wyoming, to Yellowstone. While nearing a stream near the south entrance where camp was to have been made, the strange event occurred. Escher, 29, was carrying a shotgun across his knees while managing the horses, and somehow the weapon fell from his lap, its hammers striking a moving wagon wheel. The shotgun discharged and both barrels slammed into Escher's chest. "With one groan, he died instantly," stated the *Pocatello Tribune*.

Then began a terrible drama for the remaining three people, which the newspaper headlined as "Brave Woman Keeps Wolves from Body of Dead

Husband." Hardly able to function, the two young women and the little boy built a huge fire to keep animals at bay and as a marker for the relief party. The *Tribune* intoned:

> With gentle hands the dead man's body was lifted from the wagon seat and laid on the ground by the stricken widow and her girl companion. The latter, mounting one of the horses, rode bareback to a ranch house which had been passed that afternoon, nine miles south, to summon help. Timber wolves and coyotes attracted by the scent of human blood, howled in the darkness of the surrounding forest, where Mrs. Escher, guarding the body of her husband, stood guard with a revolver. Help came at last, and the dead man was loaded into the wagon and driven to Jackson, Wyo., forty miles distant, in the dark of the night. Without sleep, suffering from the awful shock of a catastrophe which few women have ever experienced, Mrs. Escher accompanied the remains of her husband on another long drive to St. Anthony, the nearest railway point, where friends from Pocatello, met her and brought the body.

One instinctively wonders whether this very long wagon trip was made over Teton Pass to reach Saint Anthony. Regardless, W. L. Escher's funeral in Pocatello was large, for he was well known. Because Escher was a veteran of the recent Spanish war in the Philippines, military honors were accorded him. Attending were the Grand Army of the Republic local post, numerous Spanish-American War veterans, the Knights of Columbus, and the Retail Clerks' Union. War veterans fired a salvo of rifles over Escher's coffin at the interment.[8]

A self-defense shooting occurred in 1911 at the old Cinnabar townsite, northwest of Gardiner, and involved "Specimen" Schmidt. Schmidt was probably the "Specimen Schultz" discussed by Aubrey Haines in *The Yellowstone Story* (2:104–5) who, in the 1890s, sold specimens at the Cinnabar train station with a sign that said "For sale—specimens from out of the park." When the park superintendent angrily rushed down to confront the vendor, Schmidt said, "Captain, I vas careful mid dot sign; you see it says specimens from *out* of the park not from *in* the park!" That story was told to Aubrey Haines by Jack E. Haynes, who apparently got the name wrong, as the German's name was Schmidt.

"Specimen" Schmidt continued to live on the old Hoppe ranch at Cinnabar for years after the town disappeared in 1902, becoming known as "the mayor of Cinnabar" and its only resident. He lived in the same cabin that he had occupied when he tended his specimen shop near the train depot. His full name was August "Specimen" Schmidt, and the newspapers revealed that he had been at Cinnabar for at least thirty years. He might have arrived as early as

1879, for an 1894 newspaper article stated that he had been there fifteen years then and was called only "Old Specimen."[9]

On the evening of August 6, 1911, Andrew McCune went to Schmidt's house to celebrate Schmidt's seventy-fourth birthday the following day. Schmidt sent him to Gardiner to get some whiskey, and McCune came back with "a liberal amount both inside and out." The two got "gloriously full," and when morning came on August 7, they were still "lit up like a church."

The men had a series of quarrels. After the first one, Schmidt put Mc-Cune in a nearby cabin to sleep it off, but in the morning Andy started another quarrel. Schmidt talked him out of it, but Andy drank some more and again began to "chew the rag." He struck Schmidt over the head with an iron cane. Schmidt got to his feet and Andy hit him again and then again, beating him about the head and arms. Schmidt backed into his cabin with McCune following, picked up a shotgun sitting just inside the door, leveled it at McCune's chest, and pulled the trigger. McCune, shot in the heart, died instantly. Schmidt then started for Gardiner, but passed out drunkenly on the way. Picked up by a passing vehicle, he reported the killing to Deputy Sheriff Welcome. In a subsequent hearing, Schmidt was freed on grounds of self-defense. The injuries to his face and left arm, from wrist to shoulder, attested to the truth of his self-defense story, and his foe had long been known as a troublemaker when drinking. This time Andrew McCune had truly found trouble.[10]

One of the most interesting of Yellowstone's wintertime stories involved the shooting of a U.S. Army soldier by his superior. It is a story of the "nerve-racking, monotonous life of the winter guard" in Yellowstone long before there were open hotels, snowmobiling, and snowcoach tours.

Winter as a season for visitors in Yellowstone did not really take off until the first hotel was kept continuously open during the winter of 1971–1972. Prior to then, a few snowmobilers and snowcoaches braved snowdrifts, and the Mammoth Hotel had been kept open a season or two in a short-lived experiment, but generally Yellowstone did not have a winter season.

During the army era, 1886–1918, tourist wagons and automobiles did not travel through the park in winter because of deep snow. Army soldiers referred to the park as having three seasons: July, August, and winter.[11] A Chinese laundryman noted about 1910, when asked what kind of climate existed at Yellowstone Park: "It is nine months winter and three months bad sleighing."[12] Park rangers, who arrived in 1916, long referred to wintertime as their period of "Nine Months Rest."[13]

But even without visitors, the army was on duty in the park in winter before 1916, and at times the duty was long and dreary. The story of the 1912 shooting illustrates Yellowstone's worst case of winter cabin fever.

In the winter of 1911–1912, as with many winters in early days, the Sylvan Pass Soldier Station, near the east entrance, was isolated from the rest of the park by the ten-thousand-foot peaks of the Absaroka Range. Captain R. C. Foy said later that "on account of the location I considered it the most difficult station in the Park to manage." Four privates and a sergeant were stationed there in the cold and dark. A venomous hatred developed between Sergeant Clarence A. Britton[14] of First Cavalry, Troop E, and the four men he was in charge of: privates Frank Cunningham, Frank L. Carroll, William H. Mutch, and a man known only as Private May. As the winter wore on, the five "snarled and quarreled" with each other until they refused to speak at all. The telephone to headquarters at Mammoth was in working order, but none of the men ever used it.

As winter dragged on, the men grew more morose and angry. The four privates conspired against Sergeant Britton. Private Cunningham questioned the sergeant when ordered to do anything, and Carroll, Mutch, and May always backed Cunningham. Hatred between Britton and Cunningham grew to a fever pitch.

One day on or about March 29, the sergeant took off skiing, but broke a ski pole when he was just a short distance out. Returning to the station carrying the broken pole, Sergeant Britton found the four privates engaged in conversation about him. Another soldier wrote this account of what happened next:

> When he opened the door of the cabin and stood there with the club in hand, Cunningham asked him gruffly what he was going to do with it, whereupon the sergeant told him it was none of his business. Cunningham then told him if he did not drop the club he would drop him, at the same time advancing towards the sergeant. The latter immediately pulled out his pistol and fired, the bullet striking Cunningham between the eyes, killing him instantly. Another private, named Carroll, advanced behind Cunningham, and the sergeant fired at him, the bullet penetrating the left arm, nearly severing the large vein. As no other man advanced, the sergeant ordered one of the remaining privates, who had previously been in the hospital corps, to put a torniquet [*sic*] on Carroll's arm, which no doubt saved his life.[15]

A look at the station log reveals the troublemaking nature of Private Cunningham, who was physically a very large man. In January he had gone to Cody, Wyoming, gotten drunk, and shot up the Irma Hotel, for which he was fined fifty dollars and costs. Cunningham could not raise the money, so he languished in jail at Cody for a month before returning to duty on February

The March 1912 shooting of Private Frank Cunningham by Sergeant Clarence Britton, at Sylvan Pass station (from Thomas M. Connery, "The Winter Tragedy of the Yellowstone," *World Wide Magazine*, June 1919, p. 146)

3. Captain Foy reported that Cunningham also broke a lock on the Cody jail, snapped his empty gun on Private May, and kicked a small boy on the streets of Cody. Those incidents plus his earlier finding of Private May when he was lost probably had done much to antagonize Sergeant Britton and unite the four privates against Britton.

Following the shooting, Cunningham's body was transported east on a sled to Holm Lodge, pulled by soldiers wearing skis, and then to Wapiti, Wyoming, where the wagon road was open to Cody. At Cody, the group was met by other soldiers from Fort Yellowstone who placed Sergeant Britton and Private Mutch under arrest. Privates May and Carroll were also later arrested. After a trial at Mammoth Hot Springs, Sergeant Britton was found not guilty of homicide on grounds of self-defense. Carroll received three years imprisonment for mutiny and privates Mutch and May received two years each. Cunningham, of course, was dead.[16]

A self-defense shooting at Gardiner in 1914 involved longtime resident George Mack, the father of Otho Mack, who became Gardiner's barber for much of the twentieth century. George Mack, aged 59 when the incident oc-curred, owned a saloon which was partially inside Yellowstone Park. On the evening of April 27, 1914, Mack was tending his bar when another Gardiner resident, Charles Huntsman, 22, got drunk and picked a fight. Huntsman was heard to say, "I am going to get that long-whiskered fellow!" meaning Mack, and he continued to drink heavily. At one point, Huntsman, who outweighed Mack by over fifty pounds, knocked him to the floor and then threw him through a window. Mack pulled his gun and shot Huntsman in the right temple. Gardiner resident Gay Randall had just tied his horse at the hitching rack outside when Mack came crashing through the window to land on the board sidewalk only a few feet from him. Randall wrote:

> I recognized him immediately as the town's local barber, George Mack, who was pinch-hitting for the regular bartender. Immediately after him came another stocky form, who proceeded to kick and stomp poor old George in the belly and ribs. George groaned and turned on his side, his right hand flashed from under him, and he fired three of the fastest shots I have ever heard directly into the face and forehead of his tor-mentor. The shots were so fast that Charley Huntsman, a young town boy that I knew well, took them all directly as aimed before he fell on top of George. I was so close that I could see each bullet tear the flesh and bone on his forehead, as Huntsman's facial muscles twitched on his surprised face. The trouble had started over George Mack refusing Huntsman credit for more drinks.[17]

In a subsequent trial, Mack was exonerated on self-defense grounds.

There probably are other examples of self-defense and accidental shoot-ings from Yellowstone's gateway towns that have been lost to history, but these are typical.

20

MALICE IN WONDERLAND
YELLOWSTONE MURDERS

It's a hell of a thing, killin' a man . . .
You take away all he's got and all he's ever gonna have.

—Clint Eastwood as William Munny in *Unforgiven,* 1992

WILLIAM MUNNY IN THE MOVIE *Unforgiven* exemplified a character who was closer to real life than most Hollywood representations—a man who was a mixture rather than strictly good or bad. Most of the murder incidents that occurred in and around Yellowstone National Park contained similar characters and elements, ones with shades of gray rather than all black or white. Only eight murders are known to have happened inside Yellowstone National Park, but at least thirteen others occurred nearby in the towns of Cooke City, Gardiner, Aldridge, Jardine, and Horr, Montana.

It is not surprising that the first known murder in the Yellowstone region happened in its oldest town. Cooke City, Montana, is the only town in the Yellowstone area that has any claim to being older than Yellowstone National Park itself. The town was founded in the summer of 1870 when Adam "Horn" Miller, James Gourley, A. Bart Henderson, and Ed Hibbard made the gold discovery that became the town. For the first couple of years, Cooke City had very few residents, but if one wishes to consider four men with picks and shovels a "town," then Cooke City is indeed older than Yellowstone Park.

On Tuesday, July 10, 1883, Frank Young shot Dan McCarthy at Cooke City in the central camp of the Clark's Fork mining district, and as often happens the incident involved alcohol. The *Livingston Enterprise* reported the story six days later from the coroner's inquest, and it went like this. Frank Young had been drinking and was lying on McGonnegal's bed in a tent complaining that his pocket book containing four dollars was missing. Meanwhile, Alex McKenzie was sitting in his nearby tent when he noticed that Dan McCarthy and another man were standing outside next to a wagon. McKenzie stated that McGonnegal came out of his own tent and told them that the one who had Young's money had better give it to him. McKenzie denied having the money. McCarthy then entered McGonnegal's tent, and McKenzie heard someone say, "Give me that four dollars" and heard McCarthy say, "I will give it to him when he gets sober." "McCarthy then came into my tent," said McKenzie, and "showed me the four dollars in silver and a key to a faucet. He said he found them on the floor in the other tent and he would be a pretty son of a bitch of a fool if he did not put them in his pocket. He said the four dollars belonged to the man that was in the other tent, drunk, and [that] I [McCarthy] would give it back when he got sober."

McCarthy then said to McKenzie, "He has gone for a gun, have you got one?" and left the tent.

About five minutes later McKenzie heard a horse come up close to the door of the tent and heard someone shout, "Stop!" and then the sound of a rifle shot. Excited, McKenzie left the tent to encounter Frank Young with Mc-Gonnegal, and heard Young exclaim: "I have shot the son of a bitch! For four dollars he cannot rob me in daylight." Young hung the Sharps rifle on his horse, walked to McCarthy's still body, and took back the four dollars.[1]

It was all straightforward enough, but subsequent events got complicated because Frank Young had some powerful friends and because territorial lawyers got the case shifted into federal court. Frank Young was sentenced initially to prison by the U.S. District Court but was subsequently sentenced to be hanged at Bozeman on December 27. Suffering sleepless nights in jail, Young was encouraged when his influential relative, F. F. Berrisford, showed up from Saint Paul to help him.[2] As late as December 20, newspapers were reporting Young's hanging still scheduled. Territorial governor John Crosby refused clemency, but on December 21, the Helena *Independent* reported that President Chester A. Arthur had overruled Crosby and granted Young a sixty-day reprieve to appeal to the Montana Supreme Court. The appeal failed and Young's execution was rescheduled for February 27, 1884. Meanwhile Young's cellmate, John A. Clarke, was hanged in January for a separate murder. That hanging must have given Frank Young a few more sleepless nights.[3]

Berrisford's efforts on Young's behalf ultimately paid off. Territorial law was known to be primitive, and it was not trusted by everyone. In November of 1884, President Arthur commuted Frank Young's sentence to life imprisonment for the murder that he had committed a year and four months earlier.[4] So ended that Cooke City case.

The second known murder in the Yellowstone region, like the first, attracted much attention, but this time it happened in the three-year-old town of Gardiner. On Monday afternoon, August 20, 1883, at about 4:00 p.m., George Weber (known to locals as the "crazy Dutchman" or "mad Dutchman") got into an argument with John Zutavern, age about 26, at Mammoth's National Hotel. The two, both employees of the Yellowstone Park Improvement Company, fell out over a trade they had made of some blankets and a razor in which there was a difference of about four dollars. Weber accused Zutavern of stealing the razor from him and refused to give up the blankets.

The quarrel was renewed in front of Charley's beer hall in Gardiner. Words were exchanged, then fists, and then Zutavern beat Weber over the head with a rock. Weber responded by pulling out his revolver and shooting Zutavern in the left breast. Weber then sat on a nearby rock, watched Zutavern die, and fled to the Yellowstone River.

Weber was a shady character who had been a member of a gang at Miles City. It was at first believed that he drowned crossing the river, but friends correctly thought that he had escaped. In fact, Weber had sneaked along the river into the park.

Two professional hunters, Bill Germayne and George W. Grow, were camped in the park when they met a man at Willow Park walking rapidly. Thinking it a strange place for someone to be afoot, they made inquiries as to his condition. He replied that he had lost a horse but declined offers of assistance. Later that morning, the three, now traveling together, met a soldier who told them of the murder at Gardiner, and who also listened to the walking man's story that he was looking for his horse. The soldier offered assistance, and again the man on foot declined it.

Germayne and Grow became convinced that the man they were traveling with was the culprit. Apparently alarmed, the man lost them at a curve in the road by ducking into the forest. So the two men continued toward the geyser basins, determined to catch the solitary walker. They made camp, hastily cooked supper, put out their fire, and waited secretly in the darkness. They took turns sleeping and watching, and about 12:30 a.m. both heard footsteps approaching. Guns drawn, Germayne and Grow confronted the man and arrested and disarmed him. At first he denied everything, but eventually he confessed to the shooting, claiming self-defense.

After spending the night, the two took Weber, their prisoner, back to Mammoth and then started toward Livingston. Weber was "greatly afraid of being lynched" by angry Gardiner townsfolk. At Mammoth, park superintendent Conger told Germayne and Grow of Judge D. H. Budlong's presence at Gardiner.

The illustrious 1883 tourist party of park entrepreneur Rufus Hatch happened onto Messrs. Germayne and Grow at Cinnabar, Montana, while they were holding Weber at gunpoint and waiting to take him to jail at Livingston. One of the English tourists in the party described Weber as "docile as a lamb, and the least formidable of the three."[5]

Meanwhile, citizens buried Zutavern in the Mammoth civilian cemetery, thus adding his grave to the three or four already there.[6] Judge Budlong ordered Zutavern exhumed, to the consternation of local citizens who were his brothers in the Odd Fellows order and who had already divided up his estate. The judge also ordered all of Zutavern's property returned for distribution by law. After disputes over these things, the body was disinterred for the inquest and the property distributed legally.[7]

George L. Weber was tried at Bozeman, convicted of second-degree murder, and sentenced to twenty years at the Montana prison. After serving less than five years, Weber was pardoned by President Grover Cleveland, apparently because the German consul put in a good word for him.[8]

One of the most gruesome of all Yellowstone death incidents was a murder that occurred June 3, 1899, and it involved one of the park's most prominent families. On that day, Mrs. George (Margaret Gleason) Trischman slashed her youngest child's throat with a hunting knife. The story is little known but can truly be called riveting.

George Trischman was the wheelwright and post carpenter at Fort Yellowstone. At the time he took the job, his wife Margaret and four children were living at Billings, Montana. His children were Harry, Anna, Elizabeth, George T., and Joseph. Margaret had not been well mentally. One day during the late winter or early spring, she went to a cowshed behind the family's Billings home with a large butcher knife and attempted to cut her own jugular vein, inflicting a ghastly wound in her throat. Upon regaining consciousness, Mrs. Trischman claimed that she had been assaulted by a strange man, but authorities doubted her story and in fact proved it false. As a result, she was committed to the Montana mental hospital at Warm Springs.

A few months later, asylum physicians announced that Mrs. Trischman had recovered. Elated at the prospect of having his family reunited, George Trischman traveled to Warm Springs on May 28, 1899, to pick up his wife. He had decided to move the family from Billings to Fort Yellowstone, so his children were placed on the train to Livingston. The family met in Livingston, and on Tuesday, May 30, they all rode the train to Cinnabar.

Mrs. Trischman's recovery was regrettably temporary. Four days later, on Saturday evening, June 3, at about 5:00 p.m., Mrs. Trischman seized 5-year-old Joseph, the youngest of her children, and cut his throat with a large hunting knife. In the presence of his brother and sisters, his head was nearly severed from his body. Margaret G. Trischman then chased her other three children with the knife in an attempt to do the same to them. They ran in terror to the home of a neighbor, and the woman, giving up the chase, returned home. She was found a short time later, calm but insensible to her surroundings, and in a state of mind that prevented her from understanding the deed she had done. Heartbroken, George Trischman allowed her to be confined in the guardhouse at Fort Yellowstone.[9]

U.S. District Attorney T. F. Burke arrived from Cheyenne a few days later to conduct an investigation, and Mrs. Trischman was ultimately determined to be quite insane.[10] Placed on the train bound for the government hospital at Washington, DC, she jumped from it on July 8 between Point of Rocks and Dailey's ranch in Paradise Valley and landed in the Yellowstone River. Although the train stopped and backed up in order that Deputy James Morrison and Mr. Trischman could look for her, no trace of her was found, even though the search continued for many months.[11] A year and a half later, George Trischman even traveled to Glendive, Montana, to examine a body that had been found in the river in hopes that it was that of his wife. It was not.[12]

The Trischman affair was desperately sad, but the surviving children remained in the park for many years. Had their mother succeeded in killing them, the history of Yellowstone would have been indelibly changed. Harry Trischman became one of the park's foremost civilian scouts and later rangers, and the man for whom Trischman Knob was ultimately named. Anna and Elizabeth Trischman ran a very important curio store and soda fountain in the park continually from the early part of the twentieth century until 1953. Beginning in 1924, those two ladies ran the unique refreshment stand on the upper terraces known as the Devil's Kitchenette.[13] Elizabeth never married. The three must have carried these haunting memories with them all of their lives.

The Trischman story classically illustrates the historical reaction by some men and women to traveling and living in the "hostile Western wilderness": men become savages and women go insane. Mrs. Trischman was a victim of that insanity, along with the most ultimate horror that could happen to a woman in the American West—violating her bond with her child by killing it. That larger story of the West was microcosmed in her affair at Yellowstone.

This heart-wrenching tale was concluded, if only physically, with the burial of little Joe Trischman in the southwest corner of the Mammoth army cemetery. Even today we can see in this sepulchre the enduring love George Trischman had for his young son, Joseph. The grave, still surrounded by nineteenth-century iron poles and chains, bears a carved headstone with a child's sculptured marble shoes as its cap. The inscription reads:

Joseph
Son of Geo and Margie Trieschman[14]
Born July 29, 1893
Died June 3, 1899

The story of "17"-year-old "Henrietta Ross" may be the Park's spookiest and most bizarre all-time death of any kind. Was it a freezing (hypothermia), a drowning, a death from alcohol and prescription drugs, or a murder? We will probably never know definitively. But the FBI thought it a murder, even if they lacked the evidence to prove it. So I have placed it in this chapter with murders.

On August 24, 1947, at around 10:30 p.m. at night, four men—park visitors from Oregon heading to Old Faithful to find a place to stay—were driving along the west side of West Thumb of Yellowstone Lake. The driver, Edward M. Callaghan, 34, stated later that "a young lady moved into my headlights and waved for me to stop." Appearing in front of him was a wet, bedraggled young brunette woman with striking blue eyes. "She said she had been thrown in the lake,"[15] wrote Callaghan, "and was very cold and could we please take her and warm her up." The woman was dripping wet, suffering from chills, incoherent, and "appeared very drunk." During the trip to Old Faithful, she talked a great deal, some of it incoherently, telling the men that her name was Henrietta Ross, that she was a former carnival employee who had worked in carnivals in Texas, California, Oregon, and Washington, and that she was 17 years old. She gave no home address in reply to their questions and repeated that "she just wanted to get warm and dry." She begged them not to turn her over to the police; she said she had done nothing wrong but "had lost her money and billfold" and was afraid she would be detained because of that fact. Edward Callaghan continued:

> She said she would be all right as soon as she was warmed up; she seemed to be drunk and jabbered almost all the way to the inn; all I could gather from the conversation was the fact that her name was Henrietta Ross and [she] had lived in Texas, and had been married there; she had been traveling with a carnival called west shows and lived with a man and his wife by the name of . . . Cash and had travelled from California to Yellowstone with them in a two room trailer drawn by a green Pontiac sedan; she had had an argument with them and they threw her in the lake; another time, she said she had jumped in and tried to commit suicide; she also said this man Cash was taking his wife to Georgia and was [then] going to marry her, Henrietta[.] [T]he girl, seemed to be very drunk and unable to talk to[o] steadily.

The four men drove her to Old Faithful Inn, where she obtained a towel to dry her hair, and then they went to Old Faithful Lodge, rented a double cabin for all of them (with her in one side and them in the other), and lit a fire so that she could dry off. ("It was a cold night," said brother John Callaghan.)

They watched as she stood by the stove until she was quite dry and then got into bed, giving them instructions to "please wake her up" in the morning. "At this point she still was quite drunk," wrote passenger Vern LaFave. John Callaghan stated, "At this time in the [cabin's] light we could see [her] clearly for the first time. To me she appeared drunk; her hair was dish[ev]eled and [she was] a sad sight." Both John and LaFave remembered her emphasizing that she drank only wine and gin.

When the four men knocked on her door at 7:00 a.m. the following morning, they found her in a coma, so they took her immediately to Old Faithful Ranger Station. Rangers then transported her to the Mammoth hospital, where she remained in the coma for three days until she died on August 28. Dr. Clemmen at Mammoth stated that the cause of her death was unknown.

Officials from several jurisdictions scratched their heads over this case for months. Rangers turned it over to the FBI to determine whether the woman had been the victim of foul play. Newspaper coverage resulted in the park receiving many letters from relatives of missing children who were asking if Henrietta could be their relative. On August 29, FBI agents took the girl's body to Cody, Wyoming, where a county autopsy was ordered and a coroner's jury was impaneled to hold an inquest. Dr. E. C. Ridgway's initial autopsy could not determine a cause of death. He believed that bronchial pneumonia had set in, possibly from exposure or hypothermia, and he thought that the traces of barbiturates he found were not enough to cause death by themselves. Buried at Cody on September 6 in Riverside Cemetery, "Henrietta Ross" remained unidentified. On September 18, Park County stated that the case was closed, with the girl still unidentified, but could be reopened if the FBI uncovered anything else.

Months later, the FBI came through, discovering that Henrietta Ross was actually Henrietta Ross Bailey (her maiden name from Texas, which was ultimately placed on her grave marker at Cody) and that her story was desperately sad. Eventually, the coroner's jury labeled her cause of death as "excessive use of sleeping powders, exposure, and drink." The FBI labeled her file as a "Crime on Government Reservation (Murder)," so it appears that they believed it a murder but apparently could not marshal enough evidence to prosecute the perpetrators, because the exposure death was colored by sleeping pills and drink. And they found that there was much more to the story.

Henrietta Ross Bailey was born in Louisiana on December 1, 1926 (thus her age was twenty, not seventeen), and she was apparently raised in Houston, Texas. Her parents were deceased, and an uncle was her legal guardian. Suffering at age 16 from some kind of mental illness, she spent nearly four years being treated in the state hospital at Abilene, Texas. Released in the summer of 1947, Henrietta married someone in Texas but left him there to travel with carnival shows, eventually landing in "West Coast Shows" of California. Various interviewees from the shows described her as a "tramp" who "dated various men" in the towns where the carnival played, and they alleged that she had contracted a venereal disease and also had been "subjected to an abortion." The nurse assigned to Henrietta's care following her release engaged a Dr. James of Chicago to prescribe phenobarbital for her, apparently for epileptic seizures and anxiety, and Henrietta carried those pills with her to Yellowstone. The carnival went to Oregon, and there she met Rex Abbot Cash and his common-law wife Wanda Jean Parker. Henrietta developed a crush on Cash and ended up traveling with the couple on an auto trip with the intended destinations of Kansas City and eventually Georgia.

But first they drove into Yellowstone Park, entrance not specified. Cash and Parker later denied separately and jointly any foul play with reference to the victim but admitted that she had been traveling with them. On the night in question, said the Cashes, they parked off the road just east of West Thumb at about 7:30 p.m. to prepare dinner. The interviewing FBI agent stated:

> An argument ensued which was not unusual in that Wanda Parker was somewhat "miffed" at the attentions of Rex Cash to the victim. During this time, Henrietta Ross, as they knew the victim, stated that she was going to leave and start hitchhiking. According to Cash and his wife they attempted to persuade her otherwise; however, she left, taking with her only a small box of medicine. [The] Victim left with the Cash family a suitcase containing her clothes and other personal articles. After dinner was finished, Cash and his wife advised that they proceeded on eastward through the Park, thinking that they would drive in the night to avoid the heat of the day. Within a short distance they [claimed to have] passed the victim hitchhiking on the road eastward. They honked their horn, and Cash played his spotlight on her, but [the] victim paid no attention to them. Cash and his wife both denied that they stopped to talk with the victim at that time.

The Cashes' story does not hold water with me, and it apparently did not with the FBI either, for their report labeled the incident as a "murder." The time frame does not work, for there were three hours unaccounted for between the couple's dinner and Henrietta's wet walk on the road. Secondly, it makes little sense that Henrietta would suddenly decide to start hitchhiking on a cold night in a wilderness area (with which she was unfamiliar) and where darkness was approaching, especially without her suitcase or at least a warm coat. (On the other hand, she was a bit crazy.) Thirdly, her crush on Rex Cash arguably makes it less likely that she would have suddenly left, even if an argument occurred with one or both of her companions. When picked up on the road by the Callaghans, she must have been a bit fearful of traveling with four strange men at night, so it is possible that that was the reason she told them she was only 17 and continued using her essentially false name.

Because of the autopsy results (death by "excessive use of sleeping powders, exposure, and drink"), the FBI could not make the murder charge stick against the Cashes for probably causing the exposure part by throwing Henrietta Ross Bailey into the lake (and who knows what else). The combination of phenobarbital and alcohol is well known to be a deadly mixture, so that clouded the cause of death. Notwithstanding the inconsistencies in the Cashes' stories and the word "murder" in the report's title, the FBI was therefore forced to state that "there was no evidence that [the Cashes] were implicated in any foul play." Another bit of sadness occurred when Henrietta Bailey's guardian uncle was contacted in Texas but did not show up for the coroner's jury. The ultimate result was a heartbreaking ending to the overwhelmingly sad life of a girl who appears to have had no real chance from her earliest days.[16]

An unnamed infant girl became a murder victim in Yellowstone on September 13, 1952. On that day Mary Jacqueline Larson, 18, a blonde, unwed mother from Hot Springs, South Dakota, strangled her newborn by tying a piece of bedsheet around her neck in the girls' dormitory at Fishing Bridge. Larson, a Yellowstone Park Company cabin maid whose parents were visiting her there, then stuffed the body under Fishing Bridge cabin 5, where it was found later that day by housekeeper Verna Humecke.

Arrested the same day, Larson at first denied that she had been pregnant or that she knew anything about the incident. She was arraigned in the Cheyenne, Wyoming, federal district court on a charge of second-degree murder. Larson then admitted to the FBI that she strangled the newborn to keep her from crying, wrapped her in a newspaper, and stuffed her under a cabin behind the Fishing Bridge cafeteria. She pleaded guilty to second-degree murder and was sentenced to five years' probation. The woman told the court that she "became extremely panicky when the child cried out." Perhaps she was another woman "gone crazy" in the West. Her story, too, carried shades of gray.[17]

Seventeen-year-old James Lee Hamar of Susanville, California, was traveling with a juvenile companion in 1978 in Yellowstone when he was murdered. The two youths were swimming or preparing to swim at the Boiling River north of Mammoth Hot Springs at 7:00 p.m. on June 10, 1978, when they got into an argument and his juvenile companion shot Hamar once in the back. Bleeding and stumbling from the Boiling River parking area to the main road, Hamar told a passing motorist that he had been shot. Rangers responded quickly, taking him to the Mammoth clinic, where he died. The 17-year-old runaway, also from California, was charged with the murder at Cheyenne,

Wyoming. He was captured by police at Norris Geyser Basin, after wrecking a car. He pleaded guilty to involuntary manslaughter under the Juvenile Delinquency Act and was confined for three years in Wyoming.[18]

A more recent murder in Yellowstone took place in 1985 at Old Faithful. In the early morning hours of September 6, 1985, Michael Lane Nickelson, 19, of Livingston, Montana, and Randy Dean Reddog, 22, of Wolf Point, Montana, were partying together at Old Faithful. The two were seen together by witnesses between 2:00 a.m. and 2:45 a.m. Nickelson was overheard to say that he and Reddog were going up to Observation Point. Both men were seasonal employees of T. W. Services, Nickelson being a kitchen worker at Four Seasons Snack Shop and Reddog a kitchen helper at Snow Lodge. It is strange that the two would have been "partying" at that time in very cold weather. Tour guide Leslie Quinn remembers that on that particular early morning the temperature at Old Faithful dropped to six below zero.

That afternoon a park visitor at Observation Point was startled to find Randy Reddog's body near the trail to the point. He had been bludgeoned to death with a blunt object. An autopsy indicated he died of massive brain injuries and skull fractures. In this affair, after a fashion, Euripides had again been proven correct in his assertion that men must fight.

Nickelson was a hard case. At the time of the murder he was on probation from Gallatin County, Montana, for felony theft and had been detained once by park rangers in an unrelated incident. He was charged with the murder and also with a September 7 burglary of a grocery store in Livingston. In searches of his room, officers found his bloodstained shoes as well as items linking him with the Livingston burglary. Arraigned on October 8 in Cheyenne, Wyoming, on murder charges, Nickelson initially pleaded not guilty, and his trial date was set for February 10, 1985. He was convicted and sent to prison.[19]

If the Nickelson incident was straightforward, the Baker–Schlosser affair was not. One of the Yellowstone region's most macabre, memorable, and grisly murder incidents, it just missed happening inside the park in 1970, because all park campgrounds were full that night. Instead, it occurred a few miles north of Gardiner, Montana, on U.S. Highway 89 near the Devil's Slide.

On the afternoon of July 10, 1970, James Michael Schlosser, 22, a Montana welfare worker from Roundup, Montana, picked up two hitchhikers, probably just east of Livingston. Unbeknownst to Schlosser, the hitchers were ne'er-do-wells Stanley Dean Baker from Story, Wyoming, and Harry Allen Stroup of Sheridan. Baker, who called himself "Jesus," would later admit to cannibalism, Satanism, and other occult practices. He was high on LSD at the time, although Schlosser did not know it, but even without drugs, Baker would later admit that "I haven't been the same" since suffering an electrical accident at age 17. Stroup seemed only along for the ride.

The three headed toward the park north entrance, intending to camp in Yellowstone, but gate ranger Adolph Peterson told them all campgrounds were full. Had this not occurred, the murder of Schlosser would probably have happened at Mammoth Campground or another park campground. So the three headed back north to find a campsite outside of Gardiner.

Schlosser was known as a quiet, kind individual who would go to lengths to help others out. On this night, he and Baker camped about four miles north of Gardiner across the Yellowstone River from Devil's Slide. While Schlosser slept in his sleeping bag, Baker shot him twice in the head with a .22 pistol, and then dragged the body to the river, where he cut it into six parts with a twelve-inch sheath knife. He cut off several fingers and beheaded and otherwise dismembered the corpse, and then cut out the heart and ate it. Scattering some parts and throwing the rest in the river, Baker took Schlosser's car and drove north. Stroup and Baker would both later claim that Stroup was not along on this part of the affair, but a jury would not believe them.

Baker and Stroup drove west in the car they had stolen from Schlosser, a 1969 gold Opel, through Montana, Idaho, Washington, and Oregon, and then south into California. Near Big Sur, they were involved in a hit-and-run incident and were apprehended by the California Highway Patrol. Baker thereupon blurted out to police officers, "I have a problem; I'm a cannibal!" In the pockets of both men, officers found human finger bones.

Meanwhile, Gardiner fisherman Dick Miller had discovered Schlosser's torso in the Yellowstone River. The torso had no head or arms, the legs had been cut off at the knees, and the heart was missing. There were twenty-seven stab wounds in the chest and abdomen. Alert California police officials hooked up with Montana officials, and Baker and Stroup were extradited to Montana. For two months, the Yellowstone-area media fairly screamed the bizarre story. In October, Baker pleaded guilty to murder and was sentenced to life in a Montana prison. Stroup received ten years for manslaughter.

Stroup was paroled several years later and returned to Sheridan, Wyoming. Baker came up for parole in 1985, but failed to obtain it until the 1990s. In 1991, he was paroled and moved to Minnesota. But television programs such as *A Current Affair* reported his moves, and public outcry was so great he dropped out of sight.[20]

So went that murder story, but murders occurred in the Yellowstone region quite early, and there are probably more murder stories than just the following ten that we know.

An 1898 murder just north of Yellowstone Park in Aldridge, Montana, involved a woman who was burned to death. John Webster, about 38 years of age, arrived in Aldridge, Montana, in 1897. He advertised in a marriage journal called *Heart and Hand* for a wife, and a Lizzie M. West of Providence, Rhode

Island, came to Aldridge to meet her future husband. West, age about 50, took up housekeeping with Webster, who failed in his promise to marry her, instead spending her money and drinking. Violent quarrels began to occur between the two, and eventually each determined to leave the other. Webster's violent tendencies would soon appear, for he was a bad and scary person.

On Sunday April 10, 1898, another quarrel erupted, and Lizzie declared that she was going to show Webster's true light to the world, or "expose his Easter egg," as she put it. Sure enough, she went to a Mrs. Fairgraves's house where Webster was, called out for him, and assaulted him by tearing off his vest and chopping his hat into pieces with an ax while yelling, "Now go and buy a new hat, you son of a bitch!" She then returned home, and Webster continued drinking in several Aldridge saloons.

On the following night at about 10:30 p.m., Webster's house was discovered to be on fire. Bar owner Thomas Kane pointed it out to Webster, who responded by looking out, seeing the fire, returning to the bar for a swallow, and remarking that he guessed it would all be all right now. Earlier, Webster had told Kane that he was expecting some trouble with a woman, and told bar manager Sam Pullman that "the old woman" had had him on his knees with a rifle aimed at him. Townsfolk who responded to the fire found Lizzie West dead inside, her face and neck badly burned and her tongue protruding. Webster, of course, was arrested and professed his innocence loudly and continually.

At Webster's trial several people testified to the many quarrels between the two and to the fire situation at their house. John "Bombay" Reese stated that he walked past Webster's on the night of the fire and both heard and saw a quarrel in progress wherein the defendant and his woman were throwing chairs at each other. Tom Williams said he had heard Webster threaten to kill the woman that morning. William North, one of the first at the fire, stated he found a trail of oil and grease extending from the inside of the house over the doorstep and out onto the ground.

The jury convicted John Webster of murder in the second degree. Claiming innocence to the end, he was sentenced to life in a Montana prison. If Lizzie had "gone crazy," perhaps Webster had driven her to it.

Spookiest of all in this story was the photo of John Webster that Aldridge schoolgirl Mary Parish (later Mrs. Mary Criswell) had forgotten that she saved in a scrapbook for nearly seventy years. When historian Doris Whithorn pointed the man out to her in the photo, she flashed on his picture as the man she had so "feared and disliked" during her grade-school days in Aldridge, Montana. She remembered that in 1898 he had choked his common-law wife and then set their house on fire to hide the crime.[21]

At least three murders have occurred just outside of Yellowstone Park to the north at Jardine, Montana. An 1885 murder there involved a mining dispute. Frank Kannis and Jack Stevenson were both miners above Gardiner in the area that would later become Jardine. Kannis, about 45 and of German extraction, was part owner in the "Homestake" mine there. Stevenson was a nearby neighbor, and the two were using the same arrastra in the gulch to crush ore from their respective claims. One day Kannis accused Stevenson of taking some of his amalgam out of a gold pan, and a hot dispute arose, which then temporarily cooled.

On Sunday July 5, 1885, Kannis was still a little drunk from the Independence Day celebration the day before, and in fact was drinking from a keg he had taken home. Stevenson went to Kannis's house in Gardiner with a third party, a German, and the argument was revived. Stevenson said they would settle the matter, so he went to his own cabin a short distance away and got his rifle. As the *Livingston Enterprise* reported on July 11, 1885:

> Advancing to within 75 feet or less of Kannis' cabin he called to Frank to come out and come "heeled." The German tried to dissuade both men from violent action but without effect. Kannis came to the door with a revolver in his left hand and stood on the threshold with his right foot outside. Against the right door post on the outside hung a saddle at about the height of Kannis' head. Stevenson's station was at the right so that the saddle obscured him from Kannis' view. While the parties to the tragedy were in this relative position Stevenson fired and the ball entered Kannis' body in the left breast below but in the immediate vicinity of the heart and came out behind. Kannis fell backward.

Kannis died about twenty minutes later and Stevenson took off, probably into the mountains to the northeast. A notice in the local newspaper three weeks later stated that no trace of Stevenson had been found and that he had probably "made good his escape." But law enforcement eventually caught up with him. He was found guilty of manslaughter and sentenced to five and a half years in Montana Territorial Prison.[22]

Independence Day festivities and mining disagreements seemed to bring out the worst in miners at Jardine, as well as at Aldridge, Montana. On the night of July 4, 1899, at the newly named town of Jardine, Mark "Mickey" Terrell walked out of Jarvis's saloon at about midnight with George Jacka and two other men. They found George Welcome, Henry Rockinger, and another man fixing up a stand to use in firing rockets in front of Welcome's store. Apparently, there had been animosity between the men before, for when Jacka spoke to Welcome, Welcome struck Jacka across the head with a hammer. Jacka began yelling and Terrell said, "Welcome, don't do that," only to receive a blow in the head as Rockinger pistol-whipped him. Terrell tried to defend himself, but Rockinger shot him twice with a .38. The bullet struck his left side, ranged upward to a lower rib, coursed inward, and lodged in his abdomen. He died three days later.

From witnesses, it appears George Welcome may have egged on the affair, for he is known to have said to Rockinger, "Shoot the son of a bitch!" and "What do we pay you to carry a gun for?" At any rate, Rockinger, about 48 years of age, who had earlier been arrested for poaching in Yellowstone Park, was arrested, tried, and convicted of voluntary manslaughter for the shooting of Terrell. Rockinger was sentenced to no more than ten years in prison. He did his time (or was paroled) and was back in Yellowstone Park working for the U.S. Engineers by 1903. Interestingly, William Brown and Thomas Williams, two men who were peripherally involved in this incident, were subsequently convicted of blackmail for trying to extort fifteen hundred dollars from George Welcome to buy their silence in the Rockinger trial.[23]

Disagreements between miners who just plain did not like each other were responsible for another weekend murder at Jardine, this one in 1907. There was bad blood between the "company faction" there (the supporters of the Kimberly-Montana Mining Company) and another group of men who were opposed to the policies of the company. Tom Lannan, a miner from Butte who had been in Jardine for seven years, was a member of the former group, and Barney Hanlon, another old-time prospector, was in the latter. Hanlon had been appointed to guard a ditch that belonged to Mrs. George Welcome, a prominent resident of Jardine, and the company men did not like him or the ditch.

On the night of June 5, 1907, company members dynamited the ditch, and immediately a riot broke out in Mrs. Welcome's saloon between the two groups, who shot out the mirrors, broke windows, rifled the cash register, and knocked out bartender Joe Wells with a rock.

The following morning, activity began early when members of the company group arrived at Hector McDonald's saloon at 6:30 a.m. All drank heavily until 8:00 a.m., bolstering their courage and anger with fifteen to twenty drinks total. Tom Lannan openly displayed his .32- and .38-caliber revolvers and stated that he would probably need them.

Quincy Davison then went over to Welcome's wrecked saloon, the gathering place for the Hanlon faction, where he found Barney Hanlon wearing a large six-shooter. He heard Hanlon say, "Kid, they had better leave me alone, as I have the goods to do it with."

Three hours later, after much drinking, Hanlon and Lannan ran into each other in the street in front of the Bear Gulch Hotel with a bunch of other men, and words about the preceding evening were exchanged. In the presence of others, Lannan called Hanlon to one side and the two walked behind the barbershop and began a heated conversation. Both were intoxicated, and according to one witness, Lannan asked Hanlon to have a drink with him and Hanlon refused.

One of Lannan's faction, Joe Menisto, known as the "dago kid," then walked up to Lannan and handed him a whipstock about three feet long and an inch wide. Witnesses saw Lannan scratching the dirt with the stick, saw him raise it and strike Hanlon, and then saw Lannan back away quickly. Hanlon drew his revolver and fired at least three times at the fleeing Lannan, who reached the back of the nearby barbershop and tried the door before a bullet hit him. The bullet entered his chest five inches above his left nipple, coursing backward and severing his aorta.

Charles Campbell, the barber, was dressing at 11:35 a.m. when he heard three shots, looked out his second-story window, and saw Lannan fall from the steps of his barbershop to the ground. Mrs. G. S. Kirby, the company clerk, who had also seen everything, ran to Lannan and cradled his head on her lap, only to see Hanlon aim his gun at Lannan again. Instead of firing, Hanlon yelled at a man named Quinlan, "You sent that dago after me!" and Quinlan ran away. When Hector McDonald and others ran to the scene, Hanlon yelled at them, "I will shoot you sons of bitches!" He stated that if any of Lannan's friends wanted any of it, he would give it to them.

Sheriff E. L. Robertson of Gardiner went up to Jardine and arrested Hanlon and the seven men who had torn up Mrs. George Welcome's bar,[24] amid threats by townsfolk to lynch Hanlon. Robertson put them all in the stone jail below today's bridge at Gardiner. At Hanlon's trial it developed that Hanlon had been gunning for Lannan for weeks. He was sentenced to thirty years in prison.[25] Nearby Hanlon Hill probably received its name from this man or his family, and the name may have even originated with this shooting incident, although the history is obscure on that point.[26]

Only a month later, during Independence Day festivities at Aldridge, Montana, some three miles north of the park north boundary, another killing happened during a free-for-all fight. The identity of the perpetrator appears to have been hidden for all time from the authorities by Aldridge townsfolk.

Many of the Austrians employed at the Montana Coal and Coke Company went to Mammoth Hot Springs to celebrate the Fourth. When they returned, they found George Zoberts and his wife seated in a buckboard. Six of the men jumped into the rig and beat him over the head with a club in response to an earlier argument. Sheriff Robertson arrested the six men and placed them in the jail at Gardiner.[27]

Later that evening, Austrian John Flere (newspapers called him John Ferry) was shot after a saloon row at Aldridge. Flere was returning to his home "above the Catholic church over what is known as the 'Hog Back,'" when a bullet struck him in the side. Perhaps he was hit by a stray bullet from the general fusillade of celebration.

More likely he was the victim of mistaken identity. Doris Whithorn interviewed many Aldridge old-timers for her book *Photo History of Aldridge*. She says just about anyone who grew up then in Aldridge could tell the story. A big group was drinking at Yrella's saloon and there was some trouble between a certain man and the Spek family. The certain man got his gun and laid in wait for one of the Speks to go home along the "Hog Back." John Flere by chance went home that way that night, and Mr. X shot him by mistake. Mr. X was never named by anyone in Aldridge, nor was he prosecuted.

When the sheriff arrived, he found that Flere was still alive, and a week later Flere was saying he did not know whether he was accidentally or purposely shot. A month later they moved Flere to the county poor farm for care, and on October 3 he died at Aldridge. The identity of Mr. X was never disclosed by Aldridge residents. He and his family continued to live there and in nearby Horr. Doris Whithorn thought that she had found a photo of his funeral, but later decided the photo she included in her book *Photo History of Aldridge* was the funeral of a miner killed in an electrical accident. The Flere murder, plus the known tendency of Aldridge residents to poach animals in Yellowstone, caused the park superintendent to disparage the town by remarking a few days later that Aldridge residents were "rather disregardless of human and animal life."[28]

Speaking of Horr, at least three murders by shooting occurred in that town (later called Electric) in Montana, in the years 1892, 1895, and 1898. Horr was located less than a mile north of the park's boundary at Reese Creek.

Was the Northrup–Durgan shooting of September 10, 1892, murder or self-defense? Charles Northrup, a foreman of the Park Coal and Coke Company's timber camp, fired employee Daniel Durgan in early September, and Durgan went to nearby Horr and got liquored up. While he was drunk, Durgan threatened to whip Northrup, who heard of the threat and armed himself. When the two men met at the upper works of the company's operation, Durgan stated that he was there for the purpose of "doing up" Northrup and started for him. Northrup ordered him to come no closer, drew a revolver, and began firing. The first shot passed over Durgan's head, and the second one entered near his navel. Durgan turned to retreat, and the third shot struck him in the back, shattering his spinal column. He was thus paralyzed and could only move his arm and head. He lingered until Wednesday morning, September 14, saying several times, "I am a gone gosling; he has fixed me." Durgan's grave today is one of the unmarked ones at Horr.

Charles Northrup stood trial three times for this homicide, the first trial being deadlocked. In the second trial he was found guilty of second-degree murder, a verdict that was overturned on appeal. At the third trial in January 1894, defendant Northrup "twisted his mustache rather nervously, chewed tobacco vigorously and expectorated freely." The jury brought back a not-guilty verdict on the self-defense fact that Durgan was out to get him, a decision greeted with hisses. This one was a close case, as it could be argued that Northrup went beyond self-defense. Many observers considered the verdict a travesty. Northrup proceeded to leave town quickly on the train to East Helena, the newspaper stating on February 1: "It is perhaps just as well that he didn't delay his departure . . . for there was strong talk of holding an indignation meeting and giving him a taste of the old-time vigilante medicine. Some went so far as to suggest the organization of a neck-tie party."[29]

The Tracy/Anderson homicide that happened at Horr in 1895 "at the old Sommerville lodging house" in "Tin Town" resulted from a fatal Christmas joke. Jack Tracy, 46, shot Chris Anderson on December 26. Anderson, 35, had formerly managed saloons at Forsythe and Red Lodge, Montana. Tracy had a reputation for drinking and fighting with his women. The *Livingston Enterprise* reported the affair as follows:

> The fatal quarrel arose over a turkey purchased by Anderson for his Christmas dinner. Anderson and his wife occupied one side of a cabin and in the other Jack Tracy and Mrs. Ray were living together. [Mrs. Ray proved to be Frances Arnott.] The men had been chums and were drinking together a greater portion of the time. Anderson purchased a turkey and ordered it delivered to his shack. The delivery man who went with the turkey found Anderson's door fastened and left the turkey in Tracy's apartment. Tracy and Mrs. Ray conceived the idea of appropriating the turkey and having a Christmas dinner and joke at Anderson's expense.
>
> The following morning Anderson discovered that his turkey had not arrived and went to the market to make complaint. He was told that the turkey had been hung up in Tracy's room because his door had been found locked. He immediately returned to the shack and, entering the room occupied by Tracy and Mrs. Ray, demanded to know what had become of his turkey. Mrs. Ray made some reply which incensed Anderson and the three were soon involved in a quarrel which resulted in blows. Mrs. Anderson, who was in the adjoining room which was separated by a door over which boards had been nailed and a curtain hung, was attracted by the disturbance and, pushing aside the curtain, saw her husband in the corner of the room with Tracy pummeling him with his fists and Mrs. Ray striking him with a hatchet. She screamed and this had the effect to temporarily disconcert the assailants of

Anderson, who took advantage of the lull in hostilities to seize a stove poker with which he dealt Tracy a severe blow on the head. Anderson then made his escape and retreated to his own side of the house. He was suffering from a scalp wound inflicted by the hatchet in the hands of Mrs. Ray and told his wife he would go to the doctor and have his head dressed. She remonstrated with him by telling him he had better wait and have his dinner.

He consented to his wife's request and was sitting at the table when Tracy, who had gone to [L. H.] Van Dyck's house and secured a revolver which he knew was kept at that place, returned and, breaking open the door which was fastened with a button, began shooting at him. He fired two shots, the first taking effect in the groin and the other in the abdomen. Anderson fell to the floor and Tracy started toward town, when Anderson regained his feet and started for the door, followed by his wife who urged him to come back. At this juncture Mrs. Ray appeared upon the scene and fearing Anderson might still be able to avenge himself, she called to Tracy to return and shoot the _____ _____ again. Tracy, however, had proceeded some distance from the house by this time, where he met Dr. [W. H.] Allen, to whom he stated he had "got him." When interrogated as to his meaning, he replied that he had shot Chris Anderson. Dr. Allen disarmed Tracy and took him to George Welcome's where he was locked up to await the arrival of Deputy Sheriff Bellar from Gardiner.[30]

That was the account of an attorney who investigated the incident, and the subsequent trial testimony was about the same. But Mrs. Ray, who was called a "repulsive old hag" by one of the newspapers, gave testimony that made Anderson look like the villain. She recounted that on the morning of December 26, Chris Anderson was beating his wife, so she knocked on the partition and told him to stop it. Tracy was asleep at the time, but their voices woke him up and he told her to stay out of it, that Anderson could do what he wanted to in his own home. She kept yelling, however, and Anderson finally yelled back: "I will come in and give you some of the same kind if you don't shut up." Anderson then pried the boards off the partition and entered Tracy's room. He was ready to hit Mrs. Ray when Tracy countered with, "No, Chris, you don't strike her." Anderson had a hatchet in his hand.

"Tracy stepped in between us," continued the witness, "and I had a dish pan in my hand. I reached over Tracy's shoulder and struck Anderson on the head. He then said he would go home and behave himself, but instead of doing that he picked up a poker that we used to fasten the door with, and struck Tracy over the head. As soon as Tracy was hit, he fell to the floor and remained stunned for about five minutes. I then helped him on with his clothes and he started for the doctor's to have his head dressed. I didn't see the shots fired."

Tracy certainly needed his head dressed, for Anderson's blow "laid bare the skull from the top of the head to the forehead, producing a scalp wound which took five stitches to close." Bleeding, he made the mistake of telling a couple of people on his way to Van Dyck's meat market (where he worked as a butcher) that he was "going after a gun" to kill Anderson. He then came back, kicked the door in, took aim at Anderson, and yelled, "You damned son of a bitch, I've got you now!" Chris Anderson's dying declaration was admitted at trial, and it said that Tracy struck him first and then the mistress hit him with a hatchet. Tracy's temporary insanity defense probably helped his case a bit, but a jury found him guilty of voluntary manslaughter. He was sentenced to ten years at the Montana prison plus court costs.[31]

Mrs. Willard Ray (Frances Arnott) was, according to another local newspaper, also known as "Old Ray" and was a "woman of very unsavory reputation," so stated by the newspaper at a time when editors cared less about libel lawsuits. In fact, the Anaconda newspaper outrageously proclaimed that "in appearance she is absolutely repulsive, and looks as though she had seen 20 years of sin and shame." After the shooting, she ran out of the house following Jack Tracy and yelling, "Come back and shoot him again, for the son of a bitch ain't dead yet!" Mrs. Ray was taken to jail with the intent that she be prosecuted for striking Chris Anderson twice in the head with an ax. After she spent more than a month in jail, charges against her were dismissed. Thus ended a tale involving some less-than-reputable citizens.[32]

Another Horr murder, the Rolla–Cortese case, involved several Italians and some disparaging racist remarks. On March 27, 1898, Mike Rolla, 45, a small Italian man of five feet, four inches and 135 pounds, had an argument with three other workers at the Horr coke ovens. Later that evening Peter Cortese, Servius Cortese, and Frank Vitro came to Rolla's cabin and made threats. To Vitro, Rolla said, "Where are you leading them Spanish dogs?" apparently referring to the two men. After getting a translation, Peter Cortese drew a razor and, with Servius Cortese, got Rolla between them. B. Yearlo, who happened to be nearby, told Peter not to advance or "I'd hit him with an ax." When Rolla went for his Winchester, the three men ran, Peter yelling, "Brother, run, he went after a rifle!"

From 140–160 feet away, Mike Rolla fired four times at the two fleeing Corteses, hitting Servius Cortese with two shots just as he reached the railroad tracks at the coke ovens. One shot entered just below the right shoulder blade and the other six inches above the right buttock. Both bullets traveled upward and exited from the unfortunate Cortese, who yelled something like "I'm dead!" and then died of internal hemorrhaging. Rolla took to the hills, heading for Dailey, Montana, some fifteen miles to the north. Officers apprehended him there in an abandoned cellar. Frank Vitro claimed Rolla had called them "Spanish dogs," which was supposed to be derogatory toward all Italians.

Rolla was tried in April 1898, found guilty of second-degree murder, and sentenced to fifty years. A Supreme Court appeal gave him a new trial, which resulted in a guilty verdict of first-degree murder charges. A new trial was again granted, but before that third trial could ensue, Rolla pleaded guilty to second-degree murder and was sentenced to life. He died seven months later in prison at only about 35 years of age, leaving a wife and two children in Italy. His victim left a wife and two children at Horr.[33]

A 1903 murder in the Yellowstone region, probably just outside of the park to the north, is one that we are not sure even happened. A short newspaper article that was picked up and run by many newspapers in early June of 1903 read as follows: "Hospital Steward F. C. Ross, of Fort Yellowstone in the National park, went to Chico on a three-day leave of absence two weeks ago and has not returned. As Ross handled considerable money it is believed he was killed for it and the body thrown into the Yellowstone River." Nothing more is known.[34]

A spectacular early murder and suicide in the Yellowstone country involved a quarrel between man and wife in the Absaroka Range of mountains west of Cody, Wyoming, and just east of the park boundary. The story was long forgotten until this author encountered it in newspapers. Aaron Edward Swanson, born about 1856, spent his early life in Illinois and Omaha, Nebraska, but moved to Wyoming on the heels of the founding of the town of Cody in 1895–1896, arriving in or about 1895. That he was a "new arrival" then was attested to by historian Lucille Patrick in her book about Cody's first twenty years, *Best Little Town by a Dam Site*. His nephew Andrew Larson followed him to Cody a year later to open the town's first meat market; meanwhile, his uncle Aaron had education enough to get appointed as an area judge. Their prospects seemed bright.

A. E. Swanson, age about 40, loved the country and had money, so he bought the Cherry Spring Ranch at the small settlement of Ishawooa, Wyoming. That tiny hamlet was near the spot where Ishawooa Creek meets the South Fork of the Shoshone River, and according to *Wyoming Place Names* the creek's name was the Shoshone Indian word for "lying warm." In this beautiful spot Swanson was lonely for more than a decade, so he purchased a "mail-order" bride from Saint Louis named Rose Hennesey and married her in mid-May of 1906. Bringing her 5-year-old retarded son and a sister with her, Rose Hennesey entrained to Cody and married A. E. Swanson on the day that she met him.[35]

Affairs seemed well enough for many months until Rose Swanson's darker side emerged. Described as an "adventuress" by the local newspaper,

Rose, after two and a half years of marriage, did something to arouse extreme jealousy in A. E. Swanson. Perhaps her exploits, whatever they were, plus the financial and social strains of the extra family members made him crazy, for on Sunday morning, August 2, 1908, Aaron Swanson walked into the room of their ranch house where Rose was sleeping, shot her to death, and then blew out his own brains. Rose's "imbecile son" Gus Holtz and her sister were at the ranch when the event took place, but we do not know whether they were inside or outside of the house. One newspaper stated that the crime was "planned minutely." Another editor wondered whether Swanson was "temporarily insane from family trouble and worry," but nothing else was stated about the reasons behind the murder-suicide of the mail-order lovers. That the affair was desperately sad to the Cody community was attested to by the *Stockgrower*, which stated that "every one of [Swanson's] neighbors has a good word for him." The editor closed with this comment: "A good many things might be said about this sad affair; but the *Stockgrower* believes that it is best to allow Death to draw the mantle of charity over the frailties of human nature." Perhaps this statement helped to shroud the event in quiet, for it has been little known in area history.[36]

A murder on September 9, 1913, at West Yellowstone, Montana, technically occurred inside the park and involved the Monida-Yellowstone Stagecoach Company. At that time the town was known simply as Yellowstone. Dan Coffee was a barber in the town and was also a gambler. He moseyed into the park one evening to participate in a poker game at "Riverside," where Frank Haynes's stage company kept its large barns, offices, coaches, and horses. Coffee met up with Doc Long (a veterinarian), Roxy Bartlett, Parley Croft, and probably some others in the blacksmith shop and garage where coaches were worked on. "Various personal assets passed back and forth," stated Sam Eagle much later, and "at one point the stakes in the game became a bear hide . . . won by Doc Long." After some teasing and delay, the bear hide was produced, then "spirited away" several times and returned, only to disappear again. Doc Long had had enough, so he pulled his pistol and shot Dan Coffee dead. The closest police were ninety miles to the north at Bozeman, Montana, so Doc Long had a head start on running. County sheriff W. S. Evans telegraphed Sam P. Eagle saying he would be there soon and to "wire me at once description of Doctor Long and the direction he went if possible." Evans caught the doctor about a week later.[37]

A St. Anthony, Idaho, newspaper picked up the details from the *Pocatello Tribune*:

> Details of a killing that occurred at Yellowstone on the 9th have just
> reached Pocatello, when a Montana sheriff came down from Bozeman

and took Dr. Long, a veterinarian for the M-Y Transportation company into custody. It appears that a row took place over the raffle of a bearskin in which several parties had engaged in ["]jobbing" one of the party. Following the circumstances a quarrel arose between Dan R. Coffee and Dr. Long, both employees of the transportation company, and Coffee, who is a large man, gave the veterinarian two or three beatings. A scrap had just occurred between the two men, and at its finish, Dr. Long, who was not the physical equal of Coffee, drew a gun and fired four bullets into his opponent, and it is said that a hand would cover the four holes where the bullets entered Coffee's stomach. They were later taken from his back. Coffee died several hours after he was shot, and the shooting occurred in the blacksmith shop and garage. Coffee was buried at [West] Yellowstone.[38]

In a subsequent trial, the prosecution had trouble finding people to testify against Doc Long, because Dan Coffee did not seem to be popular.

One of the more interesting park-area murders involved an army private from Fort Yellowstone, the Gardiner resident that he stabbed in 1914, and a saloon that was on the boundary of Yellowstone National Park if not partially inside it.

On the night of March 5, 1914, Private Ola A. Haverson of Troop G, First Cavalry, from nearby Fort Yellowstone, entered Melchert's saloon with George A. Hosley, a Private Fritz, and probably one other man. The men had been drinking in several other saloons, and here they ordered drinks and something to eat. Bartender Walter A. Semple, age about 30, told them that the cook was gone. He brought them some sardines and crackers, and then pointed to a sign that read, "Sardines, 25 cents per can."

Bystander George Mason later testified that the men caused trouble, and newspaper accounts stated that these soldiers from Company F had caused trouble before in Gardiner bars. They refused to pay, and Hosley called Semple all kinds of names. Semple told Hosley to get out, and Hosley replied by inviting him to step outside. Haverson commented on what they would do to Semple outside. Semple grabbed a billy club, and all went to the sidewalk in front of the bar. There the argument, now technically inside the park, continued. Witnesses differed on exactly what happened then, but agreed that Semple struck Hosley with the club, and Haverson pulled his knife and began stabbing Semple. After the incident, said witness Mason, Haverson was heard to say, "I'm a good cutting _____."

Semple sustained severe knife wounds in the face and chest. One wound ran from his temple to the point of his jawbone, a second ran horizontally along his neck, a third traveled from the left of his nose onto his cheek, and a fourth ripped open the right side of his chest, penetrating his lung. Semple died from his wounds.

Deputy Sheriff George Welcome chased the men two miles into the park, caught them, and was taking them back to Gardiner when about one hundred angry citizens met the party and demanded the men for a lynching. Welcome calmed the citizens down by coolly stating, "If you had caught them before I did I would have nothing to say. I arrested them and they are mine." He took the men to the Gardiner jail on the Yellowstone River. In May, with Gardiner townspeople in attendance, a jury convicted Private Haverson of manslaughter, and a judge sentenced him to eight years in Montana prison.[39]

A 1980s shooting near Gardiner, Montana, involved a woman and was deemed a negligent homicide. Two hunters, Steven Keys, 31, and Rodney Schultz, 28, were carrying rifles and looking for black bears on the night of June 26, 1982. In near darkness at Eagle Creek campground, just north of Gardiner, the two saw a yellow tent belonging to Shannon Weatherly, 28, and a male friend. Schultz and Keys said later they thought the tent was a bear, and Schultz fired into it. His bullet struck Shannon in the head, killing her instantly and terrifying her friend. Schultz and Keys were arrested. In subsequent trials, they were found guilty, Schultz of negligent homicide and Keys of the lesser charge of creating a hazard. Strangely, both received only fines and a period of separation from firearms. A later civil suit brought by Shannon Weatherly's mother named the two plus the National Rifle Association.[40]

The park's most recent murder occurred on August 11, 1997, at Frog Rock, about six miles east of Mammoth, and it was a murder-suicide. The story of Norma Jean Reimann, 69, and her son Ronald Robert Reimann, 48, both of Blackfoot, Idaho, can be characterized as pathetic. Both were eluding law enforcement officials in Valley County for grand theft, and they had been involved in a check-fraud scheme in the Pacific Northwest. Suffering from extensive credit problems, the two had become "bored with life," and to make matters worse, Ronald had suffered a stroke. On Sunday morning, August 10, park rangers found their pickup truck with camper shell parked at Frog Rock parking area and checked the vehicle, but could not see inside due to tinted windows. They thought nothing seemed amiss. On Sunday night, rangers again checked the vehicle and again could find nothing unusual but did not open it. Sometime earlier, perhaps on August 10, Ronald Reimann took a .357 Magnum, shot his mother Norma twice in the head, killed the family's pet cat, and then shot himself once in the head, while all occupied the back of the pickup. On Monday morning when rangers again attempted to contact the owners of the vehicle, they detected the smell of decay, so opened the truck and discovered the bodies.[41]

Each of these stories offers insights into human behavior, some of them gray, but there is a larger lesson here about Yellowstone itself: people live their lives here like everywhere else. In addition to being a wilderness, Yellowstone is a human place, too, with all the deep history of anywhere else.

21

POWERLESS IN EDEN
DEATHS FROM SUICIDE

Those who commit
suicide are powerless souls.

—Spinoza, 1632–1677

WITH THOSE WORDS, a Spanish philosopher characterized suiciders. Re-markably, at least twenty-three such powerless persons have suffered from the dark machinations that preceded their suicides in Yellowstone, plus numerous others just outside the park. Most have been park employees. Perhaps they chose Yellowstone in which to suicide because it was an idyllic or famous place to die. Or perhaps for some reason they wanted their deaths inextricably linked to nature. Regardless, any suicide is doubly tragic when it occurs in a place as beautiful as Yellowstone.

The torment that ultimately plunges a suicider into death is uniquely personal, with tentacles that then touch the rest of us. William Styron, in his prize-winning book entitled *Darkness Visible* (1990), calls the suicider's world "an interior pain that is almost indescribable." Afterward the toll falls upon the remaining family and friends, leaving a smear of negativity. The suicider's private act of nullity somehow invades our own grasping and often tenuous sense of meaning in existence. It is a kind of abandonment which makes those of us left behind feel a vague sense of being somehow less protected against the surreal void of nothingness. As long ago as the 1830s, famous novelist Edgar Allen Poe dealt with unwanted impulses such as suicide in an essay called "The Imp of the Perverse." Poe noted that the impulse could increase to a wish, then to a desire, then to an uncontrollable longing. "There is no passion in nature so demonically impatient," he wrote, "as that of him who, shuddering upon the edge of a precipice, thus meditates a plunge." "The suicide does not play the game, does not observe the rules," wrote novelist Joyce Carol Oates. "He leaves the party too soon, and leaves the other guests painfully uncomfortable."

The first known suicide in Yellowstone was Emily Moore, age 27, who killed herself January 27, 1884, at Mammoth Hot Springs with a morphine overdose. The woman lived at Mammoth with her husband and son in one of the old McCartney Hotel buildings and appears to have been prosperous. She was suffering from painful neuralgia, and so she sent her son to Gardiner to R. A. Bell's store to procure morphine. Apparently on purpose, she took too much of it. Assistant Superintendent D. E. Sawyer wrote: "Mrs. Moor[e] that lived in the Gulch cabin and moved to Gardner [*sic*] committed suicide last Saturday night. She was buried Monday on the hill north of the Hotel" in the Mammoth civilian cemetery.[1] At that time, morphine was sold without restrictions, so fatalities from its use were not uncommon.

Phillip Bassett, whose family left their name on a creek north of the park, followed Emily Moore to the Mammoth civilian cemetery on May 1, 1884. He killed himself at Cinnabar, Montana (inside the present park), using an unspecified poison.[2] We know nothing else.

The story of the noted army scout Ed M. Wilson (1851–1891) is an important and very sad one. It is not known exactly when Wilson arrived in the park, but it was probably in 1885, when he was hired by Superintendent David Wear as a "mountaineer assistant." That year in August and November, Wilson made the first arrests in park history for poaching, taking George Reeder and John Ferguson into custody at Lower Falls and five other men into custody in the northwest corner of the park.[3] In January of 1887, Wilson accompanied F. Jay Haynes and Lieutenant Frederick Schwatka on what has been called the "first winter trip through Yellowstone,"[4] and as such he appeared in several of Haynes's photographs from that trip. That summer, Wilson was employed as a regular scout in the park upon the resignation of scout Jack Baronett. In February of 1888, he made the first winter patrol for protective purposes, thus establishing that winter travel was feasible in Yellowstone's backcountry.[5]

Wilson was quite active in protecting the park from poaching, and much ballyhooed for his park expertise. Superintendent George S. Anderson was particularly high on him:

> On [Superintendent Boutelle's] departure, there was only one man left here familiar with the Park and its needs, and that was Ed Wilson, the scout. He had been a trapper himself, and was thoroughly familiar with every species of game and its haunts and habits. He was brave as Caesar, but feared the mysterious and unseen. He preferred to operate alone by night and in storms; he knew every foot of the Park, and knew it better than any other man has yet known it; he knew its enemies and the

Ed Wilson on skis, n.d. (photo 65249.89, YNP Collections)

practical direction of their enmity. He came to me one morning and reported that a man named Van Dyck was trapping beaver near Soda Butte; that he spent his days on the highest points in the neighborhood, and with a glass scanned every approach; and that the only way to get him was to go alone, by night, and approach the position from the rear, over Specimen Mountain. To this I readily assented, and at 9 that night, in as bad a storm as I ever saw, Wilson started out for the forty-mile trip. He reached a high point near the one occupied by Van Dyck, saw him visit his traps in the twilight and return to his camp, where at daybreak the next morning Wilson came upon him while sleeping, photographed him with his own kodak, and then awakened him and brought him to the post.[6]

Wilson seems also to have made a practice of carefully watching the Fort Yellowstone army soldiers who themselves occasionally engaged in poaching in the park. From a long letter he wrote on the subject to G. L. Henderson, one has to wonder if these activities so added to his unpopularity in the park among the officers and enlisted men that Wilson was influenced in his decision to commit suicide.[7]

Those things may have added to his unpopularity in the park, but the real impetus for his suicide was something else. By 1891, scout Ed Wilson was in love. He had fallen hard for the youngest daughter of park hotel keeper G. L. Henderson. Pictures of Mary Rosetta Henderson make it clear that she was a beautiful young woman. Ed Wilson had watched her mature from age 16 (in 1886) to a statuesque beauty at age 20. Mary did not return his attentions. Wilson was an imposing physical character. He was five feet ten inches tall and weighed two hundred pounds. One would have thought that his dark blue eyes, dark hair streaked with gray, and dark brown mustache would have made him naturally appealing to any lady. Instead, Ed Wilson, age about 37, the consummate man of the wilderness who had pioneered so many firsts in Yellowstone, walked up a hill above the village of Mammoth Hot Springs on the evening of July 27, 1891, carrying a bottle of morphine. He sat on the hill, pondered his life, and apparently drank the entire bottle.

He was missing for nearly a year. Great searches were instituted to find him and reward posters were circulated, for Wilson was thoroughly missed. The newspapers ran notices of his disappearance, but nothing was heard about why he was missing for eleven months.

On June 12, 1892, while she was picking wildflowers, the little daughter of Willis Wyatt found Ed Wilson's clothed skeleton on a hill above Mammoth with the empty morphine bottle lying nearby. "It lay about one mile due north of the hotel," wrote a newspaperman, "in a small clump of quaking asp willows, the head being distant some 50 feet, undoubtedly dragged there by ravenous coyotes." Found with Wilson's skeleton was a package of letters addressed to him. A woman had rendered him powerless. He was buried in Livingston, Montana, probably by the Masons and only fifty feet northwest of Jack Baronett, whom he replaced as scout. At nearly this same time Mary Henderson married Henry Klamer, an employee of her father's who a few years later would establish the lower store at Old Faithful. Ed Wilson's story is hugely intriguing, and I earnestly wish we knew more. On the back of his photograph in the Yellowstone Park photo archives someone has handwritten a note that he killed himself over Mary Henderson.[8]

Another clothed skeleton was found August 21, 1900, near the Gardiner cemetery on Tinker's Hill, a location inside the park. The cemetery had been without burials for long periods, so it was (and still is) not unusual for time to go by with no one visiting the site. On May 3, 1900, Frank Pepper, age about 30, a stage driver who drove the Cinnabar–Jardine route for A. T. French, drove his team back to Cinnabar, walked around town giving away everything he had, purchased a gun from Hall's store, told others he was going to quit his job, went to the Gardiner cemetery, and shot himself in the head. The cemetery, even today, is somewhat remote, so no one found Pepper for nearly four

$200 REWARD.

Disappeared from Mammoth Hot Springs, Yellowstone National Park, Wyoming, on the night of July 27, 1891,

EDWARD M. WILSON,

height about 5 feet 10 inches, florid complexion, dark blue eyes, dark hair, slightly mixed with grey, cut pompadour, dark brown mustache, weight about 200 pounds; wore navy blue coat and vest, with light grey pants and black Stetson hat.

For a number of years past he was employed as a government scout and held that position at the time he disappeared.

It is thought that he was suffering from aberration of mind at the time and for several days previous to his leaving.

I am authorized by his friends to offer the above reward for information, satisfactory to them, that he is alive.

JAMES H. DEAN,

Mammoth Hot Springs,
Yellowstone National Park, Wyo.

Reward poster offered for Ed Wilson's return, 1891 (Anderson Collection, YNP Research Library) months. In late August, a tourist at the cemetery "came across the skeleton of a man with the flesh almost totally rotted off his bones, with a ghastly gaping hole in his head and a six-shooter lying by his side telling the story of his death in words most unmistakable and terrible in their import." Pepper had disappeared from Cinnabar on May 3 and was talked about for some time after that.[9] He was probably buried in the Gardiner cemetery and likely is in one of the unmarked graves today. The reasons for his suicide remain unknown, but he, too, had grown powerless.

Another Gardinerite killed himself close to the park if not in it. Dan Bowman, about 45, was a teamster employed by businessman Larry Link. He was described as "one of the best known residents of Gardiner." At 5:00 p.m. on July 13, 1905, Bowman, who "had been drinking heavily of late," drove his team to the barn, fed and watered them, took a packet of letters to Mrs. Jobb nearby, went back to the barn, lay down on a cot, and shot himself in the head with a .38 Colt revolver. The reasons for his suicide remain unknown.[10]

Otto Wiggins's story is strange in that he was on his way to Yellowstone by train. At Saratoga, Wyoming, on May 18, 1906, while "eating breakfast in a tent," Wiggins drew a pistol from his "companion's pocket" and, saying only the word "Good-bye" to his 12-year-old son, shot himself through the head. Wiggins, a barber from Pearl, Colorado, had just started a vacation trip and was traveling with his son and a companion.[11]

Eugene Clark's story is sad, but also very romantic. We have few facts on his death at Mammoth Hot Springs because it did not make the local newspaper, but we know that he died of carbolic acid poisoning. Carbolic acid was commonly used in his day as a means to commit suicide. It could be easily purchased at any drugstore for fifteen cents an ounce, and one ounce was all that was needed to do the job.[12] Eugene W. Clark, an assistant electrical engineer in the park, apparently killed himself on November 9, 1906. Perhaps he was despondent over the death of his infant daughter Sarah, who had died at Fort Yellowstone on October 26, 1905. At any rate, both were buried in the Mammoth army cemetery.[13] We know nothing more about their deaths.

The affair, however, was not to come to a complete close until fifty-one years later. On May 8, 1957, Jeannett Clark, age 73, died in San Francisco, California. Her will directed that she be buried beside her husband and daughter in the army cemetery at Mammoth. She had apparently never remarried. The romantic sorrow of this story is immediately touching and at the same time mysterious. What must Jeannett Clark have felt at the time of the deaths of her husband and daughter, and indeed for the rest of her life? Why did she not remarry? What were the circumstances of her departure from the park, and when did it occur? The questions are Poelike in their melancholy. Jeannett Clark was buried at Mammoth on May 15, 1957, her interment becoming the first burial there in thirty-three years and the Fort Yellowstone cemetery's last.[14]

As one might imagine, despondency was the usual reason for suicides in the park, and, interestingly, most suicides have been park employees. So it was with James P. Jackson, 39, of Lewistown, Montana, a Yellowstone Park Camps Company employee, who slashed his own throat with a razor from ear to ear and bled to death at the long-razed Mammoth Lodge sometime between April 30 and May 3, 1927.[15] So it was also with Frederick Alfred Olson, 60, a carpenter for Yellowstone Park Company, who hanged himself in room 225 of the Gardiner bunkhouse on March 2, 1951;[16] and apparently with a soldier at Fort Yellowstone, a private with Troop F, First Cavalry, who shot himself in the head with his army .38 revolver on October 11, 1911, at 2:00 in the morning while drunk. The soldier from Ohio was a close friend of prominent Gardinerite Jerry Melloy and had only recently come to the post. The man's name was not picked up by local newspapers, but he was Private Herman F. Felix. An army board determined that Felix "was a good soldier of ordinarily quiet, well disposed and cheerful demeanor but addicted to drink; that he was sometimes obsessed with the idea that he might kill himself when drunk; further, that he had upon several occasions expressed a purpose or idea of killing himself."[17] He was the second soldier to kill himself at Fort Yellowstone that year, for Thomas King, aged 22 and trumpeter in Troop F, had shot himself twice in the abdomen on the afternoon of June 27, 1911. King left two notes: one to his mother and the other unaddressed and pinned to his shirt. The first said only, "I am through, goodbye," while the second was a request to be buried in civilian clothes. Apparently life in the army had not treated him well, even though he had been enlisted for less than a year. King's body was shipped to his relatives in Dryden, Utah.[18] Another despondent park-area employee was Charles W. Anderson. His body was found in an old prospector's tunnel just outside the park on September 30, 1906. Anderson, 59, of Gardiner and Cooke City, had placed a sawed-off Winchester to his right ear and fired. Nothing else is known.[19]

With park ranger Judson M. Rhoads of Covelo, California, the despondency was due to debts. A graduate of the University of California in forestry, Rhoads, 31, had been a Yellowstone ranger for four years when he shot himself at the west entrance on January 9, 1938. His wife heard the gunshot that ended his life. A ranger who knew Rhoads recalled later that he had gotten himself into serious debt and had been depressed since a trip to California wherein he lost a 380-dollar car in a mudslide. His grandson, who shares his name, believes that he was also depressed because he was underemployed, and certainly that happened to many people during the Great Depression. Judson Rhoads's tombstone in Covelo says "presented by the National Park Service, Yellowstone, N.P."[20]

Fear of his father's looming punishment may have been the reason for 13-year-old Pud Robinson's suicide on November 15, 1938, but we do not

Body as viewed from the door on arrival

Drawing of the suicide of Frederick Alfred Olson, 1951, in Gardiner (YNP Archives)

know that for certain, and his shooting could have been accidental. For that reason, I have chosen to place the story in the "Deaths from Accidental and Self-Defense Shootings" chapter (see chapter 19).

At this writing we do not know the reasons why Garr Nelson of Ogden, Utah, hanged himself in his Yellowstone Park Company quarters at Old Faithful Lodge on August 30, 1959,[21] nor why Shirley Pitkin Clark, 36, another park employee, killed herself by drinking lye on November 19, 1962, at the Mammoth trailer village. Clark died two days later at Livingston Hospital.[22] Nor do we know for sure why Frank M. Deckard, 56, killed himself in his cabin on Deckard Flats (near Jardine, Montana) on October 19, 1930, but folks who knew him said it was because he was depressed over the government's eminent domain taking of his land there. His family left their name on the flat just north of the park boundary. This was the same Frank Deckard that twenty-five years earlier had been so badly kicked by a horse at Cinnabar that the newspaper reported it. It also reported that his father Alexander Deckard had been killed in a wagon accident the preceding autumn (see chapter 18).[23]

Yellowstone tourists have only rarely done themselves in. Robert Eikin Jr. was a park visitor from Buena Park, California, whose suicide at age 43 was a mystery. He was found in his car on the Mammoth–Gardiner road on August 14, 1960, with a gunshot wound to the chest.[24]

Glen C. Reaser must have left a big impression on a park visitor at Fishing Bridge campground. Reaser, 59, a National Park Service maintenance employee from Southwick, South Dakota, chose that campground's comfort station utility room to hang himself in on July 17, 1964. His body was found by a very startled camper.[25]

Another NPS maintenance employee shot himself in the head on June 8, 1967. "Bernie's committed suicide," said laborer George Clark to ranger Gerald Mernin when Mernin arrived the following day. Bernard Walter Bayne, 23, was found with a bullet hole in his right temple on June 9 in the government bunkhouse at Canyon Village. On the table against the north wall was a pint bottle of whiskey, empty except for a half-inch remaining. Although Bayne had mentioned suicide, his fellow employees had not known him to be depressed.[26]

Getting fired was probably the trigger for April W. Cruse's suicide on June 3, 1978. Cruse, 32, had been working at the Mammoth reservations office and then at Lake Hotel as a housekeeper. She was fired on June 2 by the Yellowstone Park Company from the latter position, and the following day she was found in front of the "Cliff" houses near the old Mammoth Lodge site with a self-inflicted gunshot wound to the head. The man whose house she died in front of was probably the man she blamed for her firing.[27]

One of the more interesting "suicides" in the park was one that never happened. Workmen employed "on the roads on Sepulcher Mountain" (probably the old Mammoth–Gardiner road) in August of 1901 found a note which pointed to the possible suicide of employee B. F. Weaver. It read: "The writer, B.F. Weaver, came here to die. Some one please drop a line to my mother, Susan E. Weaver, Buffalo, Kansas. The finder of this note will do me a favor if he will write. My name is B. F. Weaver. Left home 1892."

Weaver had been employed in the park for several days the preceding spring, but disappeared and had not been heard from since, so his death was supposed. However, Weaver soon showed up at the Mammoth post office to pick up his mail. He was very much alive.[28]

Speaking of the Mammoth post office, one of its postmasters and an employee killed themselves, probably in late 1939. The details of these two deaths are obscure, but Claude W. Anthony (who took over as postmaster on January 20, 1936) killed himself "as a result of the malfeasance of a minor employee [and] . . . while under a suspension." Another career employee of that post office, name unknown, took his own life at nearly the same time in connection with the same event. Details are not currently known about either of these suicides, but historian Aubrey Haines, who lived in the park at that time, stated of the two men that "neither was culpable, yet both *felt* responsible" for whatever the event was. A search of newspapers has failed so far to turn up the circumstances of this bizarre event.[29]

Of course, a number of (probably many) suicides occurred just outside the park, including that of Henry Gillotte, who killed himself at Jardine, Montana, in April of 1905.[30] Another, also at Jardine, was Frank Selon, a teamster aged 28, who shot himself in the forehead on Saturday, November 23, 1940.[31] Yet another was Joseph R. Charrell, who was found hanging from a tree in Cooke City in early July of 1940.[32] Cooke City, like Jardine, can be a cold and (probably more importantly) dark place in the winter, because the sun does not peek into it until later most mornings, so one instinctively wonders whether that darkness has been a factor in suicides. Two more are known at Jardine, although details are sketchy. Earl Johnson of Roundup, Montana, says that "Dead-eye" Dick Meyers killed himself at Jardine and so did Joe Tribble, both in similar fashions, and both men were miners. Meyers lived on a small homestead bordering Bear Creek. "He always told me and other people," said Johnson, "that when the time came, he would save the county the trouble of a burial; filled his cabin with wood, soaked it with kerosene, set it on fire, then shot himself. Did a very good job as the bones were hard to find!" That incident, which killed 80-year-old prospector Meyers, occurred on July 15, 1949. The next one "happened before my time," said Earl, who was born in or about 1921. Joe Tribble, whose picture is in Doris Whithorn's book *Photo History of Gardiner, Jardine, Crevasse* (p. 36), "lived on a homestead several miles up main Bear Creek from Jardine, [and] he did himself in much the same way" as Meyers. The year of Tribble's suicide is unknown.[33]

An intriguing suicide attempt occurred at Firehole Hotel (formerly Marshall's Hotel) in Lower Geyser Basin in the summer of 1885. John Howard, 19-year-old son of the well-known U.S. Army general Oliver Otis Howard, shot himself there. Park tour guide G. L. Henderson talked with General Howard at the hotel after the affair. The general told him that he, his son James, a Miss Chase of Omaha, and the general's sister-in-law (a Mrs. Howard) all entered the park from its then difficult southern side. At Shoshone Lake they were met by John Howard, who had been betrothed to Miss Chase for about a year, and who had been in the park all summer employed on the roads under Lieutenant Dan Kingman. John and James had a disagreement about Miss Chase, but General Howard said she had done nothing coquettishly to deserve it. The general supposed that the lovers had a quarrel. On August 20, at Firehole Basin, John left the party, and a few minutes later they found that he had shot himself through the breast. The rest of the party immediately left the park, and John Howard survived his self-inflicted wound.[34]

And there have been recent suicides in Yellowstone National Park. I have already mentioned the 1997 murder and suicide perpetuated by Ronald Reimann, who killed himself after he killed his mother Norma. Another suicide occurred that same year. James William Karhi, 60, of Lewistown, Montana, was driving on U.S. Highway 191 on December 31, 1997, at a point about eight miles north of West Yellowstone (inside of, or very near to being within, the park) when he suddenly slid and became stuck in snow fifteen to twenty feet off the road. A park ranger responded and asked Karhi for his insurance and registration information. Karhi reentered his car to retrieve that material and instead grabbed a .38-caliber revolver and shot himself in the head. The man had admitted moments before that he had been drinking and taking prescribed medication while driving.[35]

Yellowstone National Park ranger Don Unser, 47, killed himself at Grant Village, the place he worked, on April 6, 2001. Nothing more was learned.[36]

Dr. James Clement Jeffery, 40, of Lake Charles, Louisiana, hiked up Slough Creek before killing himself. Rangers found several notes in his abandoned red Chevrolet Blazer at a Slough Creek parking area on October 12, 2003, indicating his intention to commit suicide. They became more interested after discovering that Jeffery was suspected of faking his own death in Pensacola, Florida. Officials there reported finding his unoccupied boat banging against bridge-pier pilings after Jeffery missed his own divorce hearing for a property settlement. They then learned that Jeffery purchased a red 2000 Chevy Blazer and closed his bank account two days before that disappearance. When Jeffery's vehicle was still at Slough Creek on October 15, twelve park staff and two dog teams began searching for him. They found his body on October 16 at a point two miles north of Slough Creek Trailhead. This time his disappearance was not a fake.[37]

Wayne Skertich was a former park employee, a resident of nearby Jardine, Montana, a man that I knew personally, and a local musician who was troubled at the end of his life. He was a bit of a recluse with some marital problems, but that sounds like a lot of otherwise normal people. A builder by trade who was passionate about music, Wayne played fiddle, piano, bass, and guitar and spread a lot of happiness that way. But on Thursday night, April 7, 2005, Wayne and his wife got into an argument. She left the house at Jardine and called 911. Wayne bolted the door, refused to talk to police, and began walking around his house with a rifle in his hands. He held thirty-five officers and many, many friends and neighbors at bay for twenty-six hours. His friends "talked until [they] were blue in the face" to him. His wife and daughter stated that Wayne's troubles really had begun eight years earlier when he fell from a work scaffold and fractured his head. His accident was a bad one, and he never fully recovered, sometimes flying into irrational rages when he would forget things. It made him reclusive, but he still had lots of friends. "He must have been hurting a lot more than we realized," said one of them, and another noted that Wayne was not crazy. Instead, he had a physical injury over which he had no control.

On Saturday morning, April 9 at 2:00 a.m., after twenty-six hours of holding what seemed like the entire world at bay, Wayne Skertich shot himself in his cabin. Some thought the police had overreacted with the big show at his home. Some blamed the police, but most did not. In fact, Wayne's wife had nothing but good words for law enforcement.

Ultimately Wayne Skertich's last days were desperately sad. As one of his friends wrote, "I think Wayne's song could have played out a lot differently." But Skertich brought a lot of joy with his music to residents of the northern Yellowstone nation. "Don't remember him for the last thirty hours of his life," said his daughter, who gave us warm and heartfelt advice. "Remember him for who he was, and understand that isn't who he was becoming."[38]

Nicholas Jeffrey Mostert picked what may be Yellowstone Park's most spectacular individual spot for his demise. The Brink of Lower Falls has long been celebrated as nearly an entry point into the pearly gates themselves. Great paeans have been written to it, both in prose and poetry, effervescing about the canyon's great depths and analogizing the whiteness of the falls to the robes of angels. Artist Alfred Lambourne in 1884 thought that the spot was personally "one whose images would hold a place and whose influence would be felt through all the days remaining of my life." Edward Wessel in 1891 called it "as beautiful a scene of rugged nature as is possible to behold anywhere," and he described the waterfall ominously and a bit presciently as "losing itself in a vapory grave beneath." Traveler Henry Estabrook that same year tried vainly to describe what he saw and felt from there as he looked over the precipice. He knew that he was terrified:

> The waters here divided into three emerald strands, which only began to braid together ere they blossomed into foam that flung itself headlong into the abyss. How far did it fall? I was curious to know, and so, catching firm hold of the railing, craned my neck, beyond the verge. Holy

Moses! I started back, every fiber trembling in affright. What had I seen? I scarcely know. It was like gazing into the burning bush, into the secret places of the earth, into the arcana of heaven. I remember that it was so high, so very high, that my eyes swam in their sockets and seemed to drop out of my head. It was so white, so very white, that it seemed itself a source of light.[39]

Nicholas Jeffrey Mostert's death at this place was desperately sad. He was 20 years old, from Salt Lake City, Utah, and was a gifted musician, lyricist, and composer. He was passionate about hiking, snowboarding, and the environment, and family members say that he "felt most at home in nature." On June 16, 2009, Nicholas descended the trail to the Brink of Lower Falls, near Canyon Village, to see the monster waterfall at its top. The waterfall was carrying more than forty-four thousand gallons of water per second as it fell 308 feet into the Grand Canyon of the Yellowstone. While other visitors watched, horrified, he climbed over the retaining fence and jumped into the river at its drop. He was immediately swept over the brink, falling more than three hundred feet in the water of Lower Falls to the rocks and river below. His body was not immediately recovered.[40]

Park spokesman Al Nash attempted conciliatorily to explain the suicide. "Parks hold a special place in people's hearts," he said. "There are some individuals who feel it's important to have that kind of connection in those final moments." Another commentator was out of line in my opinion. Claiming that it was Yellowstone's "sixth suicide since 1997," a politically conservative writer only thirteen days later denounced "liberals" and "green-oriented folks" like Mostert for killing themselves in such a "wasteful" and "selfish" manner, because taxpayers have to pick up the tab for recovery and because "in a twisted way it's the ultimate statement in support of the environment."[41] This seems to me like an unreasonable, political swipe at liberals, because conservatives kill themselves too, and they too can be "environmentalists."

Another recent suicide was Peter Louis Kastner, a self-imposed and horribly sad death caused by post-traumatic stress disorder. Kastner was 25 years old and a decorated U.S. Marine. Raised in Minnesota, he enlisted in the military right out of high school. He scored a perfect three hundred on the Marines' rigorous physical test during basic training and then deployed to Iraq. Injured in at least two roadside-bomb attacks, he was promoted to sergeant and earned the Combat Action Ribbon and the Purple Heart for head injuries, once having to pick up the exploded remains of a fellow soldier. Discharged in 2007, he returned to Minnesota, where he and his wife suffered a car wreck that left him with a concussion. That exacerbated his postwar stress. "He couldn't focus, couldn't concentrate, and couldn't remember things," said his mother

Sara, while his father Larry Kastner observed that he "became more difficult to connect with and more difficult to have a logical conversation with." Following a divorce, Peter moved to Oklahoma City to pursue a college degree in accounting at the University of Oklahoma, my own alma mater, so that is one more item about this particular incident that rips at me.

In the spring of 2010, Kastner went to Yellowstone, parked his rental car at the Hellroaring Trailhead west of Tower Junction, and hiked into the back-country. Park rangers found his car on May 31, but Kastner was missing. For nearly three weeks, officers investigated his disappearance, speaking to Kastner's family and searching with air and ground teams and dog teams. On July 14, a group of park researchers working off-trail on Garnet Hill came upon Peter Kastner's remains. He was dead from a self-inflicted gunshot wound. Larry Kastner attributed his son's death to "the monster that is PTSD."[42]

Suicides are ugly and desperately sad occurrences anywhere, and certainly powerlessness knows no locale or political affiliation. Suicides somehow violate the unspoken covenant we all have with each other to affirm life, even when there may be little left to affirm. Perhaps these persons wanted their last moments to be spent in a beautiful or famous place, or perhaps they wanted their deaths to be somehow inextricably linked to nature. No doubt several of these deaths occurred only because the suiciders happened to live in Yellowstone, for geographic location is irrelevant to many such despondent persons. Instead what is foremost to these actors is "the stage inside the mind upon which they enact life's loneliest agony."[43]

There is greater sadness, even irony, in self-inflicted deaths in a place as idyllic as Yellowstone. Suicides can happen anywhere, even in an Edenic place where one would think the victims would find a reason not to kill themselves.

On the other hand, suicide is an extremely personal thing. Perhaps for some, Yellowstone was the right place for it.

22

MISSING AND PRESUMED DEAD

. . . what have you done with the disappeared?

—Argentinian protest chant, 1982

THAT QUESTION HAS BEEN asked about LeRoy R. Piper for nearly a hundred years. On July 30, 1900, Piper, 36, of Saint Marys, Ohio, was staying at Yellowstone's Fountain Hotel at Lower Geyser Basin. He purchased a cigar from the cigar stand, stepped out onto the porch of the hotel, and was never seen again.

Piper, a bank cashier, had been en route to San Francisco to settle his deceased uncle's estate. He was wearing a blue suit with a dark check about one inch wide, no vest, a soft white shirt with the initials LRP embroidered in red at the bottom of the front, black laced patent leather shoes, two diamond rings, one Knights Templar emblem, a Shriners button in the lapel of his coat, and a dark derby hat. He was carrying a considerable sum of money with him as well as valuable jewelry. Friends feared that "his mind became unbalanced," detachments of cavalry searched for a month for him, his brother-in-law came to the park to conduct a personal search, and a one-thousand-dollar reward was posted for his return, but it was all to no avail. Lieutenant Amos and scout Peter Holte gave up looking on September 5 after "deciding that the search is useless." In December, Piper's residence in Ohio gave him up for dead as well.[1]

Nearly a year later, a San Jose newspaper ran the long story headlined "Where Is Leroy Piper?" Other relatives were wondering whether Piper had been kidnapped to be held for ransom. He was, after all, the nephew of former congressman William Adam Piper, who had died in August of 1899 and whose estate Leroy Piper was heading to California to help settle. That estate was worth two to three million dollars, although estimates varied. The newspaper carried the story of Piper's brother-in-law, a Dr. Sheets of San Jose. Dr. Sheets learned that a number of other park visitors were with Piper when he went onto the hotel's porch to smoke but eventually all went inside, leaving Piper alone there. The story continued:

> The next morning Mr. Piper did not come down to breakfast. Late in the forenoon it was discovered that he was not in his room. Inquiry was made among the guests. No one had seen him since the night before on the hotel porch. It was ascertained that his entire luggage was in his room; that he did not have his overcoat with him, which would have been the case had he intended going any distance from the house. Search was at once instituted by the attaches of the hotel. The guests joined in the search. No trace of him could be found. A dispatch was then sent to his relatives in San Jose. On his arrival in Yellowstone Park Dr. Sheets began a systematic search. He engaged a large number of men. They went in every direction, searched every place where there seemed to be the most remote possibility that the missing man could have reached. All to no purpose; not a trace of him could be found. It was as though that night on the porch of the hotel he had vanished into air . . . Dr. Sheets continued the search in Yellowstone Park for a month. In that time nothing was heard of Mr. Piper, or his possible captors. So that theory was abandoned.[2]

I have my own theory as to what happened to Piper. I believe he walked out into the night and inadvertently stumbled into one of the many hot springs that were and are located nearby. Persons who fall into hot springs disintegrate, and there is often no recovery of them. Two hot springs there, Gentian Pool and Deep Blue Geyser, are very large and very deep, and I believe that a search of them or other springs there, could it be done, would yield Piper's silicified bones, perhaps covered over by years of hot-spring deposits.

One hundred years later to the night, on July 30, 2000, chief park tour guide Leslie Quinn led his fellow Yellowstone guides to the old hotel site and lit cigars in commemoration of the strange disappearance of L. R. Piper.[3]

Little Joe Osimic (or Zimec) disappeared from the area just north of Yellowstone Park on October 29, 1915. He was a woodcutter from Aldridge, Montana, and after his disappearance all the places he had worked were searched. Several years later, Edward Wright Jr. saw a skull near a lake in the backcountry just north of Aldridge and ran home to tell his father. When the elder Edward Wright arrived at the lake, the skull was gone. The lakeshore was searched many times after that, but it was not until August of 1924 that the human skull was again found. Although it was never positively identified, many of the area locals believed for years that it was that of Little Joe. Today that lake just north of Yellowstone National Park is known as Little Joe Lake.[4]

A young boy who disappeared in Yellowstone Park in 1966 has never been found despite one of the most intense National Park Service searches in Yellowstone history. On July 12, 1966, at about 1:30 p.m., Dennis Eugene Johnson, aged 8, of Inyokern, California, walked away from his parents and siblings at Cascade picnic area near Canyon Village and was never seen again. The NPS searched for him by ground and air and with the use of dogs for three weeks. The search consumed thousands of man hours, but Dennis Johnson was truly gone. His brother stated just before the search was called off that he thought the NPS had done everything possible. In subsequent months, the family procured the services of a "psychiater" who professed to be able to divine the boy's whereabouts. He told them Dennis had drowned in a shallow ditch near the location where the boy disappeared or perhaps had fallen into the canyon. Ranger Gerry Mernin, who was involved in the intensive investigation, referred twenty-seven years later to Dennis's disappearance as "still very mysterious." Mernin thinks it possible that Dennis was picked up by someone on a park road but admits that the boy's disappearance is one of Yellowstone's great unsolved mysteries.[5]

But then all disappearances are unsolved mysteries. Tracy Cray's was no less of one when it occurred, even though it was solved seven years later. Cray, 25, of Billings, Montana, disappeared near Gardiner, Montana, while hunting with his father and brother on February 13, 1983. The three men were hiking near Little Trail Creek. They split up, and Tracy's family never saw him again. Searchers looked for him for two weeks, slogging through waist-deep snow before giving up, but Tracy Cray was simply gone. He was missing for seven years before two elk hunters found his remains in 1990. Investigators believe Cray died of hypothermia from heavy snowfall the night he disappeared.[6]

Dan Campbell was engaged in illegally hunting for antlers in Yellowstone when he was lost. Campbell, 42, of Big Timber, Montana, and his dog (illegal to take into Yellowstone's backcountry) were dropped off by friends at the Hellroaring trailhead in early April of 1991. He apparently intended to hike through to Jardine, Montana, illegally collecting antlers and/or recovering a previously cached stack of antlers. A search for Campbell was instituted by park rangers on April 9, and the search was discontinued after nothing was turned up. Helitack foreman Andrew Mitchell, who was chief of the search, and ranger Paul Miller, who participated in the search, both believe that Campbell's bones are lying somewhere in the Yellowstone backcountry.[7]

A disappearance in 1993 involved a park employee who probably drowned. Daren "Franny" Dixon, a second-year employee at Roosevelt Lodge, was an avid fisherman and well liked by everyone there. He quit his job as a

HAVE YOU SEEN THIS PERSON?

DAREN "FRANNY" DIXON
20 YEARS OLD
6'1"   170 LBS.
AVID FISHERMAN
LAST SEEN: 7/4/93 COOKE CITY,
MONTANA AND LAMAR AREA
YELLOWSTONE NATIONAL PARK

IF YOU HAVE SEEN DAREN SINCE 7/4/93, CONTACT THE YELLOWSTONE COMMUNICATIONS CENTER AT (307) 344-2133

Reward poster, July 1993, circulated by Yellowstone National Park in Daren "Franny" Dixon case (author's collection) busboy there and left on July 2, 1993. Two days later Dixon disappeared. His car and wallet were found in the Lamar area. Despite a season-long search by rangers and park fire personnel, no trace of Dixon was found, and it is believed that he drowned.[8] He too remains an unsolved mystery today and one of the disappeared.

In 1994, reporter Joe Paisley of the *Bozeman* (MT) *Chronicle* became interested in these disappearances and wrote a story about them entitled "Unsolved Mysteries in Yellowstone Park." His story included news that the remains of Tracy Cray, missing for seven years, had been discovered north of Gardiner and that the remains of an unnamed Canadian man missing for five years had been recently discovered in Shoshone National Forest some five miles east of the park boundary. Perhaps the remains of others in that strange category of "disappeared" will someday turn up in the Yellowstone country.[9]

23

DEATHS FROM GAS STOVE EXPLOSIONS AND STRUCTURAL FIRES

Some say the world will end in fire . . .

—Robert Frost

MARGUERITE (MRS. H. P.) KNAPP, 36, of Chicago, was fatally burned to death when her family's gas stove exploded at Canyon auto camp on July 12, 1925. Her family of four had finished dinner and was preparing to wash dishes. Knapp was standing a few feet from the stove with her back to it when it exploded, spraying her with the flaming oil from its tank and igniting her clothing. She made the mistake of running and fanning the flames. Although she was immediately wrapped in a blanket by her family, she died the following afternoon from burns over 75 percent of her body.[1]

Likewise, Ida Florence Williams, 72, of Phillips, Texas, was killed on July 18, 1957, from flash burns to her face, chest, and hands that occurred when a gas heater exploded in her tent at Lewis Lake Campground.[2]

Both of these explosions were unusual incidents. In a similar vein, structural fires have occurred in Yellowstone Park buildings since earliest days. Two early hotels at Norris and one at Old Faithful burned completely, and a number of buildings at other locations have suffered various fires, but I have been able to find only two fires that resulted in fatalities. One occurred shortly after midnight on November 2, 1911, in a little house situated between Dean's saloon and Ford's blacksmith shop in Gardiner, Montana. The place burned fiercely, but the volunteer fire department controlled the blaze only to find the charred remains of an unknown man, "burned to a crisp and utterly unrecognizable." In time the man was identified as John C. Kelly, a 42-year-old laborer who had been jailed in Livingston several times for drunkenness.

The second fire occurred right on the park boundary at Gardiner, Montana, during the early morning hours of August 9, 1950. The fire totally destroyed the Park Hotel (formerly the Shaw and Powell Hotel) on Park Street, then located on the site of the present Town Cafe. At 3:15 a.m., a neighbor of the hotel across the alley to the north saw flames and smoke and reported the fire. Hans Ficksdahl, 60, the hotel night clerk, ran up and down the halls yelling, "Fire! Fire! Get out!" Sixteen-year-old Donalene O'Neill's aunt Agnes and uncle Roy Wilson owned the nearby Wilson Motel, and their dog Redcoat woke up Donalene by barking. She remembers that she "looked out just in time to see the flames at the back of the hotel and watched as the fire flashed in seconds to engulf the whole building!" A number of people jumped from upper windows, and others saved themselves by running into the night wearing little or nothing. But Mrs. Charles Hay of Troy, New York, and Al Durochie of Casper, Wyoming, were both killed in the fire. According to Otho Mack, chief of the Gardiner Fire Department, Mrs. Hay died when she rushed hysterically back into the flames to get her purse.[3]

Finally, one incident involving exploding gas in the coal mine at Horr is known from 1895. Cornelius "Con" Lowney, described as "one of the pioneers of Cooke City and a Grand Army veteran," was killed in the Montana Coal and Coke Company's coal mine at Horr from an explosion of gas. On January 25, 1895, Lowney, about 58, was in the mine at 8:00 a.m. with his partner Eugene Underwood. As the two walked into their work "room" about four hundred feet from the mouth of the tunnel, they smelled gas and began fanning it with their coats. Just then their supervisor walked up to them with another man. All noticed too late that the second man was wearing a flame-lit lamp on his helmet, and everything exploded. Lowney was killed instantly and his partner and supervisor were injured. The man who caused the explosion escaped injury.[4]

Other persons have been injured in gas-stove explosions or structural fires, but no one else is known to have been killed in Yellowstone in strange incidents such as these that ended in flames.

24

DEATHS FROM
CARBON MONOXIDE POISONING

AT LEAST SEVEN PEOPLE HAVE BEEN killed by carbon monoxide poisoning in or near Yellowstone National Park. Interestingly, in two separate incidents of this type three people were killed each time.

One of these occurred in the heavy snow and cold just after midnight on December 9, 1923. Three employees of Yellowstone Park Transportation Company—David Sroka, Edward J. Wright, and Dale A. Spears—were unable to get through deep snowdrifts between Canyon and Norris in their truck, so they decided to wait it out in the vehicle at a point about five and one-quarter miles west of Canyon. They left the engine running, went to sleep, and died from carbon monoxide while they slept. Then the truck caught on fire and all three bodies burned beyond recognition. The bodies were moved by sleigh to Mammoth.[1]

A similar incident happened on June 20, 1947, just outside the park to the northeast. A late snowstorm occurred in the Beartooth Mountains, and three NPS employees named Vernon E. Kaiser (55), John P. Baker, and Richard W. Huckels gave aid all day long to stranded motorists. It grew dark, so the three decided to wait out the night in their truck. They went to sleep with the engine running and did not wake up.[2]

After I published this story in 1995, the eminent park historian Aubrey Haines wrote me a letter to add details. He can tell the story better than I, so I will let him. And besides, he was working in the park in 1947 and knew the men involved. The official report gave asphyxiation as the cause, but Haines indicated he always wondered whether freezing was part of it.

> Those three men were true heroes and they deserve having the whole story told. They were the rotary plow crew from the park road camp on the Cooke City side of the [Beartooth Pass] summit. There was one of

those early summer snow storms, lots of snow and the east side camp near Red Lodge didn't get the gate shut soon enough. About 20 cars and a Park coal truck got past and into the storm. The coal truck was heavy-loaded and slow, so it became tail-end Charley of the procession, but it had good chains and enough power. As the truck moved onto the summit stuck cars kept showing up; they got them in line behind the truck with it slowly breaking trail. This caravan of vehicles got over the top and was on the downgrade toward Cooke when they came to a through-cut, the one with the 180 degree curve below it, and there was a car and its trailer house stuck solid in the cut. That stopped the procession. Before noon the Park rotary plow from the Camp where the road starts up from Clark's Fork (that was Keiser's [*sic*] outfit) reached the blockage. They thought they had room to get around the trailer, but the plow put its wheels in the ditch and high-centered. The two men in the service vehicle helped the operator; they worked all afternoon but couldn't get the plow back on the road which was blocked solid, AND no radio in those days. The boys wore themselves out and all they could do when night came was to bunch the people in a few cars, tell them not to run their engines and rely on body heat. Then the three crewmen got in their vehicle to tough-out the night. When the plow didn't come in that evening, the camp called engineering and that was the first news we had. Suspecting a breakdown, another rotary was started from Mammoth. It arrived at the cut the next morning—and found the crew dead in their truck. The whole through cut had blown full of snow so that all the vehicles were nearly covered, but the coal truck and all the people were all right. I was assistant park engineer at that time and I can tell you that was a terrible thing; besides, Vern Keiser [*sic*] was one of our good foremen. I thought the truck crew had died from total exhaustion depleting their body resistance.[3]

An 11-month-old infant was left in her parents' car with the engine running. Lois Christyne Fenner of Firth, Idaho, died at Madison Campground on September 8, 1946.[4]

In former years, internal combustion engines were notorious for leaking carbon monoxide into passenger compartments. They are safer today, but the best advice remains not to fall asleep inside a running vehicle.

25

TRAVEL IN WONDERLAND
DEATH ON THE ROAD AND IN THE AIR

Carriages without horses shall go,
And accidents fill the world with woe.

—Mother Shipton, 1500s

As on the ground, so also in the air
planes collide with disquieting consequences.

—John Kenneth Galbraith

THE AUTOMOBILE WAS OFFICIALLY admitted into Yellowstone National Park in August of 1915, and the park has been completely motorized since the summer of 1917, when one hundred eleven-passenger and seventeen seven-passenger buses replaced all horses and stagecoaches. At one point a few years later, the Yellowstone Park Transportation (YPT) Company boasted that it had 365 buses, one for each day of the year.[1] The Yellowstone transportation system had begun in 1880, with the first commercial stagecoach tour through the park, and it lasted in large form through 1990, when T. W. Services began to scale the buses back dramatically.

Of course, travel deaths include those caused by automobiles and airplanes. Automobile deaths, as mentioned earlier, are legion and considered ordinary, so I have elected to omit them.[2] Suffice it to say that Yellowstone National Park today sees about zero to five auto fatalities per year. Airplane travel to Yellowstone began in 1935, when an airport was established at West Yellowstone, Montana.

From the beginning of bus tours in 1917, park buses, like private autos, were occasionally involved in wrecks.[3] However, unlike automobiles, buses

273

were not often involved in fatal accidents. The few we know of tend to stand out.

Only four years after motorization, a park bus wreck killed a woman. At 5:30 p.m. on July 15, 1921, YPT driver Harry Dooley was driving ten-passenger bus number 157 eleven miles east of Fishing Bridge junction—then called Lake Junction—and traveling "a little fast but not twenty miles an hour." For some inexplicable reason, perhaps a mechanical failure, the bus left the road and went over an embankment. Ten persons suffered minor injuries, but Emma B. Childers, 38, of Wichita Falls, Texas, was killed instantly when her neck was broken. All of the passengers were united in stating that the driver had been very cautious and was not to blame.[4]

A park bus driver was killed on August 25, 1931. At 6:45 p.m., bus driver Delbert McConnaha, 24, of Butte, Montana, driving YPT Company bus number 205, was "deadheading" (driving without passengers) from Tower to Mammoth. At a sharp right turn between the five- and six-mile posts out of Tower, the bus left the road about halfway into the turn, skidded sideways about twenty feet, jumped sixteen feet, rolled once, and landed on its top or side. McConnaha was thrown twenty feet down the slope below the bus. He broke his neck, crushed his face, and collapsed his chest, all instantly. The cause of the wreck was determined to be driving too fast.[5]

Finally, a 1949 bus accident killed a 52-year-old bus passenger at Gibbon Meadows. Gertrude Rettenmeyer of Meriden, Connecticut, was killed and thirteen other persons injured at Gibbon Meadows on July 12, 1949.[6] This was the first serious wreck "in many years" that involved a YPT Company bus, here a "706" model. The wreck also involved a Peter Kiewit and Sons tractor-trailer rig and a third car. Mrs. Rettenmeyer was killed when she was caught under the overturned YPT bus and suffered a skull fracture.

Travel deaths include those caused not only by stagecoaches and buses but also by airplanes. At least eight airplane crashes with twenty-two associated human deaths have occurred in Yellowstone National Park, in 1943, 1963, 1970, 1978, 1987, 1991, 1995, and 2003. Some of these were military planes and some were private planes. None were commercial flights.

The air crash with the largest number of deaths was also the first one to happen in the park. On May 23, 1943, a U.S. Air Force B-17 bomber, aircraft 42-30260, was en route from Marysville, California, to Lewistown, Montana, where it was stationed. Planes of this type were sometimes referred to as the most powerful U.S. weapon in the war against Adolf Hitler. Near Reno, Nevada, the pilot, Lieutenant Roy E. Thompson, climbed to an altitude of fifteen thousand feet. Near West Yellowstone, Montana, he ordered the crew to bail out. His order was interrupted by copilot James Highley's simultaneous order over the headphones, "Get out now! Get out now!" But most of the crew was sleeping, lulled by the four 1,200-horsepower Cyclone engines.

On the ground, park ranger Tom Ela heard the trouble. "My wife, Betty, and I'd been to a birthday party and had just gotten home when we heard the plane go over. I went to the window because I knew it wasn't sounding right. We could hear it go into a scream as it went down." Ela rushed to a nearby observation spot and saw the sky light up with flame.

The plane was seen by at least two ground witnesses who claimed it was on fire while in the air. The plane's bombardier, Lieutenant William McDonald, 24, was sleeping right by the hatch with his parachute on. When he heard the frantic orders in his headphone, he sleepily rolled out the hatch and pulled the ripcord. "The next thing I remember," said McDonald later, "I was way up in the air coming down in my parachute. I could see two big flames below where the plane crashed." Only seconds elapsed between the time McDonald jumped and the crash. Almost immediately McDonald's chute snagged in a clump of trees, and he hit the ground hard in a snowbank. "I had no idea where I was. It was pitch black in the woods, so I curled up on the ground and waited until daylight before moving."

For the next two days, Bill McDonald ate snow to keep from dehydrating and tried to keep walking to stay warm. He wondered if the sounds in his headset had only been a nightmare and he had bailed out by mistake. When he saw a search plane on the second day he managed to attract its attention by waving his shirt on a stick. The plane dropped him some canned food, but McDonald did not have a can opener. He got colder and colder.

Meanwhile, Ranger Ela went with searchers looking for survivors of the crash. On the third day, Ela climbed a tree and yelled "Halloo!" for what seemed like the thousandth time. But this time an answer came back.

"He said his name was McDonald," remembers Ela. "He was very, very cold, and he asked 'Where am I?' because he had no idea. He told me he'd been sleeping right by the hatch with his parachute on."

Ela and others were able to find the crash site with a compass reading. "There wasn't much left except a smoking hole and pieces of bodies lying around," says Ela. He found an airman's foot still strapped in its boot. A short distance away was a body with its parachute still on. Ranger Bob Murphy saw another body nearby, also still strapped in its parachute. At least one other airman had been wearing his chute but had been unable to eject due to the suddenness of the crash. Bob Murphy, Paul Hoppe, and Tony Grace took out ten bags of body parts on pack animals. In the following days the local newspapers did not publish information about the incident, apparently because it was wartime. The Air Force was very quiet about the crash.

The B-17 had crashed into the rugged park country just northeast of Jack-straw Basin, some three miles southeast of West Yellowstone. Ten crew members were killed instantly. They were Sergeant Willard S. McCune, 28, West Orange, New Jersey; Staff Sergeant Lawrence W. Medlin, 19, Chattanooga, Tennessee; Staff Sergeant Leo E. Thorn, 30, Lake Charles, Louisiana; Staff Sergeant Donald W. Rice, 21, Henrietta, New York; Staff Sergeant Gilbert E. Underwood, 37, West Orange, New Jersey; Staff Sergeant Alexander G. Jurkowski, 21, Brook-lyn, New York; Lieutenant Roy E. Thompson, 23, Mount Pleasant, New York; Lieutenant James Jerome Highley, 22, Oklahoma City, Oklahoma; Lieutenant George A. Brash, 23, Roosevelt, New York; and Lieutenant Robert K. Edwards, 37, Philadelphia, Pennsylvania.

The plane's wreckage stayed on the crash site for more than forty-five years. A few years after the crash, a park ranger salvaged aluminum from the site, from which he made a snowplane. In 1988, the great fires of Yellowstone caused many persons to enter the remote and trailless area and allowed for manpower and helicopters to finally carry out much of the wreckage. The cause of the crash was determined to be icing of the plane's carburetors.[7]

The 1963 crash of an Air Force bomber in the Bechler area of the park killed three U.S. Air Force airmen and sent a fourth one on an adventure he would never forget. On Friday, May 3, 1963, a B-47 bomber containing a crew of four was involved in a training mission from Idaho's Mountain Home Air Force Base south of the southwest corner of Yellowstone National Park. At 7:16 p.m., the plane was attempting a refueling at twenty-seven thousand feet with a KC-135 tanker plane, and in trying to maneuver into position, the pilot, Captain Frank Gerard Zumbra, got too close to the tanker and struck it in midair. The plane's right wingtip and vertical stabilizer broke off in a flash, and the craft went into a flat spin. Crew members on the tanker saw the B-47 disappear into a cloud bank and knew it was doomed.

When the copilot, Captain Bruce A. Chapman, 33, saw the altimeter read-ing of only ten thousand feet, he immediately ejected. He felt himself travel-ing up and away from the plane and then felt the thump as his chute opened. Chapman had time to swing only once in the chute before he hit the top of a pine tree.

The spiraling B-47 struck the earth in a small clump of trees some 250 yards northeast of Chapman, and the pieces of it remained fairly consolidated. Unbelievably, there was neither explosion nor fire damage to the plane, but impact damage was so extreme it caused parts of the aircraft to totally dis-integrate. Pilot Frank Zumbra, 32; Staff Sergeant Lawrence E. Harrison, 35; and Captain Loren R. Matthews, 30, were killed instantly. Why they had been unable to eject was later a mystery to Chapman. The crash site was near the

Continental Divide in the rugged Madison Plateau country, 1.6 miles west of Douglas Knob and 1.9 miles south of Trischman Knob.

But Chapman knew none of this as he climbed out of the tree in the twilight. He knew only that the snow seemed very deep and that he had work to do to survive. He began sending Mayday signals out on the portable radio that was in his survival kit. These he continued to send every hour all night long, ceasing at 5:00 a.m., in fear of exhausting the batteries. In Idaho Falls, the Federal Aviation Administration control center heard the signals and started a search for him.

Chapman spent a less than comfortable night in that area, and the following day gathered necessary gear and began walking in a southerly direction. Walking through deep snow was extremely difficult; after he fell through the snow crust all the way to the ground, he fashioned himself a pair of snowshoes from tree branches. Later, when it rained, he built a shelter from his parachute and portable life preserver. With these and a fire, he protected himself all the rest of the day and through the night.

Early on Sunday morning, Chapman spotted one of the military search aircraft and was able to call them on his radio. He was instructed by them to lay out his orange-and-white canopy and was finally seen from the air. Plucked from his makeshift camp safe and sound, Chapman stated later that he had gotten so hungry that he was watching some squirrels "pretty closely." Military searchers found the bodies of Zumbra and Harrison in the plane's wreckage on Saturday, but due to the tangled mass of the debris, the body of the navigator, Captain Loren Matthews, was not found until late on Sunday.[8]

The plane's wreckage remained on the site for more than thirty years. In September of 1993, amid much press coverage, members of the U.S. Army and the National Park Service removed the wreckage from its remote site south of Trischman Knob.

A mountain downdraft might have been responsible for a plane crash that killed four persons on Top Notch Peak on August 22, 1970. Dr. Dean Jack Tiller, 53, and his wife Kay Tiller, 55, of Wichita, Kansas, along with their daughter, Jacque Paula, 24, and son-in-law, Joseph M. Biddenger, of Englewood, Colorado, took off on Saturday, August 22, at noon from the Sheridan, Wyoming, airport in a Cessna 210 en route to Vancouver, British Columbia. Dr. Tiller was to deliver a speech at a medical conference there, and he had scheduled a stop at West Yellowstone, Montana. For unknown reasons, perhaps a stall while the plane was attempting to turn, they crashed into the east face of Top Notch Peak in the stream bed of upper Middle Creek. The wreckage was found two days later by a twelve-man recovery crew that included chief ranger Ben Estey and ranger Gerald Mernin. All four occupants of the plane were killed.[9]

Remains of Dr. Jack Tiller's airplane near Sylvan Pass, where it crashed on August 22, 1970 (NPS photo 27073, YNP Archives)

A 1978 crash on Mount Washburn killed one of the two occupants of a small plane. The single-engine Cessna 206 crashed into the southeast side of that mountain on July 3, 1978, at 12:57 p.m. The pilot, Jim D. Thompson, 39, of Pacific Palisades, California, died at the scene of massive head and chest injuries. A passenger, Sandy Vincent of Manhattan Beach, California, survived. Thompson had apparently rented the plane in California.[10]

A 1987 air crash occurred in the south part of the park near Mount Hancock. On the evening of February 1, 1987, Horace H. "Shorty" Koessler, age 78, was piloting a white, single-engine Cessna from Missoula, Montana, to Jackson, Wyoming, via Idaho Falls, Idaho. Radio contact with Koessler was lost by Jackson authorities when he was some miles northeast of Jackson. For unknown reasons, he crashed into the mountainous countryside two and a half miles southeast of Mount Hancock at an elevation of 9,200 feet. Five airplanes, three helicopters, and several skiers all searched four days for Koessler's plane. High avalanche danger, bad weather, and a snowpack of seven feet all hampered searchers. Koessler's body was found in the wreckage on February 5. He had apparently died on impact.[11]

A 1991 plane crash in Yellowstone led to a death caused by drowning. On July 4 of that year, Donald Jerrell, 43, and his son Keith took off in their homemade aircraft from West Yellowstone, Montana, at around 8:45 a.m. The aircraft was designed so that the pilot sat in front of the passenger. Jerrell issued a Mayday call fifteen minutes later. In trouble, he tried to make an emergency landing in a meadow near Shoshone Lake, but missed. Instead, he crashed into five-foot-deep water in Moose Bay, flipping the aircraft upside down and submerging the pilot's seat. Keith Jerrell, 15, survived the impact and tried for fifteen minutes to free his trapped father. Finally he gave up and waded to shore. Donald Jerrell, apparently fearing he would drown on impact, had undone his seatbelt, and consequently was thrust forward in his seat, breaking both of his legs. Being underwater guaranteed that drowning would seal his fate.[12]

A deputy sheriff from Denton, Texas, crashed his plane on Independence Day of 1995 into the five-hundred-feet-deep canyon of Middle Creek. He was Kirtland Brown Watkins, who flew from Cody, Wyoming, over the park's east entrance during late morning and lost power six miles inside the park's boundary and just south of the main road. Two companions of the victim, flying in separate planes nearby, witnessed the crash, which caused the plane to burn completely before park rangers arrived. Rangers obtained permission from the Federal Aviation Administration to remove Watkins's body from the crash before its investigators arrived because of worries that grizzly bears were feeding in the area.[13]

An airplane crash in 2003 involved the history of aeronautics. James Wright, 53, of Cottage Grove, Oregon, was a history buff who built a replica of the 1935 H-1B racer plane that millionaire Howard Hughes flew during that decade. Wright first flew it successfully in July of 2002. On August 4, 2003, at around 6:30 p.m. he was flying it over Yellowstone National Park from south to north in the Old Faithful area. At Midway Geyser Basin and flying at about treetop level, Wright encountered trouble of some kind and, in the presence of park visitors, crashed his plane into a spot on the east side of Firehole River near the park's main road. The airplane burst into flames upon impact, killing Wright, flinging its engine and a wing into the river, and strewing debris about the area. Friends stated that Wright started his flight at Gillette, Wyoming, and was headed for Eugene, Oregon.[14]

Travel to Yellowstone now results in more than three million visitors per year. Considering the mountainous nature of the region, one would think that airplane crashes would occur even more frequently than they have. Perhaps the fact that very few commercial air routes cross the Yellowstone plateau is a factor, leaving only occasional private or military planes to sometimes crash. As for buses, the crowded nature of Yellowstone's roads, the small number of bus fatalities, and the high number of auto fatalities all tell of the need for mass transportation to reappear in the park. A 1993 transportation study of Yellowstone, commissioned by the National Park Service, concluded that a mass transit system of some kind should be returned in large scale to the park, whether by buses, trains, or a monorail.

Perhaps the halcyon days of hundreds of bus or stagecoach drivers are destined to return to the travel scene in Wonderland.

PAY ATTENTION AND DON'T SANITIZE THE WOODS

THE TOTAL OF VIOLENT DEATHS in Yellowstone, by nature and by man, 1839–2012, is over three hundred fifty, not including automobile and snowmobile wrecks that probably add another couple of hundred.

Stories like these are too soon gone from memory. In 1926, the *Livingston Enterprise* newspaper, in editorializing about the death of Grace Crans, who had fallen into the Yellowstone canyon, stated: "Tragedies of this sort are too soon forgotten and too soon some other person with a venturesome spirit is likely to duplicate the terrible story told concerning the unhappy ending of a Park vacation trip."[1] We can count on this loss of remembrance to happen, but hopefully the stories told here will add a modicum of reasonable care to the mindset and activities of those who read them.

Nature demands of us that we pay attention. This society has sheltered us from nature, and one of the reasons why places like Yellowstone are remarkable is that they are "nature in your face." National parks help to ease the lives of stressed-out city dwellers, and that is valuable. But with wilderness come inherent dangers. In February of 1993, the nation followed media accounts of five cross-country skiers who survived alive after four nights without shelter in the subzero, twelve-thousand-foot Colorado backcountry. The three men and two women were thought to have surely perished in huge avalanches that had plagued vast mountain areas that winter. Those survivors had things to say about inherent wilderness perils. "You entertain the possibility of these dangers when you go out there," said Ken Torp, an expedition leader. "We could have done a lot more group communication before we left in terms of equipment and what we needed out there."

Someone enters a wilderness area practically every day without adequate preparation for its dangers. But unlike the judge in the Walker case, most persons would not want their wilderness sanitized. At least I hope they would not. Wilderness is not just another product or commodity to be made safe to prevent product liability litigation. For without those dangers, it would not really be wilderness. Remember, the icy sidewalk in the city that someone slips on is owned by someone else. The bear and the hot springs are owned by you.

At the time of the Andy Hecht incident in 1970, both Yellowstone and the National Park Service offices in Washington received numerous letters commenting on the incident. While many decried the "lack of safety" in parks, just as many commented on the failure of visitors to watch their children and to respect the wilderness and its rules. "I have yet to go to Yellowstone and not see one of the regulations set up by the National Park Service being broken by one or more persons," wrote J. A. Frederick to the secretary of the interior. "People take too many chances in the Park. Then, when something happens and a person dies, the Park is held responsible for their actions. Hogwash!" Another letter attested to seeing abuses:

> We feel there are plenty of signs which tell people to stay on the walks . . . So many times we saw people off the boardwalks or traipsing along paths that stated *no trail*. Do people think the signs are there for everyone else but them? We would hate to see fences put up everywhere. It would certainly take away from the beauty of the park. It's a shame so many people who love Yellowstone or the Tetons or other lovely places will have to suffer because of a few who do not obey the signs put there as warnings.[2]

The Park Service developed some fairly standard words to answer the many letters it received on the Hecht incident, explaining why fences could not be erected around all of the hot springs in the park:

> The national parks were set aside to enhance man's sense of freedom and identification with his natural environment. The wilderness environment has always contained certain dangers and to remove them would require alterations so sweeping that the scene would cease to be refreshing.

> The possibility while hiking a trail of suddenly encountering a wild animal; or of making a river crossing on wet, slippery rocks; or becoming lost in the woods; or trees falling in sudden windstorms all have the potential for tragic results, as does a boardwalk by any method or manner in a thermal area. These known and unknown hazards cannot be completely eliminated by signs, rails, fences, regulations, or any other method any more than traffic hazards can be completely eliminated in

a large city with signs and regulations. Every effort is made to eliminate or reduce the possibility for accidents [by] potential hazards and [yet] avoid destroying the aesthetic value that can be enjoyed without the . . . restricting evidence of manmade objects and infringements.[3]

These ideas had been legally recognized in 1964 when the Eighth Circuit Court of Appeals ruled in *Ashley v. U.S.* that the federal government is not an insurer of the safety of visitors to its parks. A park may be held accountable only if it is negligent.[4]

Another letter, this one from a thermal spring expert, acknowledged some of the relevant considerations of the Park Service in not erecting extra fences or signs: "It is understandable that the Park Service does not wish to unduly restrict the activities of visitors, to intrude on the beauty of the environment with excessive signs, fencing and guard rails, to display frightening messages

Courtesy of the *Cody Enterprise*, 2004

at each public area, or to distribute gory descriptions of burns and agonizing deaths."[5] That letter recognized the problem of balance between adequate warnings and personal responsibility, between safety and letting a wilderness area remain wilderness, between reducing the possibility for "accidents" and yet preventing inordinate, city-style clutter in the woods.

But most importantly, the Tenth Circuit Court of Appeals' recent *Elder* case, as discussed in chapter 1, now backs up this proposition with applicable case law. And the older U.S. Ninth Circuit Court of Appeals *Walker* case has left us some citable common law on these matters. Both of these cases present material that is quite usable in future cases. The significance for the national parks of having these words written in black and white in appellate court decisions cannot be overstated. The *Walker* court noted:

> To require the Park Service to post signs and warnings on every boardwalk, path or trail every few hundred feet throughout a park as extensive as Yellowstone would not only be prohibitive in cost but would destroy the park's beauty as well. To require the Park Service to search out from among the 25,000 daily visitors on the days [Walker] and Bradberry were in the park those two and any others who had entered the park without paying and without receiving the warning bulletins and to hold that failure to warn such individuals as actionable negligence is for the Congress and not for the courts . . . Congress has not intended such broad coverage.[6]

Dangers are simply a part of wilderness. And when one enters wilderness, one must take it on its own terms. As Dr. Don Despain said long ago, the resource at Yellowstone is not forty thousand elk or four thousand bison or ten thousand hot springs or two hundred lakes. "The resource is wildness." And unlike a zoo or a museum or an amusement park, the worth of that wildness depends almost totally on its wholeness. Dangers are a part of that wholeness.

While appreciating its wholeness, we must never abandon a healthy respect for wilderness. Wilderness is impersonal. It does not care whether you live or die. It does not care how much you love it.

So while we are loving the Yellowstone wilderness, while we play in it, indeed revel in it, taking it on its own terms and helping to protect it, we foolish mortals must always remember to respect it. For not only can it bite us, but, indeed, it can devour us.

Chronology

Parentheses indicate cause of death.

Parentheses around names indicate an occurrence outside Yellowstone National Park.

Car wrecks and natural deaths are not included.

1839 Five unknown trappers (Indians).

1869 (Jack Crandall, _____ Dougherty, Indians).

1877 Charles Kenck (Nez Perce Indians), Richard Dietrich (Nez Perce Indians), two unnamed prospectors (Nez Perce Indians), unnamed teenaged Indian (Nez Perce Indians), unnamed Nez Perce woman (Bannock Indians).

1880 Matthew J. Carey (drowning).

1881 Unnamed man (freezing).

1883 John Zutavern (murdered); John H. Fogerty, Thomas P. Parker (drowning); unnamed workman (fall); (Dan McCarthy—murdered); (Chancey Butler—falling tree).

1884 Jacob Hess (avalanche), Emily Moore (suicide), Phillip Bassett (suicide).

1885 M. D. Scott (lightning), (Frank Kannis—murdered), (Thomas Hefron—poison gas).

1886 (John Hartz—horse), (Charles Carpenter—self-defense shooting), Sarry Bolding (freezing).

1887 (Anthony Wise, Clarence Martin—avalanche), Alexander "Mormon" Brown (freezing).

1888 Thomas Horton (wagon).

1889 Thomas Brennen (drowning), (Gus Nelson—drowning).

1890 James Joseph Stumbo (hot spring), J. L. Sanborn (horse runaway).

1891   Sergeant James P. Pruitt (horse kick), Ed Wilson (suicide).

1892   (William Chick—murdered), (Daniel Durgan—murdered).

1893   Private Andrew Preiber (freezing), Private Ellis Lingard (horse wreck), Ike Barrows (falling tree), Patrick Sheahan (falling tree).

1894   Bayard T. "Curley" Rogers (lightning); Private David J. Matthews (freezing); Henry Hubbard, James Wilder, Ed Vinage (drowning); Lieutenant Lunsford Daniel (horse runaway); Mrs. Louis Helbut (drowning); (Lee Mallison—bear); John Nunley (avalanche).

1895   (Chris Anderson—murdered), Aaron P. Bliss (thrown from a wagon), (Alexander Deckard—thrown from a wagon), (Cornelus "Con" Lowney"—gas explosion), (W. A. Babcock—horse wreck).

1896   Joseph Mullery (freezing), unknown man first thought to be Bud Williams (fall?), H. Jehnsen (wagon wreck).

1897   Private John W. H. Davis (freezing), L. V. Brigham (wagon wreck), George Williams (wagon wreck).

1898   Charles Walter Pring (hot spring), Private Harry E. Donaldson (drowning), (Lizzie M. West—murdered), (Servius Cortese—murdered).

1899   Louis Jongenel (drowning), Mrs. Joseph Lippman (stage wreck), Isaac Rowe (lightning), Joseph Trischman (murdered), Jessie Lane (accidental shooting), unnamed Monida employee (drowning), (Maurice O. Bucke—wagon wreck), (Mark Terrell—murdered).

1900   R. N. Adams (falling tree), Charles Baldwin (wagon wreck), Frank Pepper (suicide), LeRoy R. Piper (missing).

1901

1902

1903   Philip Sheldon (wagon wreck), Emil Johnson (wagon wreck), F. C. Ross (murdered or drowned?).

1904   Private Richard R. Hurley (freezing), John Murphy (fall), Christ H. Martin (avalanche), William Eaton (runaway team), Dr. Blank (stage wreck).

1905   Fannie A. Weeks (hot spring), Ed W. Davies (drowning), Frank Rose (wagon wreck), Dan Bowman (suicide), (Henry Gillotte—suicide), Oliver Adkins (drowning), (Lester LaDuke—hot spring), (Vera Downs—drowning).

1906   Eugene W. Clark (apparent suicide); W. B. Taylor, Private Harry E. Allen (drowning); (Charles W. Anderson—suicide); Peter Christensen (drowning).

1907   Peter Hanson (cave-in), (Tom Lannan—murdered), (John Flere—murdered), (Axel Hill—self-defense shooting).

1908 Private Presley H. Vance (freezing), (W. L. Escher—accidental shooting), (Rose Hennesey Swanson—murdered), (Aaron Edward Swanson—suicide).

1909

1910 Private Frank F. Monaghan (drowning), D. E. MacKay (stage wreck), Miss Ross Bodge (stage wreck), Dick Hull (horse), (Bill Jones—freezing), (Ora Tuttle—freezing), (Bert E. Corbin—freezing).

1911 Thomas King (suicide), Herman F. Felix (suicide), (Andrew McCune—self-defense shooting), John C. Kelley (structural fire).

1912 (John Graham—bear), Private Frank Cunningham (self-defense shooting), Robert Launsberry (horse).

1913 Dan Coffee (murdered).

1914 (Charles Huntsman—self-defense shooting), Walter A. Semple (murdered), (Edna Durrell—freezing).

1915 (Joe Osimic—missing).

1916 Lieutenant Joseph McDonald (avalanche), Frank Welch (bear).

1917 John W. Havekost (falling rock).

1918 Sergeant Arthur S. Brewer, Private Victor Manterfield (drowning).

1919 James Baxter Hughes (hot spring), Louis D. Boatman (diving).

1920 Unknown man (freezing).

1921 Emma B. Childers (bus wreck).

1922 (Frenchy Duret—bear).

1923 David Sroka, Edward J. Wright, Dale A. Spears (carbon monoxide).

1924 Earl J. Dunn, Mrs. Earl J. Dunn (fall).

1925 Gertrude L. Tomasko (drowning), Isadore M. Kisber (fall), Ernest Hansen (drowning), Walter Shaw (drowning), Marguerite Knapp (gas explosion).

1926 Gilbert A. Eakins (hot spring), Grace Crans (fall), Albert Collins (drowning).

1927 Rollo Gallagher (hot spring), Charles Phillips (poison plant), James P. Jackson (suicide).

1928 C. H. Brown (hot spring), Harry Asche (drowning).

1929 Georges Landoy (hot spring), Robert Wright (lightning).

1930 (Frank Deckard—suicide).

1931 Delbert McConnaha (bus wreck).

1932 Joy Hanny (hot spring).

1933 Edgar A. Gibson (hot spring); Christopher Gray (drowning); Abraham Yancovitch (fight); Dr. Shaen S. Magan, Bobby Magan, George Steckel (drowning).

1934

1935 Glenn Howard (hot spring), Charles Strombaugh (drowning).

1936   James W. McFerson (hot spring); Robert R. Walker (falling tree);
Charles Stewart, Thomas A. Cavenaugh (drowning).

1937   Kenneth Chandler (drowning), Wilfred Karls (drowning), Fred W.
Gonder (drowning).

1938   James Walker (drowning), Robert LeRoy Robinson (accidental
shooting or suicide), Judson M. Rhoads (suicide).

1939   Wesley Hunt (drowning), Bill L. Nelson (poison gas), Claude W.
Anthony (suicide), unnamed postal employee (suicide).

1940   James Hester (forest fire), Jack Davis (fall), (Frank Selon—suicide),
(Joseph R. Charrell—suicide).

1941   J. T. Flock (drowning).

1942   Martha Hansen (bear), C. L. Anderson (drowning).

1943   Willard S. McCune, Lawrence W. Medlin, Leo E. Thorn, Donald W.
Rice, Gilbert E. Underwood, Alexander Jurkowski, James Jerome
Highley, Roy E. Thompson, George A. Brash, Robert K. Edwards
(airplane crash).

1944

1945   (Charles C. White—fall), Lloyd J. Weikel (drowning).

1946   Lois Christyne Fenner (carbon monoxide).

1947   Henrietta Ross Bailey (probably murdered); Lee Monson
(drowning); Lois Pallesen (drowning); John P. Adams (drowning);
Gerry Monihan, Jacob W. Gotwals (drowning); Gene Reidiman,
Robert Clark, Herman Hutton (drowning); Herbert J. Kleine, M. C.
Baldwin (drowning); Ernest F. Shaw, Dr. Karl G. Avery, Jack Metzler
(drowning); (Vernon E. Kaiser, John P. Baker, Richard W. Huckels—
carbon monoxide).

1948

1949   Karen Lee Anderson (hot spring), Robert Kasik (hot spring),
Gertrude Rettenmeyer (bus wreck), (Dick Meyers—suicide).

1950   Leo Wester, Henry Thomas (drowning); Oliver Schmoker, Zellar
Ellen Hensley (drowning); (Mrs. Charles Hay, Al Durochie—
structural fire).

1951   Arnold Van Heuvelen (drowning), Frederick A. Olson (suicide).

1952   Ralph L. Johnson (drowning), unnamed infant (murdered).

1953   George R. Miller (fall), George R. Anderson (falling tree), Carl
George Mihlberger (drowning).

1954

1955   Robert L. Landram (fall); Charles M. Brower, Philip Brower
(drowning); Terry Lee Prince (drowning); David Gaskell (drowning).

1956   Diana Alberta Schramm (horse).

1957

1958   Danny Lewis (hot spring), Lee Burrows (drowning).

1959 Garr Nelson (suicide).

1960 Robert Eikin Jr. (suicide).

1961 Clark M. House (drowning), Thomas Hughes (drowning), Paul Ray Ingebretson (drowning).

1962 Shirley Pitkin Clark (suicide).

1963 Joseph P. Speitel (drowning); Frank G. Zumbra, Lawrence E. Harrison, Loren Matthews (airplane crash).

1964 Steven Robert Bailey (fall), Glen C. Reaser (suicide).

1965 Marita Eilers (fall), Roy Milton Barth (drowning).

1966 Stephen Athan (falling tree), Dennis Eugene Johnson (missing).

1967 Brian Parsons (hot spring); Billy B. Arnold (drowning); Steve Smith, Kenneth Ables (drowning); Bernard Walter Bayne (suicide).

1968 Leonard Szuberla (drowning).

1969 David Rasmussen (fall).

1970 Andy C. Hecht (hot spring); (James Michael Schlosser—murdered); Dean Jack Tiller, Joseph Biddinger, Kay Tiller, Paula Biddinger (airplane crash).

1971 Marvin Lesley Schrader (bison), James H. Hambrick (drowning), Charles F. Wright (drowning), Mrs. Thomas Ward (drowning), Virginia Hall (poisonous plant?), (Hugh D. Galusha—freezing).

1972 Lorrie Grewe (falling rock), Harry Walker (bear), Lloyd V. Ryan (drowning).

1973 Victor I. Songer (fall); Mrs. Jean-Claude Chabanis (fall/drowning); Bob Safran, Burris Wollsieffer, Darwin Seamons, Tom Gower (drowning).

1974 Anthony Haschke (fall), Gary Steven Chase (drowning).

1975 Donald Watt Cressey (hot spring), Brenton Kirk Jr. (lightning/drowning), James M. Thompson (drowning), Louis Stephen Majosy (drowning).

1976 Lawrence Crawford (fall).

1977

1978 Lois J. Mayer (fall); Van Lyle Hansen, Lane Potter (drowning); April W. Cruse (suicide); James Lee Hamar (murdered); Jim D. Thompson (airplane crash).

1979 Orville Sigrist, Pearl Sigrist (drowning).

1980 Raymond Guntz (fall); Duane McClure (drowning); William Bo Bess, Michael Dale Bitterli (drowning).

1981 David Allan Kirwin (hot spring), Kenneth Fullerton (drowning).

1982 James Brent Wilkerson (drowning), Lisa Cavagnaro (drowning), George Palermo (drowning), Scott Olson (drowning), William A. Frank (drowning), (Shannon Weatherly—murdered).

1983   Alain Jean Jacques Dumont (bison), Tom Pearse (falling rock), Laurie Miller (fall), (Roger May—bear).

1984   David Haller (fall), Brigitta Fredenhagen (bear), Matthew Tighe (drowning), (Carol Ann Keller—falling tree).

1985   Albert Paul Knight (fall); Keith Marsh (poison plant); Randy Dean Reddog (murdered); Kent Shane Rich (fall); LeRoy Stuppy (drowning); David Carter, Caleb Carter, Dustin Carter (drowning).

1986   William Tesinsky (bear).

1987   Christopher Lee Quintana (drowning), Horace H. "Shorty" Koessler (airplane crash).

1988   John Mark Williams (hot spring), Dennis B. Rumple (fall), (Brendan O'Connor—fall).

1989

1990   David Childers (fall), Charles Tom (drowning).

1991   Greg Felzien (avalanche), Don Jerrell (plane crash).

1992   (Robbie Ruby—avalanche).

1993   Daren "Franny" Dixon (missing—presumed drowned).

1994   Ryan Francis Weltman (drowning).

1995   Gary Lee Brockway (fall), Milan Kapusta (fall), Kirtland Brown Watkins (airplane crash).

1996

1997   Rick Hutchinson (avalanche), Michael D. Divine (drowning), Steven A. Divine (drowning), Norma Jean Reimann (murdered), Ronald Robert Reimann (suicide), James William Karhi (suicide), (Christian David Bowers—lightning).

1998

1999   Paul Hudson (freezing), Norma Norton Vaughan (fall).

2000   Sara Hulphers (hot spring).

2001   Don Unser (suicide).

2002   David Graham (drowning), Quinn Graham (drowning).

2003   Lisbeth Clair Skollingsberg (drowning), James Clement Jeffery (suicide), James Wright (airplane crash).

2004

2005   Luke Sanburg (drowning), Candace May Kellie (drowning), Drew Webster Speedie (fall), Brent Quinn Speedie (fall), Joseph R. Miller (drowning), (Wayne Skertich—suicide).

2006   Deborah Chamberlin (fall), (James Byrd—fall).

2007   Charlotte Harrison (fall), Fred Kisabeth (drowning), Charles Peters (drowning).

2008

2009   Heidi Llewellyn Smith (drowning), Nicholas Jeffrey Mostert (suicide), (James E. Burns—freezing).

2010   Mark William Ehrich (fall), Michael Alan Kellch (fall), Frank Jaszcz (drowning), Lin Ching-Ling (drowning), Peter Louis Kastner (suicide), (Erwin Frank Evert—bear), (Kevin R. Kammer—bear).

2011   Brian Matayoshi (bear), John Lawrence Wallace (bear), Christopher Johnson (drowning), (David Lee Gaillard—avalanche), (Jody Ray Verhasselt—avalanche).

2012   Maria "Masha" Sergeyevna Rumyantseva (fall), Carl Dullmaier (thrown from horse).

2013   Ernest Trim (drowning), Joseph Austin Parker (fall), Ella Marie Tucker (accidental shooting).

APPENDIX A
MAMMOTH CIVILIAN CEMETERY

T HE MAMMOTH CIVILIAN CEMETERY, located on a windswept summit north of the village of Mammoth and above the park helipad at an elevation of 6,534 feet, received its first burials in 1883. That was the year that the new National Hotel was built on the site of the present Mammoth Hot Springs Hotel and real activity began at Mammoth. The cemetery contains fourteen graves. Five of the graves contain five identified individuals. And we know the names of five others buried here even if we do not exactly know which graves contain whom. Only one monument still stands, identifying two graves, those of Mary J. Foster and Sarry E. Bolding, in graves 7 and 8, respectively.

According to that tombstone, Mary J. Foster, 33, was the "first [person] to be laid to rest at Mammoth," and this occurred on June 10, 1883. The double-marked stone says she hailed from Madison County, North Carolina, and historian Haines believed that she was an employee of the Mammoth Hotel, which was then being built. But we now know a bit more thanks to researcher M. Evelyn Rose of San Francisco. Mary Foster seems to have been in the Mammoth area because of her father, Samuel M. Foster, who owned mining properties in Cooke City and Red Lodge, Montana. The family appeared in the 1860 and 1870 censuses of Madison County, North Carolina, the former indicating Mary's birth year as in or about 1852. They moved to Benton County, Arkansas, by 1880 and shortly afterward to Montana. Descendant Shirley Rush has added a bit more, her information coming from her grandmother, Mildred Sawyer Tillquist (1900–1988). Mildred's grandparents were the aforementioned Samuel and Millie Foster of North Carolina. Mildred stated to Shirley that when her grandparents went to Montana, they stopped (probably on their way to Cooke City) at Mammoth and there, for some reason, Mildred's Aunt Mary

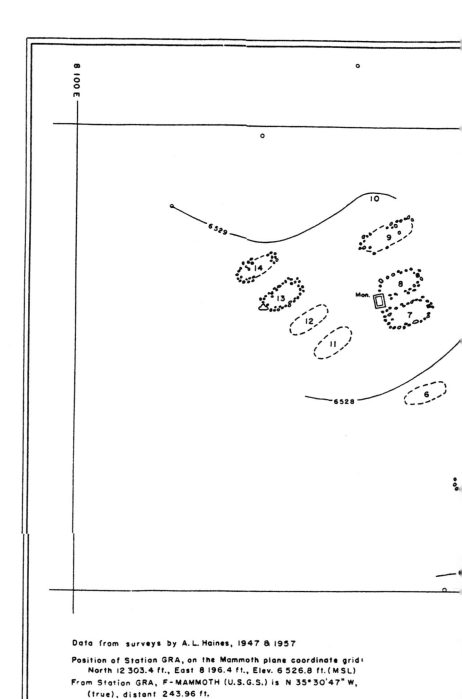

8 200 E

12 400 N

12 300 N

NOTES

(Including data from other sources)

Grave No. 1: No identification.

Grave No. 2: No identification.

Grave No. 3: Portion of a concrete block at the west end has "T.P." on one face and "J.F." on another (adjacent); two pieces of headboard, when fitted together, showed "J.F."

Grave No. 4: A headboard lying 5 feet SE was marked "T.P. 1885"

Grave No. 5: No identification. Possibly O.S. Johnson.

Grave No. 6: No identification.

Grave No. 7: "Mary J. Foster, Died June 10, 1883, Age 33 yrs., First to be laid to rest at Mammoth." Footstone of gray granite marked "M.J.F."

Grave No. 8: "Sarry E. Bolding, Died Feb. 25, 1886, Age 25 yrs." Footstone of gray granite marked "S.E.B."

Grave No. 9: No identification.

Grave No.10: No longer visible.

Grave No.11: No identification.

Grave No.12: No identification.

Grave No.13: No identification.

Grave No.14: No identification.

The monument is a cut and polished headstone common to graves 7 & 8. It is marked on top "Born in Madison Co."

A wooden headboard marked "O.S. Johnson Born Oct. 29, 1878 Died Aug. 8, 1897," lay west of the Foster-Bolding headstone; it probably belongs to grave 5.

4

3

2

1

N

SCALE, 1 inch = 10 feet

C. I. = 1 foot

△
GRA

A PLAT OF THE CIVILIAN GRAVEYARD
ON THE HILL NORTH OF MAMMOTH

IN

YELLOWSTONE NATIONAL PARK

1961

(Foster) died. Said Shirley Rush, "Grandma's mother's sister died and was buried at Mammoth." We do not know the cause of her death.[1]

The victims of Yellowstone's first drownings, John Fogerty and Thomas P. Parker, were the next burials; they died on August 15, 1883, and were buried a year later by a relative, Dan Parker. The two were buried in graves 3 and 4.[2] Today only a single footstone with the initials TPP and JF marks the site.

John Zutavern, a murder victim who died on August 20, 1883, was interred there next. His body was exhumed once for legal reasons and apparently reinterred (see chapter 20, "Malice in Wonderland: Yellowstone Murders").

Two suicides and an avalanche victim were next: Emily Moore (died January 27, 1884), Phillip Bassett, died May 1, 1884, and Jacob Hess, died February 21, 1884. These stories are chronicled in chapters 21 and 7.

As for Sarry E. Bolding, who died February 25, 1886, and was buried in grave number 8 with the same gravestone as Mary J. Foster, the best information to date is that Sarry Bolding froze to death. That information comes from Mira (Myra) Adeline Robison Tuck (1896–1990), who told her granddaughter Janice Weekley a story that apparently her parents told to her. Her parents, Martha Elizabeth Teel and William Addington Robison, lived in the Gardiner–Mammoth area "in the coldest year" of the 1880s. They told their daughter that Sarry Bolding did not come home one cold night. "The men" went out to search for her, said Mira Robison, and "found her sitting under a tree dead." They thought she had fallen through ice into a stream. While the "legendary" cold winter was the winter of 1886–1887, the winter of 1885–1886 was probably plenty cold enough to kill someone.[3]

O. S. Johnson died August 8, 1897, of unknown causes and was buried in grave number 5.[4]

Thanks to Edith Ritchie's memories,[5] we know that a Barney Elliott, whose husband worked on park wood and ice crews, was buried there sometime before 1888. And a short squib in the local newspaper makes it clear that Thomas Brennen, who drowned in Bath Lake on June 24, 1889, was also interred there. The newspaper stated that Brennen's body was taken to "the cemetery on the hill" for burial.[6]

These are all of the known persons buried in the Mammoth civilian cemetery. I can offer some educated guesses as to who the other three persons might be, however. The unknown workman who fell from a scaffold on June 7, 1883, during the construction of the National Hotel would be a candidate, except for the fact that Mary Foster's tombstone claims she was the first person laid to rest at Mammoth. If the unknown workman was buried after June 10, perhaps he indeed does rest there. Other possibilities are any or all of the three men who drowned in Yellowstone Lake in 1894: Henry Hubbard, James Wilder, and Ed Vinage. Two other possibilities are Louis Jongenel, who drowned in 1899, and Frank Rose, who was killed by a runaway team in 1905. None of these persons was buried in the other (Fort Yellowstone) cemetery.

But these are only guesses. We do not know for certain who the other three persons were.

APPENDIX B
FORT YELLOWSTONE ARMY CEMETERY

THE FORT YELLOWSTONE ARMY CEMETERY, located south of the village of Mammoth Hot Springs proper near the present concessioner horse corral, was the site of fifty-eight burials, 1888–1957. Twenty of the graves were moved to the Little Bighorn Battlefield near Crow Agency, Montana, on July 9, 1917.[1]

Those interred were U.S. Army soldiers and members of their families and civilian employees of the army along with members of their families. Here is a list of those burials in the order in which they occurred. Numbers represent grave numbers. Except for bracketed material, this is a copy of *Record Book of Interments at the Post Cemetery, Fort Yellowstone*, item 155, Yellowstone National Archives. Names on this list which do not appear on the accompanying map were removed to Little Bighorn Battlefield.[2]

1. Thomas Horton, Private, Company C 22nd Infantry, died October 1, 1888. [Died when he fell from a wagon that subsequently ran over him.]
2. Celia Henz Venneinan [descendants spell it *Vennemann*], daughter of Hospital Steward Venneinann [*sic*], died March 30, 1891.
3. Henry Miller, Private, Co. I, 6th Cavalry, died August 23, 1891.
4. James P. Pruitt, Sergeant, Co. E, First Cavalry, "Died from kick by horse in abdomen," September 11, 1891.
5. Andrew Preiber, Private, Co. I, 6th Cavalry, died March 14, 1893 (buried March 15). "Died from [alcoholism and] exposure near Gardiner."
6. Harry Wilson, child of Henry Wilson, commissary sgt., U.S.A.
7. Ellis Lingard, Private, Company D, 6th Cavalry, died August 2, 1893 (buried August 3).

8. Lunsford Daniel, Second Lieutenant, Company I, 6th Cavalry, died May 31, 1894 (buried June 1). "Died from injuries rec'd in runaway." "Remains disinterred and shipped to Thomasville, Geo. Dec. 15, 1894."

9. David J. Mathews, Private, Company D, 6th Cavalry, buried June 12, 1895. "Perished from exhaustion and exposure."

10. Mrs. M.C. Stevins [Margaret McRee Stevens, born 1824; wife of Joel King Stevens, Surgeon, United States], died November 17, 1895 (buried November 20).

11. Ellen Francisco, died January 7, 1897 (buried January 8).

12. John W. H. Davis, Private, Company D, 4th Cavalry, died December 15, 1897 (buried December 23). "Perished by freezing Dec. 15th, 1897, between Lake and Thumb Stations. Remains brought to Fort Yellowstone and interred Dec. 23rd, 1897."

13. L. V. Brigham, civilian, died December 28, 1897 (buried December 29). "Teamster—Q.M.D. died from injuries sustained by [being thrown?] from wagon."

14. Harry E. Donaldson, Private, Company D, 4th Cavalry, died April 10, 1898 (buried April 11). "Drowned in Bath Lake, near Fort Yellowstone, Wyo. April 10th, 1898."

15. Joseph Trieschman [Trischman], child of George Trischman Post Wheelwright, died June 3, 1899 (buried June 4).

16. Isaac Rowe, civilian, died June 19, 1899 (buried June 20). "Killed by lightning near Golden Gate pass."

17. Charles Baldwin, civilian, died October 19, 1900 (buried October 21). "Teamster, Q.M.D. Killed by runaway team."

18. "Unknown baby, no record can be found of date of death, age or identity."

19. Philip Sheldon, civilian, died July 13, 1903 (buried July 15). "Killed by runaway team between Fort Yellowstone, Wyo. and Gardiner, Mont."

20. Emily Sivert, daughter of Chaplain Herman A. Sivert, 9th U.S. Cavalry, died August 13, 1903 (buried August 14). "Died at Mammoth Hotel, Y.N.P. and buried in grave #8."

21. Christ H. Martin, Corporal, Company C, 3rd Cavalry, died February 17, 1904 (buried April 20). "Killed by snow slide in the Gallatin valley in Yellowstone N.P. Feb. 17th, 1904. Remains recovered Apr. 16th, 1904, and brought to Fort Yellowstone, Wyo. and interred Apr. 20, 1904."

22. Richard R. Hurley, Private, Company F, 3rd Cavalry, died May 3, 1904 (buried May 11). "Died at Thumb Emergency Cabin." "Bo_ _ell, Oct. 5, '20." [This entry seems to indicate two persons buried in position

22. The second entry reads "Bourell" or "Bomrell." [Ed Moorman ("Yellowstone Park Camps History," p. 18) has identified this person as their caretaker at the Willow Park camp of Yellowstone Park Camps Company who died in bed there one night.]

23. William Eaton, civilian, died May 30, 1904 (buried June 1). "Killed by runaway team at Mammoth Hot Springs, Y.N.P."

24. Dead-born infant of J. Landrigan, civilian. Buried June 11, 1904.

25. N. F. Elliot, civilian, died June 23, 1905 (buried June 27). "Employee of the Yellowstone Park Association. Died at the Canyon Hotel, Y.N.P. of Heart Disease. Remains shipped to Chicago, Ill., Aug. 15, 1905."[3]

26. Nellie Auditto, servant, died August 11, 1905 (buried August 12). "Employee of the Y.N.P. Association. Died at the Norris Hotel, Y.N.P. of Diphteria [*sic*]."

27. Sarah Clark, infant child of E.W. Clark, civilian employee, died October 26, 1905 (buried October 27). "Died at Fort Yellowstone, Wyo. from _____."

28. Eugene W. Clark, civilian employee, died November 9, 1906 (buried November 11). "Died at Fort Yellowstone, Wyo. from poisoning (carbolic acid). Ass't Electril. Engineer."

29. William S. Miller, Private, Company I, 6th Cavalry, died January 1, 1907. "Died at Fort Yellowstone, of spinal mengitis [*sic*] and pheummonia [*sic*]. Relation of J. A. Miller, Jearoldstown, Tennessee."

30. Floyd M. Wheate, infant child, died April 8, 1907. "Age 11 hours, child of J.M. Wheate, Const. Surgeon, U.S.A. Buried Apr. 9, '07."

31. Peter Hanson, civilian employee, engineering department, died May 13, 1907. "Killed on Cap't. Hill by embankment cave in. Asphyxia. Buried May 15, '07."

32. John O'Brien, civilian employee, Q.M.D., died May 30, 1907. "Died of pneumonia at post hospital. Buried June 1st, 1907."

33. William M. Johnson, colored, civilian employee of Major Pitcher, died June 21, 1907. "Died of double catarrh/pneumonia, post hospital. Buried June 23, 1907."

34. William Maher, civilian employee, Const. Q.M., died September 15, 1908. "Died of acute pulmonary congestion right side, with acute cardiac dilatation [*sic*]."

35. Don Wales, child of F. E. Wales, employee, Const. Q.M. "Died Sept. 30, 1908 of Marasmus. Immediate cause, exhaustion."

36. Presley H. Vance, Private, Company H, 8th Cavalry, died October _____, 1908. "Died from freezing, probably while under the influence of intoxicating liquor. Date of death not known. Body found in Elk

Park, Yellowstone National Park, October 16th, 1908. Buried at Fort Yellowstone, Wyo. October 19th, 1908."

37. William H. O'Connor, civilian employee, Q.M.D., died January 28, 1909. "Died of pulmonary oedemia."
38. John M. Symonds, employee, Const. Q.M., died March 14, 1908. "Exhaustion following broncho-pneumonia."
39. Ralph David Korn, son of Adam Korn, Sergeant 1st Class, Hospital Corps, died July 1, 1909. "Toremia caused by scarlet fever."
40. Infant child of W. J. Elliott, electrical engineer, died October 14, 1909. "Dead-born. Named Katharine Dana Elliott."
41. Walter Harper, Private, Company C, 3rd Cavalry, died November 22, 1902, at Snake River, Y.N.P. "Disinterred and buried in post cemetery, September 30, 1910."
42. Frank Schmidt, infant child of Joseph Schmidt, employee Yellowstone Hotel Association, died December 26, 1910. "Lobular pneumonia. Dr. Kellogg. Remains taken up Sept. 3, 1919, by Dr. Selby, undertaker from Livingston, and removed to Roslyn, Wyo."
43. Frank F. Monaghan, Private, Company H, 1st Cavalry, died November 22, 1910. "Drowned in Gardiner River about one mile from Gardiner, Mont. about Nov. 22, 1910, while intoxicated. Body was found about Jan. 8, 1911. Buried Jan. 9, 1911. Soldier was reported as deserter Dec. 1, 1910."
44. Infant child of second Lt. Harry L. King, 1st Cavalry, died February 5, 1911.
45. Jesse Slanson [Slauson], civilian employee, Engineering Department, died August 31, 1912. "Died from typhoid fever."
46. Infant child of William J. Elliott, electrical engineer, Q.M.D., died September 29, 1912.
47. Mrs. Grace A. Hislop, died May 26, 1913 (buried May 28). "Cause of death, general pirintonctis."
48. Reece Collins, civilian employee, engineering department, died August 31, 1913 (buried Sept. 2).
49. Madison Stedman, civilian, died March 17, 1914 (buried March 18). "Headstone furnished by relatives. Died of arterial selerosis [sic]." [Descendant Sally Kloppenburg says that he was from Helena, Montana, born 1842, Maine; married Nellie (Ellen) Goff; they had one child, Marion Grace Stedman, born June 13, 1890.]
50. Miss Victoria Venobles [Venables], employee Y.P. Hotel Company, died July 22, 1914 (buried July 23). "Died from lobar pneumonia." [Age about 35; waitress at Canyon Hotel.]
51. Samuel K. Fishel, civilian employee, saddler, Q.M.D., died November 15, 1915 (buried November 17). "Cause of death—senility and endocarditis."

52. Frank Welch, engineering employee, engineering department, died September 11, 1916. "Cause of death—injuries inflicted by a grizzly bear."
53. Harry Dicks, cook, Pack Train #5, Q.M.D., died September 28, 1916 (buried October 1). "Cause of death—Aortic insufficiency aggravated by chronic alcoholism."
54. Henry Brown, civilian employee, assistant wagonmaster, died November 27, 1916 (buried November 28). "Cause of death—cancer of bladder. Intestinal obstruction."
55. Baby Ellis, died July 4, 1925. Small wood cross.
56. Jeanett Clark, died May 8, 1957. Wife of E. W. Clark and mother of Sarah Clark.
57. Unknown baby. No information known.
58. [John Murphy, civilian, engineering department, died August 10, 1904. Fell eight hundred feet into a side canyon of Grand Canyon of the Yellowstone while supervising a road crew on Mount Washburn. Remains shipped to Chicago, Illinois.]

Historian Aubrey L. Haines produced a revised cemetery list in 1947 that showed the thirty-seven graves then in place and still present today in the Fort Yellowstone cemetery. He renumbered the graves and thus we include his list here, which corresponds with his map shown here.

1. (Infant) Ellis. Died July 4, 1925. Small wood cross [in 1947].
2. Emily Sievert. September 19, 1901 to August 13, 1903. Daughter of Capt. H.A. Sievert.
3. Joseph Trieschman. July 29, 1893 to June 3, 1899. Son of George and Margie Trieschman.
4. Isaac Rowe. Died June 19, 1899. Civilian.
5. Philip Sheldon. Died July 13, 1903. Civilian.
6. Wm. Eaton. Died June 1, 1904. Civilian.
7. N.T. Elliot. Died June 27, 1905. Civilian. (Remains sent to Chicago, August 15, 1905). Headstone still in place but it is probably no longer a grave.
8. Nellie Audito. Died August 12, 1905. Stone sunken.
9. Harry Wilson. Died May 3, 1893. Son of Commissary Sergeant Wilson, U.S. Army.
10. (Child) Landrigan. Born dead, June 11, 1904. Child of J. Landrigan.
11. (Infant) Elliot. Died October 14, 1909. Child of W.J. Elliot. (See #37, as it appears same, although spelling of last name is different.)
12. (Infant) Arthur Mallory. Died July 13, 1924. No evidence of grave. [Falls at site of 1.]

13. Margaret McRee Stevens. 1824 to November, 1895. Mother of Captain Stevens, U.S. Army, and wife of Joel King Stevens, Surgeon, Fourth Louisiana Volunteers, Mexican War.

14. Eugene Clark. (W.) 1859 to November 9, 1906. Electrical engineer, Quarter Master Division, Spanish War Veteran.

14a. Jennette Clark, Wife of Eugene W. Clark, buried May 15, 1957.

15. Peter Hanson. Killed May 13, 1907. Civilian employee of Engineering Department.

16. W. M. Johnston. Died June 23, 1907. Civilian (colored).

17. William Maher. Died September 15, 1908. Employee Quarter Master Division. Spanish War Veteran.

18. Don Wales. Died September 30, 1908. Child.

19. Frank Schmidt. Child.

20. (Infant) King.

21. Unknown. Fenced with pipe.

22. Jesse Slauson. Employee, U.S. Army.

23. Grace A. Hislop.

24. Reece Collins. Employee.

25. Madison Stedman. April 13, 1842 to March 17, 1914.

26. Victoria Venables.

27. Frank Welch. Died September 11, 1916. Civilian employee, U.S. Engineers. Grave number 52.

28. Unknown. Baby.

29. L.V. Brigham. Died December 28, 1897. Employee, Quarter Master Division.

30. Sarah Clark. October 8 to October 10, 1905. Daughter of E. and J. Clark (see 14 and 14a).

31. Jno. Symonds (John M.). Died April 14, 1909. Civilian employee, Construction, Quarter Master Division.

32. Ralph D. Korn (David). August 10, 1895 to July 1, 1909. Son of Adam Korn, Sgt., 1/c Hospital C.

33. Celia Venneman. Died March 30, 1891. Civilian.

34. Unknown. Baby.

35. Floyd B. Wheate. Died April 8, 1907. Child of Dr. J. M. Wheate, C.S., U.S. Army.

36. Ellen Francisco. Died June 7, 1893. Civilian.

37. Katharine D. Elliott. Died October 14, 1909. Child of W. J. Elliott. (See 11.)

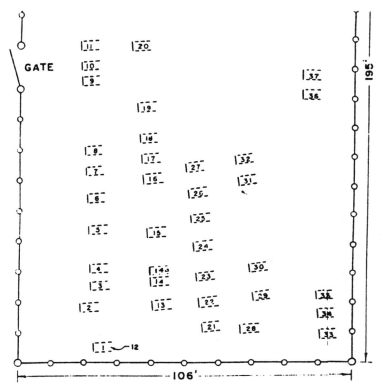

Map of the Fort Yellowstone cemetery, Mammoth Hot Springs, Wyoming, showing graves that remain there today (drawing by Aubrey L. Haines, August 1947.

APPENDIX C
GARDINER CEMETERY ON TINKER'S HILL

IT IS NOT KNOWN EXACTLY when the Gardiner cemetery was established, but it was probably just after the founding of the town in 1880. The cemetery at that time was outside of park boundaries. Today it is inside park boundaries and still privately owned by the Eagles' Club of Gardiner, Montana. That club has recently disbanded, and its representatives are trying to get Yellowstone National Park to accept the cemetery, which it ought to do because this is an important and much cherished cultural site.

Sadly, nearly all of the 1880s and many of the 1890s graves are today unmarked, the headstones having long ago fallen from years of neglect. The official cemetery map (once maintained by the Gardiner Eagles Club) is lost, but we recently have found the "sales list," and from it the author has constructed a new burial list. As a result of neglect there are at least fifty and perhaps as many as seventy-seven unmarked graves in the cemetery, all representing lost history (the "sales list" has given us possibilities as to what persons occupy some of the unmarked graves). The earliest marked graves are those of Fannie Fitzgerald and her baby, who died fifteen days apart in 1888, but many of the unmarked graves are no doubt older. The cemetery continues to receive burials today.

Edith Ritchie, a Gardiner resident beginning in 1888, remembered that what she thought was the first burial in the cemetery was a tinker (a worker in tin). She stated that this burial was responsible for the name of the hill (Tinker's Hill) on which the cemetery sits, and that it occurred following "a shooting over water." So far, research has failed to turn up this affair (if it occurred 1880–1882, there would be no newspaper record unless it appeared in Bozeman newspapers, because the Livingston newspaper did not exist until 1883), but a German tinner or tinker named John Hartz is known to have been buried here in 1886.[1]

A number of important early-day Yellowstone figures are buried in the cemetery, among them "Uncle" John Yancey (1826–1903), who ran Yancey's Hotel in the park; Herb French (1887–1969), a pioneer stage driver in the park; Andy Wald (1853–1933), a sand artist in the park; "Geyser Bob" Edgar (1843–1913), a park stage driver well known for his humorous stories; Larry Link (1860–1918), an early Gardiner businessman; James McBride (1864–1942), first chief ranger in the park; and "Little Gus" Smitzer (1849–1931), one of the park stagecoach robbers. The wife of early assistant park superintendent S. M. Fitzgerald is buried there with a double tombstone and room for him, but strangely his name is not on the tombstone.[2]

Several persons whose stories appear in this book are also buried on Tinker's Hill. They are Axel Hill (shot by "Buckskin" Jim Cutler), Charles Huntsman (shot by George Mack, who also is buried here), Henry Rockinger (who was involved in Mark Terrell's murder), Emil Johnson (killed in a wagon rollover), Frank Deckard (a suicide), and Alexander Brown, who froze to death.

APPENDIX D
OTHER GRAVESITES IN YELLOWSTONE PARK

A T LEAST TEN SINGLE GRAVES are known at various locations around Yellowstone Park. The count would be eleven if the Park's first and oldest known formal grave-occupier had not been disinterred, so we will start with it. Adell Gross Romey (born in France, October 29, 1829), age 42, was traveling through "what is now the National Park" in 1872 with her husband Lucien Romey. According to the local newspaper, she took ill, died on October 14, and was buried somewhere at Mammoth Hot Springs, before its cemeteries were established. The spot was "marked by a monument of stones and had remained undisturbed" until September of 1892. In that month, her son T. L. Romey of Virginia City, Montana, exhumed her remains and moved them to Virginia City where they were supposedly reinterred. The family did indeed show up in the U.S. Census for 1870 at Virginia City, and the story was reported in "Local Layout," *Livingston Enterprise*, October 1, 1892, p. 5.

The well-marked grave of Mattie S. Culver (1859–1889) is located near the Nez Perce picnic area. The wife of the winter keeper of the then nearby Marshall's Hotel, she came to the park with tuberculosis and died of it shortly afterward. Her body was placed in two barrel halves and covered over with snow until spring, because the ground was too deeply frozen to dig a grave. The grave was later fenced and maintained by the wife of a park concessioner, and Mattie's 18-month-old daughter was sent to live with relatives.[1]

Two graves are known on Mount Everts. According to information in the park photo archives, one is of an unknown teamster buried there in the 1890s. We do not know who is buried in the other one or the stories associated with either of them, although historian Aubrey Haines says one of these graves contains a man named Buttrick.[2]

A grave near the park south entrance was that of a "tourist girl" according to army scout Ray Little's reminiscences, but a descendant says that more

Mattie S. Culver's grave (courtesy of Yellowstone National Park)

correctly she was "an emigrant pioneer." Information in the park photo archives with a photo of the grave states that her name was Bessie Rowbottom. She came to the park as a 2-year-old girl who was a member of a large party of Wyoming residents that entered the park's south entrance on July 17, 1903, and she died the following day. "Family tradition attributes her death to pneumonia," says descendant Gary Bradak, who gave her dates of life as September 24, 1900, to July 18, 1903. Her father Lorenzo Rowbottom, a coal miner and small rancher from Almy, Wyoming, was traveling with his large family in three wagons to Calgary, Canada, to start a ranching business. The family spent at least one year in Canada before returning to Wyoming.[3] Descendant Earl Felix adds the following story, dictated to him by his grandmother, Mary Maria Rowbottom, who was an older sister of Bessie and who was present at the time the family buried her:

> We entered Yellowstone National Park on 17 July 1903 by the South entrance and on 18 July 1903 my younger sister Bessie Rowbottom died. My father went to the U.S. Army camp and received permission to bury her in the park. At this time another group of travelers came into our camp and saw that we were getting Bessie ready to be buried. With their help, we made a wooden box and lined it with oil cloth and dressed her in a nice white dress . . . A lady from the group sang the

song "Little Children Who Love Their Redeemer." Father dedicated the grave. My older brother went back to Almy and retrieved the footstone from the grave of my brother Lorenzo Rowbottom, Jr. and had it made into a head stone for Bessie. After the head stone was placed on her grave we left the park and went on to Calgary.[4]

A grave on Hellroaring Creek is that of the unidentified man who froze to death there in 1920 (see chapter 7, "Lying in the Snow: Deaths from Avalanches and Freezing").[5]

A grave in the area of Round Prairie and Pebble Creek campground is one of an unknown person. Scout Ray Little mentioned it but gave no information on its occupant. Haines says the wife of one of the park road crew was buried there in or about 1903. Park road crews found the grave in the 1950s, but Haines was never able to find it himself.[6]

A grave located between Lake Hotel and the gas station is that of Dave Edwards, the winter keeper for E. C. Waters's boat operations, who died of a heart attack while rowing in a boat on the lake on November 12, 1906. Edwards was rowing out to the new steamer *E. C. Waters*, and his body was found by soldiers at the Lake station. According to Haines, the real gravesite is under the asphalt of the service station, while the "grave" in the woods is a false one erected as a monument. At the time of Edwards's death, Waters intended to disinter Edwards's remains and return them to the dead man's home at Alta, Iowa, but apparently that never happened. Deate White, one of the road crewmen who was assigned to move Edwards's grave to a spot just east of Lake Hotel, told Haines that he never did it and that the grave remains next to the service station. A skull found in 1907 on Stevenson Island and thought to belong to one of the two men drowned in 1906 at West Thumb was buried next to Dave Edwards.[7]

A grave near the park's north boundary at Reese Creek supposedly contains a cowboy named Corwin who was killed by a bucking horse. We do not know his story.[8]

About this event, historian Aubrey Haines says: "[Park Ranger] Lee Coleman told me of the death of a cowboy at George Reese's ranch about 1905 and said he had been buried near the ranch house. He didn't know the name or anything else about him except that he had been thrown from a horse. I scouted the vicinity of the old Reese place (foundations still there) and exactly where I would make a burial, on a prominent, sagebrush-covered knob about five hundred feet from the house, I found what appeared to be a grave—a low mound of small stones and rock, roughly six feet by two feet. Thus, I felt Lee's story was confirmed by physical evidence even though there was no record of burial and no Reese family members surviving."[9]

A partial grave bearing pieces of Private Harry Allen who drowned in Yellowstone Lake in 1906 was located a year later just north of West Thumb Geyser Basin, between the road and the lake, and was marked by carved crosses on two trees (presumably for its head and foot). The story is chronicled in chapter 14 on drownings.

Two possible graves are known as existing on the "prominent knob" opposite the Cinnabar town site, but nothing is known as to their occupants, who were presumably residents of that town, which existed 1883–1902.[10]

And the grave of Dick Hull, who was thrown from his horse in 1910, may still be located somewhere in the mountains near Soda Butte (see chapter 18, "Wild Horses: Deaths from Horse, Wagon, and Stagecoach Incidents"), if it is not the grave at Round Prairie.

Finally, the location of the grave of C. J. Carpenter is not known, but it is known that he died in 1886. Jim Hepburn of Emigrant, Montana, located about thirty miles north of Yellowstone's north boundary, called the author on June 20, 1995, to give the information that his father had found C. J. Carpenter's grave marker floating in the Yellowstone River, with the notations on it that Carpenter was born in 1846 and died in 1886. Not knowing what else to do with it, the Hepburns nailed the wooden marker to their barn, and it remains there today.[11]

NOTES

INTRODUCTION TO THE SECOND EDITION

1. Nor does this book cover the difficult-to-categorize accidental deaths, such as that of a 2-month-old baby (Lance Richards) on August 13, 1967, near Lewis Falls. Jim Barton of Three Rivers, California, wrote me to report that he was a ranger at Lewis Lake that summer when he was called to Lewis River Bridge to a visitors' vehicle where a baby had somehow crawled out of its baby seat and died with its head caught between the seat and the car door. According to Barton, whether strangulation or a broken neck caused the baby's death was never determined. (Jim Barton to Lee H. Whittlesey, e-mail communication, July 10, 2009. The incident is mentioned in "Chief Ranger's Monthly Report," August 1967, box N-158, Yellowstone National Park [YNP] Archives.) Another freak accident occurred at Old Faithful Inn in 1974, when an employee named Johnson died when he fell from a ladder (box W-124, YNP Archives). Yet another occurred in June of 2009 when a concessioner employee died at Lake when weights fell onto his chest while he was exercising (Al Nash, National Park Service Public Affairs Office, e-mail to Lee Whittlesey, July 10, 2009). A fourth happened in August of 2011, when an unnamed park visitor in his mid-eighties choked to death on food in Pleasant Valley during the Roosevelt Lodge cookout (squad notes, August 30, 2011, Yellowstone National Park, p. 5). And historian Aubrey Haines (letter to Lee H. Whittlesey, September 27, 1995, YNP Archives) related to me one freak accident involving a park ranger in 1945. Ranger George Harris (a single man)

> went down to Gardiner for a pub-crawl, stayed until 2 am or later and probably left quite drunk for the hike back to Mammoth. He was found dead on Soap Hill. His body lay in the up-lane parallel with the roadway and on his back, and his head was terribly smashed. The best guess was that he lay down in the road and was aroused enough by an upcoming car to raise his head up so that some part of the underneath smashed his face and head. No one ever admitted to running over him; maybe the driver didn't even know it, as those on the road at 2:30 to 3am could have good reason to be "foggy."

2. *YNP@Work*, Yellowstone National Park employees' electronic newsletter, July 30, 2012, p. 2.

3. *Livingston* (MT) *Post* quoted in *Fergus County Argus* (Lewistown, MT), April 14, 1892, p. 3, column 3.

4. John E. Sheridan, "Dangers of the Yellowstone Park Where a Washington Woman Has Just Lost Her Life," *Washington* (DC) *Times*, September 17, 1905, magazine section, p. 48.

ORIGINAL INTRODUCTION AND RECENT ADDITIONS

1. Author's conversations with Melanie Ruesch and Anne Shepherd, Sequoia National Park, CA, August 19, 1993; Bob Wood, Zion National Park, UT, August 20, 1993; and Kitty Manscill, Great Smoky Mountains National Park, TN, August 20, 1993; Ronald B. Standler, "Lightning Strikes to People and the Legal Duties to Warn and to Protect," August 7, 1998, posted at http://www.rbs2.com/ltgwarn.pdf, citing *Schieler v. United States*, 642 F. Supp. 1310 (E.D. Cal. 1986), 15.

2. Timothy Egan, "Nature without the Nanny State," *Opinionator* (blog), *New York Times*, August 20, 2011.

3. Associated Press, "Lawsuit over Fatal Olympic National Park Goat Attack Dismissed," October 16, 2012, http://www.kplu.org/post/lawsuit-over-fatal-olympic-national-park-goat-attack-dismissed.

4. On the other hand, individual facts in a case can completely change the outcome, as in the 1994 case where the National Park Service was held liable for a lightning fatality on Mount Whitney, California. The victim's family was awarded 1.7 million dollars where lightning had struck an NPS stone hut on the mountaintop many times and where the NPS had broken its own regulations by failing to lightning-proof the hut even after it had much notice of the danger. *MacLeod, et al. v. United States*, C.D. Cal. 1994, as cited in Standler, "Lightning Strikes to People," 16.

1. DEATH IN HOT WATER

1. "Californian Dies Trying to Save Dog," *Billings* (MT) *Gazette*, July 22, 1981; "Man Dies of Thermal Burns," National Park Service, park press release 81-40, July 21, 1984; "Board of Inquiry into the Death of David Allen Kirwan," August 20, 1981, box A-114, file 7623, Yellowstone National Park Archives; author's interview with Bob Carnes, Lake Mead National Recreation Area, NV, November 9, 1992; Tony Sisto, "In Print—*Death in Yellowstone*," *Ranger: The Journal of the Association of National Park Rangers*, Fall 1995, 26. The inquiry board speculated that the dog was of a breed prone to jump into water to cool off when overheated. Ratliff admitted later that the men did not see the warning signs in the area. Kirwan at some point peeled off his shirt before making his dive and was probably in the water twenty to thirty seconds. No one can explain why he dove. Perhaps he was simply overcome by the plight of the dog and did not realize how hot the water was.

2. T. C. Everts, "Thirty-Seven Days of Peril," *Scribner's Monthly*, November 1, 1871, 6. A more detailed version of this with notes and sources is Lee H. Whittlesey, ed., *Lost in the Yellowstone: Truman Everts's Thirty-Seven Days of Peril*.

3. H. B. Calfee, "Calfee's Adventures—He and His Companion's Blood Curdling Trip to the Park over a Quarter Century Ago," manuscript made from newspaper clippings about 1896, YNP Research Library, 3 (these are from the *Bozeman* [MT] *Chronicle*, January 5, 12, 19, and 26, 1899); Calfee, "Adventurer Tells of Trip Through Yellowstone in 1873 [*sic*]," *Bozeman* (MT) *Daily Chronicle*, August 9, 1964, p. C-l.

4. "A Remarkable Story," Bozeman (MT) *Avant Courier*, September 7, 1882.

5. "Local Layout," *Livingston* (MT) *Enterprise*, November 24, 1883.

6. G. L. Henderson, "In Hot Water," *Helena Daily Herald*, April 25, 1888, p. 3. I have expended considerable space and more citations elaborating about this injury to Senator Conkling in an upcoming book. The incident is important for its relationship to early hot-spring bathing at Mammoth. See "'This Modern Saratoga of the Wilderness!': A History of the Mammoth Hot Springs and Mammoth Village in Yellowstone National Park," manuscript written for National Park Service, awaiting publisher, 2013, pp. 112–14.

7. "Local Layout," *Livingston Enterprise*, August 4, 1884, has Mr. Crossman. The young boy is in J. Herbert Roberts, *A World Tour, Being a Year's Diary, Written 1884–85*, p. 37.

8. "Dangerous Pots," *Livingston Enterprise*, August 4, 1888.

9. Maturin M. Ballou, *The New El Dorado: A Summer Journey to Alaska*, 41.

10. J. Sanford Saltus, *A Week in the Yellowstone*, 37; "Local Layout," *Livingston Enterprise*, August 9, 1890.

11. "Taking in the Park," *Anaconda* (MT) *Standard*, August 22, 1893, p. 6; "Falls in Boiling Spring," *Waterloo* (IA) *Evening Courier*, September 18, 1913, p. 1; Lyle and Geraldine Richmond, photo album, 1913 and 1915, untitled and undated newspaper clipping, 1913, accompanying their photo album, YNP Archives.

12. John L. Stoddard, *John L. Stoddard's Lectures*, 10:242.

13. Private Thomas Berger was burned in a spring near Castle Geyser and treated by G. L. Henderson in the same way Henderson treated Roscoe Conkling in 1883. "Berger's Geyser," *Livingston Post*, March 8, 1900. A copy of this article is in the Ash Scrapbook, 21a, YNP Research Library.

14. Charles M. Taylor Jr., *Touring Alaska and the Yellowstone*, 332. According to Taylor, this soldier was severely burned and his horse killed.

15. "A Serious Accident," *Livingston Post*, July 11, 1901; "Local News," July 18, 1901; "Local Layout," *Livingston Enterprise*, July 13, 20, 1910.

16. "Local Layout," *Livingston Enterprise*, July 13, 20, 1901; G. L. Henderson, "From the Park," August 17, 1901; "A Serious Accident," *Livingston Post*, July 11, 1901; "Fell Waist Deep into Hot Mud," *San Francisco Chronicle*, July 10, 1901; Superintendent's Journal, Ledger 143, July 6, 1901, YNP Archives; "Mrs. and Miss Zabriskie Fell into Boiling Clay," *Brooklyn* (NY) *Eagle*, July 9, 1901, p. 1; "Zabriskies Will Recover," *Brooklyn* (NY) *Eagle*, July 10, 1901, p. 3; "The Zabriskies at Home," *Brooklyn* (NY) *Eagle*, July 27, 1901, p. 16; Gardner S. Turrill, *A Tale of the Yellowstone, or in a Wagon Through Western Wyoming and Wonderland*, 99–100. G. S. Turrill traveled through the park in August 1898, and he says his brother-in-law Fred told him the (Zabriskie) story. Turrill

apparently added it to his text just before his book was published in 1901, even mentioning correctly that the mother and daughter were from New York and that the incident occurred at Thumb Paintpots. Turrill added that the two women died, and when their husband/father learned of the affair he became violently insane and never recovered his reason. This last statement was patently false, as later newspaper reports made clear. The women returned home to Brooklyn (Flatbush), New York, Louise living to age 99. Mrs. Zabriskie's husband had passed away before the women's trip to Yellowstone.

Turrill's trip occurred in 1898, three years before the incident happened, so he could not have known about it until just before his book was published. Sure enough, a check of Turrill's original newspaper account reveals that the Zabriskie story is not there. *The Souvenir* (Jefferson, Iowa), August 27; September 3, 17; October 1, 15, 22; November 5, 12, 22, 1898.

17. "Yet Sing's Natural Boiler . . . Scalded to Death," *The News* (Frederick, MD), February 4, 1889; "Four Less Chinamen—A Slumbering Geyser Awakes and Boils Over Drunken Celestials," *Galveston* (TX) *Daily News*, Febraury 4, 1889, p. 2; "Their Laundry over a Geyser—It Unexpectedly Spouted—Boiled Chinamen in the Yellowstone Park Region," *Illustrated Police News*, February 16, 1889, pp. 6, 13. The fable about "Chinaman Spring" (today called Chinese Spring) is explained in Aubrey L. Haines, *The Yellowstone Story* 2:17–18, 121, 390n28.

18. Park County Historical Society, *History of Park County, Montana 1984*, p. 457; Gladys Stermitz, "1st Annual Historical Tour. (Sponsored by the Park County Historical Society), August 10, 1985," 3; author's interview with Bruce Graham, Livingston, MT, August 19, 1993; author's interview with Isabel Squire, Seattle, WA, August 19, 1993. James Stumbo died during the winter, and it is unlikely that his immersion in a hot spring would have occurred then. Perhaps he was badly injured in late summer or fall of 1889 and lingered until February of 1890.

19. "Local Layout," *Livingston* (MT) *Enterprise*, October 15, 1898, p. 5.

20. "The Local News," *Livingston* (MT) *Post*, October 13, 1898, p. 3.

21. "Local Layout," *Livingston Enterprise*, July 29, 1905, says this child was a little girl but fails to give her name.

22. *Gardiner* (MT) *Wonderland*, July 27, 1905.

23. Some newspapers gave her first name as Martha, and others listed her last name as "Wickes" and her age as "22." These were all incorrect. "Woman Killed in Geyser," *New York Times*, September 7, 1905, p. 1.

24. A. L. Haines interview with Jack E. Haynes, December 9, 1963, audiotape 63-5, YNP Research Library.

25. "Death in a Geyser—Miss Fannie A. Weeks Scalded in Yellowstone Park," *Washington* (DC) *Post*, September 7, 1905, p. 1; F. V. Hayden, *Twelfth Annual Report of the United States Geological and Geographical Survey of the Territories . . . for the Year 1878 . . . Part II. . . .*, 1883, 210. At least two newspaper stories stated that Weeks weighed "200 pounds and her weight caused her to break through a thin crust." "Woman Boiled Alive," *Stevens Point* (WI) *Daily Journal*, September 7, 1905, p. 2; "Flesh Was Cooked in Boiling Spring," *Fort Wayne* (IN) *Weekly Sentinel*, September 13, 1905, p. 6; "Girl Is Boiled in Hot Spring," undated [September 1905], unknown newspaper clipping from Denver, Colorado, copy in possession of author.

26. *Gardiner* (MT) *Wonderland*, September 7, 1905; "Local Layout," *Livingston* (MT) *Enterprise*, September 9, 1905; "Badly Scalded," August 26; "Woman Boiled to Death in Hot Spring," *Pensacola* (FL) *Journal*, September 8, 1905, p. 3; "Miss Weeks' Body Expected Today," *Washington* (DC) *Times*, September 9, 1905, p. 9 (with photo); "Body of Miss Weeks Reaches Washington," *Washington* (DC) *Times*, September 10, 1905, p. 5; Letter to author from Rock Creek Cemetery, Washington, DC, October 17, 1992; Haines interview with Haynes. There is much more to Fannie Weeks's story. She spent six years as a teacher among the Ute Indians in Utah and as a result possessed a fabulous collection of Indian artifacts that passed to the Smithsonian Institution at her death. See "Death in a Geyser," *Washington Post*, as cited, p. 2; and "Famous Indian Relics," *Logansport* (IN) *Pharos*, October 31, 1905, p. 2.

27. Robert B. McKnight, "Do You Recall Your Walk in Geyser Basin?" *Yellowstone News* (Wylie Way newspaper), 1, no. 1 (Spring 1915): 4.

28. George Thomas, "My Recollections of the Yellowstone Park," 7, YNP Research Library.

29. G. L. Henderson, *Yellowstone Park Manual and Guide*, 2.

30. Theodore Gerrish, *Life in the World's Wonderland*, 186.

31. Charles J. Gillis, *Another Summer: The Yellowstone Park and Alaska*, 24.

32. *Annual Report of the Superintendent*, 1919, 92–93. A thermal injury from about the same period is in "Woman Steps into Paint Pots," *Livingston Enterprise*, August 6, 1913.

33. Picture postcard 4287, HHT Co., Norris Geyser Basin.

34. "Thermal Accidents 1919–1980," information paper, YNP Research Library; *Annual Report of the Superintendent*, 1919, 92–93; "Burns to Death in Geyser Water," *Livingston Enterprise*, July 20, 1919.

35. Wendell S. Keate, "In Re: The Rev. Gilbert Eakins," August 27, 1926, box A-44, file 146.13, YNP Archives; monthly report of superintendent, August 1926, 27; "Wyoming Minister Scalded to Death in Boiling Spring," *Livingston Enterprise*, August 26, 1926. In a letter to the director of the National Park Service, Superintendent Albright stated that Reverend Eakins "was not using ordinary (reasonable) care." Pattie Eakins to Horace Albright, November 23, 1926; Albright to Pattie Eakins, October 28, 1926; Albright to director, October 28, 1926, box A-44, file 146.13, YNP Archives.

Rocco Paperiello, an expert on West Thumb thermal features, believes that Reverend Eakins fell into present Winter Spring, then located next to a pier, and today sometimes submerged by lake water.

36. Monthly report of superintendent, August 1927, 23.

37. Monthly report of superintendent, August 1928, 24; "Funeral Services for Geo. H. Brown Thursday," *Lampasas Leader*, August 31, 1928; "Park Charges Stories Being Sent Out . . . Hurt Name," *Livingston Enterprise*, September 9, 1928; "Texas Man Boiled to Death in Geyser," Casper, WY, newspaper clipping, no date, about August 28, box W-11, file 149.1, YNP Archives.

38. Monthly report of superintendent, July 1929, 22; George Baggley, "Report of Injury," July 3, 1929, box A-44, file 146.13, YNP Archives; Old Faithful Ranger Station logbook entry, July 3, 1929, box W-34, YNP Archives.

39. "Body of Landroy [*sic*] Sent to Brussels," *Livingston Enterprise*, July 7, 1929; *Annual Report of Superintendent*, 1929, 6–7.

40. There also are discrepancies in the spelling of the man's name (Landoy versus Landroy), but the death certificate spells it Landoy, in box A-44, file 146.13, YNP Archives.

41. Roger Toll to director of NPS, August 9, 1929, box W-11, YNP archives; Horace M. Albright and William T. Ingersoll, "The Reminiscences of Horace M. Albright," transcript on microfilm of a series of recorded interviews with Albright by Columbia University, 1962, YNP Library microfilm, pp. 246–47.

42. Lee H. Whittlesey, *Yellowstone Place Names* (1988), p. 23; 2006 edition, p. 49.

43. Toll to director of NPS, August 9, 1929; Walter H. Saunders to NPS, July 6, 1929; various letters in same file from park landscape division, box W-11, YNP Archives. Interestingly, the West Thumb Geyser Basin seems to have had at least some boardwalks in the 1920s, before many other thermal areas. Horace Albright stated with regard to the Eakins incident, "We have built board walks all through this hot spring basin and where there are not board walks, there are well defined paths used daily by hundreds of people." From this we get the impression that the West Thumb area was used as a model for other thermal areas. Albright to director of NPS, October 28, 1926, box A-44, file 146.13, YNP Archives.

44. Monthly report of superintendent, June 1927, and numerous others; archive documents 3997–3998, 1901, YNP Archives.

45. Monthly report of superintendent, July 1932, 24; "Small Visitor in Park Dies," *Livingston Enterprise*, July 17, 1932; death certificate, box A-44, file 146.13, YNP Archives.

46. "Log of Events, Old Faithful Ranger Station," July 13, 1932, box W-34, YNP Archives. Temperature of the spring the following day was 66.5 degrees Celsius.

47. Monthly report of superintendent, July 1933, 22; "Log of Events, Old Faithful Ranger Station," July 19, 1933 (day after), box W-34; Roger Toll telegram to director of NPS, July 27, 1933; Sidney Born to Arno Cammerer, July 31, 1933; A. E. Demaray to Sidney Born, August 8, 1933, all in box A-44, file 146.13, YNP Archives.

48. Handwritten letter, Aune Frederickson to Elvie Fagerstrom of Winlock, WA, July [27], 1933, copy sent by Kimberly Mohney to author, June 5, 1997.

49. "Park Geyser Victim Dies from Burns," *Great Falls* (MT) *Tribune*, July 28, 1933; "Burn from Park Pool Ends Life of Tulsa Youth," *Livingston Enterprise*, July 26, 1933. These accounts gave his age as seventeen. See also "Burns Prove Fatal," *Tulsa* (OK) *World*, July 26, 1933; Aune Frederickson to Elvie Fagerstrom, July [27], 1933, via Kimberly Mohney to author, June 5, 1997.

50. "Died from Burns," *Worden* (MT) *Yellowstone*, August 22, 1935; "Youth Burned in Park Pool Dies," *Livingston Enterprise*, August 16, 1935; "Geyser Claims Boy," *Pocatello* (ID) *Journal*, August 16, 1935; Naturalists' Log Book, West Thumb Geyser Basin, August 14, 1935, YNP Research Library; death certificate, box A-44, file 146.13, YNP Archives.

51. Monthly report of superintendent, July 1936, p. 16; "Burns Prove Fatal to Ogden, Utah Man," *Kalispell Interlake* (MT), July 4, 1936; "Yellowstone Visitor Severely Burned in Fall into Hot Pool," *Livingston Enterprise*, July 4, 1936; *Annual Report of Superintendent*, 1937, 47; rangers' monthly reports, August 1936, box W-85, YNP Archives. The spring McFerson fell into may have been present Mantrap Cone, which has been the site of several injuries to fishermen, hence its name.

52. Whittlesey, *Yellowstone Place Names* (1988), 57.

53. Monthly report of superintendent, June 1921, 21.

54. Irvin Lloyd, "Special Incident Report," July 15, 1949, box W-98; Phillip R. Kasik to James Hecht, August 20, 1974, box A-78, file A7623, YNP Archives; "Boy Fatally Burned in Park Pool," *Livingston Enterprise*, July 15, 1949; "Park Hot Pool Burn Is Fatal to Young Boy," *Cody* (WY) *Enterprise*, July 19, 1949; *Annual Report of Superintendent*, 1950, 26.

55. Old Faithful Ranger Station logbook, September 13, 1949, box 33; Phillip R. Kasik to James Hecht, August 20, 1974, box A-78, file A7623, YNP Archives; "Girl Burned Fatally in Park Pool," *Livingston Enterprise*, September 14, 1949; *Annual Report of Superintendent*, 1950, 26; "Thermal Accidents 1919–1980," YNP Research Library. The logbook states that Karen Anderson fell into "the boiling fissure at the right of the Emerald pool walk[way] where it leaves the parking area." Probably she fell into the superheated geyser immediately east of Ragged Spring.

56. "Boy Fatally Scalded in Park Pool," *Livingston Enterprise*, June 16, 1958; monthly report of superintendent, June 1958, 6; *Annual Report of Superintendent*, 1958, 33; author's telephone interview with Jean Lewis Ryland (sister of Danny Lewis), June 23, 2003.

57. "Park Burn Victim Still 'Critical,'" *Billings Gazette*, July 16, 1967; "Thermal Injuries 1961–1969," YNP Research Library; Edward A. Hummel to Richard McCarthy, July 31, 1970, in Andy Hecht file, box W-53, YNP Archives; Alan Dunefsky, e-mail to author, February 1, 2006; Mark Rockmore, e-mail to author, February 1, 2006.

58. J. M. Thompson, T. S. Presser, R. B. Barnes, and D. B. Bird, "Chemical Analysis of the Waters of Yellowstone National Park, Wyoming from 1965 to 1973," U.S. Geological Survey Open-file Report 75-25, 30.

59. Author's e-mail communications with Sandy Farncomb Bennett, Norma Shannon Bruce Wilson, and Barbara Oxford Bettevy, November 2, 2012.

60. Roger Manning, case incident 75-630, July 3, 1975, box W-102, YNP Archives; "Body Found in Park Pool," *Billings Gazette*, July 4, 1975; author's interview with Bob Carnes, Lake Mead National Recreation Area, November 9, 1992; "Body Found in Hot Pool," *Livingston Enterprise*, July 3, 1975; "Man's Death Ruled Accidental," *Livingston Enterprise*, July 7, 1975.

61. Earl and Miriam Selby, "Andrew Did Not Die in Vain," *Reader's Digest*, August 1973, 134–37; "Safety First," *Newsweek*, June 10, 1974, 95.

62. The area was closed and the pool closely watched for several days. Initially, the spring was made to erupt in an attempt to get objects to rise to its surface. When that failed, pumping was attempted, and finally some remnants of the body rose to the surface. Only parts were recovered. The case incident report describes these activities.

63. "Report of Accidents Other Than Motor Vehicle," field report 1037, June 28, 1970; "Interview with Mrs. Carol Lake Regarding the Fatality Accident of Andrew Hecht on June 28, 1970"; and other attachments in box W-53, YNP Archives. In 2001, a park visitor named Earl Richbart left the following touching message taped to a sign near Old Faithful Visitor Center: "It was 31 years ago when Andy didn't come back to play baseball with us. He was our 3rd baseman. I was 2nd base. We were all told what happened . . . Today I shed a tear for our 3rd baseman as one of my sons is Andy's age.

He fears nothing but today Dad's hand will hold his tighter [than] it's ever been held . . . I still miss Andy." Tom Farrell to author, June 16, 2001, appending Earl Richbart's note. As of 2012, there was a small notation on an Upper Basin wayside exhibit that mentioned Andy Hecht, by way of a memorial.

64. James L. Hecht to Secretary of Interior, June 29, 1970; Hecht to secretary, August 11, 1970; in box W-53, YNP Archives. "Son Dies in Yellowstone; Parents Push for Safety," *Chicago Tribune*, November 18, 1970, 6; "Boy Dies in Yellowstone Pool," *Jackson Hole Guide*, July 2, 1970; Ann McFeatters, "I Write This to Give Meaning to Andy's Life," *Washington Daily News*, August 19, 1970.

65. "Engineer Urges Park Safety before Congress," *Livingston Enterprise*, April 20, 1971.

66. "Father Sues Government," *Billings Gazette*, May 26, 1971. I must say that information on fatalities in the national parks is, or was anyway, material that the NPS has not ever kept tabs on or otherwise had readily available, as evidenced by my own difficulties in finding such items for this book. Dr. Hecht's suspicions that the NPS was somehow stalling in giving him the statistics he wanted were unfounded. The service just did not have the stuff without special research.

67. James L. Hecht to Edward I. Koch, August 3, 1972, box A-74, YNP Archives. Hecht then petitioned the Park Service to erect a memorial to Andy at Crested Pool.

68. "Dead Child's Kin Push for Yellowstone Safety," (Butte) *Montana Standard*, November 12, 1970. The Cameron Smith case resulted in a lawsuit in which the plaintiffs were unsuccessful. "Court Considers Suit," *Livingston Enterprise*, September 5, 1974.

69. "Thermal Injuries 1961–1969," YNP Research Library.

70. This happened as early as 1924, when Fountain Geyser, at Lower Geyser Basin, erupted suddenly, scalding two persons. "Special Incident Report," July 28, 1924, box W55, YNP Archives. Again on July 28–30, 1952, Fountain Geyser erupted, scalding nine persons, and the walkway was relocated. Monthly report of superintendent, July 1952, 14. I remember similar walkway relocation in 1978, the result of Silex Spring's sudden eruptions to heights of fifteen feet, which splashed nearby visitors.

71. "Thermal Accidents 1919–1980."

72. "Campaign for Safety in National Parks," *Casper Star-Tribune* (WY), April 26, 1971.

73. Hugh B. Johnson v. U.S.A., 90-8060, 1990.

74. Paul Schullery, *Mountain Time*, 123.

75. "Public's Role in U.S. Park Safety Cited," *Sunday Oklahoman*, June 27, 1971.

76. Quoted in Schullery, *Bears of Yellowstone*, 96.

77. Miss J. Laguerenne to park superintendent, September 11, 1911, in item 103, folder 313, YNP Archives.

78. "Hazards of Wilderness," *Billings Gazette*, May 30, 1971.

79. "Park Visitor Burned by Fall in Hot Pool," *Livingston Enterprise*, August 28, 1978; Scott Wonder, Bellevue, WA, to author, no date [1996–2005]; Pam Haner, Redmond, WA, phone call to author, August 14, 2001.

80. "Young Boy Burned," National Park Service, Yellowstone National Park news release 05-48, July 3, 2005; "Park Visitor Burned in Yellowstone National Park," 01-39,

July 27, 2001; "Boy Who Fell into Hot Pool Expected to Make Full Recovery," July 5, 2005, http://tv.ksl.com/index.php?nid=39&sid=216710.

81. "Another Thermal Accident," *Billings Gazette*, August 14, 1981.

82. Steve Johnson, interview with Bessie Haynes Arnold, January 19, 1974, audiotape 74-4; C. P. Connally, "Yellowstone Park.," n.d. [1895?], 75.

83. Letter to author from Andrea Paul, January 31, 1993; author's interview with Andrea Paul, Mammoth Hot Springs, WY, April 20, 1993; letter to author from Melanie Weeks, March 1, 1993; letter to author from Jill Fitterer, March 15, 1993; author's interview with Bruce Blair, November 16, 1992; letter to author from Bonnie Gafney, January 17, 1993; "Man Dies after Thermal Pool Fall," *Livingston Enterprise*, February 10, 1988; National Park Service, park press release, February 9, 1988; author's interview with Jeff Henry, November 14, 1992; author's interview with Steve Blakeley, December 9, 1992; Jill Fitterer, "May There Be Mountains," n.d. [1990]; Dan R. Sholly with Steven M. Newman, *Guardians of the Yellowstone*, 188–99. John Mark Williams's monument in Yellowstone is the Lake-area employees' pub, which is today known as Henry's Bar from Williams's habit of calling his customers there Henry and being called Henry himself.

84. "Three Park Employees Seriously Burned," National Park Service, Yellowstone National Park press release 00-68, August 22, 2000; "Additional Information on Three Park Employees Seriously Burned," 0071, August 23, 2000; "Judge Dismisses Lawsuit by Yellowstone Burn Victim," January 30, 2004, www.ksl.com/?nid=148&sid=86639.

85. "Yellowstone Outing Turns Deadly," Idaho Falls *Post-Register*, August 23, 2000, p. 1; "Park Has Had Other Hot Springs Fatalities," *Post-Register*, August 23, 2000, p. A3; "Tragedy in Yellowstone," no date, http://www.outdoorplaces.com/Features/Backcountry/thermal/.

86. Michael Milstein, "Employee Killed in Hot Spring," *Billings* (MT) *Gazette*, August 23, 2000, pp. 1–2.

87. Elaine Jarvik, "Son's Recovery Elates Mom," *Deseret* (UT) *News*, December 2, 2000; Linda Ashton, "Young Woman Remembered for Spreading Love and Joy," *Moscow-Pullman Daily News* (ID), August 25, 2000, p. 10A; "Yellowstone Burn Victim [Montague] Goes Home," *Deseret* (UT) *News*, November 27, 2000.

88. "One Dead, Two Hurt at Thermal Pool," *Salt Lake* (UT) *Tribune*, August 23, 2000, p. 1; George Marler, *Inventory of Thermal Features of the Firehole River Basins*, p. 578.

89. *Elder v. U.S.*, 312 F. 3d 1172 (10th Cir. 2002); 141 F. Supp. 2d 1334 (2001); "Yellowstone Hot Springs Burn Suit Going Forward," September 1, 2002, http://www.freerepublic.com/focus/news/742809/posts; Rick Rinehart and Amy Rinehart, *Dare to Survive: Death, Heartbreak, and Triumph in the Wild*, pp. 161–63. I note here that the Tenth Circuit's jurisdiction and decision of December 3, 2002, applies only to the 96% of Yellowstone that is located in Wyoming. The 4% of the park located in Montana and Idaho is not included in this decision because those states are in the Ninth Circuit. However, many district courts' decisions in those states are headed toward this same result, even if there is currently no comparable Ninth Circuit decision.

90. *Elder v. U.S.*, 312 F. 3d 1172, December 3, 2002.

91. "Fall into Park Thermal Pool Severely Burns Park Worker," *Jackson Hole Guide* (WY), July 24, 1991; National Park Service, park press release, July 18, 1991.

2. "THESE ANIMALS ARE NOT REAL"

1. Nolie Mumey, *Rocky Mountain Dick (Richard W. Rock) Stories of His Adventures in Capturing Wild Animals*, 71–77; "History of Dick Rock," *Livingston Enterprise*, April 19, 1902. The stagecoach/buffalo incident in Hayden Valley is chronicled in MLA, "Our Summering of 1890," manuscript at University of Colorado, Boulder, CO, 21, wherein the unidentified woman author noted on July 18, 1890: "All of yesterday's wild grandeur had fled, and there was nothing in any way exciting met with, except, perhaps, the occasional fording of a creek, or the momentary expectation of an attack from buffaloes which had, even since we had entered the Park, made a reputation for themselves by attacking and almost demolishing one of the Park stages, giving the contents thereof quite a shaking up."

2. National Park Service, park press releases, 1983–1994.

3. National Park Service, park press release, June 30, 1987.

4. National Park Service, park press release, June 3, 1992.

5. National Park Service, park press release, August 14, 1978; author's interview with Beverly Bittner, Sun Valley, Idaho, March 22, 1993; "Moose Killed after Attack at College," *Altoona* (PA) *Mirror*, January 15, 1995, p. 9.

6. "Woman Attacked by Cow Elk Protecting Calf," *Idaho Falls Register*, June 3, 1991.

7. Monthly report of superintendent, November 1942. Former ranger naturalist Norman Bishop's e-mail to author, January 20, 2003, details five different coyote "attacks" in Yellowstone.

8. Monthly report of superintendent, May 1945, 4.

9. "Local Layout," *Livingston Enterprise*, July 10, 1886.

10. "Buffalo Kills Tourist," *Livingston Enterprise*, July 13, 1971; "Three Die in Parks," *Billings Gazette*, July 14, 1971; National Park Service, park press release, July 13, 1971, box K-22, YNP Archives.

11. Vernon E. Hennesay, "Board of Inquiry (on Marvin Schrader)," October 21, 1971, and death certificate, box A-88, file A7623, YNP Archives. See also box A-2.

12. Leon Brunton, interview with author, December 26, 1992, Mammoth Hot Springs, WY.

13. Mike Pflaum, interview with author, Mount Rushmore National Memorial, February 14, 1993.

14. "Bison Gores Yellowstone Tourist," *Billings Gazette*, August 2, 1983; National Park Service, park press release, August 1, 1983; "Tourist Attacked by Bison," *Livingston Enterprise*, August 2, 1983.

15. This incident was recorded by a professional camera crew and appears in the videotape *Winter in Yellowstone* by Wolfgang Bayer.

16. The philosophy in a national park is to keep things as natural as possible. Man's role in a national park is supposed to be nondisruptive. Bison and other animals die in winter; that is natural. When they die, they become a gift of life for other animals: ravens, magpies, eagles, coyotes, and others feed on the carcasses. So the National Park philosophy is one of noninterference with natural processes.

17. Author's interview with Bobbie Seaquist Hobbs, West Yellowstone, MT, December 15, 1992. Seaquist served as a Young Adult Conservation Corps volunteer before working as a park ranger.

18. Related to author by visitor at Albright Visitor Center, November 1992.

3. HUMAN DEATHS FROM BEARS

1. Steve Johnson, interview with Bessie Haynes Arnold, January 19, 1974, tape 74-4, YNP Research Library. At Canyon, bears and humans were thrown together in garbage dumps as early as 1888. Bear-human confrontations probably began in 1883, with dumps at the first park tent camps, although we currently have no documentation of these until 1888.

2. Schullery, *Bears of Yellowstone*, 292–93.

3. "Speaking of Bear," *Livingston Enterprise*, December 26, 1903.

4. Paul Schullery, ed., *Yellowstone Bear Tales*, 55–58; "Attacked by a Bear," *Salt Lake* (UT) *Tribune*, September 7, 1902, p. 1; "Torn by a Bear; Michigan Man Received Probably Fatal Injuries," *Jackson* (MI) *Citizen Patriot*, September 9, 1902, p. 2; "Clawed by a Bear; R.E. Southwick of Hart Comes to Grief in Yellowstone Park," *Grand Rapids* (MI) *Press*, September 9, 1902, p. 3; "Attacked by a Bear," *Muskegon* (MI) *Chronicle*, September 9, 1902, p. 5.

5. The initial story was "Our Local Field," *Gardiner* (MT) *Wonderland*, August 20, 1904, p. 5. Then came all the following: "Bear Kills Two Men," *Bay City* (MI) *Times*, October 10, 1904, p. 1; "Travelers Killed by Bear," *Saginaw* (MI) *News*, October 7, 1904, p. 2. The same story also appeared in the following newspapers: *Grand Forks* (ND) *Herald*, October 8; Cleveland (OH) *Plain Dealer*, October 8; *Washington* (IN) *Democrat*, October 8; *Sedan* (KS) *Lance*, October 14; *Cleveland* (OH) *Gazette*, October 15; *Seattle* (WA) *Daily Times*, October 7; Charleston (SC) *Evening Post*, October 7; *Daily* (Springfield) *Illinois State Register*, October 8; San Diego (CA) *Evening Tribune*, October 8; and others. Only the *Washington* (DC) *Post* (October 8, 1904, p. 6, "No Bear-hunting in the Park!") and the *San Francisco Call* (October 7, 1904, p. 1, "Bears in Yellowstone Park Kill Two Men") stated that the two men were employees of Lake Hotel and not tourists.

6. Attributed to *Field and Stream* magazine, this article appeared in the *Anaconda* (MT) *Standard*, November 25, 1904, p. 10, headlined "Are Tame Yet Dangerous." It also appeared in *Ft. Worth* (TX) *Star Telegram*, November 8, 1904, p. 3; *Rockford* (IL) *Republic*, November 18, 1904, p. 3; and *Muskegon* (MI) *Daily Chronicle*, December 30, 1904, p. 6. A check of the original article ("Yellowstone Park Bears," *Field and Stream*, November 1904, p. 80) shows that the newspapers quoted it completely and verbatim. That something unusual with Yellowstone's bears, or at least a perception of something unusual, was occurring in August of 1904 is apparent from a front-page newspaper article in the *San Francisco Call*. It stated that "bears have become so plentiful as to almost interfere with the pleasure of camping parties." The article complained that "no provisions are safe" from the animals and that they "visit camps at night, ransacking everything in reach." The article, apparently written from the park as a "special dispatch," griped that

bears had lost all fear of man, lamented that they emerged at night "from the forests like droves of pigs," and reported that a tourist named James Reynolds had been "severely injured" by one of them. See "Bears Raid the Tents of Campers; Animals Annoy Yellowstone Visitors," in *San Francisco Call*, August 28, 1904, p. 1. Thanks also to Jeff Henry, who pointed out to me that the 1904 "meathouse" was probably the present yellow building behind Lake Hotel, which is the residence today of Dale Fowler, winter keeper for the hotel.

7. Armed with this information, I became really interested in the possible truth of the story of two human fatalities at Lake from bears and whether some conspiracy to cover it/them up occurred (as the two newspapers stated). I immediately asked myself why such a conspiracy might have occurred and came to the conclusion that one possibility was because park officials did not want anything to get in the way of ongoing bear-feeding activities for tourists and employees at hotels. Such activities were entertaining and fun for nearly everyone—akin to a circus—not to mention stimulating to park tourism by word of mouth. After all, President Theodore Roosevelt—even though he was a hunter—was known to be sympathetic to animal protection in reservations such as Yellowstone. Perhaps Pitcher or other officials worried that Roosevelt or others high up in the federal government might shut these bear-feeding shows down.

But if word of bear attacks scared people, it could also have worked *against* tourism. Thus another possible reason for a cover-up might have been that authorities feared hurting visitation. The loss of revenue from tourism because tourists were too scared to go to the park could have been a pretty big thing in the minds of some concessioners, park officials, and politicians. Recall that park officials two years earlier had witnessed the injury of R. E. Southwick at Lake Hotel and had seen it dragged through the newspapers. Paul Schullery has noted in his *Yellowstone Bear Tales* (p. 55) that Southwick's injury went "from a possible fatality, to a serious injury, and finally to a case of misconduct on the part of the victim," all spearheaded by Acting Park Superintendent (Major) John Pitcher. Perhaps Pitcher or others did not want a repeat of this story, especially if it might have meant that it would hurt tourism.

After all, Pitcher had written in 1902 that bears "are harmless while left alone and kept in a perfectly wild state but when fed and petted they lose all fear of human beings, cause damage to property . . . and are dangerous . . . to [those who] trifle with them." (*Annual Report of Superintendent*, 1902, pp. 6–7, quoted in "Yellowstone Bears Are Dangerous Only When Tame," *Colorado Springs* (CO) *Gazette*, November 9, 1902, p. 11.)

Of course this idea of a cover-up is all speculative and theoretical and may never have happened. But treating the cover-up story as kindly as possible, I went to the U.S. Army soldiers' logbook for Lake Soldier Station during the summer and fall of 1904 as well as to the monthly reports of the station for that same period in the park archives. Both the logbook—a large single volume containing handwritten entries for many years—and the monthly reports, which consist of individual pages, were kept by noncommissioned officers who were in charge of the station (generally corporals but sometimes sergeants). In the continuous logbook for that summer and fall, the entries make no mention of any such bear-related event during the ongoing and somewhat mundane activities of horse patrolling, repairing phone lines, noting the presence of game (especially buffalo), and recording the weather. But in the monthly reports—where through time there are occasional mentions of "other" events—I noticed something a bit suspicious. The August and September reports by Corporal Lawrence Creekbarry are extremely neat and uniform with none of the insertions or uneven lines that appear in the June, October, November, and December reports. Even the pages for August and September are cleaner than those of the other months. Smudges and other dirt appear on the fronts of many of these pages (probably from fingers touching a woodstove before touching the pages) but not on those of August and September. It would have been difficult for purposeful changes to have been made to the large, ongoing logbook, but not at all difficult to change the single pages of the monthly reports. Therefore we must leave open the possibility—dependent, as is all of history, on discovery of further documents—that Corporal Creekbarry was ordered by superiors to help cover up the bear-mauling incident by rewriting his reports for August and September 1904. On the other hand, perhaps it is a mere coincidence that the August and September pages are cleaner than the others.

I also examined the *Livingston* (MT) *Enterprise*, all front pages from April 30 through December 31, 1904, and found no story on the incident. (A story involving the deaths of two people from a bear mauling would almost certainly have appeared on page 1, *if* the story found its way to Livingston.) And I examined all interior pages of this newspaper from August 1 through October 7 and found no mention of it in local-news columns. But interestingly, I did find the above-quoted story from *Field and Stream* magazine—again headlined "Are Tame Yet Dangerous"—running on page 1 of the *Livingston Enterprise* for December 3, 1904. One would think that the *Enterprise*, upon discovering this story, would have made efforts to ascertain its truth, but if the editors pursued it, I have not found the story.

8. E-mail discussions of this alleged event among historians Paul Schullery, Jeremy Johnston, and author, January 1–17, 2013.

9. F. Dumont Smith, *Book of a Hundred Bears*, 44.

10. Clifton Johnson, *Highways and Byways of the Rocky Mountains*, 224–25.

11. Schullery, *Yellowstone Bear Tales*, pp. 55–58.

12. "On Lofty Grand Teton," *The* (NY) *Sun*, January 6, 1895, p. 1, column 5.

13. A story of "Lee Millison" being missing is in "Local Items," *Livingston Herald*, July 25, 1894, p. 3. The death stories are "Millison's Remains Discovered," *Livingston Enterprise*, September 14, 1895, p. 4; "Died in the Timber—Bleached Bones of Lee Mallison Found on Elk Creek," *Livingston Post*, September 11, 1895, p. 3; "A Mystery Cleared—Lee Mallison's Remains Found on Elk Creek," *Livingston Herald*, September 12, 1895, p. 3; and "The Bear Turned on Him—Mallison's Remains Are Found—He Was Pursuing a Wounded Bear in the Natural Bridge District," *Minneapolis* (MN) *Journal*, September 14, 1895, p. 3. The *Livingston Enterprise* called him "Lee Millison," while two others called him "Mallison" and the *Herald* used Millison at first and Mallison later. For context on the mining there, see "In the Mining World—Natural Bridge Gold District," *Minneapolis Journal*, October 26, 1895, p. 12; and "The Boulder District," *Livingston Post*, September 18, 1895, p. 2.

14. "Well Known Local Man Succumbs at Hospital Sunday," *Livingston Enterprise*, March 12, 1935. This story states: "The deceased was clawed about the abdomen several years ago by a grizzly bear in Yellowstone National Park, and these injuries

brought about his death, it was said." The March 13 edition has his obituary. The mauling remembered by Walt Stebbins was recorded in H. C. Benson, *Report of the Acting Superintendent of the Yellowstone National Park . . . 1910* (Washington: GPO, 1910), p. 10.

15. Walt Stebbins, interview with author, Gardiner, MT, February 15, 1993.

16. Haines, *Yellowstone Story*, 2:86; *Annual Report of Superintendent*, 1916, 36–37; J. A. McGuire in Schullery, *Yellowstone Bear Tales*, 59–67. George B. Link, a stage driver for Wylie, knew Frank Welch personally and stated later that "he was attacked by the bear on the Cody road, and died at Mammoth a few days afterward. It was a surprise to me, for I had never heard of a bear attacking a man sleeping under a wagon, for I have done so a great many times in Yellowstone. This particular place was reported to be a bad camping place on account of a very large and troublesome grizzly." Mary Link, New Berlin, WI, to author, June 26, 1996, quoting letter from her father-in-law George B. Link to her mother, written November 29, 1916.

17. Statement of Amos Fries, September 14, 1916, and death certificate of Frank Welch, item 64, file 313, YNP Archives; McGuire in Schullery, *Yellowstone Bear Tales*, 62; "Bear Kills Man in Yellowstone," *Ogden* (UT) *Daily Standard*, September 19, 1916, p. 10.

18. "Yellowstone Bear Kills F. Welch of Corwin," *Livingston Enterprise*, September 12, 1916.

19. Herb French in A. L. Haines interview with Henry Mallon et al., July 5, 1961, audiotape 61-2, YNP Archives. Interestingly, these old stagecoach drivers all remembered the Welch incident as occurring right at noon. Perhaps they were remembering the explosion.

20. Ernest Thompson Seton, *Lives of Game Animals* 2, part 1, p. 53; Horace M. Albright and William T. Ingersoll, "The Reminiscences of Horace M. Albright," transcript on microfilm of a series of recorded interviews with Albright by Columbia University, 1962, YNP Library microfilm, pp. 246–47; "Bear Kills Man in Yellowstone," *Ogden* (UT) *Standard*, September 19, 1916, p. 10.

21. William Rush, *Wild Animals of the Rockies, Adventures of a Forest Ranger*, 63–64.

22. Ibid., 67–69.

23. Monthly report of superintendent, November 1928, 19.

24. Monthly report of superintendent, September 1934, 14.

25. Donalene O'Neill of Neihart, MT, letter to author, April 9, 1999; Rocco Paperiello, interview with author, Gardiner, MT, January 31, 1993.

26. Schullery, *Bears of Yellowstone*, 106; D. H. Bremer, "Special Incident Report" and "Individual Bear Injury Report," August 23, 1942; Dr. G. A. Windsor, "Individual Bear Injury Report," August 23, 1942; T. R. Terry, handwritten statement, no date, attachment to Bremer, all in possession of author; "Victim of Attack by Bear Dies at Park Hospital," *Livingston Enterprise*, August 28, 1942; *Annual Report of Superintendent*, 1943, 18.

27. Dr. Stephen Herrero, *Bear Attacks*, 22.

28. *Annual Report of Superintendent*, 1944, 17. See also "Mrs. Christine Hansen," in 78th Cong., 2d Sess., Sen. Report No. 785, February 7, 1944, pp. 1–6.

29. Schullery, *Bears of Yellowstone*, 106.

30. Monthly report of superintendent, November 1958, 4.

31. Herrero, *Bear Attacks*, 54–55. The investigation photos from this incident are in the park photo archives.

32. Schullery, *Bears of Yellowstone*, 41; Dennis G. Martin, as Administrator of the Estate of Harry Eugene Walker. v. U.S.A., 392 F. Supp. 243 (C.D. Calif. 1975).

33. Schullery, *Bears of Yellowstone*, 128.

34. Ibid., 141–42.

35. Ibid.; Schullery, *Mountain Time*, 123.

36. Estate of Harry Eugene Walker v. United States of America, Civil No. 72-3044AAH, January 9–February 21, 1975, trial transcript, p. 1741, YNP Research Library.

37. Ibid., 1633–35.

38. Schullery, *Mountain Time*, 122. This judge was A. Andrew Hauk, who died at age 91 in 2004. He was controversial for other reasons as well, having routinely made in his courtroom "insensitive or demeaning remarks about women, homosexuals, environmentalists, and others." Claudia Luther, "Federal Judge Whose Comments Raised Some Hackles," *Los Angeles* (CA) *Times*, November 12, 2004.

39. Dennis G. Martin, Administrator of the Estate of Harry Eugene Walker v. U.S.A., 546 F.2d 1355 (9th Cir.1976).

40. Frank C. Craighead, *Track of the Grizzly*, 212–13; "From an anonymous employee of the Department of Veterans Affairs who fears he has transgressed in the area of privacy" to author, November 19, 1996, "Subject Possible Bear Death, Herbert Muller."

41. Schullery, *Bears of Yellowstone*, 292–93.

42. Floyd Klang, backcountry permit 84-7N-806, attachment to case incident report 84-2913.

43. John Lounsbury, interview with author, Lake, WY, January 12, 1993.

44. Mark Marschall, "Initiation and Results of Search," July 31, 1984, case incident 84-2913; Mark Marschall, handwritten entry for August 1, 1984, in Pelican Springs Patrol Cabin Logbook, YNP Archives.

45. Dr. Lee K. Hermann, "Final Autopsy Report," AB4, August 2–19, 1984, Cody, WY.

46. Mike Pflaum, interview with author, Mount Rushmore National Memorial, February 14, 1993.

47. David Spirtes, "Investigation of Scene at 5-W-1," from CI 84-2913, July 31, 1984, Yellowstone National Park, WY, in box N-328, YNP Archives; "Bear Kills Woman in Yellowstone Park," *Livingston Enterprise*, August 2, 1984.

48. David Spirtes, "Investigation of Scene at 5-W-1," from CI 84-2913, July 31, 1984, Yellowstone National Park, WY, in box N-328, YNP Archives; "Bear Kills Woman in Yellowstone Park," *Livingston Enterprise*, August 2, 1984.

49. Sholly, *Guardians of the Yellowstone*, 125.

50. Ibid., 128; Scott McMillion, *Mark of the Grizzly*, 97.

51. Jeff Henry, interview with author, Cinnabar Basin, MT, November 1, 1992; Alice Siebecker, interview with author, Lake, WY, February 20, 1993.

52. Ibid.; John Lounsbury, conversation with author, August 29, 2002.

53. Ibid.; McMillion, *Mark of the Grizzly*, p. 99.

54. Kerry Gunther, Yellowstone Center for Resources, personal communication with author, February 13, 2013.

55. National Park Service, park press release, December 15, 1992; McMillion, *Mark of the Grizzly*, 90–109.

56. David Page and Pat Navaille, in U.S. Department of the Interior, National Park Service, case incident report 11-2587 of fatality/bear attack, August 2, 2011, with many supplemental attachments, www.nps.gov/aboutus/foia/foia-frd.htm; National Park Service, Investigation Team Report, "Fatality of Mr. Brian Matayoshi, from a Bear Attack on the Wapiti Lake Trail, Yellowstone National Park on July 6, 2011," www.fws.gov/mountain-prairie/species/mammals/grizzly/Yellowstone.htm; National Park Service, "Yellowstone Visitor Killed by Grizzly Bear," Yellowstone National Park news release 11-073, July 6, 2011; "Identity of Bear Mauling Victim Released," 11-075, July 7, 2011; "Yellowstone National Park Talking Points [for human fatality from bear]," no number, July 7, 2011; "Report Released on July Fatal Bear Attack in Yellowstone," 11-100, September 20, 2011; "Fatal Attack by Yellowstone Grizzly Possibly Triggered by Running, Yelling," *Bozeman* (MT) *Daily Chronicle*, September 21, 2011, p. 1; "Couple's Screaming May Have Triggered Grizzly Mauling," *USA Today*, September 21, 2011.

57. "Another Hiker," *Daily Mail Reporter* (United Kingdom), August 29, 2011, online as *Mail Online*.

58. Anna Simovska, "Friends Remember 59-Year-Old Victim of Grizzly Bear Attack," *Upper Michigan's Source*, August 30, 2011; Laura Zuckerman, "John Wallace, Yellowstone Bear Attack Victim, Called Himself a 'Grizzly Expert,'" *Huffington Post*, March 5, 2012.

59. National Park Service, "Grizzly Bear Captured and Euthanized," Yellowstone National Park news release 11-105, October 3, 2011; "Grizzly Bear Killed After DNA Links to Second Mauling," *Bozeman* (MT) *Daily Chronicle*, October 4, 2011, p. 1; "Seven Bears Captured in Yellowstone Mauling Probe," *Livingston* (MT) *Enterprise*, September 28, 2011, p. 1; Assistant Superintendent Steve Iobst, conversation with author, September 2011.

60. Board of Review report, "Fatality of Mr. John L. Wallace from a Bear Attack on the Mary Mountain Trail in Yellowstone National Park on August 25, 2011" (NPS Case Incident 11-4555), dated January 30, 2012, http://www.fws.gov/mountain-prairie/species/mammals/grizzly/WallaceBoardOfReviewReport03022012.pdf. I note that this report's map of "Trap Locations—Mary Mountain Incident" depicts where the bear trap was placed and not the actual location of the incident. The incident appears to me to have occurred on the Mary Mountain Trail about one mile north of Glen Africa Basin. See also Kerry Gunther, National Park Service, "Forensic Evidence—Human Fatality Along the Mary Mountain Trail of Yellowstone National Park on August 25, 2011," January 12, 2012, http://www.nps.gov/aboutus/foia/upload/WallaceBearAttackFatalityDocumentsForWeb.pdf; National Park Service, "Identity of Dead Hiker Released," Yellowstone National Park news release 11-090, August 29, 2011; and "Investigation Continues into Fatal Bear Attack," 11-093, September 2, 2011.

61. A. L. Haines, interview with Henry Mallon et al., July 5, 1961, audiotape 61-2, YNP Research Library.

62. A. L. Haines, interview with Edith Ritchie, November 7, 1961, audiotape 61-3, YNP Archives.

63. The donation occurred in 1941. YNP Museum catalogue record 1402, accession number 328 of skis "used by sadistic bear hunter of Jardine area who would pepper trapped bears with buckshot til dead; he once miscalculated and was killed by a not yet dead bear. [His] Skis found along north [park] line the following year."

64. A. L. Haines, interview with Henry Mallon, Herb French et al., July 5, 1961, audiotape 61-2, YNP Archives. The 1900 census gave Graham's birth year as 1848.

65. Acting park superintendent to Dr. T. S. Palmer, May 27, 1912, item 103, file 313, YNP Archives; L. W. "Gay" Randall, *Footprints Along the Yellowstone*, 139–43, 161–63. It is possible that this bear was the same one that later killed Frank Welch (1916), because the Welch bear did indeed have some toes missing from a hind foot. Haines, *Yellowstone Story*, 2:87. But this bear could not have been the same one that killed Frenchy Duret in 1922, because the Welch bear was blown up with dynamite in 1916. Nevertheless, Old Two Toes may have been responsible for two human deaths: Graham and Welch.

66. "John Graham Meets Death in Fight with Bear," *Livingston Enterprise*, May 6, 11, 1912. Perhaps the fact that the newspaper elected to run the same story twice was the reason why the longtime Gardiner residents mentioned earlier, Herb French and Henry Mallon, also claimed to remember a "second" human fatality caused by a bear and also near Crevice Mountain. Nothing further was said about this alleged "other" bear attack in the Mallon interview.

67. Albright to W. J. Newbro, September 19, 1969, in YNP manuscript file under "Horace Albright"; Aubrey Haines, two-page history of Duret and his land, no date, in YNP manuscript file under "Silver Tip Ranch"; Doris Whithorn, "A Grizzly Got Frenchy," typescript, no date, YNP Research Library.

68. Monthly report of superintendent, June 1922, 35–36; [Horace Albright?], "A Bear-Faced Robbery," *Literary Digest*, June 9, 1923, 64–65; Randall, *Footprints along the Yellowstone*, 161–63. Randall says the man who found Frenchy was a neighbor of his named Charley. Interestingly, following Duret's death, French heirs contested his will with a lawsuit against his widow in their unsuccessful attempt to get his prime, near-the-park property. "Jury Holds Joseph Duret Will Valid," undated clipping, box A-44, file 146.13, YNP Archives. Duret was buried half a mile from where his body was found in a simple service attended only by his widow, Hutchings, and Denhoff.

69. "Huge Bear Devours Trapper in Montana," *Ogden* (UT) *Standard Examiner*, June 15, 1922, p. 1; "Slain by Grizzly," *The Herald* (New Orleans, LA), September 14, 1922, p. 5 (this story was also in *Kalamazoo* [MI] *Gazette*, August 22, 1922, p. 9; *Bradford* [PA] *Star Record*, September 1, 1922, p. 7; and others); "Trapper Loses Terrific Death Battle with Huge Grizzly Bear; Mutilated Body Bears Evidence [of] Desperate Fight," *Anaconda* (MT) *Standard*, June 15, 1922, p. 1; "Meets Tragic Death in Fight with Bear; Gruesome Find Near Yellowstone Park," *Twin Falls* (ID) *News*, June 15, 1922, p. 1; "Killed in Fight with Bear," *Bourbon News* (Paris, KY), August 4, 1922, p. 7; "Grizzly Kills Bear Hunter after Fierce Fight in Park," *Colorado Springs* (CO) *Gazette*, June 15, 1922, p. 8.

70. These appeared in the New Orleans *Herald*, *Twin Falls News*, and *Anaconda Standard* stories, cited in the previous note. The Theodore Roosevelt information came from historians Paul Schullery, Bozeman, MT, and Jeremy Johnston, Cody, WY, e-mails to author, December 27, 2012.

71. "Simple Services Mark Obsequies of Bear's Victim," *Twin Falls* (ID) *News*, June 16, 1922, p. 1.

72. "Final Report—Grizzly Bear–Roger May Incident June 25, 1983," October 31, 1983, Gallatin National Forest, West Yellowstone, MT; "Grizzly Kills Man Near West Yellowstone," *Livingston Enterprise*, June 27, 1983.

73. Gordon Stenhouse et al., "Investigation Team Report: Fatality of Erwin Evert from a Bear Attack in Kitty Creek on the Shoshone National Forest on June 17, 2010," July 16, 2010, http://www.fws.gov/mountain-prairie/species/mammals/griz zly/EvertInvestigationTeamReportFinal.pdf; Kelly Burgess, "Grizzly Bear Kills Hiker near Yellowstone," *Los Angeles Times*, June 21, 2010; obituary of Erwin Frank Evert on findagrave.com, accessed January 1, 2013; Ruffin Prevost, "DNA Tests Match Dead Bear to Mauling," *Billings Gazette*, June 19, 2010.

74. C. J. Baker, "Judge Rules for Government in Bear Mauling Suit," *Powell* (WY) *Tribune*, October 25, 2012, http://www.powelltribune.com/news/item/10271-judge-rules-for-government-in-bear-mauling-suit?tmpl=component&print=1. At the time of this writing, the unsuccessful plaintiff had not appealed the decision.

75. Amanda Ricker and Karrin Ronnow, "'It Was Hunting Me'; Survivor Recounts Mauling," *Bozeman Daily Chronicle*, July 30, 2010, p. 1.

76. U.S. Fish and Wildlife Service and Montana Fish, Wildlife, and Parks Department, "Investigation Team Report: Attacks by a Grizzly Bear in Soda Butte Campground on the Gallatin National Forest on July 28, 2010," August 13, 2010, http://www.fws.gov/mountain-prairie/species/mammals/grizzly/SodaButteCampgroundAttacksInvestiga tionTeamReport.pdf; Matthew Brown, "Survivor of Soda Butte Bear Attack Says She Played Dead," *Bozeman Daily Chronicle*, July 29, 2010; Ricker and Ronnow, "'It Was Hunting Me,'" *Bozeman Daily Chronicle*, July 30, 2010, p. 1; Brett French, "Bear Attack Leaves One Dead," *Billings Gazette*, July 29, 2010, p. 1.

77. Matthew Brown in Associated Press dispatch, "Yellowstone Employee Attacked by Grizzly," e-mailed from Yellowstone Public Affairs Office, September 10, 2007.

78. Dave Hurteau, "Montana Bear Attacks: Could They Have Been Avoided?" *Field and Stream*, January 9, 2008, http://www.fieldandstream.com/pages/montana-bear-attacks-could-they-have-been-avoided.

79. National Park Service, park press release, June 21, 1994; Randy Ingersoll, interview with author, Gardiner, MT, September 6, 1994.

80. National Park news release 13-065, August 15, 2013.

81. For an involved, documented study of bear injuries/deaths including some of the ones mentioned here, see Herrero, *Bear Attacks*.

82. Ibid., 92–93.

4. DEATHS FROM POISONOUS PLANTS

1. Information for this section is from National Audubon Society, *Audubon Society Field Guide to North American Mushrooms*, and John M. Kingsbury, *Deadly Harvest: A Guide to Common Poisonous Plants*.

2. "More Lives Lost," *Cody* (WY) *Enterprise*, August 6, 1947.

3. Kingsbury, *Deadly Harvest*, 61–62.

4. "Death of Ranger Charles Phillips," *Yellowstone Nature Notes* 4, no. 4 (April 30, 1927); "Poisonous Plants," *Yellowstone Nature Notes* 4, no. 5 (May 31, 1927): 3; George Miller, "Memorandum for Chief Ranger's Files: Incidents Relative to the Death of Charles Phillips," April 20, 1927, box W-73, file 145, YNP Archives.

5. Monthly report of superintendent, April 1927, 14–15; Frederic Van de Water, "Nine Months Rest," *Saturday Evening Post*, November 12, 1927.

6. "Man Dies After Eating Water Hemlock," *Jackson Hole* (WY) *Guide*, August 7, 1985; "Poisonous Plant Kills Man in Park," *Livingston Enterprise*, August 5, 1985; Brian O'Dea, interview with author, Mammoth Hot Springs, WY, August 5, 1993.

7. Death certificate of Virginia Hall and autopsy report A-43-71, box A-74, file A7623, YNP Archives.

5. NOXIOUS FUMES AND A DEATH FROM POISONOUS GAS

1. Whittlesey, *Yellowstone Place Names* (2006), 82.

2. Ibid., 88, 205, 240–41.

3. G. L. Henderson, "A Wonderland," January 30, 1884, in Ash Scrapbook, YNP Research Library, 4.

4. "Singular Fatality" [from *Billings Herald*], *Livingston Enterprise*, February 21, 1885, p. 1.

5. "Mrs. Crew Receives Bronze Medal for Son's Heroism," *Gardiner* (MT) *Gateway Gazette*, November 7, 1940, p. 1.

6. S. H. Ash and W. W. Kessler, "Investigation of Gas Hazards at Proposed Bridge Foundation Sites in the Yellowstone National Park" and attachments, U.S. Bureau of Mines, unpublished report, n.d. [1939], YNP Research Library; Earl Johnson, Roundup, MT, letter to Lee H. Whittlesey, September 25, 1995. We have to wonder why no visitors from 1872 to 1938 reported gas problems in Devil's Kitchen. Tours of the cave were given routinely. Perhaps natural conditions in the cave changed. An earthquake could have opened new passageways for gas, or hot-spring activity (which produces gases) could have shifted.

6. DEATHS FROM LIGHTNING

1. Whittlesey, *Yellowstone Place Names*, p. 97; Whittlesey, *Wonderland Nomenclature*, 460–61; author's conversation with Jim Peaco, Swan Lake Flats, WY, August 13, 1993.

2. Traveler W. H. Dudley passed by the spot soon after and stated, "While at the lake, I saw the boat; the sail was badly burned and the mast shattered." Dudley, *The National Park from the Hurricane Deck of a Cayuse*, 73.

3. A passerby observed: "All would have lost their lives had not the boat, which was fortunately near the shore, drifted in, for the electric current had made a hole in the

bottom." Alfred Gurney, "A Ramble Through the United States, February 3, 1886," unpublished manuscript, Montana State University, 18–19.

4. E. T. Allen, "Early Yellowstone Incidents," *Yellowstone Nature Notes* 7, no. 5 (May 1930): 25.

5. John H. Renshawe, November 14, 1926, in Marguerite Lindsley, "Acoustic Phenomena over Yellowstone Lake," in National Park Service, *Ranger Naturalists' Manual* (National Park Service, 1928), Yellowstone National Park Library, pp. 120–21.

6. This was according to the local newspapers and John Renshawe. Elwood Hofer passed by the spot in February 1887, and noted that the grave was still there: "On a hill to our left was the grave of a man struck by lightning while out on the lake in a boat. He was connected with the Geological Survey. The wind had drifted the snow away from the grave, leaving it in plain sight." Probably Hofer saw only the remains of the grave and did not realize that the relatives had claimed the body. Hofer, "Winter in Wonderland," *Forest and Stream*, April 28, 1887, 294.

7. [G. L. Henderson], "Park Letter . . . Death by Lightning," *Livingston Enterprise*, September 12, 1885; "Noticed in Park," *Livingston Enterprise*, September 19, 1885, p. 1; "Local Layout," *Livingston Enterprise*, September 26, 1885; E. T. Allen, "Early Yellowstone Incidents," *Yellowstone Nature Notes* 7, no. 5 (May 1930): 25; Haynes, *Haynes Guide Handbook of Yellowstone National Park*, 119; and J. H. Renshawe in National Park Service, *Ranger Naturalists' Manual*, pp. 120–21. Meteorologists state that so-called "bolts from the blue" on seemingly clear days often originate in clouds that are a long distance from the spot where the lightning eventually strikes.

8. "Local Layout," *Livingston Enterprise*, September 24, 1887. Lamartine gave no date for this story.

9. Whittlesey, *Wonderland Nomenclature*, 124.

10. "Killed by Lightning," *Livingston Enterprise*, September 1, 1894; "'Curley' Rogers Killed by Lightning," *Livingston Post*, August 30, 1894; "Local Matters," September 6, 1894; *Gardiner Wonderland*, August 24, 1905.

11. "Local Layout," *Livingston Enterprise*, June 24, 1899; "Local Matters," *Livingston Post*, June 22, 1899; "Record Book of Interments at the Post Cemetery, Fort Yellowstone," item 155, YNP Archives, p. 2. The notation says "killed by lightning near Golden Gate pass."

12. Monthly report of superintendent, August 1926, 26–27.

13. Monthly report of superintendent, July 1929, 23; death certificate of Robert S. Wright, box A-44, folder 146.13, YNP Archives.

14. "Tragedy Hits Park Visitors," *Billings Gazette*, August 8, 1975. There are also two articles about this incident in the *Livingston Enterprise*.

15. James V. Court, letter to author, January 13, 1997.

16. Mike Pflaum, interview with author, Mount Rushmore National Memorial, February 14, 1993; Brian O'Dea, interview with author, Mammoth Hot Springs, WY, August 5, 1993; Lee Silliman letter to author, June 20, 1995.

17. National Park Service, park press release, July 9, 1986.

18. "Lightning Kills Gardiner Cyclist," *Livingston* (MT) *Enterprise*, September 8, 1997, p. 1; Cheryl Matthews, Yellowstone National Park news release 05-33, June 21,

2005, YNP Archives; "Park Visitors Hurt by Lightning at Old Faithful," *Livingston Enterprise*, June 22, 2005, p. 1; "Lightning Victim Mending," *Livingston Enterprise*, June 23, 2005, p. 1.

7. DEATHS FROM AVALANCHES AND FREEZING

1. "Butte City Locals," from *Butte* (MT) *Daily Miner*, quoted in Bozeman (MT) *Avant Courier*, January 20, 1881, p. 3, column 3.

2. Aubrey L. Haines, personal papers at Montana State University, interview with Ernest Murri and Ward W. Reynolds, May 5, 1968.

3. "Park Notes," *Livingston* (MT) *Enterprise*, February 26, 1884, p. 2, [G. L. Henderson]; "Up-River Mishaps. A Fatal Snowslide," *Livingston Enterprise*, February 23, 1884, p. 3.

4. Haines, *Yellowstone Story*, 1:325; clipping from unknown newspaper, 1884, in Ash Scrapbook, YNP Library, p. 33.

5. Lee Whittlesey, interview with Janice Weekley of Tulsa, OK, a Xanterra Reservations employee, July 13, 2007. A check of the *Livingston Enterprise* for January–March 1886 does not turn up this incident, nor does it show up so far in other area newspapers. A check of Ancestry.com shows that Mira Adeline Robison and Ralph Tuck were not born until the 1890s, so probably Janice misunderstood and Adeline was quoting something that her own parents told her about themselves. Her parents were Martha Elizabeth "Eliza" Teel (1869–1929) and William Addington Robison (1859–1949) who were married in Benton County, AR, in 1884.

6. Haines, *Yellowstone Story*, 2:6; "Buried in a Snowslide," *Livingston Enterprise*, January 15, 1887; "Local Layout," January 15, 1887, p. 3.

7. "Death from Exposure," *Livingston Enterprise*, January 15, 1887, p. 3; Haines, *Yellowstone Story*, 2:6.

8. "Caught by an Avalanche—John Nunley Buried under 15 or 20 Feet of Snow," *Anaconda Standard*, September 14, 1894, p. 1,

9. "Local Matters," *Livingston Post*, January 18, 1894, p. 3; "Local Layout," *Livingston Enterprise*, January 20, 1894, p. 5; "Local Matters," *Livingston Post*, January 25, 1894, p. 3; "In Virginia City," *Anaconda Standard*, January 22, 1894, p. 6.

10. "Local Layout," *Livingston Enterprise*, May 9, 1886, and May 30, 1896; "Local Matters," *Livingston Post*, May 6, 1886, and May 13, 1896; "How Mullery Was Found," May 20; "Died of Exposure," *Livingston Herald*, May 14, 1896.

11. "Record of Death and Interment," pasted into inside front cover of *Record Book of Deaths and Interments*, item 155, YNP Archives.

12. *Annual Report of Superintendent*, 1895, 7; original "Record Book of Interments," handwritten note pasted into inside front cover. His remains were identified by his clothes and watch.

13. Haines, *Yellowstone Story*, 2:195.

14. Haines, interview with Jack Haynes, December 9, 1963, tape 63-5, YNP Archives.

15. George S. Anderson, "Work of the Cavalry in Protecting the Yellowstone National Park," *Journal of the United States Cavalry Association* 10 (March 1897).

16. "Perished from Cold in the Park," *Livingston Enterprise*, December 25, 1897; George Whittaker, scout diary, December 21, 1897, in *Annual Report of Superintendent*, 1898, 33; Elwood Hofer, "Yellowstone Park Notes," *Forest and Stream*, January 8, 1898, 25; Haines, "A Yellowstone Winter Tragedy," *Yellowstone Interpreter* 2, no. 3 (May–June, 1964): 45–47.

17. Hofer, "Yellowstone Park Notes," January 8, 1898, 25; Lieutenant Elmer Lindsley to park superintendent, January 1, 1898, documents 1457–1458, YNP Archives.

18. Apparently this hill is located just across the Gallatin River from "BM 6912" on the 1955 Crown Butte 15-minute quadrangle map. The Martin avalanche probably occurred somewhere near "6922," just south of there.

19. "Death in Avalanche," *Livingston Post*, February 25, 1904. The date of February 17 for the event is given in "Soldier Buried in Snowslide," *St. Paul* (MN) *Globe*, February 23, 1904, p. 2.

20. Edward H. Moorman, "Yellowstone Park Camps History," April 2, 1954, p. 11, YNP Research Library.

21. Record of Interment, 3; Haines, *Yellowstone Story*, 2:197; R. A. Waagner, March 1904, documents 7435–7436, YNP Archives.

22. E. C. Anderson, scout diary, April 20, 1909; S. M. Fitzgerald, scout diary, uses "Sn [*sic*] over Slide" in 1907.

23. Record of Interment, 3; Sergeant Patrick Durkan, Lake Soldier Station, monthly report, May 3, 1904, YNP Archives; Ed Romey to John Pitcher, May 3, 1904, document 7203; Samuel Martin to commanding officer, April 27, 1904, document 7241, YNP Archives. Peter Holte also chronicled this version in his "Catching Buffalo Calves," *Forest and Stream*, September 17, 1910, 449.

24. Haines, interview with Raymond Little, April 21, 1961, audiotape, YNP Research Library; Haines, *Yellowstone Story*, 2:198.

25. Haines, interview with Ted Ogston, June 20, 1966, audiotape 63-5, side 2, YNP Research Library.

26. Memories of William Wiggins, Herman Biastack, John Bauman et al., box 3, audiotape 57-2, YNP Archives. This last sentence from Ogston makes a great story, but it cannot be true, as Harry Trischman did not enter government service until several years after 1904.

27. Post circular, National Archives, record group 98, October 18, 1908, as quoted in Richard A. Bartlett, *Yellowstone: A Wilderness Besieged*, 273–74. See also Record Book of Interments, 4; and William Nichols to H. W. Child, October 21, 1908, box YPC-97, YNP Archives.

28. "Body of Scout Jones Found in Bear Creek," *Livingston Enterprise*, July 10, 1911.

29. Stephen Carpenter, U.S. Land Office, to commanding officer, December 17, 1910; and major [Lloyd Brett] to E. U. Tuttle, December 21, 1910, both in box 28, item 58, file "180 Lost, Stolen, or Strayed," YNP Archives; "Shoe Leads to Finding Remains of Lost Hunter," *Anaconda* (MT) *Standard*, October 10, 1913, p. 11.

30. Pronounced "Ray's," this pass was named for one of the area's earliest residents, George Rea.

31. Bert Corbin's story is taken from the following sources: "Body of Corbin, the Missing Banker, Found Lying in Deep Snow Near the Summit of Reas Pass Near the Park Line," *Idaho Register* (Idaho Falls, ID), December 13, 1910, p. 2; "Banker Perishes Pursuing an Elk," *The Call* (San Francisco, CA), December 12, 1910, p. 1; "Banker and Faithful Horse Die Together," *Evening Standard* (Ogden, UT), December 13, 1910, p. 8; "Body Found in the Snow," *Salt Lake Herald-Republican*, December 12, 1910, p. 1; "Heart Failure May Have Been Responsible," *Idaho Statesman* (Boise, ID), December 13, 1910, p. 1; "Finding of Body Clears Up Mystery Surrounding Disappearance of Corbin," *Idaho Statesman*, December 12, 1910, pp. 1–2; "Scouring Hills for Missing Boise Man," *Idaho Statesman*, November 25, 1910, p. 1; "Corbin's Wife May Join in Search," *Idaho Statesman*, November 26, 1910, p. 1; and "U.S. Soldiers Join in Hunt for Corbin," *Idaho Statesman*, November 28, 1910, p. 1.

32. Sergeant James P. Brooks, weekly outpost report, March 31, 1914, in item 126, YNP Archives; "Wyoming News," *Big Piney* (WY) *Examiner*, April 9, 1914, p. 2.

33. Max Haw's story is taken from the following sources: "Lost in Yellowstone Park," *Galveston* (TX) *Daily News*, April 9, 1906, p. 3; "Skied through Yellowstone," *Riverside* (CA) *Independent Enterprise*, March 14, 1906, p. 1; "Tours Yellowstone Park in Winter," *Seattle* (WA) *Daily Times*, March 15, 1906, p. 11; and "Arrives at Helena," *Duluth* (MN) *News-Tribune*, March 25, 1906, section II, p. 4.

34. Bartlett, *Yellowstone: A Wilderness Besieged*, 269.

35. "An Army Officer Meets Tragic Death," *Livingston Enterprise*, January 10, 1916; death certificate in item 64, file 313, YNP Archives.

36. Copied pages from Bessie Haynes Arnold diary, handwritten entry, no date, and untitled newspaper clipping dated January 22, 1916, in same diary, YNP manuscript file; Marguerite Lindsley Arnold, "Early Impressions," *Yellowstone Nature Notes* 11, nos. 3–4 (March–April 1934): 16. Bessie Arnold stated that the accident occurred at Minerva Terrace, which is probably an error. This incident is also mentioned by Ray Little in his interview. See also "Army Officer Killed in Snowslide Mishap," *Oakland* (CA) *Tribune*, January 10, 1916, p. 10.

37. Haines, "Landscape Alterations Map 1870 to 1967," National Park Service map 6316, September 1967, site 233.

38. Monthly report of superintendent, April 1920, 19–20; *Annual Report of Superintendent*, 1920, 137; "Discovery of Body Clears Up Track Mystery," *Livingston Enterprise*, April 24, 1920.

39. Hugh Galusha's story is taken from the following sources: "Galusha Loved the Country Where He Died," *Independent-Record* (Helena, MT), February 2, 1971, p. 1; Jim Klobuchar, "Snowmobile Trip Ends with Death," *Billings Gazette*, February 1, 1971, p. 1; "Tragedy Blamed on Freezing Rain," pp. 1, 6; "Hugh Galusha Dies in Snow Cave," *Independent-Record* (Helena), February 1, 1971, p. 1; "Tragedy Strikes Snowmobilers," *Billings Gazette*, February 2, 1971, p. 3; and Jim Klobuchar, *Where the Wind Blows Bittersweet*, pp. 32–77.

40. Author's interviews with Dr. Bob Crabtree, April 1, 1993, Bozeman, MT; Kerry Murphy, April 7, 1993, Mammoth, WY; and Andrew Mitchell, November 12, 1993, Mammoth, WY.

41. Author's interview with Diane Ihle [Renkin], Gardiner, MT, December 6, 1992.

42. "Researcher Killed in Park Avalanche," *Bozeman Chronicle*, February 24, 1992; "Avalanche Kills Man," *European Stars and Stripes* (Darmstadt, Germany), February 26, 1992, p. 7. The case incident report for this incident is in box W-222, YNP Archives.

43. "Avalanche Claims Cut Bank Teen," *Billings Gazette*, February 16, 1993; "Two-Top Avalanche Takes Life of Young Montana Rider," *West Yellowstone* (MT) *News*, February 25, 1993.

44. Marsha Karle, National Park Service, Yellowstone National Park news release 99-33, May 29, 1999, YNP Archives.

45. "Man Found Dead Along Roadway," *Livingston* (MT) *Enterprise*, December 8, 2009, p. 1; "Man Found Dead Alongside Road ID'd," *Livingston Enterprise*, December 9, 2009, p. 1; "Park County Releases Name of Man," *Missoulian* (MT), December 10, 2009.

46. "Bozeman Man, One Other Killed in Cooke City Avalanches," *Bozeman* (MT) *Daily Chronicle*, January 2, 2012, p. 1; "Cooke City Avalanche Victims Had Been Warned to Turn Back," *Missoulian* (MT), January 6, 2012; "Obituaries David L. Gaillard," *Bozeman Daily Chronicle*, January 4, 2012.

47. My story of Rick Hutchinson's death is culled from the following sources: John Lounsbury and National Park Service, case incident record 97-0442, in box W-222, folder "Hutchinson SAR, 1573-0703-HMR," YNP Archives; National Park Service, "Search Takes Place in Yellowstone National Park," park press release 97-29, March 5, 1997; "Yellowstone National Park Employee Dies in Accident," 97-30, March 6, 1997; "Second Avalanche Victim Found in Yellowstone National Park," 97-31, March 7, 1997; "Leading Geologist Missing," *Billings Gazette*, March 6, 1997, p. 1; "Geyser Expert Missing," *Livingston Enterprise*, March 6, 1997, p. 1; "Missing Park Worker Found Dead," *Bozeman Chronicle*, March 7, 1997, pp. 1, 8; "Geologist's Body Found," *Livingston Enterprise*, March 7, 1997, p. 1; David Talbot, "Avalanche Victim's Friends Hail Her as Adventurous," *Boston* (MA) *Sunday Herald*, March 9, 1997, p. 16; Jeff Koechling, letter to author, March 22, 1997, YNP Archives.

8. DEATH BY CAVE-IN

1. Record book of interments, YNP Archives, 4.

9. DEATHS FROM FALLING ROCKS

1. George W. Wingate, *Through the Yellowstone Park on Horseback*, 1886, p. 80.

2. Aubrey L. Haines, *Yellowstone Story*, 2:143; Aubrey Haines interview with Ray Little, April 21, 1961, audiotape, YNP Archives; Aubrey L. Haines to Julie Gayde on Ray Little, December 11, 1992, in possession of author.

3. Chester Lindsley to director, August 13, 1917, item 64, file 313, YNP Archives, and death certificate of John W. Havekost in same file.

4. "Rock Injures Girl in Park," *Livingston Enterprise*, July 14, 1972; "Girl Seriously Hurt in Yellowstone Park," *Billings Gazette*, July 14, 1972; John E. O'Dea, "Report of

Accident Other Than Motor Vehicle," field report 1444, July 11, 1972, box A-91, file A7623, YNP Archives.

5. Mike Pflaum, interview with author, Mount Rushmore National Memorial, February 14, 1993.

6. National Park Service, park press release, August 29, 1983; park press release, August 8, 1983; "Victim of Falling Rock Identified," *Billings Gazette*, August 10, 1983; "Illinois Boy Killed in Hiking Accident," *Livingston Enterprise*, August 8, 1983; Board of Inquiry on Pearse, box A118, file 7623, YNP Archives.

10. YELLOWSTONE'S DEATHS FROM FALLING TREES

1. "Accidental Death" [Sheahan], *Livingston Enterprise*, May 20, 1893, p. 1; "Northrup Acquitted" [Barrows], *Livingston Post*, January 25, 1894.

2. "Local News," *Livingston Post*, December 20, 1900.

3. "Local News," *Livingston Post*, January 30, 1902; "Local Layout," *Livingston Enterprise*, February 1, 1902.

4. "Fatal Accident at Cooke City," *Livingston Enterprise*, November 17, 1883, p. 1, A. J. M.; "Local Miscellany," Bozeman *Avant Courier*, November 22, 1883, p. 3.

5. Monthly report of superintendent, July 1936, 16; *Annual Report of Superintendent*, 1937, 47; "Local Boy Is Killed as Tree Falls in Park," *Billings Gazette*, July 9, 1936; "Child Killed and Three Persons Hurt in Wind Storm in Yellowstone," *Butte Standard*, July 9, 1936.

6. Monthly report of superintendent, July 1932, 22, 24; monthly report of superintendent, July 1937, 2.

7. "Massive Cleanup," *Livingston Enterprise*, June 29, 1970.

8. At least five different witnesses saw the funnel cloud and proclaimed it a tornado. I, too, personally saw it, and I possess a photograph of that funnel cloud taken by Norris thermal VIP (volunteer in park) Rocco Paperiello. The tornado's spiral winds snapped numerous trees in their centers at the west end of Elk Park and on the hill west of the Ice Lake trailhead. See National Park Service, park press release, July 12, 1984.

9. Roy Renkin, "A History of Hazard Trees," *Buffalo Chip*, September–November 1992, 24–25.

10. Monthly report of superintendent, October 1953, 12; "Park Worker Killed by Falling Tree," *Livingston Enterprise*, October 31, 1953.

11. "Cooke City Girl Dies in Accident," *Livingston Enterprise*, July 30, 1984.

12. *Lawrence E. Middaugh, Administrator of the Estate of Stephen Athan v. U.S.A.*, Civ. No. 5148, D. Wyoming, May 29, 1968, pp. 34–37.

13. Lee H. Whittlesey, "Governmental Tort Liability in Recreation: A City and Its Parks (With Some Words about Federal Parks)," legal manuscript citing cases, April 23, 1987, YNP Research Library.

14. National Park Service, park press release, May 30, 1984.

15. Department of the Interior, *Where Are the Trees?* National Park Service information pamphlet (Department of the Interior: Yellowstone National Park, 1984).

11. DEATHS FROM FALLS

1. Monthly report of superintendent, July 1924, 54–55; Herman Hanser, M.D., to Horace Albright, July 14, 1924, box A-44, file 146.13; C. P. Donohoe to Horace Albright, July 15, 1924, box W55, YNP Archives. See also "Plunges 1000 Feet into Grand Canyon," undated clipping from *Minnesota Independent* in scrapbook "General 1923–1927," YNP Library.

2. Two Plunge to Death When Car Backs Down Precipice of Canyon," *Livingston Enterprise*, July 15, 1924; "The Canyon Accident," op. cit., 2; "Uncharted Park Trips," unidentified editorial [1924], in box A-44, file 146.13, YNP Archives.

3. "Local Layout," *Livingston Enterprise*, June 30, 1883; "Local Layout," July 10, 1883.

4. Monthly report of superintendent, August 1940, 12; "Wyoming Man Killed in Accident in Park," *Livingston Enterprise*, August 30, 1940; *Annual Report of Superintendent*, 1941, 12.

5. Item 64, file 313, YNP Archives.

6. Monthly report of superintendent, July 1953, 13.

7. "Gardiner Man Dies in 85-foot Bridge Fall," *Livingston* (MT) *Enterprise*, February 16, 2006, p. 1.

8. National Park Service, Yellowstone National Park news releases: 05-71, September 16; 05-72, September 17; 05-73, September 18, 2005; "Info Sought in Park Deaths," *Billings* (MT) *Gazette*, September 18, 2005, p. 28; "Pair Killed in Fall from Yellowstone Bridge," *Livingston Enterprise*, September 19, 2005, p. 1.

9. A. Bart Henderson in Haines, *Yellowstone Story*, 1:79.

10. Olin D. Wheeler, *Indianland and Wonderland*, 70–71.

11. Herman Haupt Jr., *The Yellowstone National Park*, 145.

12. WKC, "Hand of God Alone," 1897, in scrapbook 4209, 142, YNP Research Library.

13. Quoted in Chris J. Magoc, "The Selling of Wonderland: Yellowstone National Park, the Northern Pacific Railroad, and the Culture of Consumption, 1872–1903," 25.

14. *Record Book of Interments at the Post Cemetery, Fort Yellowstone*, items 154, 155, YNP Archives. Dave Bucknall's pamphlet lists Murphy's grave as number 25a in the post cemetery, but if ever there, it was only temporarily.

15. "Gov'ment Surveyor Killed," *Deseret Evening News* (Salt Lake City, UT), August 15, 1904, p. 3.

16. "Utah Youth Saves Chum from Death," *Salt Lake* (UT) *Herald-Republican*, July 11, 1910, p. 6.

17. Monthly report of superintendent, August 1926, 29; "Mrs. Grace Carps [*sic*] of Denver Plunges to Death Over Wall of Yellowstone Canyon," *Park County News* (Livingston, MT), August 20, 1926; "Re: Mrs. Grace Crans . . . Denver, Colo.," box W-11, YNP Archives; "Woman Tourist of Denver Killed in Grand Canyon Fall," *Livingston Enterprise*, August 19, 1926; "Uncharted Park Trips," August 20 editorial; "Woman Falls Thousand Feet to Death in Yellowstone," undated clipping; Lloyd P. Banker, undertaker, to Yellowstone National Park, August 20, 1926; death certificate of Grace Crans, box A-44, file 146.13, YNP Archives. The *Enterprise* stated about their route that the first two hundred feet was sloping but timbered, followed by one hundred feet of steep, bare slope, and followed finally by a nine-hundred-foot vertical drop.

18. Monthly report of superintendent, August 1964, 8; "Fall into Canyon Is Fatal," *Livingston Enterprise*, August 15, 1964. This article gave his last name as Dailey.

19. Monthly report of superintendent, November 1965, 4; "Girl from Germany Dies in Fall in Yellowstone Park," *Livingston Enterprise*, November 9, 1965.

20. "Two Missing in Park River," Idaho Falls *Post-Register*, July 2, 1973; "Special Incident Report," July 1, 1973, box A-74, file A76-23, YNP Archives.

21. National Park Service, park press release, September 2, 1983; "Board of Inquiry, Death of Laurie Miller," September 16, 1983, box A-118, file A7623, YNP Archives.

22. Mike Pflaum, interview with author, Mount Rushmore National Memorial, February 14, 1993.

23. National Park Service, park press release, August 7, 1988; "Young Boy Rescued after Tumbling 200 Feet into Yellowstone Canyon," *Livingston Enterprise*, August 7, 1988; Sholly, *Guardians of Yellowstone*, 201–2; Stephen Dobert, interview with author, Mammoth, WY, January 26, 1993.

24. Sholly, *Guardians of Yellowstone*, 200–201; National Park Service, park press release, February 25, 1990; "Local Boy Dies in Fall in Yellowstone Park," *Livingston Enterprise*, February 26, 1990.

25. "Park Kept Report on Boy's Death a Secret," *Livingston Enterprise*, June 23, 1992; "Family Gets Nothing in Park Death," *Billings Gazette*, July 3, 1993.

26. Monthly report of superintendent, July 1925, 41; "Park Visitor Attempts Perilous Side Trip," *Livingston Enterprise*, July 10, 1925; "Accident Victims to Homes with Body of Husband-Father," July 18; death certificate of Isadore M. Kisber, box A-44, file 146.13, YNP Archives.

27. National Park Service, Yellowstone National Park press release, September 17, 1995; "Man Dies from Fall in Grand Canyon of Yellowstone," press release 95-54, September 9, 1995; "Visitor Falls 400 Feet to Death," unlabeled undated newspaper clipping, about September 21, 1995, Laramie, WY.

28. National Park Service, Yellowstone National Park press release 99-62, September 5, 1999; "Billings Woman Falls to Death in Park," *Livingston Enterprise*, September 7, 1999, p. 1.

29. "Teen Dies after Fall from Inspiration Point," National Park Service, Yellowstone National Park news release 12-035, June 8, 2012; "Canyon Fall Victim's Identity Released," 12-036, June 11, 2012.

30. National Park Service, "Body of Missing Hiker Found in Northwest Yellowstone," park press release 13-055, July 18, 2013; "Angler, Hiker Die in Park," *Livingston Enterprise*, July 19, 2013, p. 1.

31. *Annual Report of Superintendent*, 1956, 15; monthly report of superintendent, July 1955, 18, and October 1955, 12; "Utah Tourist Falls into Yellowstone Canyon and Rangers Search for Body," *Livingston Enterprise*, July 20, 1955; "S. L. Tourist Killed in 500-Ft. Fall," *Deseret News/Salt Lake Telegram* (UT), July 20, 1955, p. 1.

32. "Body Is Found in Yellowstone," *Billings Gazette*, July 10, 1973, p. 14; "Florida Visitor, 18, Victim of Fall at Yellowstone," *Wyoming* (Cheyenne) *State Tribune*, June 29, 1973; National Park Service, park press release, July 10, 1973, box K-23, YNP Archives.

33. National Park Service, park press release, August 15, 1978; "Woman Falls to Her Death in Yellowstone," *Livingston Enterprise*, August 16, 1978. Interestingly, Lois Mayer's body was one of four found by fisherman Dick Miller, whose son, Paul, is a ranger

in the park. Dick Miller found Mayer's body near the mouth of Geode Creek several weeks later. He had also found the grotesque remains of the 1970 murder victim on the river just north of Gardiner, Montana. And he found two other bodies at various times during his many fishing excursions along the Yellowstone River. Said one park ranger upon hearing the Dick Miller story, "I believe I would quit fishing." Mary Lou Miller, interview with author, Mammoth, WY, November 30, 1992.

34. National Park Service, Yellowstone National Park news release 06-33, June 17, 2006; "Tourist Taking Picture Falls to Her Death," *Lawrence* (KS) *Journal World*, June 19, 2006, p. 1; National Park Service, "Friday Night Falling Victim Identified," Yellowstone National Park press release 07-96, October 1, 2007; National Park Service, "Update on Calcite Springs Incident," no date [2007], in possession of author.

35. Report in box A-78, file A7623, YNP Archives; "Park Visitor Killed in 300-foot Plunge," *Livingston Enterprise*, September 16, 1974.

36. "Youth Killed in Yellowstone," *Livingston Enterprise*, May 20, 1976.

37. Robert Bower, interview with author, Idaho Falls, ID, April 1, 1992; National Park Service, park press release, August 18, 1980; "Man Falls to Death in Park," *Livingston Enterprise*, August 18, 1980.

38. National Park Service, park press release, June 21, 1985.

39. National Park Service, park press release, August 1, 1969, box K-22, YNP Archives.

40. Jeff Henry, interview with author, Cinnabar Basin, MT, November 14, 1992; Albert F. Knight, "The Death of a Son," *New York Times*, June 29, 1986; "Yellowstone Accidents Leave 3 Dead 1 Missing," *Billings Gazette*, June 22, 1985. There is also a park press release on this incident.

41. National Park Service, park press release, July 23, 1985; Ranger Mark Marschall, interview with author, Gardiner, MT, November 29, 1992; "Body Recovered, Man Killed in Park," *Livingston Enterprise*, July 23, 1985; Kyle Hannon letter to author, July 20, 1996.

42. "Hiker's Body Found Friday on Fox Peak," *Livingston Enterprise*, July 24, 1989; "Body Found above Cooke City Identified," July 28, 1989.

43. National Park Service, internal e-mailed announcement, September 9, 1995.

44. National Park Service, "Climbing Accident Victims Removed from Canyon," Yellowstone National Park news release, 10-037, May 25, 2010. See also 10-036, same date.

45. Monthly report of superintendent, November 1945, p. 5.

46. Aubrey L. Haines, letter to author, September 27, 1995.

47. Ida McPherren, *Imprints on Pioneer Trails*, 1950, pp. 213, 353.

12. DEATHS FROM FOREST FIRES

1. Micah Morrison, *Fire in Paradise*, 208; "Firefighter Killed Battling Forest Fire," *Livingston Enterprise*, October 12, 1988.

2. "CCC Youth Killed Fighting Forest Fire in Yellowstone," *Livingston Enterprise*, June 23, 1940; monthly report of superintendent, June 1940, p. 2.

3. Whittlesey, *Yellowstone National Park Mile by Mile Guide*, 70. The Blackwater incident is also discussed by Stephen Pyne in *Fire in America*.

14. DEATHS FROM DROWNING

1. "Sandwiches," Bozeman (MT) *Avant Courier*, September 2, 1880, p. 3, column 2; "The Territories," *San Francisco Bulletin*, September 2, 1880, p. 4; "Matthew Carey Drowned," Helena (MT) *Daily Independent*, August 26, 1880, p. 3; and "Montana Melange [Carey exhumed]," *Butte* (MT) *Daily Miner*, September 11, 1883, p. 4.

2. *Livingston Enterprise*, August 28, 1883.

3. Haines interview with Henry Mallon et al., July 5, 1961, audiotape 61-2, YNP Research Library. My account is culled from "Drowned in the Park," *Livingston Enterprise*, August 28, 1883, and other items in this newspaper through the September 22 edition. See also G. L. Henderson in archive document 1448, August 10, 1884, YNP Archives, and appendix B in this book.

4. Swimming pools have long been removed from Yellowstone Park as being incompatible with the idea of naturalness in a national park. After all, Yellowstone Park is not a resort; it is a nature preserve.

5. "Local Layout," *Livingston Enterprise*, June 29, 1889.

6. "Local Layout," *Livingston Enterprise*, April 16, 1898; *Record Book of Interments*, item 155, YNP Archives, p. 2.

7. "Local News," *Livingston Post*, August 31, 1899.

8. *Gardiner Wonderland*, September 7, 1905. "Local Layout," *Livingston Enterprise*, September 9, 1905, says he was age 16 and from Sheridan, WY.

9. "Our Local Field," *Gardiner Wonderland*, July 27, 1905, p. 5.

10. "The Funeral of Oliver Atkins [Adkins]," *Gardiner Wonderland*, June 1, 1905; Lee Whittlesey, archivist, to Tamra Phelps of Somerset, KY (descendant of Oliver Adkins), February 24, 1999, in file H14, YNP Archives; "News of Nebraska," Omaha (NE) *Daily Bee*, June 6, 1906, p. 3, column 5; "New Citizens," Columbus (NE) *Journal*, March 14, 1906, p. 1, column 4.

11. Monthly report of superintendent, August 1925, 32; Vernon Goodwin to Horace Albright, September 1, 1925, box A-44, file 146.13, YNP Archives; monthly report of superintendent, July 1937, 2, 18; *Annual Report of Superintendent*, 1938, 42; *Billings Gazette*, July 8, 1937; monthly report of superintendent, August 1937, 19; "West Yellowstone Youth Dies in Pool," *Bozeman Chronicle*, August 26, 1937; *Annual Report of Superintendent*, 1938, 42; "Young Nebraska Girl Drowns. . . ." *Livingston Enterprise*, July 29, 1947; monthly report of superintendent, July 1947, 11. The official report on Palleson is "Case of Lois E. Palleson, Drowning . . . July 28, 1947," in file 207-05.1, box W-194, YNP Archives.

12. *Record Book of Interments*, item 155, YNP Archives, 5; "Fisherman Finds Body," *Livingston Enterprise*, January 9, 1911; "Dead Soldier Is Identified," January 10, 1911. This article calls him "William Monahan."

13. *Annual Report of Superintendent*, 1918, 52; monthly report of superintendent, July 1918, 15–16; "Soldiers Drown on Fishing Trip," *Livingston Enterprise*, July 24, 1918.

14. "A Sad Death by Drowning," *Livingston Enterprise*, July 8, 1899; bound volume 181, Soda Butte Station log, entry for June 26, 1899; Haines, *Yellowstone Story*, 1:305, 314. Strangely, the *Livingston Post* carried nothing on this incident.

15. Stage driver Herb French remembered it as occurring "just below" the checking station. He probably meant south of the checking station rather than north, because that is where the road crossing was in 1925. Haines interview with Henry Mallon et al., July 5, 1961, audiotape 61-2, YNP Archives

16. "Walter Shaw Meets His Death," *Livingston Enterprise*, June 20, 1925; monthly report of superintendent, June 1925, 29; Haines interview with Mallon et al., and with Ted Ogston, June 20, 1966, audiotape 63-5, YNP Archives; *Livingston Enterprise*, June 19, 1925, and subsequent issues. The Shaw family scrapbook is at the Montana Historical Society, and it contains a number of references to this drowning.

17. "Girl Drowns in Park," *Great Falls* (MT) *Tribune*, September 22, 1925; "Accident Victim Was to Have Been Married," *Livingston Enterprise*, September 23, 1925; death certificate and coroner's report, box A-44, file 146.13, YNP Archives.

18. Monthly report of superintendent, December 1926, 16–17. Collins's death certificate, in box A-44, YNP Archives, indicates that he died from a fractured skull, but the report stresses drowning.

19. Monthly report of superintendent, July 1935, 20; death certificate, box A-44, file 146.13, YNP Archives.

20. Monthly report of superintendent, June 1952, 15.

21. "Man Lost in River," *Montana Standard* (Butte, MT), June 29, 1974, p. 10; "Body Found in Log Jam," *Billings Gazette*, June 30, 1974, p. 21.

22. *Livingston Enterprise*, June 28, July 6, 1982; Jon Dahlheim, interview with author, Mammoth, WY, May 5, 1993.

23. Monthly report of superintendent, October 1936, 15.

24. Monthly report of superintendent, June 1963, 8; "Inquest into Death of J.P. Speitel, Y.P. Company Employee," audiotape in oral history collection, YNP Archives; "Park Employee Killed on Mountain Climb," *Livingston Enterprise*, June 18, 1963.

25. "Livingston Youth Drowns," *Billings Gazette*, February 14, 1982; Board of Inquiry on Olson, box A-I 16, file 7623, YNP Archives.

26. National Park Service, park press release, June 1, 1982; "Man Drowns in Park," *Livingston Enterprise*, June 1, 1982.

27. National Park Service, park press release, January 20, 1983, announcing the closure.

28. Monthly report of superintendent, August 1928, 24; L. J. Hart to H. M. Albright, September 26, 1928; Ernest Miller to Mr. Albright, received September 20, 1928; Harriet Spear to Horace Albright, September 30, 1928; Albright to Roger Toll, December 11, 1929, all in box W-11, Accidents File 149.1, YNP Archives.

29. Monthly report of superintendent, August 1937, 19.

30. Monthly report of superintendent, June 1938, 3.

31. Monthly report of superintendent, July 1947, 11; "Yellowstone Park Employee Drowns in Slide Lake," *Livingston Enterprise*, July 7, 1947.

32. Monthly report of superintendent, July 1947, 11.

33. "Yellowstone Park Worker Drowns," *Billings Gazette*, July 20, 1982; National Park Service, park press release, July 19, 1982; Board of Inquiry on Wilkerson, box A-116, file 7623, YNP Archives.

34. Todd Wilkinson, interview with author, Mammoth Visitor Center, March 1, 1993.

35. A. Bart Henderson, "Journal of Various Prospecting Trips 1871 and 1872 [and 1873]." *Yellowstone Interpreter*, May–June 1964, YNP Library.

36. National Park Service, Yellowstone National Park news release, 09-083, September 11, 2009.

37. Clyde A. Maxey, "SIR [Special Incident Report]: Drowning in Shoshone Lake Lee Burrows," June 17, 1958, in box W-98, file 2623, YNP Archives; monthly report of superintendent, June 1958, 6; "Casper Man Drowns in Park Lake," *Livingston Enterprise*, June 13, 1958. The Hofer story is in Edwin Linton, "Diary of an Expedition Through . . . 1890," pp. 59, 62, Yale Beineke Library.

38. Rodney Plimpton, interview with author, Mammoth Visitor Center, summer 1991.

39. "Park Canoe Accident Kills 2 Scouts," *Billings Gazette*, July 23, 1978; Philip Yancey, "Killer Wind at Shoshone Lake," *Readers' Digest*, June 1980, 111–15; "Report of Review Team," March 30, 1979, box A-109, file A7623, YNP Archives.

40. National Park news release 94-40, July 4, 1994; Michael Ross, interview with author, Grant Village, WY, August 22, 1994; Smokey Sturtevant, interview with author, Mammoth, WY, August 3, 1994.

41. National Park Service, "One Dies and Another Missing . . ." Yellowstone National Park news release 02-37, June 9, 2002; "Second Drowning Victim Found . . ." 02-39, June 17, 2002; "Boy Drowned, Father Missing at Remote Yellowstone [area] Lake," *Livingston Enterprise*, June 10, 2002, p. 3.

42. National Park Service, "Two Idaho Men Found Drowned in Yellowstone's Shoshone Lake," Yellowstone National Park press release 07-87, September 9, 2007.

43. "More Lives Lost in Park Waters," *Cody Enterprise*, August 6, 1947; monthly report of superintendent, August 1947, 9; *Annual Report of Superintendent*, 1947, 21.

44. Monthly report of superintendent, September 1950, 2, 15; *Annual Report of Superintendent*, 1951, 31; "Two Local Anglers Are Drowned in Park," *Livingston Enterprise*, September 11, 1950. This account calls one of the victims Harry Thomas.

45. Monthly report of superintendent, August 1955, 16; *Annual Report of Superintendent*, 1956, 15; monthly report of superintendent, October 1955, 12; "Two Feared Drowned in Lewis Lake," *Livingston Enterprise*, August 15, 1955.

46. "Fisheries Biologist Drowns in Lewis Lake," *Jackson Hole Guide*, July 6, 1967.

47. National Park Service, Yellowstone Park press release 05-50, July 8, 2005; "Search Underway. . . . " 05-47, July 3, 2005; "Search Continues. . . . " 05-49, July 4, 2005; "Body Found in Park Lake," *Livingston* (MT) *Enterprise*, July 15, 2005.

48. Case incident by Mary Lynch and Tom Briney, box W-124, YNP Archives; "Swimmer Drowns in Park," *Billings Gazette*, August 6, 1974, p. 6.

49. National Park Service, "Bozeman Boy Drowns," park press release, August 20, 1975, box K-27; letters in box A-74, file A7623, YNP Archives.

50. National Park Service, "Drowning in Yellowstone National Park," *Yellowstone National Park* news release 03-74, August 7, 2003; "Lisbeth Clair Skollingsberg—Boise," Twin Falls (ID) *Times News*, August 9, 2003, p. A-5.

51. National Park Service, "Taiwanese Woman Drowns in Yellowstone's Firehole River," *Yellowstone National Park* press release 10-083, July 28, 2010.

52. Monthly report of superintendent, September 1933, 15; *Annual Report of Superintendent*, 1933, 6; "Body of Youth Drowned in Yellowstone Found," *Livingston Enterprise*, September 19, 1933; George F. Baggley, "Special Incident Report" and death certificate, box A-44, file 146.13, YNP Archives.

53. "Body of Antler Smuggler Recovered," *Billings Gazette*, September 8, 1982; "Gardiner Horn Hunter Presumed Drowned in Park," *Livingston Enterprise*, September 2, 1982.

54. "Local Layout," *Livingston Enterprise*, July 13, 1889; "Local Layout," July 20.

55. Monthly report of superintendent, August 1939, 1, 10; *Annual Report of Superintendent*, 1940, 5, 32; "Oklahoma Resident Is Park Drowning Victim," *Livingston Enterprise*, August 23, 1939.

56. Monthly report of superintendent, August 1951, 2–3; September 1951, 2.

57. Monthly report of superintendent, July 1955, 18; August 1955, 17; *Annual Report of Superintendent*, 1956, 15; R. J. Murphy, "SIR: Drowning of David Gaskell," August 7, 1955, box W-98, file 2623, YNP Archives. Gaskell's father stated: "He managed to yell, 'Help! Dad!' I ran downstream a short distance, and attempted to reach him . . . but my plastic waders pulled me down. This was the last time I saw him." The body was not immediately recovered.

58. Monthly report of superintendent, August 1955, 16; *Annual Report of Superintendent*, 1956, 15; "Another Boy Drowns in Yellowstone," *Livingston Enterprise*, August 16, 1955.

59. J. W. B. Packard, "SIR: Drowning of Paul Ray Ingebretson," August 31, 1961, box W-98, file 2623, YNP Archives.

60. Monthly report of superintendent, July 1961, 4; unnamed newspaper clipping furnished by descendants, "Davenport Resident Drowns Saving Boy," Bettendorf, IA, July 10, 1961, p. 1; nephew Dale Dose, interview with author, Davenport, IA, February 13, 1993.

61. Kenneth Ashley, memorandum A7623, July 26, 1965, in box A-155, YNP Archives; monthly report of superintendent, August 1965, p. 7.

62. National Park Service, park press release, July 30, 1968.

63. "Man Missing," *Livingston Enterprise*, June 29, 1970; "Searchers Frustrated," June 30; "Two Bodies Found in Park County," July 13; Lynn D. Tucker, "Special Incident Report Involving Keith Alfred Jensen," July 2, 1970, and death certificate, box A-83, file A7616; Board of Inquiry on Jensen, box A-85, file A7623, YNP Archives.

64. "Denver Man Drowns in Yellowstone Park," *Livingston Enterprise*, August 18, 1971; Gerald Mernin, field report 1344, box W-102, YNP Archives; Board of Inquiry (on James H. Hambrick), October 22, 1971, and death certificate, box A-88, file A7623, YNP Archives. Two nearby men swam out to help Hambrick but got in trouble themselves and swam back. He had driven past a high-water warning sign.

65. Letters in box A-74, file A7623, YNP Archives.

66. National Park Service, park press releases, July 20–21, 1981; "Nebraska Man Drowns in Yellowstone," *Billings Gazette*, July 22, 1981; "Body Found in Yellowstone," *Livingston Enterprise*, August 26, 1981; Board of Inquiry on Fullerton, box A-114, file 7623, YNP Archives.

67. National Park Service, park press release, September 8, 1984; John Lounsbury, interview with author, Lake, WY, February 20, 1992.

68. "Man Missing in Park," *Livingston Enterprise*, July 3, 1985; "Body Recovered, Man Killed in Park," July 23; National Park Service, park press release, July 3, 1985.

69. Ranger Dan Krapf, interview with author, Yellowstone Heritage and Research Center, October 22, 2012.

70. National Park Service, Yellowstone National Park news release 05-38, June 25, 2005; 05-50, July 8, 2005; Paula Clawson, "Missing Scout's Shoes Found in River," *Livingston Enterprise*, June 27, 2005, p. 1; "Search for Scout Slows as Hopes of Survival Fade," *Cedar Rapids* (IA) *Gazette*, June 28, 2005, p. 5A; "When Tragedy Strikes at National Parks, Some Families Find Support Among Special Rangers," *Huntingdon* (PA) *Daily News*, July 22, 2005, p. 6.

71. "Car Goes into River," *Livingston Enterprise*, June 30, 2005, p. 3; "Park Worker Missing After River Crash," *Livingston Enterprise*, July 1, 2005, p. 3; National Park Service, "Search and Rescue in Progress for Park Employee," Yellowstone National Park news release 05-45, June 30, 2005; 05-46, "Search and Rescue Operations Continue. . . . " July 1, 2005; 05-50, July 8, 2005; 08-042, "DNA Tests Show Remains Those of Missing Belgrade Woman," June 3, 2008.

72. National Park Service, park press release, August 9, 1979; Curtis Whittlesey, interview with author, November 1992; Board of Review (on the Sigrists), August 29, 1979, box A-109, file A7623, YNP Archives.

73. National Park Service, "Montana Angler Dies in Yellowstone River," park press release 13-056, July 18, 2013; National Park Service, "Fishing Accident Victim Identified," park press release 13-057, July 22, 2013.

74. "Man Swept Away in Park While Fishing," *Livingston* (MT) *Enterprise*, July 16, 2010, p. 1; National Park Service, "Fishing Accident Victim's Identity Released," Yellowstone National Park news release 10-066, July 18, 2010.

75. National Park Service, park press releases, August 8, 1990, and August 9, 1990; John Lounsbury, interview with author, Lake, WY, February 20, 1993; Julianna Pfeiffer to Ruth Lira [Quinn], West Yellowstone, MT, April 10, 1993, original in author's possession.

76. An 1884 article repeated twenty years later, "Twenty Years Ago," *Livingston Enterprise*, August 13, 1904, p. 3.

77. "Man Dies in River Mishap," *Livingston* (MT) *Enterprise*, June 17, 2011, p. 1.

78. F. V. Hayden, *Preliminary Report of the U.S. Geological Survey of Montana . . . Fifth Annual Report*, 97.

79. W. A. Jones, *Report upon the Reconnaissance of Northwestern Wyoming*, 22.

80. Rick Fey, letter to author, September 14, 1998.

81. "Drowned in Yellowstone Lake," *Livingston Post*, July 12, 1894; "Local Layout," *Livingston Enterprise*, July 14, 1894, p. 5.

82. "Drowned in the Park," *Livingston Enterprise*, September 1, 1906; "W. B. Taylor of Bozeman," September 8; G. P. Taylor to John Pitcher, December 13, 1906, in archive document 6280, and John Pitcher to G. P. Taylor, December 17, 1906, Letters Sent, vol. 16, p. 470, YNP Archives; document 7026, August 26, 1907, YNP Archives.

83. Captain M. O. Bigelow to park superintendent, June 1907, archive document 6992. See also Sergeant Arthur Franson to C.O., June 27, 1907, archive document 7023.

84. "Permanent Station Record," vol. 185, p. 201, August 30, 1907, YNP archives.

85. Monthly report of superintendent, August 1933, 21–23; *Annual Report of Superintendent*, 1933, 6; "Three Persons Drown in Yellowstone Lake," *Livingston Enterprise*, September 1, 1933; death certificates of all three persons are in box A-44, file 146.13, YNP Archives.

86. Earl Semingsen, "SIR: Report Concerning the . . . Drowning of Major J. T. Flock"; statement of Richard H. Carmichael, box W-98 and box W-194, YNP Archives; monthly report of superintendent, July 1941, 1; *Annual Report of Superintendent*, 1942, 14; "U.S. Army Officer Drowns in Yellowstone Lake," *Livingston Enterprise*, July 24, 1941.

87. Monthly report of superintendent, August 1942, 2; *Annual Report of Superintendent*, 1943, 18; "Long Beach Man Is Drowned in Lake in Park," *Livingston Enterprise*, August 24, 1942.

88. Monthly report of superintendent, July 1947, 11; William Nyquist, "Special Incident Report," August 7, 1947, box W-193, file A7623, YNP Archives; "3 Feared Drowned Yellowstone Lake," *Cody Enterprise*, July 30, 1947; "Three Wyoming Men Feared Drowned in Yellowstone Lake," *Livingston Enterprise*, July 30, 1947; see also August 18, 1947, for discontinuance of search.

89. Dennis E. Hess, "Kleine-Baldwin Drowning," box W-98, YNP Archives; monthly report of superintendent, August 1947, p. 9; *Annual Report of Superintendent*, 1948, p. 21; "Two More Fishermen Are Drowned in Yellowstone Lake," *Livingston Enterprise*, August 2, 1947.

90. Bridge Bay Marina did not exist until 1962. Prior to then, boat activity on the lake was centered in front of Lake Hotel and at Fishing Bridge.

91. William Nyquist, "Special Incident Report," August 25, 1947, box W-98, YNP Archives; "Ernest F. Shaw, *Cody Enterprise* Owner, Drowns in Yellowstone," *Cody* (WY) *Enterprise*, August 27, 1947; "Dr. Avery Funeral in Iowa Thursday," August 27; "Rites Held for Jackie Metzler," September 3; monthly report of superintendent, August 1947, 9; *Annual Report of Superintendent*, 1948, p. 21; *Livingston Enterprise*, August 25, 1947.

92. "SIR: Schmoker-Hensley Drowning, July 10, 1950" and statement by Joseph Gentry, box W-98, YNP Archives; monthly report of superintendent, July 1950, 1; *Annual Report of Superintendent*, 1951, 31; "Two Drown as Storm Upsets Boat on Yellowstone Lake," *Livingston Enterprise*, July 7, 1950.

93. Hugh B. Ebert, "Disappearance of Lloyd J. Weikel," August 31, 1945, box W-98, YNP Archives; monthly report of superintendent, August 1945, 5; *Annual Report of Superintendent*, 1946, 22.

94. "The Disappearance and Presumed Drowning of Mr. Carl G. Mihlberger," July 20, 1953, box W-98, YNP Archives; monthly report of superintendent, July 1953, 12–13; "Search Abandoned for Drowned Man," *Park County News* (Livingston, MT), July 16, 1953.

95. National Park Service, park press release, May 23, 1980; "Ranger Missing in Yellowstone," *Billings Gazette*, May 24, 1980; Board of Inquiry, June 9, 1980, box A-113, file A7623, YNP Archives.

96. B. Riley McClelland, "SIR: Drowning of Mr. Thomas Hughes," [September 1961], box W-98, file 2623, YNP Archives; monthly report of superintendent, September 1961, 5; "Utah Man Loses Life in Boating Accident," *Livingston Enterprise*, September 12, 1961.

97. "Two Park Employees Are Missing," *Livingston Enterprise*, July 21, 1967; "Park Search Continued," July 22, 1967.

98. "Woman Drowns in Park Lake," *Billings Gazette*, August 11, 1971; "Woman Drowns in Yellowstone Lake," *Livingston Enterprise*, August 10, 1971; Board of Inquiry (on Mrs. Thomas Ward), October 14, 1971, and death certificate, box A-88, file A7623, YNP Archives.

99. "Man Drowns in Yellowstone," *Jackson Hole News*, July 27, 1972; "Man Drowned in Park Lake," *Livingston Enterprise*, July 24, 1972; Elwood Jones, "Boating Accident Report," July 26, 1972, box A-91, file A7623, YNP Archives. There is also a park press release on this incident in box K-22, YNP Archives.

100. Charles Anderson, "Report of Accidents Other Than Motor Vehicle," June 17, 1972, box A-91, file A7623, and death certificate in box A-74, file A7623, YNP Archives.

101. "'There Is a God,' Survivor of Drowning Ordeal Says," Cheyenne *Wyoming State Tribune*, July 21, 1973.

102. "Survivor Recalls Boating Tragedy," Cheyenne *Wyoming State Tribune*, July 20, 1973; H. Kim Jones, e-mail to author, January 29, 2009.

103. "4 on Scout Trip Drown in Icy Yellowstone Lake," *Billings Gazette*, July 26, 1973.

104. "Four Die, Survivor Recalls Terror of Yellowstone Thunderstorm," *Salt Lake Tribune*, July 21, 1973.

105. "Icy Waters Claim 4 in LDS Scout Party," Ogden (UT) *Standard-Examiner*, July 20, 1973; National Park Service, "Four Members of a Boy Scout Canoeing Party Drown in Yellowstone National Park," Yellowstone National Park press release, July 20, 1973, in box K-23, YNP Archives. Wollsieffer was not wearing his life jacket, which proved to be a child's model, good only for fifty pounds, and in poor shape.

106. *Salt Lake Tribune*, July 21, 1973.

107. Ranger Jerry Ryder, interview with author, Mammoth Hot Springs, WY, December 14, 1992.

108. *Salt Lake Tribune*, July 21–22, 1973. See also "Survivor Describes Lake Ordeal," *Post-Register* (Idaho Falls, ID), July 22, 1973. The investigation file on this incident is in box A-78, file A7623, YNP Archives.

109. Technically, there is a conflict as to whether Burris Wollsieffer's body was found. Rangers who participated in the postincident inquiry (box A-78) stated that it was found a few days later. But Mary Eleanor Foutz of Gallup, New Mexico, is friends with numerous people who knew the Wollsieffers personally, and they agree that the body was never found. Lee Whittlesey, letter to Mary Ann Foutz, April 6, 2001, and her response note on reverse.

110. John Dracon to author, November 14, 2008, filed in YNP Archives.

111. Audiotape cassette of inquiry into quadruple drowning, September 7, 1973, box A-78, file A7623, YNP Archives.

112. National Park Service, park press release, June 21, 1980; "Two Idaho Men Drowned in Yellowstone," *Billings Gazette*, June 22, 1980; memorandum from coroner, July 9, 1980, box A-113, file A7623, YNP Archives.

113. National Park Service, park press release, June 21, 1985; "Bodies Found in Park," *Livingston Enterprise*, July 26, 1985; Mike Pflaum, interview with author, Mount Rushmore National Memorial, February 14, 1993; Dan Reinhart, interview with author, Lake, WY, August 12, 1993.

114. "Bison 'Warns' Park Tourist," *Cody Enterprise*, June 25, 1987; National Park Service, park press release, June 19, 1987.

115. "Men Killed in Park," *Livingston Enterprise*, June 13, 1997, p. 1; National Park Service, "Two Die in Boating Accident," Yellowstone National Park press release 97-47, June 12, 1997; press release 97-48, June 13, 1997; NPS, Division of Ranger Activities, Washington, DC, "Boating Accident; Two Fatalities," incident 97-265, June 13, 1997.

15. DEATHS FROM INDIAN BATTLES

1. Haines, *The Yellowstone Story*, 1:22–24; Joel C. Janetski, *Indians of Yellowstone National Park*, 39–55. The seminal works on Indians and Yellowstone National Park are Peter Nabokov and Larry Loendorf, *Restoring a Presence: American Indians and Yellowstone National Park* (Norman: University of Oklahoma Press, 2004) and their *American Indians and Yellowstone National Park* (Mammoth, WY: National Park Service, 2002).

2. William T. Hamilton, *My Sixty Years on the Plains*, 94–95.

3. Philip Sheridan and William Sherman, *Reports of Inspection Made in the Summer of 1877*, 31–32.

4. My account is culled from Andrew J. Weikert, "Journal of the Tour Through the Yellowstone National Park in August and September, 1877," in *Contributions to the Historical Society of Montana* 3 (1900): 153–74; Janetski, *Indians of Yellowstone National Park*, 63–76; Haines, *Yellowstone Story*, 1:216–39; Mrs. Cowan in Schullery's *Old Yellowstone Days*, 19; H. D. Guie and L. V. McWhorter, *Adventures in Geyserland*, 184–86; Hiram M. Chittenden, *The Yellowstone National Park*, 134–39; Mark Brown, "Yellowstone Tourists and the Nez Perce," *Montana Magazine of Western History* 16, no. 3 (1966): 39–40; "Wonderland. Scenes of Bloodshed," Bozeman *Avant Courier*, September 6, 13, 1877, "Stewart's Story," September 27; "News from the Front . . . Charles Kenck and Professor Dietrich Dead," September 6 (see also the October 25 and November 1 editions); and H. McDonald Clark, "Horse Drawn Wagon Once Was His Dental Office," *Great Falls* (MT) *Tribune*, August 5, 1962, Montana Parade section.

5. Hugh L. Scott, *Some Memories of a Soldier*, 62. McPherren, *Imprints*, 178–79.

6. One of the Guie/McWhorter accounts says Dietrich received four bullets.

7. Mary B. Richards, *Camping Out in the Yellowstone*, 1910, p. 26. Like Kenck's, Dietrich's body would eventually be moved to Helena. Chittenden, *Yellowstone*, 138, says Weikert moved both bodies, but McCartney has also been credited. My account of Dietrich's death is culled from Haines, *Yellowstone Story*, 1: 228–33; Chittenden, Yellowstone, 134–39; Mark Brown, "Yellowstone Tourists"; Bozeman *Avant Courier*, September 6, 1877; September 13, 1877; and Guie and McWhorter, general.

8. P. W. Norris, *Fifth Annual Report of the Superintendent of the Yellowstone National Park*, 42.

9. Hiram Chittenden, *The Yellowstone National Park*, 1964, pp. 103–4.

10. Jerome A. Greene, *Nez Perce Summer 1877*, p. 176, quoting S. G. Fisher.

11. E. S. Topping, *The Chronicles of the Yellowstone*, 1968, p. 219; Greene, *Nez Perce Summer 1877*, pp. 194, 207.

12. The name of this man has long been uncertain. In his "Expedition into the Yellowstone Country 1870," James Gourley, a prospector who sometimes traveled with them, called him by a third name: "Greenleaf."

13. Topping, *Chronicles*, 76–77, says "Arrapahoes."

14. Ibid., says this spot was "on a large creek which flows into Clarke's Fork from the right, and about ten miles from where they had been left by Anderson," which was on the river above its canyon. The stream today is Crandall Creek.

15. Caroline Lockhart, "Story of Jack Crandall, Killed by Crow Indians, on Creek Which Bears His Name," *Park County* (MT) *News*, November 23, 1923; Virginia Hansen and Al Funderburk, *The Fabulous Past of Cooke City*, 3; Topping, *Chronicles*, 76–77.

16. Hugh Ebert to chief ranger, April 12, 1944, 2–3, YNP Archives.

17. Thomas Michener, unpublished history of Gallatin Canyon, 1917–1921, as quoted in Janet Cronin and Dorothy Vick, *Montana's Gallatin Canyon: A Gem in the Treasure State*, 13–15.

16. DEATHS FROM FIGHTS

1. Bartlett, *Yellowstone: A Wilderness Besieged*, 300.

2. "Yellowstone Park Camp Is Scene of Tragedy," *Missoulian*, July 15, 1933; "Youth Died of Brain Injury," *Bozeman Chronicle*, July 16, 1933.

3. Whithorn, *Photo History of Aldridge*, 164; "Killed in Fight," *Livingston Post*, May 14, 1903; "Both Bound Over," May 28; "Fight for His Life," July 9. The newspaper refers to him as Frank Chiplock.

17. A DEATH FROM DIVING

1. *Annual Report of Superintendent*, 1919, 92.

2. Monthly report of superintendent, July 1940, 10.

18. DEATHS FROM HORSE, WAGON, AND STAGECOACH INCIDENTS

1. Richard A. Bartlett, "Those Infernal Machines in Yellowstone," *Montana Magazine of Western History* 20 (1970):16–19; Haines interview with Huntley Child Sr., audiotape 61-3, 1, September 11, 1961, YNP Oral History Collection.

2. Haines, *Yellowstone Story*, 2: 143 and note 81.

3. Aubrey L. Haines, *Norris Soldier Station Historic Structures Report* (Washington, DC: National Park Service, 1969), p. 13, quoting National Archives, Post Returns, Camp Sheridan, September 1888.

4. "Fatal Accident at Cinnabar," *Livingston Enterprise*, August 16, 1890.

5. "The Ticket Agents' Excursion," *Livingston Enterprise*, September 19, 1891; *Record Book of Interments*, 2. "Sgt. Trint," is in "Local Layout," *Livingston Enterprise*, September 19, 1891, p. 3.

6. Record of Interment, 2; "Local Matters," *Livingston Post*, June 7, 1894; "Local Layout," *Livingston Enterprise*, June 2, 1894; "Accidental Death in Park," *Livingston Enterprise*, June 2, 1894.

7. "A Hunter Killed," *Livingston Post*, September 25, 1895, p. 3; "Over a Precipice—Mr. W. A. Babcock Meets Death in the Rocky Mountains," *Cleveland* (OH) *Plain Dealer*, September 27, 1895, p. 8; "Home Again—All That Remains to Earth of W. A. Babcock," *Cleveland* (OH) *Plain Leader*, September 29, 1895, pp. 1–2; "Over a Precipice—W. A. Babcock of Cleveland Meets with a Fatal Accident in the Mountains," *Livingston Enterprise*, September 28, 1895, p. 1. The quote is from "A Sad Return—The Remains of W. A. Babcock Arrive in Cleveland," *Cleveland Plain Dealer*, September 29, 1895, p. 6.

8. Record of Interment, p. 2; "Fatal Accident in Park," *Livingston Enterprise*, August 12, 1893.

9. Park superintendent to Ray and F. A. Hull, September 27, 1910, item 103, file 313, YNP Archives. It is not known whether Hull's grave was ever moved. It may be the grave we know of at Round Prairie.

10. "Lieutenant Launsberry Dies from Injuries Received in Steeplechase at Fort Yellowstone," *Livingston Enterprise*, October 2, 1912; "Fort Yellowstone Lieutenant Killed," *Anaconda* (MT) *Standard*, October 3, 1912, p. 7; "Cavalry Officer Killed," *Evening Tribune* (Albert Lea, MN), October 3, 1912, p. 1.

11. Monthly report of superintendent, August 1956, 10; *Annual Report of Superintendent*, 1957, 14; "Woman Killed in Mishap in Yellowstone," *Livingston Enterprise*, August 30, 1956; "Canyon Ranger Station, August 30, 1956," box A-83, special incident file, YNP Archives.

12. "Man Dies on Trail Ride," *Livingston* (MT) *Enterprise*, August 1, 2012, p. 1; National Park Service, Yellowstone National Park news release 12-056, July 31, 2012.

13. "Dead and Alone," *Anaconda Standard*, September 8, 1895, p. 1; "Local Layout," *Livingston Enterprise*, September 14, 1895, p. 5; "Local Matters," *Livingston Post*, September 11, 1895, p. 3. Alexander Deckard was buried at Gardiner. The newspapers had trouble with his name, referring to him as "Becker" and "Beck."

14. G. O. Cress to park superintendent, July 23, 1897, document 1330; Driscoll to park superintendent, n.d., document 1480; Driscoll to park superintendent, July 23, 1897, document 1482, YNP Archives; "Local Layout," *Livingston Enterprise*, July 31, 1897. Bliss is in "The Bear Turned on Him," *Minneapolis Journal*, September 14, 1895, p. 3.

15. Record of Interment, 2; "Killed by a Fall," *Butte* (MT) *Weekly Miner*, December 30, 1897, p. 2. This article gives his name as L. H. Brigham.

16. Ida McPherren, *Imprints on Pioneer Trails*, 1950, pp. 175–76, 271.

17. "Killed in Yellowstone Park," *Anaconda* (MT) *Standard*, October 22, 1900, p. 2; "Local Layout," *Livingston Enterprise*, October 22, 1900; Record of Interment, 2.

18. Record of Interment, 2; "Killed on the Road," *Gardiner Wonderland*, July 16, 1903; "Death on the Hill," *Livingston Post*, July 16, 1903; "Local Layout," *Livingston Enterprise*, July 18, 1903, gave the accident location as "about two miles from Gardiner."

19. "Gardiner News," *Livingston Enterprise*, December 28, 1895, p. 1; "Horrible Death," *Anaconda Standard*, December 24, 1895, p. 1.

20. *Gardiner Wonderland*, October 10, 1903; "Local Layout," *Livingston Enterprise*, October 10, 1903, says the wagon struck "a piece of timber" and capsized. Probably it was a culvert made of wood.

21. "Frank Rose Dead," *Gardiner Wonderland*, November 2, 1905; "Local Layout," *Livingston Enterprise*, November 4, 1905; memorandum, November 1, 1905, document 7032, YNP Archives.

22. Record of Interment, 3; M. C. Usher, "Record of Death and Interment," May 31, 1904, document 7034, YNP Archives.

23. "Killed in a Runaway," *Livingston Enterprise*, December 16, 1899; "Neck Was Broken," *Livingston Post*, December 14, 1899.

24. *Livingston Enterprise*, October 9, 1886; "Local Layout," *Livingston Enterprise*, June 21, 1885, p. 3; A. L. Haines interview with Edith Ritchie, November 7, 1961, tape 61-3, YNP Research Library. Ritchie says this first Gardiner death followed a "shooting over water," so if Hartz was not the first burial, he still made the name of the hill relevant.

25. "Salt Lake Woman's Most Tragic Fate," *Deseret Evening News* (Salt Lake City), August 28, 1899, p. 1; "Mrs. Lippman Killed in Yellowstone Park," *Salt Lake* (UT) *Herald*, August 27, 1899, p. 1; "Tragic Death of Mrs. Lippman," *Salt Lake* (UT) *Herald*, August 28, 1899, p. 1. See also "Local News," *Livingston Post*, August 31, 1899; and "Sad Accident in the Park," *Livingston Enterprise*, September 2, 1899, which confirms the location as near "Dwelles," but incorrectly says that it was a stage station in Yellowstone Park (Dwelles was west of the park). The *Post* article incorrectly gave the location as Riverside, inside the park.

Upon learning of the tragic event, P. B. McKenzie, the Monida and Yellowstone Stage Company's agent at Monida, MT, and also coroner for that tiny town, left immediately for the site of the incident. Speaking like a stage company representative who was worried about being sued, McKenzie told the *Deseret Evening News* the story, and the newspaper reported it on August 28 as follows.

The accident happened shortly before [illegible] by the stage being partially overturned on a dugway near Dwelle's, sixty miles from Monida. There were nine passengers on the coach. Several of them were hurt, among them Mrs. Lippman, who it is presumed became alarmed and put her head out of the window. Her head, I understand, came in sudden contact with a tree breaking her neck instantly. I cannot say how badly Mr. Lippman was hurt. His injuries, however, are probably more painful than serious. The driver was Roger Sherman, one of the oldest and safest stage drivers in the Rocky Mountain country. He has been at the business for over twenty years in Montana and never had an accident of serious consequence before. Besides he is a perfectly sober man. I cannot—he cannot account for this one. All we can say is that it was an accident. It was very dark and cloudy at the time, and the wheels seem to have slid down over the embankment, causing a partial turnover. There was, however, no runaway of the horses as reported here. The fact is the horses did not advance the length of the coach after the accident. Had the party been driven fifty yards further, it would have been out of the mountains and in the rolling country. It seems to me like a case of fate. The driver was terribly wrought up over the matter and asked to be relieved from further duty saying he could not drive a team over that road again after the death of that beautiful Salt Lake lady.

26. "Tragic Death of Mrs. Lippman," *Salt Lake* (UT) *Herald*, August 28, 1899, p. 1.

27. "Fort Yellowstone," and "Our Local Field," *Gardiner Wonderland*, October 8, 1904; "Local Layout," *Livingston Enterprise*, October 15, 1904; M. C. Usher, "Record of Death and Interment," October 4, 1904, document 7033, YNP Archives. Transportation boss Berg Clark claimed many years later that the coach driver's name was Scotty and that he had a drinking problem. Audiotape interview with Berg Clark, Gallatin Oral History Project, YNP Research Library.

28. "Stage Accident," *Livingston Enterprise*, October 5, 1907.

29. "Local Layout," *Livingston Enterprise*, August 17, 1907.

30. "List of injuries received by D. E. MacKay, August 13, 1910" and Superintendent Benson's certification, August 17, 1910, item 103, file 313, YNP Archives; "Accident in the Park—Coach Loaded with Passengers Strikes a Cave-in and Sinks," *Ogden* (UT) *Standard*, August 13, 1910, p. 7; "Road Caves in, One Dead," *Oregonian* (Portland, OR), August 14, 1910, p. 1; "Killed at Yellowstone Park," *New York Tribune*, August 14, 1910, p. 1; "A Fatal Accident," *Livingston* (MT) *Enterprise*, August 20, 1910.

31. Haines interview with Huntley Child Sr., September 11, 1961, audiotape 61-3.

32. Haines, *Yellowstone Story*, 2:143.

33. Her uncle was Amos Shaw, himself a park concessioner, who would later lose his son Walter to a drowning incident on Gardner River.

34. Herb French, a stagecoach driver, remembered many years later that this wreck happened "above the reservoir," probably just north of Silver Gate, and also that Roy Armstrong was the driver in this incident, although his compatriot Henry "Society Red" Mallon disagreed, believing the driver to have been "Nez Keef" and the vehicle to have been a Wylie stagecoach. A. L. Haines interview with Henry Mallon et al., July 5, 1961, audiotape 61-2, YNP Archives.

35. "Miss Bodge Killed," *Livingston Enterprise*, August 13, 1910.

36. Haines interview with Henry Mallon et al.

37. L. M. Brett to director [of NPS], July 25, 1916, item 64, file 313, YNP Archives; "Eight Injured in Wild Yellowstone Park Runaway," *Livingston Enterprise*, July 25, 1916; "Colonel Brett Comments on Accident," July 26, 1916.

38. Haines interview with Huntley Child Sr., YNP Archives.

19. DEATHS FROM ACCIDENTAL
AND SELF-DEFENSE SHOOTINGS

1. Monthly report of superintendent, November 1938, pp. 1–2; December 1938, p. 3; *Annual Report of Superintendent*, 1938, p. 41.

2. William L. Kearns, untitled thirteen-page reminiscence of his life at Mammoth 1934–1940 with photos, January 27, 2004, pp. 1–2, YNP Library.

3. "The Gardiner Homicide," *Livingston Enterprise*, June 26, 1886; "The Acquittal of Ferguson," October 23.

4. "The Cooke Homicide," *Livingston Enterprise*, October 1, 1892; "Malloy Acquitted," January 14, 1893.

5. "Local News," *Livingston* (MT) *Post*, August 31, 1899.

6. Park Historian Aubrey L. Haines to chief park naturalist, April 19, 1961, on "Anecdotes related by Jack Haynes this afternoon," in box H-2, file H-14 "Area and Service History, 1957–1962," YNP Archives, pp. 2–3.

7. "Held for Trial," *Livingston Enterprise*, May 11, 1907; "In Self Defense," May 18.

8. "Guarded Her Husband's Dead Body from Coyotes and Timber Wolves," *Pocatello* (ID) *Tribune*, September 5, 1908, p. 1; *Pocatello City Directory*, 1909, p. 91; "Brave Woman Keeps Wolves from Body of Dead Husband," *Salt Lake* (UT) *Tribune*, September 7, 1908, p. 3; "Pocatello, Ida," *The Intermountain Catholic* (Salt Lake City, UT), September 12, 1908, p. 3; "Remains of Late W. L. Escher Followed to Grave by Many Sorrowing Friends," *Deseret Evening News* (Salt Lake City, UT), September 12, 1908, part 2, p. 24.

9. W. F. H[atfield], "Play with the Bears," no date [probably 1894] in scrapbook 4209, p. 56, YNP Library.

10. "M'Cune Inquest on for Today," *Livingston Enterprise*, April 8, 1911, p. 1; "Schmidt Is Free," April 9, p. 1; Whithorn, *Photo History of Aldridge*, 168, 171 (photo).

11. In Elmer Lindsley, "A Winter Trip through the Yellowstone National Park," *Harper's Weekly* 42, January 29, 1898, 106.

12. Thomas M. Connery, "The Winter Tragedy of the Yellowstone," *World Wide Magazine*, June 1919, 143.

13. Frederic F. Van de Water, "Nine Months Rest," *Saturday Evening Post*, November 12, 1927.

14. Connery's account refers to the sergeant as "John" Britton, but numerous newspaper accounts call him "Clarence" Britton.

15. Connery, "Winter Tragedy," 143–47.

16. Haines, *Yellowstone Story*, 2:200–201; Connery, ibid.; "Soldier Dead from Sergeant's Bullet," *Livingston Enterprise*, April 2, 1912; "Sergeant in Yellowstone Shoots Two of Command," April 6; "Sergeant Britton's Trial to Take Place Next Monday," May 9; "Fort Yellowstone Men Under Arrest," June 10. See also "Sergeant Shot Man in Self-Defense," *Ogden* (UT) *Examiner*, May 18, 1912, p. 4; "Accused Sergeant Will Not Talk About Shooting," *Anaconda* (MT) *Standard*, April 5, 1912, p. 8; and "Additional Proceedings of a Board of Officers Convened at Fort Yellowstone, Wyo . . . April 17, 1912," in RG 393, part V, entry 11, Fort Yellowstone, WY, box 16, file 1022, National Archives.

17. L. W. "Gay" Randall, *Footprints Along the Yellowstone*, p. 86; "Charles Huntsman of Gardiner," *Livingston Enterprise*, May 2, 1914; "Trial of George Mack," May 23; "Day Spent in Arguments," May 25; "George Mack Exonerated," May 26.

20. YELLOWSTONE MURDERS

1. "Murder at Cooke City," *Livingston* (MT) *Enterprise*, July 16, 1883, p. 1. Clarence Stephens, formerly the park's assistant superintendent, and Cooke resident Zed H. Daniels served on the inquest jury. See also "Cooke City Murder—Frank Young Shoots and Kills His Partner, Daniel McCarthy," *Bozeman Weekly Chronicle*, July 18, 1883, p. 3.

2. "Dakota and Montana," St. Paul *Daily Globe*, November 11, 1883, p. 5; "Dakota and Montana," November 15, 1883, p. 5; "Brief Items," Helena (MT) *Independent*, November 11, 1883, p. 5; "Amalgam," *Daily Miner* (Butte, MT), December 13, 1883, p. 1, quoting *Bozeman Courier*.

3. "Brief Items," Helena *Independent*, December 14, 1883, p. 5; "Amalgam," *Daily Miner* (Butte, MT), December 21, 1883, p. 4; "Brief Items," Helena *Independent*, December 21, 1883, p. 5; "A Murderer Hanged," *New York Times*, December 28, 1883, p. 2; "Supreme Court," Helena *Independent*, January 8, 1884, p. 5; "Montana Matters," Helena *Independent*, February 21, 1884, p. 7.

4. "Dakota and Montana," St. Paul *Daily Globe*, June 26, 1884, p. 7; "The Territories," *Daily Miner* (Butte, MT), November 30, 1884, p. 1.

5. William Hardman, *A Trip to America*, 141; EGD [Elbridge Gerry Dunnell], "In the National Park," *New York Times*, September 10, 1883, p. 2.

6. Graves there contained Mary Foster, John Fogerty, Thomas P. Parker, and perhaps an unnamed workman.

7. My sources do not state whether or not Zutavern's body was returned to the Mammoth cemetery afterward, but presumably it was, and he apparently is thus in one of the fourteen graves still located there. See also "Another Murder," *Bozeman Weekly Chronicle*, August 29, 1883, p. 3.

8. My account is culled from the following sources: "Fatal Shooting at Gardiner" and "Local Layout," *Livingston Enterprise*, August 22, 1883; "By Telegraph. Details of the Killing at Gardiner," August 23; "Weber's Capture" and "The Gardiner Shooting Affair," August 24; "Local Layout," August 25; "Webber [*sic*] Pardoned," June 16, 1888. For more on the Trischman family, see Elizabeth A. Watry, *Women in Wonderland: Lives, Legends, and Legacies of Yellowstone National Park*, pp. 37–41.

9. "Butchered a Babe," *Livingston Post*, June 8, 1899, p. 1; "Shocking Infanticide," *Livingston Enterprise*, June 10, 1899, p. 1.

10. *Annual Report of Superintendent*, 1899, 14, says she was at first charged with murder in federal court.

11. "Local News," *Livingston Post*, July 13, 1899.

12. "Local News," *Livingston Post*, January 17, 1901.

13. Haines, *Yellowstone Story*, 2:365, 415n69, 447–48.

14. Both the gravestone and the *Livingston Enterprise* spell the name *Trieschman*. Contemporary historians Aubrey Haines and Richard Bartlett as well as the *Livingston Post* spell it *Trischman*, and this appears to be the correct spelling, because document 3615, YNP Archives, contains George Trischman's signature.

15. Edward's brother John V. Callaghan indicated that the first words out of the girl's mouth while she was standing on the road were, "I am soaking wet; they pushed me in the lake," and he wrote this with quotation marks around those words, as if he

remembered it clearly. After she was in the car, John stated the following about what she said to them: "She was very angry at the couple and said they had thrown her in the lake. She retaliated by throwing her wallet into [the] lake and then going down in [the] water [after it], and [thus] attempting suicide. She said, 'I did a poor job of it.'"

I interpret this to mean that she was in the lake twice and/or was worried that the couple would steal her wallet and/or was depressed at her own wretched condition, but regardless this was apparently how she lost her wallet. John Callaghan also stated: "She seemed to have mentioned dope sometime [at some point] and looking [at] her [I] thought perhaps she might have been dope[d]. [When] [w]e could not rouse her [that morning], [w]e all fel[t] she must not be drunk after all and took her to the Ranger Station." All of this information is carried in the written statements of the Callaghans.

16. The story of Henrietta Ross Bailey is culled from the following sources: National Park Service, "Case of Henrietta Ross, August 24, 1947," file 207-05.1, including the report of R. P. Kramer, agent in charge, Federal Bureau of Investigation, Denver, CO, February 17, 1948, in box W-194, YNP Archives; "Local Authorities Investigating Mystery Death of Carnival Dancer," *Cody* (WY) *Enterprise*, September 3, 1947; "Mystery Death of Girl in Yellowstone Park Is Probed," *Livingston* (MT) *Enterprise*, September 13, 1947, copy in box A-196, YNP Archives; "Park Authorities Seek Identification of Girl," *Billings* (MT) *Gazette*, September 13, 1947, p. 10; "Park Authorities Seek Identity of Girl Who Died Mysteriously," *Independent-Record* (Helena, MT), September 15, 1947, p. 2; "Probe into Death of Girl to Be Considered Closed," *Montana Standard* (Butte, MT), September 19, 1947, p. 9; Riverside Cemetery District, Cody, WY, burial index for Henrietta Ross Bailey, on Internet, accessed November 14, 2012. For phenobarbital and alcohol, see "One Thing Is No Mystery: Lethal Nature of a Mix," *New York Times*, http://www.nytimes.com/1997/03/28/us/one-thing-is-no-mystery-lethal-nature-of-a-mix.html.

17. "SIR: Death of Infant at Fishing Bridge," September 15, 1952, box W-98, YNP Archives; "Girl Is Held on Charge of Killing Baby," *Livingston Enterprise*, September 15, 1952; "Girl Denies Murder Charge," October 1; "Mother Accused of Killing Baby," *Deseret News*, October 2; item in box W-59, YNP Archives; monthly report of superintendent, September 1952, 15; "Unwed Mother Gets Probation in Child Death," *Wyoming Eagle* (Cheyenne, WY), November 27, 1952; "Girl Pleads Innocent in Death of New-Born Child," *Wyoming Eagle*, October 1, 1952, p. 1.

18. National Park Service, park press release, June 12, 1978; "Runaway Charged with Park Killing," *Livingston Enterprise*, June 12, 1978; Jerry Phillips to Tim Bommer, March 9, 1979, box A-111, file A76, YNP Archives. The official case incident report for this event is in box W-223, YNP Archives.

19. "Murder Victim's Body Found in Park," *Livingston Enterprise*, September 9, 1985; "Local Indicted for Park Murder," September 30; "Nickelson Enters Plea," October 9; "Jury to Hear Death Evidence," October 24; "Teen Suspect Arrested in Park Slaying," *Billings Gazette*, September 10, 1985.

20. "Two Bodies Found in Park County," *Livingston Enterprise*, July 13, 1970; "No Parts of Body Located," July 14; "Piece Together Bizarre Crime," July 15; "Waive Extradition in Torso Murder Case," July 16; "Accused Slayers Being Held Here," July 20 (see also editions of July 17, 20, 27, 31, August 3, 4, 8, 17). "Stroup Enters Innocent Plea,"

Livingston Enterprise, September 8; "Baker Pleads Guilty; Sentenced to Life," October 20; "Baker Testifies at Trial," November 19; "I Did the Crime: Baker," November 20; "Shanstrom Gives Stroup Ten Years," December 15; "Cannibal Killer Trying to Work Out Parole Plan," May 8, 1985.

21. "Another Park County Horror," *Livingston Enterprise*, April 16, 1898; "Second Degree," July 2; "Webster Sentenced," July 9. John Webster's photo and Mary Criswell's reaction to it are in Whithorn, *Photo History of Aldridge*, p. 172.

22. "Local Layout," *Livingston Enterprise*, July 25, 1885; "Twenty Years Ago [sentencing of Jack Stevenson]," April 7, 1906, p. 3.

23. "It Was Rockinger," *Livingston Post*, July 13, 1899; "District Court," October 12; "Shooting at Jardine," *Livingston Enterprise*, July 3, 1899; "His Wound Fatal," July 15; "It Was Voluntary Manslaughter," October 14; "Justice Meted to Criminals," October 21; superintendent to John Rees, October 13, 1903, item 103, file 313, YNP Archives.

24. Archive document 7954, YNP Archives.

25. "Riot and Murder," *Livingston Enterprise*, June 8, 1907; "Held for Trial," July 15, 1907; "Buried at Butte," July 15; "Hanlon on Trial," November 23; "Thirty Years," November 30.

26. The name Hanlon Hill does not appear on the 1919, 1933, or 1939 maps of "Absaroka National Forest," but was probably in local usage in the Jardine area and appears on the 1955 fifteen-minute map of Gardiner, Montana.

27. "Tragedy Number Three," *Livingston Enterprise*, July 6, 1907.

28. "A Strange Case," *Livingston Enterprise*, July 13, 1907; Whithorn, *Photo History of Aldridge*, 164, 166; S. B. M. Young to secretary, July 10, 1907, Letters Sent, vol. 17, 216, YNP Archives.

29. Whithorn, *Photo History of Aldridge*, 169; "Homicide at Horr," *Livingston Enterprise*, September 17, 1892; "Verdict of Guilty," January 28, 1893; "Not Guilty," January 27, 1894; "Northrup Acquitted," *Livingston Post*, January 25, 1894; "Local News," February 1, 1894.

30. Whithorn, *Photo History of Aldridge*, 165–66, 169 (photo); "Shot in Cold Blood," *Livingston Enterprise*, December 28, 1895, p. 1; "Fatal Christmas Joke," January 4, 1896.

31. Whithorn, *Photo History of Aldridge*, 167; "Voluntary Manslaughter," *Livingston Enterprise*, January 25, 1896, p. 1; "District Court," February 8, p. 1; "Tracy Killed Him," *Anaconda (MT) Standard*, December 28, 1895, p. 1; "About the Tragedy . . . A Repulsive Old Hag Mixed Up in It," *Anaconda (MT) Standard*, January 5, 1896, p. 9.

32. "A Killing at Horr," *Livingston (MT) Herald*, January 2, 1896; "Tragedy at Horr," *Anaconda (MT) Standard*, December 27, 1895, p. 1; "About the Tragedy—Details of the Cold Blooded Murder at Horr on Christmas Day . . . A Repulsive Old Hag Mixed Up in It," *Anaconda Standard*, January 5, 1896, p. 9; "Tracy's Plea," *Anaconda Standard*, January 26, 1896, p. 8; "Tracy's Trial," *Anaconda Standard*, January 23, 1896, p. 2; "District Court," *Livingston Enterprise*, February 8, 1896, p. 1.

33. Whithorn, *Photo History of Aldridge*, 167–68; "Homicide at Horr," *Livingston Enterprise*, April 2, 1898; "Second Degree," May 7; "Rolla Case Reversed," December 10; "A Righteous Verdict," January 28, 1899; "Death of Mike Rolla," August 19.

34. "Steward Perhaps Murdered," *St. Paul (MN) Globe*, June 12, 1903, p. 4.

35. Lucille Nichols Patrick, *The Best Little Town by a Dam Site*, pp. 36, 100; "Cherry Spring Ranch, Home of A.E. Swanson," undated, untitled newspaper clipping (with photo) in Park County (WY) Archives; "Married," *Wyoming Stockgrower and Farmer* (Cody, WY), May 17, 1906.

36. "A Sad Tragedy," *Wyoming Stockgrower and Farmer* (Cody, WY), August 6, 1908, p. 1; "Murder and Suicide," *Basin* (WY) *Republican*, August 7, 1908, p. 1; "Murder and Suicide," *Big Horn County Rustler* (Basin, WY), August 7, 1908, p. 1; "Shot His Wife Rose," *Columbian* (Bloomsburg, PA), August 13, 1908, p. 6; "Judge Kills Wife and Self," *Muldrow* (OK) *Press*, August 14, 1908, p. 2 (this also appears in *Scott County Kicker* [Benton, MO], August 15, 1908, p. 2).

37. Sam Eagle and Ed Eagle, *West Yellowstone's 70th Anniversary—1908 to 1978*, p. 2–34.

38. "Killed at Yellowstone," *Teton Peak Chronicle* (St. Anthony, ID), September 18, 1913. See also "Tells of Killing," *Salt Lake Tribune*, September 16, 1913, p. 7.

39. "Trial of Ola A. Haverson for Gardiner Murder Is On," *Livingston Enterprise*, May 19, 1914; "Haverson's Fate Will Be with Jury Before Evening; Self Defense Is His Plea," May 20; "Haverson Given 8 Years in the State Penitentiary," *Livingston Post*, May 28, 1914; "High Price of Sardines Ends with Murder," *Oakland* (CA) *Tribune*, March 7, 1914, p. 18; "Bartender Killed in Gardiner Saloon," *Anaconda* (MT) *Standard*, March 7, 1914, p. 11; "Haverson Guilty Given Eight Years," *Anaconda* (MT) *Standard*, May 23, 1914, p. 4.

40. "Woman Shot Near Gardiner," *Livingston Enterprise*, June 28, 1982; "Hunters to Be Charged Soon for Shooting Death," July 30; "NRA Added to Tent-Shooting Suit," July 7, 1983. See also the October 26 and November 26, 1982 editions.

41. National Park Service, Yellowstone Park news release 97-65, August 12, 1997; 97-66, August 13, 1997; "Mother and Son Identified Who Were Found Dead in Park," *Livingston Enterprise*, August 14, 1997, p. 2; "Murder, Suicide in YNP," *Bozeman* (MT) *Chronicle*, August 13, 1997, p. 1; "Park Identifies Couple Found Dead in Truck," *Jackson Hole* (WY) *Guide*, August 20, 1997.

21. DEATHS FROM SUICIDE

1. "In Memoriam," *Livingston Enterprise*, January 29, 1884; D. E. Sawyer to Patrick Conger, January 31, 1884, document 1544, YNP Archives; Haines, *Yellowstone Story*, 2:325; Dave Bucknall, *Cemeteries and Gravesites in Yellowstone National Park*, June 10, 1975, YNP Research Library.

2. "Local Layout," *Livingston Enterprise*, May 4, 1884.

3. "Rounding Up Offenders," *Livingston Enterprise*, August 15, 1885; "Arrested in the Park," *Livingston Enterprise*, November 7, 1885, p. 3. In a report he made called "Game in the Park," Ed Wilson called himself an "assistant superintendent." *Forest and Stream* 25, 407 December 17, 1885, 407.

4. That it was not the first winter trip is attested to by geologist Arnold Hague, who claims that Elwood Hofer made one in 1880 (Hague notebook 3869, 1891, National Archives, USGS record group 57, Field Notebooks, box 55). As well, Henry N.

Maguire made a winter trip to Mammoth Hot Springs in 1873, and H. B. Calfee also did it before 1887, although the year is not known. Maguire, *The Coming Empire, A Complete and Reliable Treatise on the Black Hills, Yellowstone and Big Horn Regions*, 128; William L. Lang, "At the Greatest Personal Peril to the Photographer," *Montana Magazine of Western History* 33 (Winter 1983): 22.

5. Haines, *Yellowstone Story*, 2:448.

6. George S. Anderson, "Protection of the Yellowstone Park," in *Hunting in Many Lands: The Book of the Boone and Crockett Club* by T. Roosevelt and G. B. Grinnell, 384–86.

7. Ed Wilson to G. L. Henderson, January 20, 1891, George Ash collection, YNP Archives. That G. L. Henderson liked Wilson is apparent from a long letter that he wrote touting Wilson's skills to the incoming park superintendent George S. Anderson. Henderson to Anderson, January 26, 1891, Anderson collection, YNP Library.

8. "Wilson's Remains Found," *Livingston Enterprise*, June 18, 1892; "Montana," *Omaha* (NE) *Daily Bee*, June 20, 1892, p. 5; "$200 Reward" poster for Ed Wilson's return, Ash Collection, YNP Archives. "Nothing but Bleached Bones," *Livingston Enterprise*, June 16, 1982, p. 3. Wilson's photo is in box D-6, YNP photo archives.

9. "Local News," *Livingston Post*, August 23, 1900; "He Committed Suicide," *Park County* (MT) *Republican*, August 25, 1900, p. 3; Wound Told a Tale of Suicide—A Ghastly Discovery at Gardiner," *Anaconda* (MT) *Standard*, August 22, 1900, p. 10.

10. "Bowman Suicides," *Gardiner Wonderland*, July 13, 1905. *Livingston Enterprise*, July 15, 1905, says the incident happened at noon.

11. "Barber Ends Life; First Says 'Good-Bye,'" *Salt Lake* (UT) *Tribune*, May 19, 1906, p. 1.

12. "Local News," *Livingston Post*, March 2, 1899.

13. Record of Interment, 3, YNP Archives.

14. *Annual Report of Superintendent*, 1957, 27. Clarence "Pop" Scoyen, who was born at Mammoth in 1895 and spent his entire life in the area, professed in 1970 to remember Eugene Clark's death at the time Scoyen was 11 years old. He remembered that Clark was an electrician but thought he died of pneumonia. In 1957, Scoyen helped bury Jeannett Clark. Merv L. Olson, interview with "Pop" Scoyen, October 6, 1970, audiotape 70-1, YNP Archives.

15. Monthly report of superintendent, April 1927, 16–17; "Jackson Takes His Own Life," *Park County News* (Livingston, MT), May 6, 1927; death certificate and coroner's report, box A-44, file 146.13, YNP Archives.

16. Monthly report of superintendent, March 1951, 9. The official report is in box W-194, YNP Archives. Olson had been a resident of Gardiner for twenty-one years. He drilled a hole in his ceiling to loop rope around a hidden stringer, stood on a chair, and jumped from the chair a distance of fourteen inches.

17. "Soldier Commits Suicide at Post," *Livingston Enterprise*, October 11, 1911; Special Orders 92, Fort Yellowstone, October 11, 1911, in record group 393, part 5, entry 11, box 15, file 860, National Archives.

18. "Fort Yellowstone Trooper Ends His Life," *Anaconda* (MT) *Standard*, June 28, 1911, p. 12; "Despondent, Kills Self with Revolver," *Livingston* (MT) *Enterprise*, June 27, 1911, p. 1.

19. "By His Own Hand," *Livingston Enterprise*, October 6, 1906.

20. *Annual Report of Superintendent*, 1938, 42; monthly report of superintendent, January 1938, 2; Haines interview with Ted Ogston, June 20, 1966, audiotape 63-5, YNP Archives; "Park Ranger Is Dead," Idaho Falls *Post-Register*, January 13, 1938; Judson M. Rhoads to author, e-mail, July 12, 2003.

21. Monthly report of superintendent, August 1959, 8.

22. Monthly report of superintendent, November 1962, 8.

23. Monthly report of superintendent, October 1930, 11; "State of Montana," *Anaconda Standard*, July 13, 1896, p. 9: "Frank Deckert, a teamster for Hoppe Brothers at Cinnabar."

24. Monthly report of superintendent, August 1960, 7; "Suicide," *Yellowstone News*, August 18, 1960, p. 2.

25. Monthly report of superintendent, July 1964, 6.

26. Gerald Mernin, "Apparent Suicide of Government Employee," June 10, 1967, box A-83, file "A76 Special Incidents," YNP Archives; Monthly report of superintendent, August 1967, 5.

27. National Park Service, park press release, June 5, 1978; Chris Scott Marshall, interview with author, Mammoth, WY, January 28, 1993.

28. "It May Be Suicide," *Livingston Post*, September 5, 1901; "Local Layout," "Additional Local," *Livingston Enterprise*, September 7, 1901.

29. Aubrey L. Haines, "Postal Service in Yellowstone Park," unpublished typescript, August 15, 1966, YNP Library vertical files, p. 7.

30. "Gillotte Suicides," *Gardiner Wonderland*, April 13, 1905.

31. "Bullet Ends Jardine Man, Saturday PM," *Gardiner* (MT) *Gateway Gazette*, November 28, 1940, p. 1.

32. "Body Found Hanging in Tree," *Gardiner* (MT) *Gateway Gazette*, July 11, 1940, p. 1.

33. Earl Johnson, Roundup, MT, letter to author, September 25, 1995; "Officers Study Death of Man [Meyers]," *Billings* (MT) *Gazette*, July 17, 1949, p. 5.

34. "Park Letter. Further Details of John Howard's Attempted Suicide. Death by Lightning," *Livingston Enterprise*, September 12, 1885; "Crossed in Love," August 29; "Lost in Wonderland," *Deseret Evening News* (Salt Lake City), August 3, 1900, p. 3. I have written a long analysis of the 1885 John Howard suicide attempt in connection with the event's location near Marshall's Hotel. See Lee Whittlesey, "Hotels on the Firehole River in Yellowstone, 1880-1891, and the Origins of Concessioner Policy in National Parks" (longer version of an article published in *Yellowstone Science*), unpublished manuscript, September 4, 2012, YNP Library.

35. "Man Who Shot Himself in Park Identified," *Billings* (MT) *Gazette*, January 3, 1998.

36. Mike Finley to YNP Employees, e-mail, April 9, 2001; "Donald 'Don' C. Unser," *Bozeman* (MT) *Daily Chronicle*, April 11, 2001.

37. National Park Service, Yellowstone National Park news release, 03-125, October 17, 2003; "Missing Doc's Car Found in Yellowstone," *Livingston Enterprise*, October 16, 2003, p. 1; "Missing Doctor Found Dead," *Livingston Enterprise*, October 17, 2003, p. 1.

38. Three letters in "In the Mail," *Livingston* (MT) *Enterprise*, April 13, 2005; Scott McMillion in "The Day the Music Died," *Bozeman* (MT) *Daily Chronicle*, April 14, 2005; John Nowakowski, "Events Surrounding Jardine Suicide Recalled," *Livingston Enterprise*, June 28, 2005, p. 1.

39. Henry D. Estabrook, "Estabrook on His Travels," *Omaha* (NE) *World Herald*, September 27, 1891, p. 10; Edward Wessel, "Seeing the Yellowstone," *Capital City Courier* (Lincoln, NE), August 15, 1891, p. 1; Alfred Lambourne, "In Wonderland," *Salt Lake* (UT) *Herald*, December 25, 1887, p. 14.

40. National Park Service, "Recovery Efforts Continue in Yellowstone for Missing Utah Man," Yellowstone National Park press release, 09-044, June 18, 2009, see also 09-043, June 17, 2009; and Nicholas Jeffrey Mostert, obituary, *Salt Lake Tribune*, June 19–20, 2009, http://www.legacy.com.

41. Bill Croke, "Don't Jump," *American Spectator*, June 29, 2009, http://www.spectator.org/archives/2009/06/29/dont-jump.

42. National Park Service, "Search Underway in Yellowstone for Missing Oklahoma Man," Yellowstone National Park press release 10-041, June 1, 2010; "Search Continues for Missing Man," 10-46, June 4, 2010; "Body of Missing Man Discovered," 10-071, July 20, 2010; "Marine Sgt Peter Kastner," *Fallen Heroes* blog, July 22, 2010, http://livinglegendteam.blogspot.com/2010/07/marine-sgt-peter-kastner.html; Kathie DiCesare, "Marine Sergeant Peter Louis Kastner Didn't Want to Live Another Day," *Wounded Times Blog*, http://woundedtimes.blogspot.com/2010/07/marine-sgt-peter-louis-kastner-didnt.html.

43. William Styron, *Darkness Visible: A Memoir of Madness*.

22. MISSING AND PRESUMED DEAD

1. "Local News," *Livingston Post*, December 20, 1900; Haines, *Yellowstone Story*, 2:117–18; Superintendent's Journal, Ledger 143, September 5, 1900, YNP Archives.

2. "Where Is Leroy Piper? His Strange Disappearance from a Hotel in Yellowstone Park," *Evening News* (San Jose, CA), May 7, 1901, p. 1; "Hon. W. A. Piper Dead," *San Diego* (CA) *Union*, August 6, 1899, p. 1; "W. P. [*sic*] Piper Dead," *Riverside* (CA) *Morning Enterprise*, August 6, 1899, p. 1.

3. Lee H. Whittlesey, "'Music, Song, and Laughter': Paradise at Yellowstone's Fountain Hotel, 1891–1916," *GOSA Transactions Journal of the Geyser Observation and Study Association* 10 (2008): 161.

4. Whithorn, *Photo History of Aldridge*, 165, quoting "Human Skull Found at Aldridge," *Park County* (MT) *News*, August 15, 1924.

5. Gerald Mernin, interview with author, June 15, 1993, South Entrance, Yellowstone National Park, WY; Mernin, "A76 Special Incident," August 8, 1966, in box A-83, file A7616, YNP Archives. This report includes maps and subsequent correspondence with the boy's parents.

6. "Search for Lost Hunter Continues," *Livingston Enterprise*, February 15, 1983; "Hunter Search Stopped," February 26, 1983; "Unsolved Mysteries in Yellowstone Park," *Bozeman Chronicle*, July 7, 1994.

7. National Park Service, park press release, April 12, 1991; author's interview with Andrew Mitchell, November 18, 1993, Mammoth, WY; interview with Paul Miller, Mammoth, WY, November 7, 1992.

8. Author's conversation with Tim Baymiller, Roosevelt Lodge, Wyoming, August 27, 1993; National Park Service, missing persons poster, July 4, 1993.

9. Joe Paisley, "Unsolved Mysteries in Yellowstone Park," *Bozeman Chronicle*, July 9, 1994, p. 1.

23. DEATHS FROM GAS STOVE EXPLOSIONS AND STRUCTURAL FIRES

1. Monthly report of superintendent, July 1925, 43; "Tourist Camp Scene of Fatal Explosion," *Livingston Enterprise*, July 15, 1925; death certificate, box A-44, file 146.13, YNP Archives.

2. Monthly report of superintendent, July 1957, 5, 7.

3. "John C. Kelly Burned to Death," *Livingston Enterprise*, November 2, 1911; "Two Killed, Three Others Hurt in Early Morning Blaze in Gardiner Hotel," August 9, 1950; author's interview with Florence Crossen, Gardiner, Montana, September 6, 1993; Donalene O'Neill, letter to Lee H. Whittlesey, April 9, 1999.

4. "That Was in Early Days," *Anaconda Standard*, January 30, 1895, p. 8; "Local Layout," *Livingston Enterprise*, February 2, 1895, p. 5; "Killed by an Explosion," *Livingston Post*, January 30, 1895, p. 3. Lowney was buried at Horr, Montana.

24. DEATHS FROM CARBON MONOXIDE POISONING

1. Monthly report of superintendent, December 1923, 13–14.

2. Monthly report of superintendent, June 1947, 2.

3. Aubrey L. Haines, letter to author, September 27, 1995. The official reports are in box W-194, compensation file, "Richard N. Huckels of Akron, Ohio"; and file 207-05.1, "Case of Vernon Kaiser, John P. Baker, Richard Huckels, Lost Their Lives on Red Lodge Cooke Road, June 21, 1947."

4. Monthly report of superintendent, September 1946, 9.

25. DEATH ON THE ROAD AND IN THE AIR

1. A panoramic photo in the office of the manager of transportation, Xanterra Parks and Resorts, Ltd., shows the fleet on September 23, 1926, stretching from the truck gate to the north entrance checking station. The Yellowstone National Park Museum collection also has this photo.

2. The only car-wreck death I am including here is one for the record, because it is the first one that ever happened in Yellowstone's history. Not surprisingly, it occurred

the very year that automobiles were allowed into the park. At 11:30 a.m. on September 3, 1915, the George Higgins family of Helena, MT, was riding in a large Maxwell car from Tower to Mammoth. Three hundred yards east of the Gardner River crossing, above the old Sheepeater Bridge and on present "Undine Hill," the car met a horse-drawn wagon and went out of control on the slick, wet road and over a sixty-foot embankment. Sarah Edith Higgins, 49, of Ringling, MT, was killed when the car over-turned and landed on top of her, fracturing her skull. Her two children safely jumped from the car, but her husband was severely injured when he was pinned under the car with his wife. "Woman Killed in Park When Auto Goes over Cliff," *Livingston Enterprise*, September 4, 1915; "First Auto Accident in Yellowstone Park Fatal to Montanan," *Missoula* (MT) *Sentinel*, September 4, 1915; "Mrs. Higgins Meets Death," *Meagher County Republican* (White Sulphur Springs, MT), September 10, 1915. See also item 103, file 313, YNP Archives.

3. The 1920s editions of the monthly reports of the superintendent chronicle numerous instances of YPT Company buses involved in nonfatality wrecks.

4. Monthly report of superintendent, July 1921, 24–26; death certificate, box A-44, file 146.13, YNP Archives. Park bus driver Gerry Pesman (1926–1942) remembers hearing about a bus fatality that occurred "before I got here (in 1926)." He was told, apparently mistakenly, that it occurred in the Cut area and that the woman's neck was broken. Gerry Pesman, interview with author, Albright Visitor Center, summer 1991.

5. Monthly report of superintendent, August 1931, 27–28; "Remains of Bus Driver Will Be Shipped to Home," *Livingston Enterprise*, August 28, 1931; death certificate, box A-44, file 146.13, YNP Archives. The newspaper gave his hometown as Harlington, NE.

6. Monthly report of superintendent, July 1949, 2, 11; *Annual Report of Superintendent*, 1950, 9, 26; author's 1991 interview with Gerard Pesman, YPT bus driver 1926–1942. The official report for this incident is file 207-05.1, "Death Mrs. Gertrude Rettenmeyer . . . July 12, 1949," in box W-194, YNP Archives.

7. *Annual Report of Superintendent*, 1943, 18–19; Andy Beck, "B-17 and B-47 Crash Sites in Yellowstone National Park, Wyoming," unpublished study with photos, summer 1984, YNP Research Library; miscellaneous letters and photos on 1943 B-17 crash, box A-76, YNP Archives; "Park Fires Bring History to Light," Idaho Falls *Post-Register*, November 30, 1988; Ross W. Simpson, *The Fires of '88*, 60–67; former ranger Bob Murphy, conversation with author, Mammoth, WY, September 13, 1993.

8. "Planes Collide Near West Yellowstone," *Livingston Enterprise*, May 4, 1963; "Body of B47 Victim Found," May 7; "Rescuers Find A. F. Survivor; 2 Dead, 1 Missing in Crash," *Salt Lake Tribune*, May 6, 1963; Dale H. Nuss, "Narrative Report of Activities of Ranger Personnel Connected with the Search, Rescue, and Investigations Operations of the U.S. Air Force B-47 Bomber Crash—May 3 Through May 9, 1963," box W-56, YNP Archives; Andy Beck, "B-17 and B-47 Crash Sites in Yellowstone National Park, Wyoming," unpublished study with photos, summer 1984, YNP Research Library. See also box A-76, general photos and reports of air crashes. The Air Force informed Andy Beck in 1984 that the causes of the B-17 and B-47 crashes and the accompanying safety recommendations were confidential in line with the government mishap-prevention program. Captain Zumbra's name is spelled *Zumba* in the Air Force incident reports.

9. Gerald Mernin, "Report of Accidents Other than Motor Vehicle," 1193, August 26, 1970, box W-98; report in box A-85, file A7623, YNP Archives; "Plane Crash Kills Four Near Sylvan," *Cody Enterprise*, August 26, 1970; "Crash Site Found," *Livingston Enterprise*, August 25, 1970.

10. National Park Service, park press release, July 5, 1978; "One Killed in Plane Crash," *Livingston Enterprise*, July 5, 1978. The case incident report for this event is in box W-222, YNP Archives.

11. "Search Continues in Yellowstone for Missing Montanan," *Livingston Enterprise*, February 4, 1987; "Plane Wreckage Found," February 5; National Park Service, park press release, February 1, 1987.

12. There were no witnesses to the crash, but rangers David and Michael Ross were first on the scene. Michael Ross to Lee Silliman (copy to author), August 9, 1991, at Shoshone Lake. "Plane Crash in Yellowstone," *Livingston Enterprise*, July 5, 1991.

13. National Park Service, Yellowstone National Park news release 95-39, July 5, 1995; "Texas Pilot Dies in Plane Crash at Yellowstone," *Deseret* (UT) *News*, July 6, 1995.

14. National Park Service, Yellowstone National Park news release 03-72, August 5, 2003; "Small Plane Crashes in Yellowstone, One Killed," *Bozeman* (MT) *Daily Chronicle*, August 4, 2003, p. 1; "Model of Hughes Aircraft Crashes, Killing Its Pilot," *Post Standard* (Syracuse, NY), August 6, 2003, p. A-8.

CONCLUSION

1. "Uncharted Park Trips," *Livingston Enterprise*, August 20, 1926.

2. J. A. Frederick to Secretary of Interior, n.d. [1970]; Mr. and Mrs. Robert Schoening to Jack Anderson, August 6, 1970, box W-53, YNP Archives.

3. Assistant Secretary of Interior Leslie L. Glasgow to Shiela Dillon on Andy Hecht, August 21, 1970; National Park Service form letter A3615, August 24, 1970, box W-53, YNP Archives.

4. 326 F.2d 449 (8th Circuit 1964).

5. Louise Brock to John Douglass, August 18, 1970, in Andy Hecht file, box W-53, YNP Archives.

6. 546 F.2d at 1361 (9th Circuit 1976).

APPENDIX A: MAMMOTH CIVILIAN CEMETERY

1. Bucknall, *Cemeteries and Gravesites in Yellowstone National Park*, p. 10; Haines, *Yellowstone Story*, 1:362n63, and "A Plat of the Civilian Graveyard on the Hill North of Mammoth," inset map; M. Evelyn Rose, e-mail correspondence with author, 2002, 2008, and 2010, enclosing census records for 1860, 1870, and 1880; Shirley Rush of Hepburn, ID, interview with author, September 14, 2006.

2. G. L. Henderson in archive document 1448, YNP Archives; Bucknall, *Cemeteries and Gravesites in Yellowstone National Park*, map.

3. Lee Whittlesey, interview with Janice Weekley of Tulsa, OK, a Xanterra Reservations employee, July 13, 2007.

4. Bucknall, *Cemeteries and Gravesites in Yellowstone National Park*, map.

5. Aubrey Haines, interview with Edith Ritchie, November 7, 1961, YNP Archives.

6. "Local Layout," *Livingston Enterprise*, June 26, 1889.

APPENDIX B: FORT YELLOWSTONE ARMY CEMETERY

1. Bucknall, *Cemeteries and Gravesites in Yellowstone National Park*, 7; "Soldiers Buried in Park to Be Exhumed," *Livingston Enterprise*, April 25, 1917; Haines, "Plat of Post Cemetery," January 28, 1948, YNP Archives.

2. *Record Book of Interments at the Post Cemetery, Fort Yellowstone*, item 155, YNP Archives; Bucknall, *Cemeteries and Gravesites*. See also the disinterments list in item 104-B, file 51, "Buildings," YNP Archives, which also has a list dated June 1, 1917, recommending thirty-two graves in Fort Yellowstone Cemetery that will be left in place.

3. This man was probably Ninian T. Elliott, born 1855 in Causey Banks, N'ld, England, son of Robert William Elliott of Tynemouth and Margaret Clark of Gateshead, Durham, England. His great-grandson, Steve Elliott, contacted me November 30, 2000, with biographical information, now placed in YNP Library, biography file, and explained the variant *T* at the end of the name as a second *T* added for religious reasons—mainly a cross.

APPENDIX C: GARDINER CEMETERY ON TINKER'S HILL

1. "Local Layout," *Livingston Enterprise*, October 9, 1886; Aubrey Haines interview with Edith Ritchie, November 7, 1961. Information on the cemetery being one of three nonfederally owned parcels within park boundaries (the other two formerly were owned by the state of Montana and the Burlington railroad) is in "Some Yellowstone Land Isn't Part of the Park," *Livingston Enterprise*, June 9, 1986.

2. List of Gardiner cemetery burials in possession of author.

APPENDIX D: OTHER GRAVESITES IN YELLOWSTONE PARK

1. Haines, *Yellowstone Story*, 2:24; information on Mattie Culver from Nan Weber Boruff, Salt Lake City, UT, who possesses Mattie Culver's autograph book and who is the author of *Mattie: A Woman's Journey West* (1997).

2. Haines, "Landscape Alterations Map 1870 to 1967," National Park Service 6316, September 1967, site number 9; Aubrey Haines, conversation with author, Mammoth, WY, August 9, 1993.

3. Haines "Landscape Alterations Map," site number 110; Haines interview with Ray Little, April 21, 1961; Gary S. Bradak of Logan, UT, letter to Lee H. Whittlesey, July 9, 1999.

4. Earl Felix of Veradale, WA, letter to author, September 27, 2008. Visitor Samuel Preston Ewing's diary entry for June 30, 1904, confirms the burial: "Camped near where a little girl had been buried in July 1903." See also David de L. Condon, "Memorandum for the files [on Bessie Rowbottom and people with her]," August 22, 1949, in box H-2, file "101 History 1937 to July 1957," YNP Archives.

5. Haines, "Landscape Alterations Map," site number 233.

6. Haines "Landscape Alterations Map," site number 224. A possible occupant of this grave is Dick Hull (see chapter 18, "Wild Horses: Deaths from Horse, Wagon, and Stagecoach Incidents"); Aubrey Haines, conversation with author, Mammoth, WY, August 9, 1993.

7. [John Pitcher], "Memo. concerning Mr. Dave Edwards," November 13, 1906, document 7025, YNP Archives; Haines "Landscape Alterations Map," site number 177; Aubrey Haines, conversations with author, April 2, 1978, and August 12, 1993; *Livingston Enterprise*, January 26, 1907. See also document 7028, YNP Archives.

8. Haines, "Landscape Alterations Map," site number 1; Aubrey Haines, conversation with author, August 9, 1993.

9. Aubrey L. Haines to author, September 19, 1977.

10. A. L. Haines to chief naturalist, April 13, 1961, in box H-2, file "H-14, Area and Service History, 1957–62," YNP Archives.

11. Jim Hepburn to author, Emigrant, MT, June 20, 1995.

BIBLIOGRAPHY

"Accident Other Than Motor Vehicle." Field report 1037, June 28, 1970. Box W-53, Yellowstone National Park Archives.

Acting Park Superintendent. Letter to Dr. T. S. Palmer, May 27, 1912. Item 103, file 313, Yellowstone National Park Archives.

Albright, Horace H. Letter to Director of National Park Service, October 28, 1926. Box A-44, file 146.13, Yellowstone National Park Archives.

———. Letter to Pattie Eakins, October 28, 1926. Box A-44, Yellowstone National Park Archives.

———. Letter to W. J. Newbro, September 19, 1969. In Yellowstone National Park manuscript file under "Horace Albright."

———. Letter to Roger Toll, December 11, 1929. Box W-11, file 149.1, Yellowstone National Park Archives.

[Albright, Horace?]. "A Bear-Faced Robbery." *Literary Digest*, June 9, 1923, 64–65.

Albright, Horace M., and William T. Ingersoll. "The Reminiscences of Horace M. Albright." Transcript on microfilm of a series of recorded interviews with Albright by Columbia University, 1962, Yellowstone National Park Library microfilm.

Allen, E. T. "Early Yellowstone Incidents." *Yellowstone Nature Notes* 7, no. 5 (May 1930): 25.

Anderson, Charles. "Report of Accident Other Than Motor Vehicle." June 17, 1972. Box A-91, file A7623, Yellowstone National Park Archives.

Anderson, E. C. Scout diary, April 20, 1909. Yellowstone National Park Archives.

Anderson, George S. "Protection of the Yellowstone Park." In *Hunting in Many Lands: The Book of the Boone and Crockett Club*, by Theodore Roosevelt and G. B. Grinnell. New York: Harper and Brothers, 1895.

———. "Work of the Cavalry in Protecting the Yellowstone National Park." *Journal of the United States Cavalry Association* 10 (March 1897): 9–10.

Annual Reports of the Superintendent of Yellowstone National Park, 1872, 1877–1883, 1885–1991, Yellowstone National Park Research Library.

Arnold, Bessie Haynes. Excerpts from her diary. Ms. file, Yellowstone National Park Research Library.

———. Interview by Steve Johnson, January 19, 1974. Tape 74-4, Yellowstone National Park Research Library.

Ash, S. H., and W. W. Kessler. "Investigation of Gas Hazards at Proposed Bridge Foundation Sites in the Yellowstone National Park" and attachments. U.S. Bureau of Mines, n.d. [1939]. Yellowstone National Park Research Library.

Ashley v. U.S. 326 F.2d 449. 4th Cir. 1964.

Avant Courier, Bozeman, MT. September 6, 13, 1877; September 2, 1880; January 20, 1881; September 2, 1880; January 20, 1881; September 7, 1882.

Baggley, George. "Report of Injury." July 3, 1929. Box A-44, file 146.13, Yellowstone National Park Archives.

———. "Special Incident Report" and death certificate. Box A-44, file 146.13, Yellowstone National Park Archives.

Ballou, Maturin M. *The New El Dorado: A Summer Journey to Alaska.* Boston and New York: Houghton Mifflin, 1889.

Banker, Lloyd P. Letter to Yellowstone National Park, August 20, 1926, and death certificate of Grace Crans. Box A-44, file 146.13, Yellowstone National Park Archives.

Bartlett, Richard A. "Those Infernal Machines in Yellowstone." *Montana Magazine of Western History* 20 (1970): 16–29.

———. *Yellowstone: A Wilderness Besieged.* Tucson: University of Arizona Press, 1985.

Baymiller, Tim. Conversation with author. Roosevelt Lodge, WY. August 27, 1993.

Beck, Andy. "B-17 and B-47 Crash Sites in Yellowstone National Park, Wyoming." Summer 1984. Yellowstone National Park Research Library. See also box A-76, Yellowstone National Park Archives.

Bigelow, Captain M. O. Letter to S. B. M. Young, June 1907. Archive document 6992, Yellowstone National Park Archives.

Billings Gazette, Billings, MT. News items from 1936–2010.

Bittner, Beverly. Interview with author. Sun Valley, ID, March 22, 1993.

Blair, Bruce. Interview with author. Philadelphia, PA, November 16, 1992.

Blakeley, Steve. Interview with author. Gardiner, MT, December 9, 1992.

Blank, Tim P. "Interviews with Family." From case incident 84-2913, July 31, 1984.

Board of Inquiry [on Bess and Bitterli]. July 15, 1980. Box A-113, file A7623, Yellowstone National Park Archives.

——— [on Kenneth Fullerton]. July 20, 1981. Box A-114, file A7623, Yellowstone National Park Archives.

——— [on Raymond Guntz]. September 17, 1980. Box A-113, file A7623, Yellowstone National Park Archives.

——— [on James Hambrick]. October 22, 1971. Box A-2, Yellowstone National Park Archives.

——— [on Keith Alfred Jensen]. September 4, 1970. Box A-85, Yellowstone National Park Archives.

——— [on David Allen Kirwan]. August 20, 1981. Box A-114, Yellowstone National Park Archives.

——— [on Duane McClure]. June 9, 1980. Box A-113, file A7623, Yellowstone National Park Archives.

———— [on Laurie Miller]. September 16, 1983. Box A-118, file A7623, Yellowstone National Park Archives.

———— [on Scott Olson]. March 11, 1982. Box A-116, file A7623, Yellowstone National Park Archives.

———— [on Tom Pearse]. August 25, 1983. Box A-118, file A7623, Yellowstone National Park Archives.

———— [on Mrs. Thomas Ward]. October 14, 1971. Box A-2, Yellowstone National Park Archives.

———— [on James Wilkerson]. August 31, 1982. Box A-116, file A7623, Yellowstone National Park Archives.

Board of Review [on the Sigrists]. August 29, 1979. Box A-109, file A7623, Yellowstone National Park Archives.

Bower, Robert. Interview with author. Idaho Falls, ID, April 1, 1992.

Bozeman Chronicle, Bozeman, MT. News items from 1933–2010.

Bremer, D. H. "Individual Bear Injury Report." August 23, 1942. Possession of author.

————. "Special Incident Report." August 23, 1942. Possession of author.

Brett, L. M. Letter to Director, July 25, 1916. Item 64, file 313, Yellowstone National Park Archives.

Brock, Louise. Letter to John Douglass, August 18, 1970. In Andy Hecht file, box W-53, Yellowstone National Park Archives.

Brown, Mark. "Yellowstone Tourists and the Nez Perce." *Montana Magazine of Western History* 16, no. 3 (1966): 39–40.

Brunton, Leon. Interview with author. Mammoth Hot Springs, WY, December 26, 1992.

Bucknall, Dave. *Cemeteries and Gravesites in Yellowstone National Park*. Pamphlet. June 10, 1975. Yellowstone National Park Research Library.

Buffalo Chip, Sturgis, SD. September–November 1992, Yellowstone National Park Resource Management Division.

Butte Standard, Butte, MT. July 9, 1936.

Calfee, H. B. "Calfee's Adventures—He and His Companion's Blood Curdling Trip to the Park over a Quarter Century Ago." Manuscript from newspaper clippings [about 1896]. Yellowstone National Park Research Library.

Canyon Ranger Station [on Diane Schramm]. August 30, 1956. Box A-83, Special Incident File, Yellowstone National Park Archives.

Carnes, Bob. Interview with author. Lake Mead National Recreation Area, November 9, 1992.

Casper Star-Tribune, Casper, WY. [About] August 28, 1928; April 26, 1971.

Census of the United States. State of Montana, 1900.

Chicago Tribune, Chicago, IL. November 18, 1970.

Child, Huntley, Sr. Interview with A. L. Haines, September 11, 1961. Audiotape 61-3, Yellowstone National Park Oral History Collection.

Chittenden, Hiram M. *The Yellowstone National Park*. Cincinnati: R. Clarke Company, 1895, 1903; Stanford: Stanford University Press, 1954; University of Oklahoma Press, 1964.

Clark, Berg. Interview, Gallatin Oral History Project, January 7, 1975. Yellowstone National Park Research Library.

Cody Enterprise, Cody, WY. News items from 1947–1987.

Connally, C. P. "Yellowstone Park." In Scrapbook 4209, 74–77, n.d. [1895?], Yellowstone National Park Research Library.

Connery, Thomas M. "The Winter Tragedy of the Yellowstone." *World Wide Magazine*, June 1919.

Crabtree, Dr. Bob. Interview with author. Bozeman, MT, April 1, 1993.

Craighead, Frank C. *Track of the Grizzly*. San Francisco: Sierra Club Books, 1979.

Cress, G. O. Letter to Park Superintendent, July 23, 1897. Document 1330, Yellowstone National Park Archives.

Cronin, Janet, and Dorothy Vick. *Montana's Gallatin Canyon: A Gem in the Treasure State*. Missoula, MT: Mountain Press Publishing, 1992.

Crossen, Florence. Interview with author. Gardiner, MT, September 6, 1993.

Dahlheim, Jon. Interview with author. Mammoth, WY, May 5, 1993.

Death certificates, autopsy reports, and coroner's reports. Miscellaneous. Box A-44, file 146.13, Yellowstone National Park Archives.

———. Grace Crans. Death certificate. Box A-44, file 146.13, Yellowstone National Park Archives.

———. Virginia Hall. Death certificate and autopsy report number A-43-71. Box A-74, file A7623, Yellowstone National Park Archives.

———. James H. Hambrick. Death certificate. August 17, 1971. Box A-88, file A7623, Yellowstone National Park Archives.

———. John W. Havekost. Death certificate. Item 64, file 313, Yellowstone National Park Archives.

———. Keith Alfred Jensen. Death certificate. Box A-83, file A7616, Yellowstone National Park Archives.

———. Isadore M. Kisber. Death certificate. Box A-44, file 146.13, Yellowstone National Park Archives.

———. Marguerite Knapp. Death certificate. Box A-44, file 146.13, Yellowstone National Park Archives.

———. Georges Landoy. Death certificate. Box A-44, file 146.13, Yellowstone National Park Archives.

———. Joseph McDonald. Death certificate. Item 64, file 313, Yellowstone National Park Archives.

———. Lloyd V. Ryan. Death certificate. Box A-74, file A7623, Yellowstone National Park Archives.

———. Marvin Schrader. Death certificate. July 12, 1971. Box A-88, file A7623, Yellowstone National Park Archives.

———. Gertrude Tomasko. Death certificate and coroner's report. Box A-44, file 146.13, Yellowstone National Park Archives.

———. Laura E. Ward. Death certificate. August 9, 1971. Box A-88, file A7623, Yellowstone National Park Archives.

———. Robert S. Wright. Death certificate. Box A-44, file 146.13, Yellowstone National Park Archives.

"Death of Ranger Charles Phillips." *Yellowstone Nature Notes* 4, no. 4 (April 30, 1927).

Dennis G. Martin as Administrator of the Estate of Harry Eugene Walker . . . v. U.S.A. 546 F.2d 1355. 9th Cir. 1976.

Dennis G. Martin as Administrator of the Estate of Harry Eugene Walker. v. U.S.A. 392 F. Supp. 243. C. D. Calif., 1975.

Deseret News, Salt Lake City, UT. October 2, 1952; July 20, 1955; July 6, 1995; December 2, 2000.

"The Disappearance and Presumed Drowning of Mr. Carl G. Mihlberger." July 20, 1953. Box W-98, Yellowstone National Park Archives.

Dobert, Stephen. Interview with author. Mammoth, WY, January 26, 1993.

Donohoe, C. P. Letter to Horace Albright, July 15, 1924. Box W-55, Yellowstone National Park Archives.

Dose, Dale. Interview with author. Davenport, IA, February 13, 1993.

Driscoll, Sgt. ___. Telegram to park superintendent [Col. S. B. M. Young], n.d. [probably July 23, 1897].

———. Letter to Park Superintendent, July 23, 1897. Document 1482, Yellowstone National Park Archives.

Dudley, W. H. *The National Park from the Hurricane Deck of a Cayuse*. . . . Butte City, CA: Free Press Publishing, 1886.

Eagle, Sam, and Ed Eagle. *West Yellowstone's 70th Anniversary—1908 to 1978*. West Yellowstone, MT: Eagle Company, Inc., 1978.

Eakins, Pattie. Letter to Horace Albright, November 23, 1926. Box A-44, Yellowstone National Park Archives.

Ebert, Hugh B. "Disappearance of Lloyd J. Weikel. . . . " August 13, 1945. Box W-98, Yellowstone National Park Archives.

———. Memo to chief ranger, Yellowstone National Park, April 12, 1944, pp. 2–3.

Estate of Harry Eugene Walker v. United States of America. Civil No. 72-3044-AAH, January 9–February 21, 1975. Trial transcript, p. 1741. Yellowstone National Park Research Library.

Everts, T. C. "Thirty-Seven Days of Peril." *Scribner's Monthly*, November 1871.

Ewing, Samuel Preston. [A Trip to Yellowstone Park 1904]. Copy of handwritten diary. Vertical files, Yellowstone National Park Research Library.

Fey, Rick. Interview with author. Lake, WY, August 12, 1993.

"Final Report—Grizzly Bear–Roger May Incident—June 25, 1983." October 31, 1983. Gallatin National Forest, West Yellowstone, MT.

Fitterer, Jill. Letter to author, March 15, 1993.

———. "May There Be Mountains," n.d. [1990].

Fitzgerald, S. M. Scout diary, 1907. Yellowstone National Park Archives.

Franson, Arthur. Letter to commanding officer, June 27, 1907. Archive document 7023, Yellowstone National Park Archives.

Frederick, J. A. Letter to Secretary of Interior, n.d. [1970]. Box W-53, Yellowstone National Park Archives.

Fries, Amos. Statement, September 14, 1916. Item 64, file 313, Yellowstone National Park Archives.

Gafney, Bonnie. Letter to author, January 17, 1993.

Gardiner Wonderland, Gardiner, MT. News items from 1903–1905.

Gerrish, Theodore. *Life in the World's Wonderland*. Biddeford, ME, 1887.

Gillis, Charles J. *Another Summer: The Yellowstone Park and Alaska*. New York: J. J. Little and Co., 1893.

Glasgow, Leslie L. Letter to Shiela Dillon on Andy Hecht, August 21, 1970. Box W-53, Yellowstone National Park Archives.

Goodwin, Vernon. Letter to Horace Albright, September 1, 1925. Box A-44, file 146.13, Yellowstone National Park Archives.

Gourley, James. "Expedition into the Yellowstone Country 1870." 1929, Yellowstone National Park Research Library.

Graham, Bruce. Conversation with author. Livingston, MT, August 19, 1993.

Great Falls Tribune, Great Falls, MT. September 22, 1925; July 28, 1933; August 5, 1962.

Greene, Jerome A. *Nez Perce Summer 1877*. Helena: Montana Historical Society Press, 2000.

Guie, H. D., and L. V. McWhorter. *Adventures in Geyserland*. Caldwell, ID: Caxton Printers, Ltd., 1935.

Gurney, Alfred. "A Ramble Through the United States, February 3, 1886." Montana State University.

Hague, Arnold. Hague notebook 3869, 1891. In National Archives. USGS Record Group 57, Field Notebooks, box 55.

Haines, Aubrey L. Conversations and tour with author. Yellowstone National Park, WY, August 9–13, 1993.

———. "History of Duret and His Land." In Yellowstone National Park manuscript file under "Silver Tip Ranch," n.d.

———. Interview with author. Bozeman, MT, April 2, 1978.

———. "Landscape Alterations Map 1870 to 1967." National Park Service, map number 6316, September 1967.

———. "Plat of Post Cemetery. . . ." January 28, 1948, Yellowstone National Park Archives.

———. "A Plat of the Civilian Graveyard on the Hill North of Mammoth. . . ." 1947, Yellowstone National Park Archives.

———. *The Yellowstone Story*. 2 vols. Boulder: University of Colorado Press, 1977; revised 1996.

———. "A Yellowstone Winter Tragedy." *Yellowstone Interpreter* 2, no. 3 (May–June 1964): 45–47.

Hamilton, William T. *My Sixty Years on the Plains*. New York: Forest and Stream, 1905.

Hansen, Virginia, and Al Funderburk. *The Fabulous Past of Cooke City*. Billings, MT: Billings Printing Co., 1962.

Hanser, Herman, M. D. Letter to Horace Albright, July 14, 1924. Box A-44, file 146.13, Yellowstone National Park Archives.

Hardman, William. *A Trip to America*. London: T. V. Wood, 1884.

Hart, L. J. Letter to H. M. Albright, September 26, 1928. Box W-11, Accidents File 149.1, Yellowstone National Park Archives.

Haupt, Herman, Jr. *The Yellowstone National Park*. St. Paul, MN: J. M. Stoddart, 1883.

Hayden, F. V. *Preliminary Report of the U.S. Geological Survey of Montana . . . Fifth Annual Report.* Washington, DC: Government Printing Office, 1872.

———. *Twelfth Annual Report of the United States Geological and Geographical Survey of the Territories . . . Part II . . . 1878.* Washington, DC: Government Printing Office, 1883.

Haynes, Jack. Interview with A. L. Haines, December 9, 1963. Tape 63-5, Yellowstone National Park Research Library.

———. *Haynes Guide Handbook of Yellowstone National Park.* Bozeman, MT: Haynes Studio, 1966.

Hecht, James L. Letter to Edward I. Koch, August 3, 1972. Box A-74, Yellowstone National Park Archives.

———. Letter to Secretary of Interior, June 29, 1970 and August 11, 1970. Box W53, Yellowstone National Park Archives.

Henderson, A. Bart. "Journal of the Yellowstone Expedition of 1866. . . ." May 18, 1871, entry. *Yellowstone Interpreter* 2, no. 1 (1962).

Henderson, G. L. Document 1448, August 10, 1884, Yellowstone National Park Archives.

———. "From the Park." *Livingston Enterprise,* August 17, 1901.

———. "In Hot Water." Helena *Daily Herald,* April 25, 1888, 3.

———. Letter to G. Anderson, January 26, 1891. Anderson Collection, Yellowstone National Park Research Library.

———. "A Wonderland." Newspaper clipping from West Union, IA, January 30, 1884. In Ash Scrapbook, 4, Yellowstone National Park Research Library.

———. *Yellowstone Park Manual and Guide.* Mammoth Hot Springs, WY, 1888.

[Henderson, G. L.]. "Park Letter . . . Death by Lightning." *Livingston Enterprise,* September 12, 1885.

Hennesay, Vernon. "Board of Inquiry [on Marvin Schrader]," October 21, 1971. Box A-2, Yellowstone National Park Archives.

Henry, Jeff. Interview with author. Cinnabar Basin, MT, November 1, 14, 1992.

Hermann, Lee K., M.D. "Final Autopsy Report, no. AB4," August 2–19, 1984. Cody, WY, case incident 84-2913.

Herrero, Stephen. *Bear Attacks.* New York: Lyons and Burford, 1985.

Hess, Dennis H. "Kleine–Baldwin Drowning. . . ." Box W-98, Yellowstone National Park Archives.

HHT Company. Picture postcard 4287, Norris Geyser Basin.

Hobbs, Bobbie Seaquist. Interview with author. West Yellowstone, MT, December 15, 1992.

Hofer, Elwood. "Winter in Wonderland." *Forest and Stream,* April 28, 1887, 294.

———. "Yellowstone Park Notes." *Forest and Stream,* January 8, 1898, 25.

Holte, Peter. "Catching Buffalo Calves." *Forest and Stream,* September 17, 1910, 448.

Hummel, Edward A. Letter to Richard McCarthy, July 31, 1970. In Andy Hecht file, box W-53, Yellowstone National Park Archives.

Idaho Falls Register, Idaho Falls, ID. June 3, 1991.

Ingersoll, Randy. Interview with author. Gardiner, MT, September 6, 1994.

Jackson Hole Guide, Jackson Hole, WY. News items from 1967–1997.

Janetski, Joel C. *Indians of Yellowstone National Park*. Salt Lake City: University of Utah Press, 1987.

Johnson, Clifton. *Highways and Byways of the Rocky Mountains*. New York: Macmillan, 1910.

Johnson, Hugh B. v. U.S.A. 90-8060, 1990. On file at Grand Teton National Park, WY.

Jones, Elwood. "Boating Accident Report." June 26, 1972. Box A-91, file A7623, Yellowstone National Park Archives.

Jones, W. A. *Report Upon the Reconnaissance of Northwestern Wyoming. . . .* Washington, DC: Government Printing Office, 1875.

Kalispell Interlake, Kalispell, MT. July 4, 1936.

Kasik, Phillip R. Letter to James Hecht, August 20, 1974. Box A-78, file A7623, Yellowstone National Park Archives.

Keate, Wendell S. "In Re: The Rev. Gilbert Eakins." August 27, 1926. Box A-44, file 146.13, Yellowstone National Park Archives.

Kingsbury, John M. *Deadly Harvest: A Guide to Common Poisonous Plants*. New York: Holt, Rinehart, and Winston, 1965.

Klang, Floyd. Backcountry permit 84-7N-806, attachment to case incident report 84-2913.

Klobuchar, Jim. *Where the Wind Blows Bittersweet*. Wayzata, MN: Ralph Turtinen Publishing Company, 1975.

Knight, Albert F. "The Death of a Son." *New York Times*, June 29, 1986.

Laguerenne, J. Letter to Park Superintendent, September 11, 1911. Item 103, file 313, Yellowstone National Park Archives.

Lampasas Leader, Lampasas, TX. August 31, 1928.

Landscape Division. Letters, 1929. Box W-1 1, Yellowstone National Park Archives.

Lang, William L. "At the Greatest Personal Peril to the Photographer." *Montana Magazine of Western History* 33 (Winter 1983): 14–25.

Lawrence E. Middaugh, Administrator of the Estate of Stephen Athan v. U.S.A. Civ. No. 5148. D. Wyoming, May 29, 1968.

Lindsley, Chester. Letter to Director, August 13, 1917, Item 64, and death certificate of John W. Havekost, file 313, Yellowstone National Park Archives.

Lindsley, Elmer. Letter to Park Superintendent, January 1, 1898. Document 1458, Yellowstone National Park Archives.

———. "A Winter Trip through the Yellowstone National Park." *Harper's Weekly*, January 29, 1898, 106.

"List of injuries received by D. E. MacKay, August 13, 1910," and Superintendent Benson's certification, August 17, 1910. Item 103, file 313, Yellowstone National Park Archives.

Little, Raymond. Interview with A. L. Haines, April 21, 1961. Audiotape, Yellowstone National Park Research Library.

Livingston Enterprise, Livingston, MT. News items from 1883–2013.

Lloyd, Irvin. "Special Incident Report." July 15, 1949. Box W-98, Yellowstone National Park Archives.

Lockhart, Caroline. "Story of Jack Crandall, Killed by Crow Indians, on Creek Which Bears His Name." *Park County News* (MT), November 23, 1923.

"Log of Events, Old Faithful Ranger Station," July 13, 1932, and July 19, 1933. Box W-34, Yellowstone National Park Archives.

Lounsbury, John. Interview with author. Lake, WY, January 12, 1993.

Magoc, Chris J. "The Selling of Wonderland: Yellowstone National Park, the Northern Pacific Railroad, and the Culture of Consumption, 1872–1903." PhD diss., University of New Mexico, 1993.

Maguire, Henry N. *The Coming Empire, A Complete and Reliable Treatise on the Black Hills, Yellowstone, and Big Horn Regions.* Sioux City, IA: Watkins and Mead, 1878.

Mallon, Henry, et al. Interview with A. L. Haines, July 5, 1961. Audiotape 61-2, Yellowstone National Park Research Library.

Manning, Roger. Case incident 75-630, July 3, 1975. Box W-102, Yellowstone National Park Archives.

Manscill, Kitty. Conversation with author. Great Smoky Mountains National Park, TN, August 20, 1993.

Marler, George. *Inventory of Thermal Features of the Firehole River Basins.* Washington, DC: National Technical Information Service, 1972.

Marschall, Mark. "Initiation and Results of Search." July 31, 1984. Case incident 84-2913, Yellowstone National Park, WY.

———. Interview with author. Gardiner, MT, November 29, 1992.

Marshall, Chris Scott. Interview with author. Mammoth, WY, January 28, 1993.

Martin, Samuel F. Letter to commanding officer, April 27, 1904. Document 7241, Yellowstone National Park Archives.

Maxey, Clyde A. "SIR: Drowning in Shoshone Lake Lee Burrows." June 17, 1958. Box W98, file 2623, Yellowstone National Park Archives.

McClelland, B. Riley. "SIR: Drowning of Mr. Thomas Hughes. . . ." September 1961. Box W-98, file 2623, Yellowstone National Park Archives.

McFeatters, Ann. "I Write This to Give Meaning to Andy's Life." *Washington Daily News,* August 19, 1970.

McKnight, Robert B. "Do You Recall Your Walk in Geyser Basin?" *Yellowstone News* (Wylie Way newspaper) 1, no. 1 (Spring 1915).

McMillion, Scott. *Mark of the Grizzly.* Guilford, CT: Lyons Press, 2012.

McPherren, Ida. *Imprints on Pioneer Trails.* Boston: Christopher Publishing House, 1950.

Meagher, Mary. "Possible Sequence of Events Relating to 5-W-1 Fatal Bear Mauling." In case incident 84-2913, August 22, 1984, Yellowstone National Park.

Memorandum from coroner, July 9, 1980. Box A-1 13, file A7623, Yellowstone National Park Archives.

Mernin, Gerald. "A76 Special Incident." August 8, 1966. Box A-83, file 7616, Yellowstone National Park Archives.

———. "Apparent Suicide of Government Employee." June 10, 1967. Box A-83, file A76 Special Incidents, Yellowstone National Park Archives.

———. Field Report w. 1344. Box W-102, Yellowstone National Park Archives.

———. Interview with author. South Entrance, Yellowstone National Park, WY, June 15, 1993.

———. "Report of Accidents Other than Motor Vehicle." August 26, 1970. Report 1193, box W-98, Yellowstone National Park Archives.

Miller, George. "Memorandum for Chief Ranger's Files: Incidents Relative to the Death of Charles Phillips." April 20, 1927. Box W-73, file 145, Yellowstone National Park Archives.

Miller, Mary Lou. Interview with author. Mammoth, WY, November 30, 1992.

Miller, Paul. Interview with author. Mammoth, WY, November 7, 1992.

Missoulian, Missoula, MT. July 15, 1933; December 10, 2009; January 6, 2012.

Mitchell, Andrew. Interview with author. Mammoth, WY, November 12 and 18, 1993.

MLA. "Our Summering of 1890." Manuscript at University of Colorado, Boulder.

Montana Standard, Butte, MT. November 12, 1970; June 29, 1974.

Monthly Reports of Superintendent of Yellowstone National Park, 1917–1967 [these are all that exist]. Yellowstone National Park Archives.

Moorman, Edward H. "Yellowstone Park Camps History." April 2, 1954, Yellowstone National Park Research Library.

Morrison, Micah. *Fire in Paradise*. New York: HarperCollins, 1993.

Mumey, Nolie. *Rocky Mountain Dick (Richard W. Rock) Stories of His Adventures in Capturing Wild Animals*. Denver: Range Press, 1953.

Murphy, Bob. Conversation with author. Mammoth, WY, September 13, 1993.

Murphy, Kerry. Interview with author. Mammoth, WY, April 7, 1993.

Murphy, R. J. "SIR: Drowning of David Gaskell." August 7, 1955. Box W-98, file 2623, Yellowstone National Park Archives.

National Audubon Society. *Audubon Society Field Guide to North American Mushrooms*. New York: Alfred A. Knopf, 1981, 1991.

National Park Service. Audiotape cassette of inquiry into quadruple drowning, September 7, 1973. Box A-78, file A7623, Yellowstone National Park Archives.

———. Form letter, n.d. [1970]. Box W-53, Yellowstone National Park Archives.

———. "Inquest into Death of J. P. Speitel, Y. P. Company Employee." Audiotape in oral history collection, Yellowstone National Park Research Library.

———. "Interview with Mrs. Carol Lake Regarding the Fatality Accident of Andrew Hecht on June 28, 1970," and other attachments in box W-53, Yellowstone National Park Archives.

———. Miscellaneous letters and photos on 1943 B-17 crash. Box A-76, Yellowstone National Park Archives.

———. *Where Are the Trees?* Information pamphlet. U.S. Department of the Interior, Yellowstone National Park, WY, 1984.

Naturalists' Log Book, West Thumb Geyser Basin, August 14, 1935. Box A-44, file 146.13, Yellowstone National Park Archives.

Nichols, William. Letter to H. W. Child, October 21, 1908. Box YPC-97, Yellowstone National Park Archives.

Norris, P. W. *Fifth Annual Report of the Superintendent of Yellowstone National Park*. . . . Washington, DC: Government Printing Office, 1881.

Nuss, Dale H. "Narrative Report of Activities of Ranger Personnel Connected with the Search, Rescue, and Investigations Operations of the U.S. Air Force B-47 Bomber Crash—May 3 through May 9, 1963." Box W-56, Yellowstone National Park Archives.

Nyquist, William. "Special Incident Report." August 7, 1947. Box W-193, file A7623, Yellowstone National Park Archives.

———. "Special Incident Report." August 25, 1947. Box W-98, Yellowstone National Park Archives.

O'Dea, Brian. Interview with author. Mammoth Hot Springs, WY, August 5, 1993.

O'Dea, John E. "Report of Accident Other Than Motor Vehicle." Field report 1444, July 11, 1972. Box A-91, file A7623, Yellowstone National Park Archives.

Ogston, Ted. Interview with A. L. Haines, June 20, 1966. Audiotape no. 63-5, side 2, Yellowstone National Park Research Library.

Old Faithful Ranger Station logbook. July 3, 1929, box W-34 and September 13, 1949, box 33, Yellowstone National Park Archives.

Packard, J. W. B. "SIR: Drowning of Paul Ray Ingebretson." August 31, 1961. Box W-98, file 2623, Yellowstone National Park Archives.

Paperiello, Rocco. Interview with author. Gardiner, MT, January 31, 1993.

Park County Historical Society. *History of Park County, Montana 1984*. Dallas, TX: Taylor Publishing Company [1984].

Park County News. Montana, August 20, 1926; May 6, 1927; July 11 and 16, 1953.

Park Press Release. August 1, 1969. Box K-22, Yellowstone National Park Archives.

———. July 10, 1973. Box K-23, Yellowstone National Park Archives.

———. July 20, 1973. Box K-23, Yellowstone National Park Archives.

———. August 20, 1975. Box K-27, Yellowstone National Park Archives.

Park Press Releases. 1978–1993. Yellowstone Public Affairs Office.

———. June 21, 1994, and July 4, 1994. Box K-22, Yellowstone National Park Archives.

Park Superintendent. Letter to Ray and F. A. Hull, September 27, 1910. Item 103, file 313, Yellowstone National Park Archives.

Patrick, Lucille Nichols. *The Best Little Town by a Dam Site*. Cheyenne, WY: Pioneer Printing, 1984.

Paul, Andrea. Interview with author. Mammoth Hot Springs, WY, April 20, 1993.

———. Letters to author, January 31, 1993, and August 15, 1993.

Pesman, Gerard. Interview with author. Albright Visitor Center, Mammoth Hot Springs, WY, Summer 1991.

Pfeiffer, Julianna. Letter to Ruth Lira and copy to author, West Yellowstone, MT, April 10, 1993.

Pflaum, Mike. Interview with author. Mount Rushmore National Memorial, February 14, 1993.

Phillips, Jerry. Letter to Tim Bommer, March 9, 1979. Box A-I11, file A-76, Yellowstone National Park Archives.

[Pitcher, John]. "Memo. concerning Mr. Dave Edwards. . . ." November 13, 1906. Archive document 7025 and letter, 7028, Yellowstone National Park Archives.

Plimpton, Rodney. Interview with author. Mammoth Visitor Center, Summer 1991.

Pocatello Journal, Pocatello, ID. August 16, 1935.

"Poisonous Plants." *Yellowstone Nature Notes* 4, no. 5 (May 31, 1927): 3.

Post-Register, Idaho Falls, ID. January 13, 1938; July 2, 1973; July 22, 1973; November 30, 1988; August 23, 2000.

Pugh, George. Item 64, file 313, Yellowstone National Park Archives.

Pyne, Stephen. *Fire in America*. Princeton, NJ: Princeton University Press, 1993.

Randall, L. W. "Gay." *Footprints along the Yellowstone*. San Antonio, TX: Naylor Co., 1961.

Rangers' Monthly Reports, August 1936. Box W-85, Yellowstone National Park Archives.

"Re: Mrs. Grace Crans . . . Denver, Colo." Box W-11, Yellowstone National Park Archives.

Record Book of Interments at the Post Cemetery, Fort Yellowstone. Items 154 and 155, Yellowstone National Park Archives.

Reinhart, Dan. Interview with author. Lake, WY, August 12, 1993.

Renkin, Diane Ihle. Interview with author. Gardiner, MT, December 6, 1992.

Renkin, Roy. "A History of Hazard Trees. . . ." *Buffalo Chip*, September–November 1992.

"Report of Review Team [on Lane Potter and Van Hansen]." March 30, 1979. Box A-109, file A7623, Yellowstone National Park Archives.

Richards, Mary B. *Camping Out in the Yellowstone*. Salem, MA: Newcomb and Gauss, 1910.

Rinehart, Rick, and Amy Rinehart. *Dare to Survive: Death, Heartbreak, and Triumph in the Wild*. New York: Citadel Press Books, 2008.

Ritchie, Edith. Interview with A. L. Haines, November 7, 1961. Audiotape 61-3, Yellowstone Research Library.

Roberts, J. Herbert. *A World Tour, Being a Year's Diary, Written 1884–85*. Cambridge, England: Trinity College, privately printed, 1886.

Rock Creek Cemetery. Letter to author. Washington, DC, October 17, post-1992.

Romey, Ed. Letter to John Pitcher, May 3, 1904. Document 7203, Yellowstone National Park Archives.

Ross, Michael. Interview with author. Grant Village, WY, August 22, 1994, regarding the drowning of Ryan Francis Weltman on July 3, 1994.

———. Letter to Lee Silliman and copy to author, August 9, 1991.

Ruesch, Melanie. Conversation with author. Sequoia National Park, CA, August 19, 1993.

Rush, William. *Wild Animals of the Rockies, Adventures of a Forest Ranger*. Garden City, NY: Halcyon House, 1939, 1942.

Ryder, Jerry. Interview with author. Mammoth Hot Springs, WY, December 14, 1992.

"Safety First." *Newsweek*, June 10, 1974, 95.

Salt Lake Tribune, Salt Lake City, UT. September 7, 1902; May 19, 1906; September 7, 1908; May 6, 1963; July 21, 1973; August 23, 2000; June 19–20, 2009.

Saltus, J. Sanford. *A Week in the Yellowstone*. New York: Knickerbocker Press, 1895.

San Francisco Chronicle, San Francisco, CA. July 10, 1901.

Saunders, Walter H. Letter to National Park Service, July 6, 1929. Box W-11, Yellowstone National Park Archives.

Sawyer, D. E. Letter to Patrick Conger, January 31, 1884. Document 1544, Yellowstone National Park Archives.

Schoening, Mr. and Mrs. Robert. Letter to Jack Anderson, August 6, 1970. Box W-53, Yellowstone National Park Archives.

Scott, Hugh L. *Some Memories of a Soldier.* New York and London: The Century Company, 1928.

Scoyen, Clarence "Pop." Interview with Mery L. Olson, October 6, 1970. Audiotape 70-1, Yellowstone National Park Research Library.

Schullery, Paul. *Bears of Yellowstone.* Worland, WY: High Plains Publishing Co., 1992.

———. *Mountain Time.* New York: Schocken Books, 1984.

———. *Old Yellowstone Days.* Boulder: Colorado Associated University Press, 1979.

———. ed. *Yellowstone Bear Tales.* Niwot, CO: Roberts Rinehart Publishers, 1992.

Selby, Earl, and Miriam Selby. "Andrew Did Not Die in Vain." *Reader's Digest,* August 1973, 134–37.

Semingsen, Earl. "SIR: Report Concerning the Drowning of Major J. T. Flock" and statement of Richard H. Carmichael. Box W-98, Yellowstone National Park Archives.

Seton, Ernest Thompson. *Lives of Game Animals.* 2 vols. Boston: Charles T. Branford Company, 1953.

Shepherd, Anne. Conversation with author. Sequoia National Park, CA, August 19, 1993.

Sheridan, John E. "Dangers of the Yellowstone Park Where a Washington Woman Has Just Lost Her Life." *Washington* (DC) *Times,* September 17, 1905, magazine section, p. 48.

Sheridan, Phillip, and William Sherman. *Reports of Inspection Made in the Summer of 1877 by Generals P. H. Sheridan and W. T. Sherman of Country North of Union Pacific Railroad.* Washington, DC: Government Printing Office, 1878.

Sholly, Dan R., with Steven M. Newman. *Guardians of the Yellowstone.* New York: William Morrow and Co., 1991.

Siebecker, Alice. Interview with author. Lake, WY, February 20, 1993.

Simpson, Ross W. *The Fires of '88.* Helena, MT: Geographic Publishing Company, 1989.

"SIR: Death of Infant at Fishing Bridge." September 15, 1952. Box W-98, Yellowstone National Park Archives.

"SIR: Schmoker-Hensley Drowning, July 10, 1950," and statement by Joseph Gentry. Box W-98, Yellowstone National Park Archives.

Sisto, Tony. "In Print—*Death in Yellowstone.*" *Ranger: The Journal of the Association of National Park Rangers,* Fall 1995.

Smith, F. Dumont. *Book of a Hundred Bears.* Chicago: Rand McNally and Co., 1909.

Souvenir, Jefferson, IA. August 27; September 3, 17; October 1, 15, 22; November 5, 12, 22, 1898.

Spear, Harriet. Letter to Horace Albright, September 30, 1928. Box W-11, file 149.1, Yellowstone National Park Archives.

"Special Incident Report." July 28, 1924. Box W-55, Yellowstone National Park Archives.

———. July 1, 1973. Box A-74, file A76-23, Yellowstone National Park Archives.

Spirtes, David. "Investigation of Scene at 5-W-1." From case incident 84-2913, July 31, 1984, Yellowstone National Park.

Squire, Isabel. Conversation with author. Seattle, WA, August 19, 1993.

Standard-Examiner, Ogden, UT. July 20, 1973.

Standler, Ronald B. "Lightning Strikes to People and the Legal Duties to Warn and to Protect." August 7, 1998, posted at http://www.rbs2.com/ltgwarn.pdf.

Stebbins, Walt. Interview with author. Gardiner, MT, February 15, 1993.

Stermitz, Gladys. "1st Annual Historical Tour (Sponsored by the Park County Historical Society), August 10, 1985." Unpublished manuscript, Yellowstone National Park Research Library.

Stoddard, John L. *John L. Stoddard's Lectures*, vol. 10. Boston: Balch Brothers Company, 1909.

Sturtevant, Smokey. Interview with author. Mammoth, WY, August 3, 1994, regarding the drowning of Ryan Francis Weltman on July 3, 1994.

Styron, William. *Darkness Visible: A Memoir of Madness.* New York: Vintage Books, 1992.

Sunday Oklahoman, Oklahoma City. June 27, 1971.

Superintendent. Letter to John Rees, October 13, 1903. Item 103, file 313, Yellowstone National Park Archives.

Superintendent's Journal. Ledger 143, July 6, 1901, Yellowstone National Park Archives.

Superintendent's Journal. Ledger 143, September 5, 1900, Yellowstone National Park Archives.

Taylor, Charles M., Jr. *Touring Alaska and the Yellowstone.* Philadelphia: George W. Jacobs and Company, 1901.

Terry, T. R. Handwritten statement, n.d., attachment to Bremer. Possession of author.

"Thermal Accidents 1919–1980." Yellowstone National Park Research Library.

"Thermal Injuries 1961–1969." Yellowstone National Park Research Library.

Thomas, George. "My Recollections of the Yellowstone Park." Manuscript, 1883. Yellowstone National Park Research Library.

Thompson, J. M., T. S. Presser, R. B. Barnes, and D. B. Bird. "Chemical Analysis of the Waters of Yellowstone National Park, Wyoming from 1965 to 1973." U.S. Geological Survey Open-file Report 75-25, 1974.

Toll, Roger. Letter to Director of National Park Service, August 9, 1929. Box W-11, Yellowstone National Park Archives.

———. Telegram to Director of National Park Service, July 27, 1933. Box A-44, file 146.13, Yellowstone National Park Archives.

Topping, E. S. *The Chronicles of the Yellowstone.* St. Paul, MN: Pioneer Press Co., 1888; Minneapolis, MN: Ross and Haines, Inc., 1968 (1968 edition with notes by Robert A. Murray).

Tucker, Lynn D. "Special Incident Report involving Keith Alfred Jensen," July 2, 1970. Box A-83, file A7616, Yellowstone National Park Archives.

Tulsa World, Tulsa, OK. July 26, 1933.

Turrill, Gardner S. *A Tale of the Yellowstone, or in a Wagon Through Western Wyoming and Wonderland.* Jefferson, IA: G. S. Turrill Publishing Company, 1901.

[Usher, M. C.?] Memorandum [on Frank Rose]. November 1, 1905. Archive document 7032, Yellowstone National Park Archives.

Usher, M. C. "Record of Death and Interment" on Charles J. Blank, October 4, 1904. Archive document 7033, Yellowstone National Park Archives.

———. Record of Death and Interment" on William Eaton, May 31, 1904. Archive document 7034, Yellowstone National Park Archives.

Van de Water, Frederic F. "Nine Months Rest." *Saturday Evening Post*, November 12, 1927, pp. 16–17, 80, 83, 85–86.

Waagner, R. A. Letter to Captain Frank A. Barton, March 2, 1904. Archive Document 7436, Yellowstone National Park Archives.

———. Letter to C. A. Lindsley, March 10, 1904. Archive document 7435-7436, Yellowstone National Park Archives.

Watry, Elizabeth A. *Women in Wonderland: Lives, Legends, and Legacies of Yellowstone National Park*. Helena, MT: Riverbend Publishing, 2012.

Weber, Nan. *Mattie: A Woman's Journey West*. Moose, WY: Homestead Publishing, 1997.

Weeks, Melanie. Letter to author, March 1, 1993.

Weikert, Andrew. "Journal of the Tour Through the Yellowstone National Park in August and September, 1877." *Contributions to the Historical Society of Montana* 3 (1900): 153–74.

Welch, Frank. Death certificate. Item 64, file 313, Yellowstone National Park Archives.

West Yellowstone News, West Yellowstone, MT. February 25, 1993.

Wheeler, Olin D. *Indianland and Wonderland*. St. Paul, MN: Northern Pacific Railroad, 1894.

Whithorn, Doris. "A Grizzly Got Frenchy." Manuscript, n.d., Yellowstone National Park Research Library.

Whithorn, Doris, and Bill Whithorn. *Photo History of Aldridge*. Minneapolis, MN: Acme Printing and Stationery, n.d. [1965].

Whittaker, George. Scout diary. December 21, 1897, in *Annual Report of Superintendent*, 1898, 33. Original in Yellowstone National Park Archives.

Whittlesey, Curtis. Interview with author. Mineral, CA, November 1992.

Whittlesey, Lee H. "Governmental Tort Liability in Recreation: A City and Its Parks (With Some Words About Federal Parks)." Legal manuscript citing cases, April 23, 1987, Yellowstone National Park Research Library.

———, ed. *Lost in the Yellowstone: Truman Everts's Thirty-Seven Days of Peril*. Salt Lake City: University of Utah Press, 1995.

———. "'Music, Song, and Laughter': Paradise at Yellowstone's Fountain Hotel, 1891–1916." *GOSA Transactions Journal of the Geyser Observation and Study Association* 10 (2008): 149–68.

———. *Wonderland Nomenclature: A History of the Place Names of Yellowstone National Park, Being a Description of and Guidebook to Its Most Important Natural Features, Together With Appendices of Related Elements*. Helena: Montana Historical Society, 1988. Microfiche and typescript, Yellowstone National Park Library.

———. *Yellowstone National Park Mile by Mile Guide*. Mammoth Hot Springs, WY: T. W. Services, Inc., 1985.

———. *Yellowstone Place Names*. Helena: Montana Historical Society, 1988; Gardiner, MT: Wonderland Publishing Company, 2006.

Wiggins, William, Herman Biastack, John Bauman et al. Memories. Box 3, audiotape 57-2, Yellowstone National Park Archives.

Wilkinson, Todd. Interview with author. Mammoth Visitor Center, March 1, 1993.

Wilson, Ed. Letter to G. L. Henderson, January 20, 1891. George Ash Collection, Yellowstone National Park Research Library.

Windsor, G. A. "Individual Bear Injury Report." August 23, 1942. In possession of author.

Wingate, George W. *Through the Yellowstone Park on Horseback.* New York: O. Judd Company, 1886.

WKC. "Hand of God Alone." In scrapbook 4209, 1897, 139–42, Yellowstone National Park Research Library.

Wood, Bob. Conversation with author. Zion National Park, UT, August 20, 1993.

Worden Yellowstone. August 22, 1935.

Wyoming Eagle, Cheyenne, WY. October 1, 1952; November 27, 1952.

Wyoming State Tribune, Cheyenne, WY. June 29, 1973; July 20, 1973; July 21, 1973.

Yancey, Philip. "Killer Wind at Shoshone Lake." *Reader's Digest,* June 1980, 111–15.

Yellowstone National Park Museum catalogue record 1402, accession number 328.

Young, S. B. M. Memo [on drowning]. August 26, 1907, archive document 7026, Yellowstone National Park Archives.

Index